Vartan Gregorian

The Road to Home

to Home

My Life and Times

SIMON & SCHUSTER

New York London Toronto Sydney Singapore

SIMON & SCHUSTER
Rockefeller Center
1230 Avenue of the Americas
New York, NY 10020

For information about special discounts for bulk purchases,
please contact Simon & Schuster Special Sales:
1-800-456-6798 or business@simonandschuster.com.

Manufactured in the United States of America

1   3   5   7   9   10   8   6   4   2

Library of Congress Cataloging-in-Publication Data
Gregorian, Vartan.
The road to home : my life and times / Vartan Gregorian.
p.   cm.
Includes index.
1. Gregorian, Vartan.   2. Educators—United States—Biography.
3. College presidents—United States—Biography.   4. Armenian Americans—Biography.
I. Title.
LA2317.G643 A3   2003   973'.0491992'0092—dc21
[B]   2003045566
ISBN 0-684-80834-X

To my beloved grandmother Voski Mirzaian,
who nourished my body, my heart, and my soul

To my sister, Ojik,
whose benevolent love has been mine since she was born

To Simon Vratzian and Wayne S. Vucinich,
and to all my teachers who made my life happen

and

To my incomparable wife, Clare,
and our three wonderful sons, Vahé, Raffi, and Dareh Ardashes,
who made my life matter

CONTENTS

The Road to Home

INTRODUCTION

My Birthplace

I was born in Tabriz, Iran, an ancient city with a turbulent and illustrious past. In his *Legend: The Genesis of Civilization,* the archeologist David Rohl claims that the Garden of Eden must have been located in northern Iran, in Tabriz, where I was born. The Book of Genesis 2:10–14 states that Eden encompassed the sources of four rivers: the Euphrates, Tigris, Gihon, and Pi-shon. Since Josephus, the first-century Jewish historian, scholars have debated the identity of the last two rivers. Rohl argues that before the advent of Islam in Iran in the seventh century A.D., the river Aras (Araxes) was known as Gaihun, the equivalent of the Hebrew Gihon. He claims the fourth river must have been Uizun, Pishon being a Hebrew corruption of the name. He believes that he may have located a village named Naqdi, which could be a trace of the land of Nod, the place of Cain's exile after he murdered his brother, Abel, referenced in the Book of Genesis as ". . . east of Eden."

I will leave it to archeologists and biblical scholars to debate the exact location of the Garden of Eden. I can assure you, however, that the Tabriz of the mid-1930s was no paradise, even though it had its share of beautiful springs, pleasant summers, gorgeous flowers, delicate gardens, delicious fruits and vegetables, exquisite Persian carpets, pure and tasty drinking water, inspiring sunrises and dramatic sunsets, and gentle breezes during its summer nights. But the city had quantities of dust and mud as well, including awful potholes. Tabriz had wet autumns, harsh winters, frightening thunderstorms, torrential rains, marble-sized hailstones, heavy snowfalls, minor and major earthquakes, and devastating plagues, including typhus and cholera, not to mention smallpox.

More than anything else, however, Tabriz had a long, rich, checkered, and sometimes glorious history. Its burden of memory included a record of centuries of struggles, adversities, triumphs, defeats, tragedies, destructions and dislocations, cycles of decline and rebirth. Situated in a valley to the north of the beautiful Mount Sahand, Tabriz was at the crossroads of expanding or contending empires and rival kingdoms. It was often a battleground or a military frontier, sometimes a center of political and economic power, other times confined to the periphery. Throughout it all, Tabriz remained the home for generations of artisans, merchants, scholars, poets, political leaders, petty rulers, kings, and even emperors.

Mentioned for the first time in Assyrian King Sargon II's epigraph in 714 B.C., Tabriz served as the capital of various rulers, beginning with Atropates and his dynasty (fourth century B.C.) and most notably Ghazan Khan, the Il-Khan of the Mongol empire in A.D. 1295. The latter's realm stretched from the Oxus to the borders of Egypt and from the Caucasus to the Indian Ocean. Ghazan Khan's conversion to Islam inaugurated a new chapter in the history of the Middle East and Central Asia by shifting international and regional balances of power. It was during his rule that Tabriz reached the height of its power. The emperor expanded the city and built major caravanserais, markets, and public baths, along with many prominent mosques and other notable public structures, including an observatory and a number of colleges and libraries that attracted scholars from all over his empire and beyond, transforming Tabriz into a great center of learning. Some fourteen thousand men worked on the construction of his mausoleum. In 1392, after the end of the Mongol rule, the city was sacked by Tamerlane.

The city, invaded by Arabs, Seljuk Turks, Mongols, Tatars, Turkomans, Uzbeks, Ottoman Turks, and Russians, suffered repeated natural disasters as well. It was destroyed by fifteen terrible earthquakes between A.D. 634 and 1936 and decimated in 1737 by plague. Yet the inhabitants in the city's remnants have always had the tenacity to build and rebuild their city and continued to preserve its commercial and strategic role in the region and its central place on the Silk Road. Tabriz's fabulous bazaar, the seat of its economic power, dazzled many contemporary chroniclers, such as Ibn Batutta (1327), Ruy González de Clavijo (1404), Giasufo Barbaro (1474), J. B. Tavernier (1632), Olearius (1637), and Jean Chardin (1641), who reported that Tabriz had some 250 mosques and 300 caravanserais.

In 1501, Tabriz became the capital under Shah Ismail, the founder of the Safavid Empire of Persia, which lasted until 1736. Shah Ismail adhered to the strictest tenets of the Shiite doctrine of Islam and made it the official state religion of Persia, formalizing the split between the Shia and Sunni realms of Islam and inaugurating more than two centuries of intermittent conflict between the Ottoman and Persian empires. During the Qajar dynasty (1784–1925), Tabriz was the residence of the crown princes of Persia, who often served as titular governors of the Azerbaijan province.

From the eighteenth through the first part of the twentieth century, Persia confronted European imperialism and became a pawn in the "Great Game" that pitted Great Britain and the Russian Empire against each other. During the reigns of Peter the Great and Catherine the Great and afterward, Russia waged aggressive wars against Persia. Tabriz was captured by Russian forces but returned to Persia after the Treaty of Turkomanchai in 1828. The treaty consolidated two decades of Russian gains. Persia lost her rich Caucasian provinces, and present-day Georgia, Azerbaijan, and Armenia were annexed by Russia. The Aras River became the frontier between the Russian Empire and the Persian Kingdom.

In the early part of the nineteenth century, Abbas Mirza, a Qajar prince and the governor of Azerbaijan, launched a modernization scheme from Tabriz. He introduced Western-style institutions, imported industrial machinery, installed the first regular postal service, and undertook military reforms. He rebuilt the city and launched diplomatic initiatives to the West, concluding a treaty with Napoleon and later with England in an effort to fend off the Russian threat. He attempted to establish a rational taxation system and fought to control corruption. His plans were visionary but his finances limited, and he died in 1833 while engaged in reestablishing Persian sovereignty over the city of Herat. From 1841 on, Great Britain and Russia established political and commercial hegemony over Persia. In 1907, the Anglo-Russian Convention divided the country into two spheres of influence, British and Russian.

During the first decade of the twentieth century, Tabriz and the province of Azerbaijan became centers of the Persian nationalist movement. Its citizens fought for and succeeded in obtaining a constitutional monarchy in 1908. In 1915, during World War I, in spite of Persia's official neutrality, Ottoman forces occupied Tabriz. Then the Russians defeated and expelled the Turko-Kurdish forces. After the Russian revolution in 1917, Russian forces withdrew, and Ottoman troops returned. They were forced out after the Allied victory. The Persian government's control was confined to Tehran and the country was bankrupt. The 1919 Anglo-Persian Treaty rendered Persia a de facto British protectorate. In 1925, Reza Khan deposed the last Qajar ruler and declared himself Reza Shah Pahlavi. Embarking upon a vast policy of modernization and Westernization, he centralized the bureaucracy, built a modern army, undertook social and educational reforms, curbed the authority of the religious and tribal leaders, and nationalized the private schools. Iran was celebrating the tenth anniversary of the Pahlavi dynasty when I was born.

The Tabriz of my childhood had the remnants of only two great historical monuments to its past glory: the Masjid-i-Ali Shah (The Mosque of Ali Shah), built between 1312 and 1322 and converted into an Arg (Citadel) during Qajar rule; and the Masjid-i-Kabud, or Blue Mosque (A.D. 1456), an architectural gem.

Iran had a polyglot society: Persians, Turks, Kurds, Baluchs, Turkomans, and Arabs were the major ethnic groups. The majority of Iranians were Shia Muslims. The Kurds and Turkomans were Sunni Muslims. The major religious minorities consisted of the Armenian and the Assyrian Christian communities and smaller communities of Jews, Zoroastrians, Bahais, and some Georgian Christians. Tabriz was a microcosm of Iran. The majority of its population spoke Turkish. In addition to the larger minorities, there were Russians, American missionaries, and a handful of French and other foreigners. The largest religious minority, and one of the oldest, was my Armenian community.

Armenia and the Armenians, off and on, were either ruled by Iran or were under its political, military, and economic spheres of influence from the sixth to the third centuries B.C. Armenian kings, princes, and their armies often served in the ranks of Persian military forces. Armenia was often a battlefield between contending empires and a highway for an endless number of invaders. Often the country was devastated and the Armenians uprooted as part of scorched earth policies. From 1048 to 1071, the Seljuks took a great number of Armenian prisoners to Iran. Fourteenth- and fifteenth-century Mongol and Turkoman invaders followed this practice. By the sixteenth century, there were Armenian communities in most of Iran's major cities.

The clash of the Ottoman and Safavid empires during the sixteenth and seventeenth centuries inaugurated a new phase of devastation. The two fought eleven major wars between 1514 (Battle of Chaldiran) and 1639 (Treaty of Zuhab). Armenia, divided between the Ottoman and Safavid Persian empires, was often the main battlefield. Towns and villages were devastated and looted, populations massacred, deported, or taken away in slavery. Some Armenians were settled in Istanbul or urban centers of Iran. In 1603, following the capture of Tabriz by Shah Abbas I, the Safavid ruler, tens of thousands of people, mainly Armenians, were deported to Iran. In the fall of 1604, as Ottoman forces advanced, the inhabitants of the Armenian city of Julfa, a major regional trade center, were forcibly uprooted by the Persians and settled in Isfahan. The Persians destroyed Julfa to prevent the Armenians from harboring any plans of return.

In the late nineteenth century, Tabriz became a major center of Armenian culture and was the seat of the Prelacy of the Armenian Church in Azerbaijan. The prelates of the province welcomed secular teachers and secular culture. Thousands of students received their education within a network of Armenian elementary and secondary parochial schools, taught by Armenian teachers, scholars, and intellectuals, educated in Russian and European colleges and universities. Their ranks included some prominent leaders of the Armenian nationalist and revolutionary movements founded in 1880 and 1890. An Armenian press published Armenian textbooks, books, and periodicals. The city also boasted an Armenian theater, the Aramian, that staged plays and welcomed foreign actors and actresses. Its repertory included Armenian and Shakespearian plays. Occasionally the Aramian also welcomed operas.

By 1906, there was already an Armenian string music band. Instructors of violin and piano educated in England, Russia, Belgium, and Germany gave private lessons and taught music classes in elementary and secondary schools. A great pride of Tabriz was the American Memorial High School, founded by American missionaries. Hundreds of Armenians, Assyrians, Jews, Turks, and Persians received their secondary education in English. The French operated Jeanne D'Arc school, where the nuns educated girls. In addition to the Memorial High School, American missionaries operated an American hospital. There were Seventh-Day Adventist, Methodist, and Presbyterian churches.

In 1935–36, the Persian government, following the order of Reza Shah Pahlavi, nationalized all private and parochial schools and in 1939 shut down the American and other foreign language schools in Persia. The Armenian language could be taught only as a language for religion. The government changed the name of Persia to Iran, which is the name of the country in Persian. It was speculated that the change was instigated by the Persian ambassador to Nazi Germany because Germany was cultivating good relations with nations of the Aryan race. Iran is a cognate for Aryan. Following in the footsteps of Mustapha Atatürk of Turkey, Reza Shah also wanted to lay the foundations of a secular Iran, break from its immediate past, reclaim its pre-Islamic legacy, and assert its independence from the

British and now Soviet spheres of influence. Reza Shah forbade traditional dress for Muslim and even Christian and Jewish communities, ordering Western-style clothing to be worn. Turbans were banned, as were veils and headscarves. Long scarves worn to conceal women's hair and necks were outlawed.

With the closing of the Armenian parochial schools, there sprang up a furtive organized campaign on the part of all the secular Armenian teachers of language, history, ethics, literature, and religion to teach their subjects in Sunday schools or through private, individual, or group lessons, or during the religious instruction that was authorized by the Ministry of Education.

CHAPTER ONE

My Family

Both my maternal and paternal grandparents migrated to Tabriz from the Armenian villages of Karadagh (Black Mountain). Whether they were the remnants of sixteenth- and seventeenth-century Armenian deportees of the Safavid shahs of Iran, or earlier thirteenth- and fourteenth-century deportees of the Seljuks and Mongols, or early inhabitants of the region, is hard to determine. When I was born, many of the peasants of the villages of Karadagh had moved to Tabriz, including my paternal grandfather, Balabeg, and his brother, Tevan, and their families. They owned a caravanserai, a bakery, and a dairy business. Ours was an extended family, and a wall separated the two branches of the Gregorian clan. My grandfather had two children: my aunt Nvart (Rose) and my father, Samuel. Tevan had one son, Grigor, and four grandsons. By the time I was born, my paternal grandmother, Anna, had died, as well as my aunt Nvart, who had married an Armenian notable in Tiflis and left her orphaned son, Bobken, with us.

My grandfather valued education enough to send my father to the American Memorial High School. The same opportunity was not afforded to my cousin Bobken, who worked in the caravanserai and the milk business. He was only able to finish elementary school and later had a terrible accident that burned half his face and body. He became a successful tailor.

My father was very young when he got married. My mother, Shooshanik

(Shooshik for short), was very beautiful, with a gentle smile, soft skin, and tender, smiling eyes. She wore practically no makeup. She had married at eighteen. My older brother, Aram, died when he was only a year old. My sister, Ojik (Eugenie), was born sixteen months after me. Our father's ambition had been to continue his education in the United States, but my grandfather had vetoed his wishes. Instead, because of his excellent English and expertise in accounting, he took a middle-management administrative position with the Anglo-Iranian Oil Company in Abadan. My sister and I were brought up by my mother and maternal grandmother.

In 1939, on the eve of World War II, a great calamity befell our family. My seventy-five-year-old grandfather was arrested and jailed on trumped-up charges that he was smuggling arms to Iran. Police searched the caravanserai, the Armenian schools, and other locations and reportedly found one or two weapons. It was not clear to whom they belonged or whether enemies or business rivals of my grandfather had planted them. He died in jail. I am sure he was tortured since there was evidently a great deal of reluctance to release his body to the family. The effort to retrieve his body was left entirely to my mother, including procuring and taking a coffin in a horse-drawn carriage to the central jail. I am told that my mother, in tears, pleaded with Fatullah Khan, chief of the Tabriz police department, for the release of my grandfather's body, so that he could be given a proper Christian burial. According to my grandmother, my mother donated all her exquisite needlework to the police chief's wife.

The imprisonment and death of my grandfather brought an end to the family business. The caravanserai and the milk business were sold. In my father's absence, my mother purchased a house near the Armenian church with the proceeds of the sale. I still remember the number: 1699 Church Street. My grandmother, mother, sister, uncle, cousin, and I moved to our new house.

I have a handful of memories of my mother: being held in her arms, being sung lullabies, being with her in an open-air movie performance in the Arg (Citadel) of the city. I remember only that it was dark, the screen far away, the images blurred, and that I was scared and shut my eyes. I remember a reception at the home of my godfather. I was instructed to behave, "to be a good boy," to take one cookie, not two, above all to be sure to thank our host. I remember following the gaze of my mother and declining seconds. Most important, my sister and I had been told to leave a small portion of whatever we were eating on the plate as a "sign of politeness." This was required etiquette, otherwise we would exhibit signs of being *gyormamish*, a Turkish adjective that describes someone who is a hick, has not "seen anything," is easily impressed and greedy, is nouveau riche, and has no savoir faire.

I remember our family's trip to Tehran and from there, by train to Abadan, to visit my father. The weather in Abadan was atrocious, very hot and humid. There were big fans on the ceiling of our bedroom but they did not seem to make much difference. I gather the journey was an attempt by my mother to save her marriage and to reconnect us with our absentee father. There were whispers of "another woman" in Abadan. The trip was memorable for another reason: I contracted malaria. After several months in Abadan, we returned to Tabriz.

My last glimpse of my mother was when my sister and I were ushered to a room where she lay motionless. She was very pale and cold. Her long black hair covered her shoulders. Her beautiful eyes were shut. She did not hug us, she did not greet us. Everyone was crying. We began crying, too. Something was strange. Something was very wrong. Everyone was extremely nice to us but wanted us to leave as soon as possible. We were told to bid good-bye to our mother because she was undertaking a long journey: she was leaving for America, a beautiful faraway land. . . . I did not know she had died. I had no clear ideas about death. I had been told people die when they are very old. But my mother was not old. She was so young, so beautiful, so tender, so warm. . . . I did not even know she had been ill.

Only a few years ago, I learned that on the way back from Abadan my mother miscarried twins, lost a lot of blood, developed pneumonia, and died without doctors or appropriate medicine. She was twenty-six. All of a sudden, my sister and I were essentially orphaned. In retrospect, it is both sad and strange that my sister and I never addressed her as Mother or Mama or our father as Father or Papa. Instead, we called them by their given names: Shooshik and Samuel. This was because we lived in an extended family where the authority was vested in my paternal grandfather, Balabeg, a widower, and my maternal grandmother, Voski (Gold). We called them Papa and Mama.

Following the death of my mother, her brother, my uncle Harootiun, age twenty-nine, died. He was devoted to his sister and had traveled with great difficulty from Tehran to Tabriz to be with her. His car had been confiscated sixty miles from Tabriz and he had to walk for some time before he was able to hitch a ride and attend my mother's funeral. He contracted pneumonia, too, and, again in the absence of proper medical care, succumbed. Within the span of less than two years, I lost my grandfather, mother, and uncle.

On August 25, 1941, military forces of the Soviet Union and Great Britain invaded Iran following Allied accusations that Iran was collaborating with the Axis and harboring pro-German sympathizers. The Soviet Army entered Iran in three columns: the first occupied Tabriz, the second occupied the northeastern border province of Khorasan, and the third occupied the Caspian coastal towns. I remember the Soviet propaganda leaflets that showered over Tabriz. The British forces occupied Iran's oilfields. Reza Shah was forced to abdicate. The Allies gave assurances that they had no designs on Iran's territorial integrity, independence, or oil, and expressed the hope that Iran would not resist the Allied advance. They did not have to worry as the Iranian opposition proved negligible. Despite the Iranian army's communiqués that boasted of the army's excellent morale and its successful resistance, the Iranian military resistance crumbled. Many officers deserted their units; many units abandoned their arms and melted away. The Allied occupation of Iran was accomplished within a few days.

My father was in the Iranian cavalry regiment dispatched to the north to face a Soviet mechanized division. I remember his departure, on a white horse. As he was getting ready to bid farewell to us, we were asked to sit down and then to get up together as one. This was to prevent the evil spirits from knowing who was leaving our home to journey to the unknown. As my father left on his horse with his rifle on his shoulder, he was asked not to look back. To ensure his safety we poured buckets of water after him. This was to cover his tracks in order to prevent the evil spirits from being able to follow him.

A few weeks later, as war broke out, panic spread throughout Tabriz over Iranian military losses. Rumors were rampant about Iranian soldiers, including Armenian ones, who had died fighting or were captured. My grandmother was told that my father was possibly a *dassaleek,* a fancy word in Armenian meaning someone who had deserted. We did not know what it meant, except that it was not good news. We all started crying. We thought our father was dead, too.

A week or so later two peasants with their donkeys were passing through our narrow street when one surprised my grandmother, who was on her way to stand in the bread line, by addressing her in Armenian and calling her Mama. Evidently my father had traded his horse and rifle and uniform for peasant's clothes and a donkey ride to town, following the decimation of his cavalry unit by Soviet mechanized forces. We were happy that he was alive but I was ashamed that he had fled. For the next month or so, my father stayed in bed or at home trying to "recover" from a "wound" caused by his rifle. People came to visit him and expressed their sympathy for his being wounded at the front.

My maternal grandmother was an extraordinary person. She was of medium height, with big, dark brown eyes. Her broad forehead accentuated her fierce, penetrating eyes and eyebrows. Her hair and neck were always covered with a black scarf. She wore several layers of cloth, covered with a long outer dress, which reached her ankles. Under these layers, she carried a flat bag holding keys, money, safety pins, needles and thread, and, occasionally, candy. She was an illiterate peasant who spoke a vernacular Karadagh dialect of Armenian, as well as Turkish.

My grandmother and her sister knew which day, week, month, and hour they were born, but, oddly, not the year. We were only told of an extraordinary event that occurred during the year of grandmother's birth: a red cow had been born in their village in Karadagh. She and her sister quarreled occasionally as to who was the younger. It was only when she died, in 1964, that we found out that she had been born in 1882. I gather she married early and had seven children. Four of her children died when they were very young, victims of epidemics.

Following the outbreak of World War I and Ottoman and Russian invasions into northern Iran, Kurdish and Turkish fighters and brigands had looted the Armenian and Assyrian villages of Karadagh and elsewhere. Thousands of Armenians and Assyrians left their villages for Tabriz. My grandmother was among those who fled with her three remaining children. Her two sisters, Manooshag (Violet) and Sophia, were part of the exodus. My grandmother and her sisters never spoke about their husbands and their fate. Were they killed? Had they abandoned them?

I remember, however, that my grandmother was very proud of her family name, Melik Mirzaian. She told me that her husband's family was part of the elite of the village—hence the title Melik, but more important, she took special pleasure in the fact that Mirza stood for "scribe" in Persian and that although she was illiterate, her family came from a tradition of literacy. It was a sore point for her that while she came from a well-known family, she had no schooling. She made sure, however, that her three remaining children would be educated. My uncle Harootiun graduated from the American Memorial High School, and my mother from the Armenian Diocesan High School. Armenag, my second uncle and an epileptic, received only a fifth-grade education, to the great chagrin of my grandmother. To raise her family and send her children to school, my grandmother worked for many well-to-do Armenian households, cleaning, baking bread, cooking, washing, and knitting.

Even though she was a churchgoing, fervent Christian, my grandmother seemed dazed by the calamities visited upon her by the loss of her husband, loss of six of her seven children, loss of her home and village, loss of a grandson. I had the impression, as I grew up, that she was angry at God or mystified by His actions, and that she lived to protest against Him. Her rudimentary argument with God was that since He is the Author, or at least it is with His consent that events take place in this world, He could have preserved at least some of her children, since she was not so sinful to deserve such a severe punishment. Her grief was private. She never complained; she cried for her sorrow, she cried for her children only in private. Her plight broke my heart.

Since my grandmother did not know how to read, she had no access to the Bible. She knew only a couple of short prayers by heart. She did not know the names of the twelve apostles, nor did she understand the lengthy Sunday sermons of the priests. She went to church to listen to the choir, observe the ceremony, receive communion, and pray. She used to light a candle and stand in front of the picture of Saint Mary, the Mother of Christ. One day after gazing at Saint Mary's picture, she shook her head. Probably they did not understand each other. Eventually she stopped her regular church attendance. Only once a year, on the eve of Good Friday, when the Church had the late-night service Khavaroom (Darkness, the Eclipse), when everyone came to mourn the death of Christ and that of their loved ones, did my grandmother attend the service, weeping in the darkness with scores of others over the loss of her children. She thought she was a "marked sinner."

After the deaths of her children, my grandmother never left Tabriz. She was fearful that she might die somewhere else and not be buried near her children. To be buried next to one's family members is a great blessing, she told us, because during Judgment Day and Resurrection, one must be near one's relatives. My grandmother believed in eternal life. Every Saturday night, she told us, belonged to departed souls. Saturday nights she kept a light on in our room and burned incense to invite departed souls to enter and rest for a while.

Thanks to my grandmother, I was acquainted with a world full of mythology, magic, and fantasy, where everything was simple, meaningful, and often beautiful. Since she could not read books to me and my sister, she spun tales. I learned that the stars were human souls, living in the sky, and that each of us could choose an exclusive star. (Naturally, I chose the North Star as mine.) These stars were our guardians. They not only protected us but had us under constant watch to see that we did the right thing. They were gifts of God, given to each of us upon our births. They served as lamps to light our inner world, enabling us to see its richness. They were the seats of our conscience. They gave us a sense of goodness, love, compassion, tolerance, and justice. The soul lived in the heart in an indefinite shape, as a body of light. The soul was also conceived to be air or breath. It was believed that when somebody died, the soul left the body through the mouth. The individual expired like a candle.

Departed souls could appear as good or bad ghosts. Good ghosts were associated with angels and holy beings; bad ghosts were souls of sinners. If someone had lived a good life, he would die with a smile. If, on the other hand, someone had not lived a virtuous life, one's death was painful, one struggled with Grogh (the writer of fate), and with the Hok-eh-ar, the taker of souls. Good and bad angels prepared their records of the dead for the ultimate Judge. If the good deeds weighed heavier, the soul went to Heaven. The bridge to Heaven (*mazer*, made of hair) was so fragile that it would break if the sins of the soul weighed it down.

During the summer nights when my sister and I slept on the roof, flanking our grandmother, we watched with awe the sky full of shining stars and an imposing moon. If we wanted to know how many people lived in the world, my grandmother would tell us, all we had to do was count their stars. When a comet streaked across the sky, it was a sign that somebody had been killed or passed away. On nights when the sky turned pitch black and the stars disappeared, my grandmother explained: "Probably somewhere in the world or here at home people have acted unfairly, unjustly, or are fighting each other like animals. That is why the stars are hurt and ashamed and have decided not to shine tonight."

The moon and the sun were brother and sister. The sun was a very beautiful girl, but shy and modest. Since she was naked, she was ashamed to appear before human beings who did not respect her privacy and stared at her constantly. She cried for many long hours. Then one day, God, pitying her, gave her needles to help her protect herself. It is since that day that we cannot look at her: she would not only blush but would also send needles into our eyes to avert our gaze. Her brother, the moon, on the other hand, was a naughty boy who constantly annoyed his sister. One day, their mother, the Heaven, who was kneading bread, could not take it anymore. She slapped him with a hand full of flour. The white spots that we see on the face of the moon are the consequences of that punishment. From that time on, it has been impossible to see the moon and the sun together—the moon is chasing his sister to punish her for having reproached him before their mother. It is, however, a futile effort. He is running after her but to this day has not been able to catch her.

In the autumn, when it stormed, we watched from our window and listened with trepidation to the violent commotion overhead. Rain lashed down and jagged lines of lightning ran across the sky, followed by bellowing, tearing thunder. The windows shook from the sound. We wondered what caused it and were afraid. On those occasions my grandmother spoke to us of the realm of spirits. There were dragons who lived high on the mountains; it is they who personified thunder, whirlwinds, and thunder clouds. The thunder was actually the scream of dragons. When the clouds gathered, my sister and I saw in the clouds giants, chariots, horses, and armies advancing and retreating, fighting and destroying each other.

My grandmother believed these spirits were everywhere and ever present. We had to follow certain rules to prevent evil spirits from harming us or interfering in our daily lives. I remember some of the prescribed precautions: boiling hot water must not be poured on the ground because it sinks into the earth and may burn the feet of the children of the evil spirits. In the evenings, you must pour no water at all on the ground because you may disturb the peace of evil spirits. Once disturbed, they may resort to vengeance or retribution. For the same reason, by night you should not sweep out the house, for you may hit the evil spirits. But if you are compelled to sweep by night, you should singe the tip of the broom so as to frighten the evil ones away in plenty of time.

Then there was a prescription for how to protect an expectant mother from the ever-present danger of evil spirits. It was recommended that something made of iron be placed under the pillow of the pregnant woman to ward off the evil spirits, since they were unable to touch iron. My grandmother believed in the evil eye. She was certain that, influenced by envy, it cast a spell that caused misfortune or illness. You had to protect beautiful babies and children from exposure to certain individuals who "possessed the evil eye." To do so, you either kept your children away from them or you used "evil eye repellents" in the form of deep-blue beads, glass or ceramic. They served as antidotes to the evil eye. As a grown-up, if you were the subject of excessive praise or flattery, you or a close friend or a relative pinched you as a precaution against the spell of the evil eye.

There were also the spirits of disease. They are small in stature and wear triangular hats and hold in their hands white, red, and black branches. If they strike with the white one, you will become ill but soon recover. If with the red, you will have to spend much recovery time in bed. If one is struck with the black branch, there is no cure. That is why parents, while talking about their children, expressing their joy that their child is healthy and cheerful, or is gaining weight, must always knock at a table of any kind of wood to frighten the evil spirits and not let them hear that the baby is healthy, because they may strike with one of their branches. It is to protect their children from such spirits that each child, from the moment of his or her birth, is given a personal guardian angel.

My grandmother was a wonderful storyteller. There were moralistic tales to teach children and youth about virtue, duty, and wisdom. These tales always started with the phrase "Once upon a time, there was," or "Once upon a time, there was not," or "There was, there was not, there was." The stories concluded that from Heaven fell three apples: "one for you, one for the storyteller, and one for the person who has entertained." The tales usually dealt with light and darkness, evil and good, selfish villains and generous souls, angels and demons, gardens, waterfalls, water fountains, treasures, cunning, greed, flattery, avarice, wicked stepmothers, actions that appeased or outwitted evil and relied on or prayed to God, human beings or animals who talked, married, had offspring, and had magical ability and imparted wisdom.

My grandmother was a disciplinarian. I remember two punishments. When I was eight or nine, I had uttered newly acquired Turkish obscenities in her presence. She washed my mouth with soap. "Your mouth will remain clean," she said. And when I was ten years old, she hit me very hard for stealing the equivalent of ten cents. As I was crying, she cried along with me. The fact that she was crying while attempting to punish me I perceived to be the sign of ultimate affection and concern for me. Her admonition was that those who are capable of stealing an egg are capable also of stealing a horse.

Grandmother taught us morality and ethics through stories, fables, and allegories. She started with basics: You must not lie, because you will lose all your credibility. Do good, but don't expect reciprocity or even gratitude. Life has its own logic, its own cycles; sooner or later you will be the object of good deeds, their beneficiary. Since life resembles a wheel of fortune, don't step on those who are down; give a helping hand, she would say, for those who are on the bottom will come up to the top one day and those on the top will go to the bottom. Therefore, one must not judge people by their current stations in life. People's circumstances may change throughout life, but who they *are* will not.

What impressed me most was how my grandmother bore so much suffering, so many losses, with stoicism, with dignity, without becoming bitter and without becoming cynical. She never gave up. She mourned privately, but she continued to work in various rich households, cooking, washing, cleaning. I did not know that she had sold all her valuables to help feed us, or even that she worked, because she was always there when we came home from school, always had food on the table, even though often she had to stand in line before dawn for five hours for three loaves of bread.

During the first two or three years of World War II, bread, sugar, butter, tea, and gasoline were rationed. We drank tea with raisins and dates for sweetening. On one or two occasions, Santa Claus was unable to visit our house to bring New Year's gifts because "he was too old, had caught cold, was ill." We believed that until we found that some of our friends in the neighborhood who were well-to-do had received visits from Santa Claus. Then, of course, there were her admonitions about hospitality. If you have guests in your house, it did not matter, she said, whether you like them or dislike them, because so long as they are in *your house,* it was a matter not of a personal but a family obligation to treat them well. Then there was the matter of thirst: If someone was thirsty and asked for water, even a leper, you must give it to him. You could not send away a thirsty person.

My grandmother admonished me about the seven deadly sins when I was twelve. I understood about Pride, Anger, and Sloth. I had no notion of Covetousness, Lust, or Gluttony. Envy impressed me most because I was told it was a bottomless pit. Certain virtues were hard to understand until later in life: humility, generosity, restraint, moderation, forgiveness, charity. Her bottomless stores of sayings were to help guide us through life. These are some that have stayed with me throughout the years:

> The stomach is an oven. If there is adequate fuel in it, don't over-
> burden it.
> You don't build a reputation or make a name for yourself on what
> you are going to do.
> An unkind word is like a thrown stone: it cannot be called back.
> The reason you have a house with walls is to keep the family news
> inside. Don't make a private matter a public one.
> Don't insult a crocodile before you cross a river.
> Those who know much don't talk too much.
> Good advice, like good medicine, is hard to swallow.

My grandmother instilled in me at an early age the notions of reputation, honor, and dignity. I learned from her, and at school as well, how to distinguish between *chakatagir* (fate, kismet, or what is written on your forehead) and *nkaragir* (character, or what is imprinted in you). Over the first, I was told, we had no control, but in the case of *nkaragir* we were fully responsible and accountable.

It was my grandmother who instructed me in the first moral lessons of life and the "right way." She was the best example of what good character means. Among the many things she taught us between the ages of seven and fifteen was that earthly belongings are ephemeral, as are, unfortunately, vigor and beauty. What endures are good deeds and reputation, one's name, one's dignity. For her, dignity embodied the true character of the individual. It was not love of the self; it was appreciation of one's true values, the essence of one's humanity, one's enduring qualities and values. She admonished us to properly guard our dignity and our honor, for they were not negotiable commodities. You are not known by what you eat, she told me, but who you are. No one will investigate the contents of your stomach, but they will scrutinize the content of your character. "Be proud, but not arrogant," she said. "Be polite, but not overbearing. Be self-sufficient: self-sufficient and self-confident people don't need to be jealous."

She taught us not to envy, because envy tends to deform character: "You must not have a hole in your eye," she used to say. That hole is bottomless, it can never be filled. Human envy is insatiable and will diminish an individual. Instead of envying individuals for what material possessions they have, high position they hold, or power they wield, one must be impressed only by who they are, respect them for values they possess and what good they do.

The teachings and musings of my grandmother, I soon discovered when I went to school, were not original. Indeed, as a choirboy and altar boy, I heard some of them during the Sunday sermons as well as at school. What was unique about my grandmother was that she practiced what she taught.

*　*　*

Our house was modest, built of bricks and separated from neighboring houses by thick, tall walls typical of other dwellings. It was walled in because privacy and security were of paramount importance. From outside, you could see and hear nothing. A heavy, solid door with a big doorknob and keyhole opened up to a hallway leading to a courtyard. On the street side of the courtyard was my father's bedroom and that of my cousin Bobken. Next to it was our spacious and formal reception and dining room, used for guests and special occasions only. That room was a showplace. Our best rugs, good china, silverware, electric lamp, small chandelier, modern, expandable dining room table, and modern chairs and sofa, were all there. The room came alive during Christmas and Easter as well as on birthdays and name days. Otherwise, it was off limits for us. Underneath this reception room there was a cistern, a reservoir for fresh water. We received fresh water two or three times a year, brought through aqueducts and distributed throughout Tabriz under the supervision of the *mirab* (supervisor of water distribution).

Next to the cistern was a basement, unfortunately damp, used for storage. Across the small courtyard was our bedroom. It was large and used for dining, study, recreation, and sleeping. It had no electricity. We used oil or kerosene lamps. The earthen floor of this room was covered with *hassir* (straw matting), which was, in turn, covered with kilims. They all served to prevent the damp from working through. In addition to curtains, during the summer months, the windows were also protected with straw shades. Our mattresses, quilts, and pillows were stored in open, recessed wall spaces, covered with colorful curtains, as were our copper dishes, samovar, everyday china, and utensils.

Twice a day, as we woke up or got ready for bed, we had to rearrange the furniture and put aside the mattresses to ready the room for other functions. Across the hall was a smaller bedroom where my uncle Armenag slept. Behind these two bedrooms was a large, multipurpose room: our kitchen. In the middle of the kitchen there was our *toneer* (tandoor) or oven. The *toneer* was central to a family's health and continuity. Indeed, the hearth fire symbolized a family's longevity. (Even today, we have a saying in Armenian: May the light of your hearth *(ojakh)* or fireplace not be extinguished.)

Every month or so, my grandmother cooked bread—called *lavash*. She placed on a large slab balls of dough and began to stretch them with a rolling pin. When they were almost paper thin, the dough was slapped against the heated side of the tandoor. On such occasions, my grandmother wore a big padded mitt over her right hand. While slapping one, she would pull another one from the other side of the *toneer*. The thin sheets of *lavash* were then stacked in tall piles and stored on special suspended bread trays. They stayed fresh for weeks. When needed, these breads were dampened with water and wrapped around a piece of meat or cheese.

The small coal burners in the kitchen were used during times of relative financial well-being to cook rice, chicken, varieties of dolmas, stuffed cabbage, quince, apple, squash, eggplant, grape leaves, or sauces that contained meat, pine nuts, and raisins to accompany the rice dishes. Occasionally, my grandmother cooked *kufta,* a huge meatball that contained an entire chicken or many hard-boiled eggs. It was served both as a soup and a main dish. On rare occasions, we were served pig's feet. This dish was cooked slowly for some twenty-four hours and was a great delicacy.

On Christmas and Easter, depending on money, my grandmother cooked *nazook,* which were unsweetened as well as sweet coffee rolls. This was an all-day event. It required the use of special yeast dough and very rich sweetened or unsweetened fillings. We carried these, along with a variety of cakes, and, with some rarity, a leg of lamb, a sturgeon, or a rabbit to the local bakery. We had to wait in line, since most families like ours, who did not have large ovens, had the same dishes in different quantities that had to be baked. The aroma of freshly cooked *nazook* was so enticing and intoxicating that there was a belief that you had to serve one to anyone who commented on its aroma, even on your way home; otherwise that person would develop a mysterious craving for it, which, if left unsatisfied, would be harmful to health.

Every Friday or Saturday night, our kitchen was transformed into a bathhouse. Plenty of water was boiled. My sister and I took turns taking "showers." We stood in the middle of a copper basin while our grandmother washed us, scrubbed us, and combed our hair. Once a month we spent an entire day in a rented unit of a public bathhouse, owned and operated by an Armenian. As I grew older, a professional scrubber was engaged to scrub me.

In the spring, summer, and autumn, when we woke up and got dressed in the mornings we filled our copper bowls with water and carried them along with soap and towels to the courtyard, where we washed our hands and faces. In the winter, we washed in the kitchen with hot water. It was only *after* we had washed our hands and faces that we could bid each other good morning.

During the winter months, we operated a wood- or charcoal-burning oven in our combined bedroom, dining, and study room. The oven provided heat and allowed us to dry our wet shoes. Occasionally we cooked on it. However, we had to open the window of the room off and on so as not to be poisoned by the charcoal.

The wood and charcoal were stacked in the main basement, under our bedroom. The damp and humid basement also stored our flour, bread, big ceramic jars that contained butter, *gaourma* (boiled and heavily salted lamb or beef), jars with homemade tomato sauce, rice, pickled cucumbers, grapes, a variety of jams, boxes of basic soap, potatoes, assorted dried beans, and pieces of *chortan,* dried yogurt, hard as a rock. Whenever we needed yogurt soup, in the absence of fresh yogurt, we placed several pieces of dried yogurt in boiling water to make instant soup. When we had the means, we replenished some of these staples, especially butter and meat.

Under my uncle's bedroom was the family's bathroom. It was a standard, spacious, clean outhouse. Water, lime, and salt were used to control the stench. Since Tabriz had no sewage system at the time, the waste was carted away once a year or every other year. Those were terrible, stinking occasions. Peasants with huge leather bags loaded the nightsoil on donkeys and carried it to the outskirts of the city. One positive aspect of the outhouse was the fact that nobody stayed there too long. There was no firm lock at the door. When we used it, we coughed a lot to indicate that we were there.

Finally, we had a courtyard with several small trees, some flowers, and a big almond tree. Unfortunately, it bore bitter nuts. We also had a temperamental peach tree which, for two or three years, refused to bear any fruit. I remember a mock trial for the tree, one relative brandishing an ax threatening to cut it down, another one pleading loudly to give it another chance because the next year surely it would bear fruit. And it did. Evidently, the threat was serious enough to scare the tree.

*   *   *

After the Anglo-Soviet occupation of Iran and my mother's death, my father, Samuel, a young widower thirty-eight years old, stayed in Tabriz instead of returning to his job with the Anglo-Iranian Oil Company in Abadan. He found employment with the Morrison-Knudson Corporation and Comsax, two international construction companies. My father was well organized, fastidious, and meticulous about his overall appearance: his suits, ties, shirts, and shoes were reflections of his conservative taste. He got regular and proper haircuts and took, what seemed to me then, an inordinate amount of time to shave. Every morning, right after early breakfast, he used to open a box of assorted razor blades, sharpen them with a new gadget, place a portable mirror on a table with a bowl of hot water, soap and a brush. There were no variations. The only novelty in his routine was the introduction of Burma Shave.

My father, alone now, had to face his responsibilities as a parent. He was lucky. So were we. My grandmother took care of us. She cooked, cleaned, washed, sewed, and knitted. We were not her only responsibility. She took care of my father, my uncle, and my cousin. My father was not a daily presence in our lives. As I grew up, one of my amazing realizations was that we had no books at home. Actually, that is not correct. We had two books: the Bible, in vernacular Armenian, and a high school world history textbook in English. Then there was a pamphlet on feminism, written by my father in his very handsome handwriting. Sometime after he graduated from the American Memorial High School, he must have lost interest in reading and writing. If there were any newspapers, they were taken in sporadically. His cousins had a radio, but we did not.

To this day, it is a great puzzle to me that my father did not take an interest in our education. He never read to us. He never visited our schools and I don't remember his helping me with homework, or playing with us, or ever telling or reading a story to us. I believe he took us to the movies on two or three occasions. I don't remember him giving us any toys. Actually, that is not completely accurate. During the course of my entire childhood, I was given a stuffed mechanical toy duck, an American soldier's hat, a football, and a dove. I lost the dove to a neighborhood pigeon trainer; the mechanical duck malfunctioned; the American soldier's hat was stolen. The football lasted for a while—the neighborhood boys, my classmates, and I put it to good use. Although my father was not interested in our schooling, he took great pride in my sister's beauty. On one or two occasions, an American or a European couple compared her to Shirley Temple and even inquired as to whether she could be given up for adoption.

What astonished and, as I grew older, angered me was that my father, who gave English-language private lessons, and translated and drafted letters, never responded to my eager request to learn English. Only once, he wrote the English alphabet for me. To demonstrate my seriousness and diligence, and to please him, I must have copied the English alphabet at least a hundred times. It was a vain effort. I remember only two occasions when my father took pride in my abilities and accomplishments: once when I was able to name the capitals of all the European and Asian countries, and when, during holiday parties and special occasions, I was asked to recite Armenian poetry and even sing a song or two.

Still, I have two very pleasant memories of my father. When I was six or seven years old, he took me to the local Armenian barbershop. There stood a big barber with his apron, scissors, clippers, and a long razor blade. A big chair faced a huge mirror. Underneath it there were many fancy bottles of perfume, alcohol, and a jar of powder. I was petrified. My father stood by my side. I thought of him as a powerful protector. My long, curly hair was cut. Per my grandmother's instructions, however, we retrieved my cut hair, which she sent to an Armenian church in Karadagh, "known for its power." Years later, I was told that these locks were placed in one of the walls of the church. My grandmother did not want my departed hair to end up in a garbage dump. (She also saved my first teeth.) I remember, also, when my father took me for my first photograph. I was obedient and well behaved and it was a memorable experience. The photographer disappeared behind a curtain several times. Then there it was. My picture!

My father's financial situation was precarious. During periods of unemployment, in the first year or so of the Soviet occupation of Tabriz, and in transitions between jobs, my mother's Singer sewing machine was pawned to Mr. Sadegh, a moneylender. That sewing machine and a carpet were her legacies. Mr. Sadegh would call on my father to ask that he repay his loan or pay additional interest. My grandmother and I would go to the door and inform him that my father was not at home. Other creditors also came to ask for unpaid interest payments. On one or two occasions, the deed of our house was also mortgaged. My sister, too, was sent home for my father's failure to pay her tuition. During these difficult interludes, it was once again left to my grandmother's wits to feed us. She had a very good reputation in our neighborhood and great credit with grocers, bakers, and butchers. All I had to do was to say in Turkish or Armenian that *Voski Bajee* (Sister Voski) had sent me to fetch foodstuffs. Meanwhile, my father, who was a proud, jovial, and sentimental person, put on a façade of nonchalance and strong self-confidence, playing backgammon, dominoes, cards, or drinking with a handful of his friends or frequenting Stepan's grocery shop. Although my father liked to drink, he was not an alcoholic. I saw him totally drunk only once. His companion, who was also drunk, was a policeman. Under the influence of alcohol, my father was being addressed as "Your Excellency Mr. Mayor." The policeman, in turn, had assumed the title of "Esteemed Colonel."

Beginning in 1946 and through 1949, there were appeals from Soviet Armenia to "working Armenian families" from the diaspora to emigrate to Armenia. My father flirted with the idea, along with his first cousin, Grigor, and his four sons and their families. In anticipation of such a move, he bought, as an investment, ten boxes of Lux soap. It was rumored that there was a big demand for it, not only in Armenia but in the entire Soviet Union. Since we did not go to Soviet Armenia, we used the Lux soap for the next few years.

Having worked for several British and American construction companies as an accountant, my father was hired to work for Barbari, the Transportation Department of the Province of Azerbaijan. When, under the Soviet auspices, an autonomous Republic of Azerbaijan was established, my father became an employee of the new "republic," which lasted for a year. In 1946, under Allied and United Nations pressure, the Soviet-supported republics of Azerbaijan and Kurdistan collapsed and the Iranian government took full control of both provinces. Iranian oil concessions to the Soviet Union were nullified. Those who had worked for the republic were investigated, including my father. The entire leadership of the Transportation Department was under suspicion for having made illicit and personal gains during the transition. My father was exonerated but it took another year or two before he found a "suitable" job.

My father, a competent and conscientious bureaucrat who believed in order, process, efficiency, and status, was a poor businessman. He tried several business ventures and all of them failed. In 1946, he made an investment in a consignment of modern design coffee cups that were supposed to be very fashionable. There was no demand for them. Then he bought, with a relative as a partner, a used U.S.-made truck. It was a venture capital deal. The driver of the truck, his partner, kept the capital and my father inherited the venture. I loved the truck and liked the driver. He allowed me to ride with him to nearby destinations. This truck had many breakdowns, in part because people believed the tonnage for which they were built could be doubled without any risk.

A third venture consisted of the concessions for the sale of refreshments at the Dideban cinema. I loved it. It meant that we could go to the movies for free with our father. Unfortunately, there was no profit in that business. My father and his partners sold the concession. While waiting for the "right job," my father gave private lessons in English and translated commercial transactions. Naturally, he never discussed any of his ventures or disappointments with us.

When the Soviet Union withdrew its armed forces from Iran in 1946, precipitating the fall of the Azerbaijan and Kurdistan autonomous "republics," the Iranian army remained in the outskirts of Tabriz for several days. Retributions were meted out by organized groups and scores were settled against former officials of the autonomous republics. Most of them fled to the Soviet Union; some were shot in the streets of Tabriz. At the time, my apolitical father demonstrated a rare act of courage. We gave shelter in our attic and food for several days to Abi, a minor official in the Ministry of Transportation. While we were all apprehensive of the consequences, I was very proud of my father.

CHAPTER TWO

Childhood

During the Soviet occupation of northern Iran (1941–1946) after the abdication and exile of Reza Shah Pahlavi, the Armenian elementary schools were reopened. For the first time, Russian was introduced as a second language and the instruction of Persian was deemphasized. Some of our textbooks came from Soviet Armenia. For a brief period, 1945–1946, when Azerbaijan was made an "autonomous" republic, Azeri Turkish was added to our curriculum, which included Armenian language and literature, history, the Russian and Persian languages, mathematics, physical education, art, and music.

The Tamarian elementary school was a sanctuary, a self-contained world. I loved my school. I had friends there and I was given books. I had good teachers who introduced me to unknown worlds and foreign languages and allowed me to learn and appreciate my mother tongue, with its unique alphabet created in the late fourth and beginning of the fifth century A.D. I was interested in everything, but above all in history and literature, singing and music. I remember my first lesson in Persian—it was about an illiterate who wants to buy a pair of eyeglasses and tests many of them until the pharmacist asks him what kind of glasses he wants. "Reading ones," he answers. "Sir," answers the pharmacist, "first you have to learn how to read."

My love of history and literature, I think, were due to the influence of my elementary school teachers, particularly Onnik Yeganian. He was a patient, passionate, and inspiring teacher. In addition, we were made aware that we were living in the midst of fast-moving historical times. There were the Soviet troops in Tabriz, with their tanks and annual parades. There was a huge map of the Soviet Union in the center of the city. Great arrows indicated the positions of Nazi and Soviet armed forces. When there were Soviet successes, the maps changed. I remember our celebration of the successful defenses of Stalingrad and Leningrad. I began collecting the pictures and biographies of famous Soviet (and Armenian) generals: Voroshilov, Budyoni, Koniev, Rokosovsky, Zhukov, Safarian, Bagramian, Admiral Isakov. We took great pride in the fact that there were so many Armenian generals in the Soviet army, and so many heroes of the Soviet Union. I had a poster of the Big Three, Churchill, Stalin, and Roosevelt, who met in Tehran in 1943.

The immediacy of war was also felt at home when we were asked on two or three occasions to send foodstuffs as a gift to orphans in Kharkov and Kiev. Notwithstanding the fact that we did not have much for ourselves, I pleaded with my grandmother, saying that since we were orphans we should help other orphans, that the school expected each of us to do our best. My grandmother gave me two kilos of rice and a kilo of raisins. She placed them in two small white bags. I copied the address given to me and the message: "To the orphans of Kharkov and Kiev, from Vartan Gregorian." I have wondered all these years whatever happened to those hundreds of packages sent by us, the Armenian children of Tabriz. Did they reach their destination? Were they simply attempts to mobilize public opinion on behalf of the Soviet war effort?

It was not only us, the children of Tabriz, who were asked to contribute to the Soviet war effort. The entire Armenian community of Iran was asked to do its share as well by contributing to the funding of a Soviet tank unit to be known as David of Sassoon (the Armenian epic hero). In the process of fund-raising, Armenians made outlandish claims about "the genius of the Armenian military." It was asserted later that it was the Armenian General Never Safarian's tank division that had captured Berlin. There was even speculation that Nazi Germany owed its initial spectacular military successes against the Soviet Union to a General Guderian, another Armenian general. He actually was not an Armenian.

While my grandmother knitted gloves, mittens, pullovers, scarves, and socks for me and my sister, all my other clothes were hand-me-downs from my father. From age eleven to fourteen, I wore my father's old suits, altered and refitted by my cousin Bobken. Easter was my favorite holiday because sometimes I was given a pair of new shoes. My shoes had to be repaired and with time I had only one pair for all seasons. I had no galoshes. Winters were very harsh, as were the rainy seasons. Every ice patch, every pothole had to be negotiated. What protected my feet were the thick woolen socks that my grandmother made. I don't remember having any new clothes until I was fourteen when my cousin Bobken gave me a suit as a gift. He also gave me my first colored crayons. My father's first cousin, Uncle Grigor, gave me my first inkpad. I remember how proud I was walking into my classroom with a shining silver-colored inkpad.

But while we were poor, my sister and I as well as our friends had an ample supply of imagination. When I learned about the importance of oxygen and the nefarious nature of carbon dioxide at age eight or nine, I thought I had made a "discovery" that would impress even the long-bearded, wise professors for I found a simple formula that would lengthen human life. I thought that since we inhaled air with our noses and exhaled through our mouths, if people did not talk, they would spare the nose and themselves from the harmful effects of the carbon dioxide and live longer. I imagined how scientists would be surprised if they heard about this discovery and would wonder how this elementary, commonsensical solution for longevity had eluded them for such a long time.

When I learned in a class about anteaters, I schemed how my sister and I could become rich quickly. I had heard that America was a very clean country. Ergo, it must not have ants, but it did have zoos and the zoos had anteaters that needed ants. So we embarked upon a business scheme. We started killing thousands of big black ants because they were more valuable, powerful, and numerous; they were "Muslim" ants. We spared the small yellow ants because they were helpless "Christian" ants. After stuffing these multitudes of ants into hundreds of matchboxes, just for the sake of insurance I told my second-grade teacher that there are those who say that there are no ants in America. "Those who say that are stupid," he retorted. Disappointed and ashamed, we organized a makeshift Christian ceremony and buried all the "Muslim" ants in front of our big almond tree.

When I was eight or nine, I became an altar boy at Saint Sarkis Church. On Sundays and holidays and special occasions, such as funerals, I carried tall candles and sometimes a religious banner. I also sang in the choir. It was a wonderful feeling to stand at the altar, wearing a beautifully handcrafted and embroidered robe, facing the congregation, next to the priest in his resplendent vestments. Not only did I feel important and useful, but I also loved the church, its liturgy, its mystery. As time went on, I appreciated my part in a ceremony that was over 1,650 years old and encompassed such a long period, times of tragedy, suffering, misery, despair, and happiness as well, times in which generations of Armenians had prayed to God and had not abandoned hope.

Until I was fourteen, I took part in the church services. Its liturgy, sometimes pleading and sometimes triumphant, captivated me. When the choir sang *"Sourp, Sourp"* ("Holy, Holy"), it was so beautiful that I was sure that it was a tribute worthy of God's attention. When the choir sang "Lord Have Mercy on Us," I observed a throng of believers transfixed with grief, anxiety, and hope, asking for forgiveness. I was sure that God heard them. And when I heard the hymn "Heavenly Jerusalem," a prayer for the rest of the souls of the departed, I remembered my mother and uncles and was moved to pray for their souls. I experienced intense emotions, a sense of communion with generations past, and an awe before the possible, mysterious presence of an omnipresent God.

In the church I found a secure world that not only lifted my spirits but gave me a sense of individuality as well as belonging. I was somebody, and the Church affirmed my importance and respected me every Sunday and every holiday, by allowing me to stand next to the priest at the altar and accompany him to every important religious ceremony. The fact that the priest, Ter Karapet, had married my parents and baptized me in the same church gave me great pride.

Every year, I waited with great anticipation for Christmas, Holy Week, and Easter. Even though I was not asked, I took upon myself at the beginning of Holy Week to clean and shine the church's wrought-bronze wreaths, which would cover, on Good Friday, the symbolic coffin of Christ. I learned the entire liturgy of the Armenian Church. So strong was the influence of the Church on me and my obsession and love for it as an altar boy and choirboy that on several occasions I horrified my grandmother and sister by sleepwalking. During these episodes, I put a sheet on my back in imitation of the priest's robes and attempted to perform a Sunday service.

I had disappointments, too, the first when I saw our priest coming out of the men's room. It shocked me. At that age, I had simple notions: God had created men and women, priests and nuns, as well as Muslim mullahs, as distinct entities. They were different. Therefore, I thought, priests could not have the same bodily needs as the rest of us. After all, they were covered head to toe with black tunics and some of them had long beards. But soon I learned that the priests were also married and had children, that, indeed, to be a priest in the Armenian Church, you must be married, unless you wanted to be a celibate member of the Church's scholarly and ruling spiritual cadre. Another disappointment awaited me. I thought Christ was Armenian, since our Church was Armenian and we prayed and read the Bible in Armenian. It came as a surprise that Christ was born a Jew and that Aramaic, the language Jesus is thought to have spoken, was not Armenian.

When I was thirteen or fourteen, I read Victor Hugo's *Les Misérables* and was deeply moved by Jean Valjean and the spirit of charity and redemption. My reading coincided with my encounter with Olinka. Mentally deranged, she was one of two or three homeless individuals who subsisted in the Armenian quarter of Tabriz. According to the lore, she was once a beautiful girl who had fallen in love, been betrayed by her lover, gone crazy, lost everything, and lived a lonely life, earning charity by singing love songs. She had a beautiful voice but was unkempt and kept cats. It was rumored that she took care of some of them, during the winters, in the warmth of her bosom. One Easter, Olinka showed up in church, minus the cats, wanting to receive communion. The priest refused her. That shocked me. I saw no Christian charity in that act, none of the redemptive qualities embodied in Jean Valjean. I was utterly disillusioned.

The lively rivalry among the three priests of our church—Father Karapet, Father Vartan, and Father Sahag—seemed shameful to us. They quarreled over who would preside over the funerals of the rich and who would bless the graves of important people's family members. As the priests read the prayers in the company of altar boys and a deacon, the relatives slipped "thank you" donations to the priests.

The church became a source of pocket money. Since funeral processions required candle bearers and banner bearers, altar boys also received small donations. Those were welcome occasions. So were Christmas and Easter, when instead of the regular collection plates for the church and the poor, there were at least four more for priests, the deacon, and the choir and altar boys. We altar boys, who carried the collection plates, were at the bottom of the totem pole. Naturally, the first two or three plates received the largest donations and the last one, the smallest. On one occasion, we were so incensed that when my friend Vahak asked me to transfer some of the bills from the third plate to the last, I responded readily. Later, I prayed for forgiveness.

In spite of its shortcomings, the Armenian Church remained the center of our religious and social life. We were told not to confuse the gatekeepers with the Church and its historical mission and spiritual essence. Besides, our Church had no real competition. On several occasions, we young boys and girls were invited to attend the Seventh-Day Adventist Church for religious services and Sunday school. We found out, to our great surprise, that the minister was Miss Satenik, a middle-aged Armenian spinster. She gave us pictures of Christ depicting several biblical stories. We were asked to shut our eyes while praying. Miss Satenik admonished me once for not doing so. My answer did not please her: "How did you know that, since you were to shut your eyes, also, while you prayed?" During a typical Sunday school, we sang unfamiliar hymns and Miss Satenik played the piano. We even sang "Farmer in the Dell." Miss Satenik had translated the words into Turkish:

> Pishig schan istar
> (The cat wants mice)
>
> Schan panir istar
> (The mice want cheese)
>
> Hallo cherrio, Pishig schan istar
> (The cat wants mice)

And on and on . . .

Miss Satenik and scores of other missionaries, who were prohibited from proselytizing Muslims, concentrated their efforts on Armenian and Assyrian Christians. While the Protestants did not convert many, they did provide excellent educational opportunities and health services to citizens of Tabriz and others in Iran. The American Hospital was one of the most respected institutions of our city. I was convinced that all Americans wore eyeglasses, since all the missionaries did. I had concluded that it was because they were well educated or read too much.

The state of medical care in Tabriz was very poor. I don't remember any medical checkups or visits to the dentist. I do remember vaccinations in our schools. My sister's and my medical needs were taken care of by my grandmother and her friends with their scant knowledge of folk medicine. Whenever we caught a terrible cold, we stayed in bed. My grandmother practiced cupping—special cups were heated from inside by fire and placed on our backs. The vacuum created in the glasses sucked our skins: the bluer the skin was, the happier my grandmother was because they were getting rid of our fever, our colds. After removing the cup, my grandmother rubbed our backs with alcohol or vodka. We sweated and our fever subsided. Only years later did I learn that cupping was a common practice among Persians, Turks, Russians, and even Jews in the United States from Eastern Europe. For whooping cough, the proposed remedy was donkey's milk. Thank God, I never had whooping cough! Several years ago, I learned from my sister that when I was nine years old, my grandmother and a friend had determined that my tongue was very short. They contemplated cutting the frenulum to let my tongue grow.

In addition to school and the church, there was the Armenian Prelacy, with its buildings, garden, and library. In the evenings, we young people went to the garden to enjoy each other's company, to see and be seen. Since it was the Prelacy, it was open to Armenians only, with a policeman or a guard at the gate. Armenian theatrical, cultural, and educational organizations held their activities in the Prelacy. In the mornings the yards were used by the David of Sassoon Armenian Sports Association. Several hundred of us young boys and girls belonged to it and wore distinctive T-shirts with the emblem of David of Sassoon, the legendary Armenian epic hero, on his magic horse, armed with his magic sword. The Prelacy's Rostom-Kaspar library had a couple of thousand books and periodicals, most Armenian. There were, however, some Russian and German volumes as well.

From age eleven on, I was a part-time page at the library, which proved to be a great oasis of privacy, peace, and occasional solitude. I loved to read and I read everything. I understood some of what I read, was bewildered by much, but over time the library introduced me to Armenia's history and literature, and Russian, English, German, and Polish novels in translation. The library opened a new world. At age fourteen, with two friends, I edited a newspaper named *Ararat* for the library's bulletin board. I wrote an editorial titled "Our Voice" and the first obituary about the late, beloved prelate of our Church, Archbishop Nerses Melik-Tanguian. At the same time, I started to write articles for the respected Armenian daily *Alik* in Tehran, beginning with obituaries and reporting on cultural events in Tabriz. I wrote under a pseudonym in order to be taken seriously by the readers. Neither the library nor the newspaper paid, but I benefited immensely from both. I was poor, but I was not alone.

I faced on a daily basis a major problem: I had no pocket money. I had no regular allowance and when I did get it, it was a pittance. It became the cause of my first overt conflict with my father. He wanted me to ask for it every Sunday. He refused to just give it, and I refused to ask for it. My sister, a generous soul, asked for her allowance with great grace and charm. She got it. She often split it with me and on an occasion or two "lent" it to me, secretly, for I had refused to "beg" for it. My grandmother gave me what she could spare, which was not much, since she had sold and spent almost everything she had on us. Occasionally, my cousin Bobken, the most generous, loving, caring male relative of mine, gave me some change. Under the circumstances, without money, I could not go to the movies with my friends, or rent a bicycle for an hour, or buy a baked potato or red beet or quince, not to mention that I could not buy books, and there were times I could not even rent books from a local stationery store, which carried Sherlock Holmes and Arsène Lupin detective stories. The shop rented by the day. To maximize its profits, it split the books into two or three parts to prevent borrowers from being able to read the entire book in one night.

Desperate, I gathered the nuts of our bitter almond tree and went from pharmacy to pharmacy, attempting to sell them. Most were not buying, and when they bought, it yielded a very meager sum. We had some fifteen or twenty pounds of surplus nails in our basement which I took then to the bazaar. There was no market for them.

I tried to earn some pocket money during the summer months by working as an "apprentice," in reality a "gofer," in the shops of two outstanding silversmiths. At the time, there were many well-known and talented Armenian silversmiths, goldsmiths, and jewelers in Tabriz. Most of these artisans were the remnants of the Armenian community of Van, in Turkey, decimated during the World War I Armenian Genocide. They had relocated in Tabriz and after two or three decades had become a dominant artisan force.

As an apprentice, I cleaned the premises, did errands, and polished the silver. The pay was very little, but I was grateful for it. My grandmother was also happy, since I was "off the streets." Once in a while a family purchased a silver set for a dowry or a wedding gift. On such occasions, the apprentices got a handsome tip, enough for one or two movie tickets. One or two summers, I served as an apprentice in my cousin Petros's tailoring shop.

Another short-lived apprenticeship was in a brush "factory," in reality a sweatshop. The compensation was small. It was not based on hourly, daily, or weekly wages but on how many brushes you finished. I was a miserable failure.

*   *   *

There were three movie houses in Tabriz: Mihan, Homa, and Dideban. Each was divided into classes: loge, first tier orchestra, and second tier orchestra. The first six or seven rows, the steerage, was the fourth class, separated from the others by a partition.

Most of the movies were in English, as they originated in Hollywood, and it took them many years to get to Tabriz. Unfortunately, they were not dubbed or subtitled. We loved Tarzan, action and adventure movies, comedies with Laurel and Hardy, Charlie Chaplin and, later, Bob Hope, Red Skelton, and Abbott and Costello. We were enthralled with space wars

(Flash Gordon) and *The Jungle Book*. Movies such as *Frankenstein* and *King Kong* gave us nightmares.

One day my friend Vartkes and I, eight and a half, went to the Mihan movie house to see a Charlie Chaplin movie. Our plan was to sneak into the movie house on a Saturday, see the movie, and come back home by five P.M. In those days you could get in and leave the movie house any time. We must have sat through two or three shows. I remember that Charlie Chaplin got out of a barrel and hit someone on the head several times. Suddenly, it was nine P.M. and the theater was closing. We were petrified. So were our relatives, who had notified the police that we were missing. With great trepidation we began our fast return home. Halfway there, we were met by scores of relatives, acquaintances, and friends with lanterns, out looking for us. Thank God, my father was out of town. My grandmother gave me the punishment of my life, hitting me very hard because she was happy that I was safe. I was grounded for several months.

Notwithstanding this terrible start, I became enamored of movies. Over the years, I saw such silent movie stars as the Keystone Cops, Tom Mix, Lon Chaney, and the Lone Ranger. The movies that left the greatest impression on me were those with Rin-Tin-Tin, *The Mark of Zorro* (1920), starring Douglas Fairbanks Sr., *The Three Musketeers* (1922), and *The Great Train Robbery* (1903). *The Sheik* (1926), featuring Rudolph Valentino, packed the movie house night after night. Although I liked the desert scenes, the beautiful horses, and the tents (they reminded me of *The Arabian Nights*), I did not like the movie. There was lots of romantic "mush" and not much action.

I became an addict of talking cowboy movies. Even though the movies were not dubbed, the themes were simple and formulaic. We all knew right away that the protagonist would not die, that the white hats were the good guys and the black hats were the bad ones. We recognized that the *Mystery of the Hooded Horseman* (1937), starring Tex Ritter, was about greed, landgrab, cattle, and justice. Occasionally we were surprised to see that Clark Gable, a former hero of Westerns, was cast in the role of a bad guy, such as in *The Painted Desert* (1931). Nevertheless, we loved William Boyd (Hopalong Cassidy) and his magnificent white horse. We were overwhelmed by John Wayne and Randolph Scott. We saw *Stagecoach* (1939) several times. We loved Ringo Kid (John Wayne) and his quest to confront his brother's murderers. In *The Man of the Frontier* (1936), we were astonished that a cowboy (Gene Autry) who exposed the saboteurs of an irrigation project was a singing cowboy. However, for weeks we hummed and whistled the tune from *Red River Valley* (1936). Several years later, we saw Howard Hughes's

The Outlaw (1943), starring Walter Houston and Jane Russell, about Billy the Kid and Doc Holliday. We did not know anything about their alleged rivalry. We admired the horse and fast gun mastery of the protagonists and, above all, we were touched by acts of loyalty and friendship. It was only years later that I realized that censors had cut out Jane Russell's sexy scene.

Western action movies had a tremendous impact on my generation. They provided us with instant and pure fantasies, a source of escape. Good characters always survived, even good people's hats never fell off. For us, used to our traditional society's didactic teachings, they were morality plays—set against the Western landscape—about loyalty, friendship, self-sacrifice, justice, and standing up for one's rights, especially the underdog's. The horses, saloons, guns, cattle drives, fearless cowboy heroes, loyal sidekicks, and trusting heroines became welcome inhabitants in our minds and memories.

We engaged in mock duels and battles with guns cut out of cardboard or wood, painted black. We made masks, à la Zorro. We called each other John, Bill, Jack, Tom, and Mack. We all became cowboys. Unfortunately, there were no heroines to be won over and, understandably, there were no Indians. We all learned to say *Hi, pardner,* and *Howdee,* with our thick Turkish, Persian, and Armenian accents.

Outer space was another frontier. The adventures of Flash Gordon captivated our imagination so much that on Saturday afternoons we played in our churchyard, using the doorknobs of the church as control wheels for the outer spacecraft we were in—starting the engines with sounds in chorus of *fsh . . . fsh . . . fsh . . .*

We also loved gangster and horror movies. George Raft, James Cagney, and Edward G. Robinson were our favorite gangsters. *Frankenstein, Dracula,* and *Fu Manchu* scared us. One had to demonstrate to his peers that he was not afraid. Occasionally we saw musicals. We did not like them, especially the kissing scenes, which embarrassed us. We viewed them as annoying interruptions. We wanted action! The dances were deemed to be unnecessary distractions, burdensome and boring. After viewing a handful of musicals, including one featuring Deanna Durbin, we concluded that Americans must be singing and kissing all the time. Another "revelation" for us was that other than bartenders, cowboys, pirates, shopkeepers, gangsters, and certainly the Indians, no one worked for a living in the United States.

Soviet movies brought us down from outer space to face the Soviet struggle against Nazi Germany, focusing on acts of individual and collective courage and self-sacrifice for the Motherland. *She Defends the Motherland* (1943), Lev Arnshtam's *Zoia Kosmodemianskaia* (1944), about the arrest and execution of the teenage partisan heroine, and *Raduga* (*The Rainbow,* 1943) were some of the movies shown to us. During the war, the Soviets revived Russian nationalist movies such as *Ivan the Terrible* (1944). In the summer, it was a treat to see *Alexander Nevski,* as well as *Peter the Great,* extolling the greatness of the Russian nation and its "heroic struggles" against "Teutonic hordes." I remember vividly the imposing and forceful figure of Peter the Great, the unifier and modernizer of the Russian nation. In the summer, we saw many open-air movies about the Bolshevik Revolution and the Civil War. One film that left a great impression on me was *Chapaiev* (1934), which dealt with civil war in Russia and the triumph of the Bolshevik Red Army.

Arabic and Indian movies were our last choices. Indian ones at least had some swordsmanship as well as singing. The plots of these movies were formulaic: a rich, fat guy wants to marry a young, beautiful girl. Her father is urging her to agree. The mother, however, wants true happiness for her daughter and she opposes the match. As it happens, the girl is in love with a young, handsome man who is, unfortunately, poor. This family conflict gives occasion to lots of singing and mourning and becomes a morality tale. The message was mainly about the fact that people should not be judged by what they have, but who they are. The right to choose one's love and mate was usually affirmed and, naturally, love always triumphed.

The movies allowed us to transcend our sorrows, misery, and anxieties, and liberated us from the oppressive, monotonous routine of daily life. As the cinema's lights were switched off and the movies began, magic took over: we got carried away to another world, a world of dreams, imagination, beauty, justice, compassion, and possibilities. If there was nothing in the outside world, the internal world, the world of imagination, became a whole world unto itself.

Other than the movies and school, cultural, and athletic activities, we looked forward to many religious and secular holidays with great anticipation. First of all, there was *Amanor,* January 1, the New Year. If we received gifts at all, we received them on the first day of the New Year. Such gifts were brought thanks to Saint Nicholas or Santa Claus, whom we never saw, since they were busy tending to all of humanity. New Year's was a secular event, not a religious one.

To mark the arrival of the New Year, we usually had a very small tree. We decorated it with tiny cotton balls (which resembled snowflakes), strings of popcorn, some decorations consisting of multicolor shiny paper and small candles lit once or twice under vigilant supervision. Grown-up, sophisticated Armenians celebrated the New Year at the Armenian Club, with music, dance, drinks, and dinner. Until his remarriage, my father was one of these sophisticated Armenians. The rest of us stayed home. No radio, no fireworks, no bells heralded the advent of the New Year.

In 1947 or 1948, I was asked to man the RCA gramophone at a dance party organized by a group of young Armenians. The apartment where they danced had pictures of Tyrone Power, Clark Gable, Alice Faye, Rita Hayworth, Dorothy Lamour, Betty Grable, Robert Taylor, and other movie stars. The couples danced to the latest tunes of Western music. I happily changed the records and learned my first song, Cole Porter's "When They Begin the Beguine." Naturally, I did not know the meaning of the words. The other tune that appealed to me was "La Paloma." For the first time, I saw couples in love dancing cheek to cheek. I was so envious that the intensity of the feeling made me feel guilty. I could not wait to get older in order to have the opportunity and the right to dance cheek to cheek. Between childhood and adulthood, there were no consolations. For my generation, there was no such thing as a teenage period or teenage culture. Everything truly exciting belonged to the adults.

In anticipation of the New Year and Christmas, Armenian families started cooking a variety of cakes, cookies, and a variety of meat and vegetable dishes and baked bread. On Christmas Eve, we had our Christmas dinner. All the members of our extended family got together. There was a variety of pilafs, dolmas, spinach, and my favorite, salty sturgeon served with rice. There was wine, beer, and *kvas* (fermented bread) to drink, as well as assorted fruit. The occasion served as the first family reunion of the year. Whereas the New Year was associated with gifts, Christmas was considered to be primarily a religious holiday.

Right after Christmas came Vartanank, the celebration of Saint Vartan. Saints' days in general and Vartanank in particular were occasions for individuals to celebrate their name days. Most people's given names were derived directly or indirectly from the name of a saint. Name days were occasions to receive gifts.

The only Persian festival that captured our attention and imagination was the Iranian New Year. Whereas Armenians, along with Europeans and Russians, celebrated the New Year on January 1, Iran, along with Tajikistan, Uzbekistan, and Afghanistan celebrated *Noe Rooz* (the New Year) on March 21, the first day of spring. *Noe Rooz* thus symbolized hope and renewal and was marked by a weeklong celebration. The last Wednesday of the old year heralded the arrival of the New Year when families gathered around the *Haft sin* table, which symbolized the blessings of the earth. The table held a mirror (symbol of light), a candle (symbol of the sun), a bowl of water (symbol of earth), wheat or lentil sprouts grown on a plate (symbol of revival or rebirth of nature), a basket of painted or colored eggs (symbol of the beginning of life), as well as assorted spring flowers: violets, narcissus, daffodils, and hyacinths. In addition, since the color white symbolizes purity, integrity, and honesty, the *Haft sin* table also held flour, bread, yogurt, cheese, and cube sugar (symbol of abundance). Then, of course, there were many sweets and assorted fruit.

The *Zadig* (Easter) that followed the Persian New Year was a major occasion of celebration, not only because it marked the Resurrection of Christ and was therefore a symbol of rebirth and hope but also because it brought family members together. It also challenged the culinary expertise and aspirations of all the families. Scores of meals had to be prepared, cakes had to be baked, cookies decorated, plates of dried and fresh fruits, chocolates, and candies had to adorn the banquet table to serve, impress, and honor relatives and friends who visited each other to celebrate Easter. New clothes were worn, along with new shoes. We got haircuts and cleaned the house. We went to church, carrying our colored eggs, we played with our friends and strangers as well, attempting to crush their eggs in a competition. We carried the broken eggs home for consumption.

Two other festivals were very dear to us young boys and girls. They pertained to love. Nine weeks before Easter, we celebrated Saint Sarkis Day, dedicated to the patron saint of lovers. We loved that holiday. Each year, it gave us, grown-ups and children as well, an occasion to find out who our true love was. On that day you ate sweets as well as salty cake or candy, especially made for the occasion. You remained thirsty and went to sleep thirsty. It was during that night your dreams might show you the right boy or the girl whom you really loved or who loved you. The one who offered water was your true love, your destiny.

Forty days after Easter, the Church celebrated *Hambardzoom* (Ascension Day). Whereas Saint Sarkis dealt with the realm of dreams, Ascension Day, in addition to its place in Church history and liturgy, also had a fortune-telling ritual concerning love and marriage, called *Veejak* (lottery). The ritual, popular in villages, later was transferred and adopted in urban communities. Seven kinds of wild flowers and water from seven brooks (the numbers dwindled in the cities) were placed in a clay jug, along with possessions from each girl who wanted her fortune told: rings, pins, necklaces, brooches. The jug was placed in full moonlight, because it was believed that stars that shone on the jug shaped man's destiny. A little (innocent) girl, representing Destiny or one's luck, retrieved from the jug the individual objects at regular intervals, as a song of prediction, or prophecy, was sung collectively. Each object was accompanied by a verse, predicting the luck of the individual.

I must also mention one practice common in both the Muslim and Christian communities of Tabriz and Iran. When people made a wish, escaped a calamity, survived an accident, were cured of an illness, gave birth, or sought a safe journey, they made offerings to God by sacrificing sheep in a ritual slaughter.

We could not afford to sacrifice any sheep. But occasionally, we sacrificed a rooster or two. One of the exciting as well as distasteful duties assigned to me was to kill the rooster by cutting off its head. Placing a foot on each wing, I held the rooster's neck and cut it with a sharp knife. The flow of blood almost made me sick. It was considered inhumane to lift your feet off the rooster. You had to wait until it stopped moving. To allow it to stagger without its head was considered to be sinful and sadistic. During my childhood and youth, you always bought live chickens, roosters, and sheep to be sure they were healthy before you slaughtered them. My grandmother always saved the rooster's heart for me. If I swallowed it, she said, it would give me courage.

CHAPTER THREE

The Armenian Community of Tabriz

The Armenian community of Tabriz lived in an invisible ghetto, a neighborhood in which there were also many Muslim shops. Armenians felt superior culturally and yet were comfortable within Azerbaijan's and Tabriz's political and economic structure, dominated by Azeri Muslims. Although the two groups had intensive and extensive business and professional ties, they did not often mix socially.

During the reign of Reza Shah and the Soviet occupation, Armenians performed the compulsory two-year military service. Armenians were allotted two seats in the Iranian parliament, one for northern Iran and one for southern. Schools were integrated, as were movie houses, restaurants, theaters, and concert halls. Workplaces were integrated, too. There were athletic competitions between Armenian and Azeri teams, especially soccer. Occasionally there were fist fights, especially if the Armenian teams won. But mostly it was live and let live.

Armenians were respectful of Muslim religious tenets. Never ostentatious, they danced and consumed alcohol within the privacy of their homes and clubs. Armenian churches were built not to tower over or outshine the mosques. During important Muslim holidays, such as Ramadan or Ashura, we were very careful in our public behavior, including eating, drinking, and music-making, in order not to offend the religious sensibilities of faithful Muslims.

Muslims tolerated us. We were *their* Christians. We had been with them for some 1,400 years. We were not newcomers or foreign imports. We were good for the economy and reputation of Tabriz. We were bridges to Europe, Russia, and India. We shared with them great pride in Tabriz and Azerbaijan. We had fought with them in their struggle to secure a constitutional monarchy in Iran. We had fought for the territorial integrity and sovereignty of Iran during and after World War I. They were *our* Muslims. The leaders of both communities did not look kindly on those who attempted to foment discord. I remember a fight between some of us, Christian boys and several Muslim kids. When a policeman arrived, Muslim boys told him that we had insulted the Prophet Muhammad. We, in turn, accused them of insulting Jesus Christ. We were all slapped and told to go home.

Even though the Armenians of Tabriz (and the rest of Iran) were an ethnic and religious minority, we did not feel inferior. On the contrary, we were better educated, we were cosmopolitan, we were modern, we were Christians. We had the legacy of the Iranian civilization *plus* our own. We had modern education, music, theater, opera, and translations of world literature alongside those in Persian, Arabic, and Turkish. There was no notion of different *civilizations*. There were different cultures, but only one *tammadon* (civilization). Every nation and culture made a contribution to that and had been doing so throughout history. Scholarship, science, and progress were universal. Plato and Aristotle coexisted with Ibn Sina (Avicenna) and Ibn Rushd (Averroës). European and Muslim architecture were part of the history of architecture.

Although the Muslim merchants in the Armenian neighborhood felt comfortable with us (considering us "People of the Book"), learned Armenian, became an integral part of the economic life of our community, and even sought to reside in our neighborhood, there were nevertheless instances of intolerance and discrimination against us as Christians elsewhere in the city. Sometimes some Muslim merchants considered us nonbelievers "dirty" by definition. When you wanted to shop at their shops, especially those that sold fruit, they admonished loudly, "Don't touch! Or else you will have to buy the whole batch." There was even a joke we uttered and laughed at in response:

> Allen verma Ermani
> Mundar olar yappani

Or, "Don't touch the dung, Armenian. It will get dirty."

In 1946, when the Soviet-backed "autonomous" republics of Azerbaijan and Kurdistan collapsed after the withdrawal of Soviet forces from Iran, there were fears in the Armenian community that the Muslim militants and nationalists, offended by the pro-Soviet behavior of some of the Armenians, would use it as an excuse to attack and pillage Armenian neighborhoods. These fears did not materialize, mostly because the local Muslim political and religious leaders opposed such action and protected the Armenian quarter. The valiant prelate of the Armenian Church in Azerbaijan, Archbishop Melik-Tanguian, even though ill, traveled some sixty kilometers to welcome, with offerings of peace—bread and salt—the commander of the Iranian armed forces, General Shahbakhti. This gesture was well received and inaugurated a new era of cooperation between the Iranian authorities and the leader of the Armenian community.

On the social scene, there were irritants and minor tensions that occasionally led to fisticuffs. The chief cause of these minor fights between Muslim boys and men and their Armenian counterparts was sexual harassment of Armenian girls and women in the form of groping. This occurred in the public park, the movie houses, and on Pahlavi, Tabriz's only paved major avenue at that time. I was determined to defend myself against assorted big bullies and bought brass knuckles. I soon realized that the best defense was offense. I cannot say why, but at the beginning of each academic year, I would pick a fight with a notorious bully. Even if I lost the fight and my nose got bloodied, I gained a protective shield for the rest of the academic year. "Don't get tangled up or mess with Vartan," the students would say. "He is tough. He cannot be intimidated. He is crazy."

As young boys, we had to assume protective "street coloring" to survive. We were always careful, always aware of our immediate surroundings. You had to have perfect peripheral vision. You had to know about the quickest shortcuts. You had to have the requisite verbal agility to provoke and defuse conflicts. You had to know the entire spectrum of Armenian, Russian, Persian, and above all Turkish cuss words. To use them was considered ordinary; to be able to refute their logic was considered an extraordinary feat. For example, if someone told us "You are a mother f——" the ideal response was "I am sorry your mother told you the sad story." If someone uttered the routine "f— you" the retort was "With what?" and on and on. The Turkish language had the most original and the richest treasury of curses and insults. One that has always remained with me was *"Aghzeve osterem Englis khefenan"* ("I'll fart in your mouth through an English-made funnel").

Whether you dealt with Armenian or Turkish boys, there was an unwritten code of behavior. There were strict rules not to irreparably humiliate your opponent. To "lose face" was terrible. To be given respect, one's proper deference, was the dominant rule. If there were breaches of this strict rule, all kinds of attempts were made to find a solution, a reconciliation. Intermediaries were used, apologies extended. Verbal arguments were preferred to a physical fight. One cardinal rule was that you must not offend your "opponent" in front of his girlfriend or younger brother, not to mention one's sister and mother.

For us, the Christian boys, and especially the girls, regular recreational opportunities outside our neighborhood were very limited. In addition to Gulistan (the public garden) with its beautiful flowers, trees, and fountains, and carousels, there was the Shah Gyoli (Shah's Lake), a small artificial lake with surrounding gardens in the outskirts of the city, and Pahlavi Avenue, which served as a crossroads for all faiths, classes, and professions. Side by side stood shops of jewelers, tailors, hairdressers, *"nouveauté"* boutiques, gunmakers, shoemakers, and drugstores belonging to Muslims and Armenians alike.

Then there was the fabulous bazaar of Tabriz. For us, it was the forbidden land. With the exception of some rug merchants and a handful of individuals involved in banking and the export of dry fruits, the bazaar was the private domain of Muslim merchants. If you wanted to smoke, eat "dirty" yet delicious kebob from street vendors, see mountains of assorted goods, smell the aroma of a multitude of exotic spices, observe beautiful girls, Muslim girls, the bazaar was the place. It captured our imagination. It was with great excitement that we observed Muslim girls and women rearrange their chadors and, for an instant, reveal their beautiful dresses, beautiful smiles, and gorgeous eyes.

When I was ten or eleven, I fell in love with Victoria, a classmate. Her sheer presence in the classroom gave me a great sensation. Her eyes, her voice, her hair, her poise, her walk, her laughter captivated me. I studied very hard not only to please my teacher but to attract Victoria's attention and, I hoped, her affection. I passed two or three poems to her in the classroom. I remember the excitement and high anxiety when, as an altar boy, I had to accompany the priest to *her* home for the funeral procession of her father's coffin. Her grief broke my heart. Now she was an orphan, too. I was pleased that I had shared, albeit vicariously, her grief and loss.

In the meantime, I told the news of my love for Victoria not only to my close friends but also to the entire Armenian neighborhood. I carved on trees and doors: *V.G.* + *V.G.* = *VG,* since my initials and hers coincided (Victoria's last name was Gurjian). The only way we boys could manifest our affection for girls was to pass notes to them, carve their names on trees, and follow them home after school. One day, as she reached her home, Victoria turned her head and smiled at me. I was overwhelmed.

Even after both of us left the Armenian elementary school, and Victoria went to Parvin School for Girls and I to Massood-e Saad School for Boys, my platonic relationship with Victoria flourished. I followed her home after my school was over. I went to cultural and athletic events, movies, anything, to be in the same location with her and to see her beautiful eyes. I was so happy during the religious holidays to see her at the church with her mother and sisters. Her smiles sustained me. My ultimate ambition was to hold her hand, or walk hand in hand and kiss her. It never happened. (Years later, I met Victoria in Beirut, Lebanon, where she was a student at the American University. Later, she married in Iran and emigrated with her family to Los Angeles. Several years ago, when the Hamazkaïn Armenian Cultural Association gave a dinner in my honor in Los Angeles, Victoria and her children were there.)

Naturally, Victoria was not the only girl who was placed on a pedestal. There were six or seven girls in our school, Eleanor, Alice, Hasmig, Geghanoush among them, who, it seemed, had captured the hearts of all the boys who followed them with devotion to their houses, to the public garden, to the movies, to the church, anywhere to catch a glimpse of their beauty and to get their benevolent attention. Sex was out of the question. Almost all the relationships were mostly or purely platonic. There was no sex education or any discussion of it, either at school or at home. You learned all about it through the underground, from your friends, friends of your friends, those who bragged that they were "experienced," from gossip, tales from the street, occasionally from books. As a general rule, parents did not discuss sex with their children. If they did, it was all about the ravages of venereal diseases. Certainly my grandmother did not talk to me about sex; neither did my father nor my cousins.

Other than occasional scenes in the movies, some of my friends and I had never seen a picture of a naked girl or a woman. They were a mystery to us. We tried the Armenian Library's encyclopedias. Unfortunately, even the Russian and the German ones only contained the anatomy of women in terms of their nervous systems and internal organs. Besides, we could not read German, nor could we understand the intricate descriptions in Russian. Once, several of us tried to take a peek at naked girls from the rooftop of our neighborhood public bathhouse, only to find out that the steam had fogged the rooftop glass.

Under such circumstances, imagine, therefore, the shock, the irony, and the excitement when we found out, in the aftermath of the Soviet occupation of northern Iran, that the official Massoud-e Saad Persian school, named for a famous medieval Persian poet, which had agreed to admit those of us who had attended five or six years of an Armenian-Russian school, was next to the red-light district. The school was private, owned and operated by Mr. Najat, who was its director. It was a huge house, with some twenty or thirty rooms and a big courtyard, but no playground. There were opium addicts and pimps near our school. Pretty soon we came to know all of the major notorious prostitute neighbors. They arrived and departed in droshkies, horse-drawn carriages, with poise and serenity befitting aristocrats. At intermissions and lunchtime, we would gather in front of the school and whistle and cheer as the imperious madams, with fictitious names like Iran Khanom (Madam Iran), Tamara Khanom (Madam Tamara), Tahra Khanom (Madam Tahra), rearranged their veils so as to give us a glimpse of their beauty and responded to our cheers and catcalls about their business. They either roared with laughter or else uttered unmentionable obscenities. It was a great, free, and unexpected spectacle.

Older boys, the "experts," advised us that if we ever had enough money and ventured to have sex with them, we should be sure that we either urinated immediately because our urine would wash out all the impurities, or else we should wash ourselves with permanganate. There were rumors that condoms were imported to Iran by American and British soldiers who used them to protect themselves from venereal diseases. There were even malicious rumors that Soviet soldiers used pages of *Pravda* and *Izvestia* as a protective device. To satisfy our curiosity, we looked for and found only one Armenian book about sexuality and sexually transmitted diseases. It gave us the impression that premarital sex was dangerous. Period.

Notwithstanding its location, Massoud-e Saad gave us a good education. It was an integrated school, open to Turkish, Persian, Kurdish, Jewish, and Armenian students. The school was kind to the Armenians, since we were a major source of revenue. They were also generous in connection with various major religious holidays. Since I was an altar boy and a choirboy, on several occasions older Armenian students coerced me into testifying that some minor religious holidays were major ones. Although the school respected our holidays, it was very harsh with those of us who broke the rules. We were subjected to severe beatings, slapped and hit with rulers and on occasion with a whip. Class solidarity with mischievous students usually resulted in collective punishment. The vice principal, a sadistic character, enjoyed the administration of corporal punishments. We had no recourse but to submit, since the alternative was to be kicked out of school. We resorted to minor acts of revenge, which resulted in further punishment.

Once we administered a sweet revenge. Several well-to-do and grown-up boys gave a prominent prostitute a "down payment" for a personal visit to our principal during the lunch break. As the prostitute went to visit the principal, only to be ejected, we cheered. We were all punished.

Although we hated the draconian rules of the school, they did not shock us or any of our relatives. Corporal punishment was regarded as a necessary instrument of discipline, and discipline a fundamental, integral ingredient of learning. There was a popular saying in Armenian and in Turkish used by parents entrusting their children to the school. They said figuratively to the principal: "The meat is yours, the bones are ours." In other words, do anything you want, but educate our children. Mr. Najat, the principal's brother, who taught us Persian language and literature, explaining it in Turkish, used to hit us on our heads with his fist and also slap us during the course of his instruction if he decided that there was an intolerable lack of attention or infraction of discipline.

Our acts of revenge against teachers included attempts to demonstrate their lack of knowledge and preparedness by studying well and going beyond them. In the case of Mr. Najat, we used to find some arcane Persian words and ask him about their meaning: *Bir Kooshen adidi Hindustanda* (the name of a bird in India). He would respond in Turkish with a great air of self-satisfaction, unwilling to admit his ignorance. At the end of the academic year, our vocabulary was enriched with names of some ten to fifteen such birds.

Our math teacher, Mr. Samii, did not resort to corporal punishment to maintain discipline in the classroom but he relied on his charisma and competence. It was rumored that he was a homosexual. Therefore, each time he put his hand on a student's shoulder, we would say in Armenian, *"Kssouma"* ("He is caressing"). Once, he asked me its meaning. I told him. He was utterly embarrassed. Before I left Iran he drew my portrait as a farewell gift.

Our physics and chemistry teacher was a frustrated soul. We had no laboratories. Hence our teacher was forced to tell us to "imagine" various experiments. We imagined . . . but we did not understand. At the time, it was my ardent ambition to be a scientist. Massoud-e Saad, through no fault of its own, killed that ambition in favor of imagination.

The teacher we had most fun with was Mr. Mehrdad, short, slim, and highly energetic, who bordered on being a manic paranoiac. He thought of himself as fearless and took upon himself the assignment to "protect" Armenian boys from Turkish or Persian homosexual "predators." He had gone to the police and lodged a complaint, demanding an investigation of the matter, calling for the protection of Armenian youth. We never missed his classes. We had great fun—unfortunately often at his expense. As a class, we decided sometimes to look at his trousers and giggle or smile. The poor man would pretend to clean the blackboard and check in the meantime whether the buttons or zipper of his trousers was all right. He would proctor his exams by piercing holes in his newspaper and pretend he was reading, while attempting to monitor us, causing howls of laughter in the classroom.

In his literature classes, as he attempted to find a yardstick by which to describe the height of the legendary heroes of Iran, he often picked himself as the measure. The heroes were described as a couple of inches taller than he. (He was five feet two inches.) We learned a lot from Mr. Mehrdad about geography, history, and especially Iranian literature. He gave life to such classical Persian poets as Saadi, Firdawsī, Hafez, Rumi, and Omar Khayyám. I learned much about Iran, its history, and the accumulated wisdom of its people. I learned about the nuances, ambiguities, elegance, splendid richness of the Persian language, literature, its subtle humor, the fact that each sentence required interpretation and clarification, and every clarification required additional clarification. I remember with great fondness and excitement some of the poems from Saadi's *Gulistan (The Garden)*. They were words of wisdom, told through exquisite lyrics, about the "science of life." Here are some of my favorite samples of Saadi's teachings:

> If a man be expert in any art, he need not tell it, for his own skill will show it.
>
> A wise man is like a vase in a druggist's shop: silent but full of virtues, and the ignorant man resembles the drum of a warrior, being full of noise and an empty babbler.
>
> A learned man, beset by the illiterates, is like one of the lovely in a circle of the blind, or the Holy Koran in the dwelling of the infidel.
>
> Intellect without firmness is craft and chicanery; and firmness without intellect, perverseness and obstinacy.
>
> I asked a wise man: "Who is the fortunate man, and who is the unfortunate?" He said, "That man was fortunate who spent and gave away, and that man unfortunate who died and left behind."
>
> Two persons labored to a vain, and studied to an unprofitable end: he who hoarded wealth and did not spend it, and he who acquired science and did not practice it.
>
> However much thou art read in theory, if thou hast no practice, thou

art ignorant. He is neither a sage philosopher, nor an acute divine, but a beast of burden with a load of books. How can that brainless head know or comprehend whether he carries on his back a library or bundled sticks of wood?

Three things have no durability without their concomitants: property without trade, knowledge without debate, or a sovereignty without government.

Two orders of mankind are the enemies of religion and state: the king without clemency, and the holy man without learning.

Nothing is so good for an ignorant man as silence, and if he knew this, he would no longer be ignorant.

When unadorned with the grace of eloquence, it is wise to keep watch over the tongue in the mouth. The tongue by abuse renders a man contemptible.

Whoever acquires knowledge and does not practice it, resembles him who plows his land and leaves it unsown.

A scholar without diligence is a lover without money, a traveler without knowledge is a bird without wings, a theorist without practice is a tree without fruit; and a devotee without learning is a home without entrance.

To tell a falsehood is like the cut of a sabre: for though the wound may heal, the scar of it will remain.

One of my favorite lines from Saadi is his description of a severe famine: "There was such a famine in Damascus that lovers forgot love."

Mr. Mehrdad taught three fundamental rules: (1) when you see a donkey carrying a diploma, don't say it is an educated donkey—it is only a donkey carrying a diploma; (2) if you see a donkey carrying gold, you should know that it is not a golden donkey, but only a donkey carrying gold; (3) if you see a donkey in a holy city, don't think it is a holy donkey, it is only a donkey in a holy city.

I remember two stories told to us by Mr. Mehrdad. It is only when I was at Stanford University that I found out that the sources of these two stories were *The Arabian Nights*.

Those who can neither forget nor forgive either themselves or others lose everything. Thus began our teacher while retelling the tale of how Abu Hassan broke wind. It was the story of a wealthy merchant who stages a wonderful wedding feast with rice of five colors, and goats stuffed with walnuts, almonds, and pistachios. While rising to join his wife, Abu Hassan lets out "a huge and deafening fart" that so shames him that he goes abroad.

Years later, returning to his hometown in disguise, he overhears a young girl asking her mother on what day she was born. "On the very day that Abu Hassan did his famous fart," the mother replies, whereupon he flees overseas again, never to return.

The other tale, a disquieting one, is that of the donkey and the ox. The donkey compares his status with that of the ox in the household of a rich landlord. Look at me, he brags to the ox. I am cleaned every day, well fed. I have a saddle. My owner uses me, infrequently, to go to market. I am kept on the shady side of the street. I have been given time to sleep and recuperate from my "work." As to you, he points out to the ox, you are dirty, you are not well fed, your sleeping quarters are a disgrace, and from dawn to dusk you carry the yoke in the field, under the hot sun, with insects attacking you left and right. "What should I do to improve my condition?" asks the ox. "Revolt," answers the donkey. "Do not cooperate with your handlers. Kick them, don't eat the miserable food, don't get up in the mornings so readily, then they'll appreciate you." The ox accepts and acts according to the donkey's prescription. After several days, the horrified ox hears his owner say, "There is something very wrong with this ox. Let us kill him."

From Mr. Mehrdad and the Iranian school system, I learned about *adab*. This was a complex tenet. It stood for culture, for politeness in manner and behavior. It stressed not only the absorption of abstract learning but the importance of its application in one's daily life as well. It insisted that true education combined a sense of culture, common sense, a knowledge of one's traditions, one's place in particular social settings, in short, one's class. It required one's understanding of the importance of correct, proper, and polite language, table manners, how to express one's appreciation, how to invite, how to decline an invitation, how to address one's elders, one's parents, one's relatives, how to be hospitable, how to be chivalrous toward women and children, how not to be eager or covetous, how to be generous without display, the importance of being familiar with historical and classical (Persian) literature allusion. In short, *adab* required the acquisition of refined manners and the knowledge of aesthetics. I learned a lot about *adab* while growing up in Tabriz and attending Persian school and reading Persian literature. I learned that Iranians, Azeris, and Armenians addressed (and still do) their parents in the formal; that you always addressed your elders by their last names; that there was only one etiquette for all. It transcended class, race, ethnicity, and religion. It was universal.

*   *   *

In 1946, my father remarried. His bride was forty-one years old, a blond seamstress who was born in Tabriz but lived in Tehran. This marriage was long overdue. For years, my grandmother and others had been urging my father to find a suitable mate. After all, he was a young man in need of affection, love, and companionship. His children needed a mother. Our illiterate grandmother was alone and ill equipped to cope with our growing needs. We observed with admiration and some envy friends of ours who had a mother, father, and normal home with all the amenities. We were at a disadvantage vis-à-vis all of them, having no mother and a father who had not been an authority figure during the first seven years of our lives. Even though I am sure he had our welfare at heart, he was not intimately involved with us. His marriage made sense.

We had been introduced to Amalia, "a very kind, pretty, and modest woman," according to my grandmother, as a possible mate for our father. We liked her. She liked us. We were led to believe that our father liked her, too, and as a matter of fact, he had been seen with her in public several times. It came as a great surprise, then, when we learned that our father had married someone we had not heard of. We were not forewarned. We were not even present at our father's wedding, which was held on my birthday. Needless to say, we were very anxious and apprehensive about the idea of a stepmother.

My father arrived from Tehran with his bride, Rozik (Little Rose). My grandmother welcomed her with open arms and urged us to do so as well. The day after she arrived, Rozik, dressed in her beautiful bathrobe, crossed the courtyard to greet us. We were ready for her. We were washed and scrubbed by our grandmother; we wore our Sunday best. We had been instructed by our grandmother to leave a good impression upon our stepmother. She was presented to us by our father as our "new mother." Rozik hugged and kissed us. We reciprocated. In all fairness to her, we did not appreciate her difficult situation. We were not old enough to understand her predicament. She had made a big leap. She had left her family and friends in Tehran, along with her clientele (she was a seamstress), and had inherited an instant family: two orphans, aged ten and a half and eleven and a half, their maternal grandmother, their uncle Armenag, and their cousin Bobken.

The promising beginning of our relationship did not last very long. There soon followed a period marked with resentment, anger, at times even hatred, resulting in my alienation from my father and stepmother. Several developments contributed to this turn of events. My father first asked, then ordered us, to call Rozik "Mother." We could not and did not. If she was to be our mother, were we supposed to cease calling our grandmother "Mother" after some twelve years? How could we call her "Mother" when we had called our mother Shooshik and were still calling our father Samuel?

Then came the second major crisis. My mother's picture, which had hung in our living room, was removed. My sister and I, not to mention my grandmother, were very upset. We felt that Rozik and our father were trying to obliterate our mother's memory and traces of her presence in our lives. We had been anticipating such a move, since we had been reading all kinds of children's stories that featured helpless orphans and wicked stepmothers. I remember vividly one story, "Gikor," by Hovhannes Toumanian, a prominent Armenian poet and writer of the late nineteenth and early twentieth century.

"Gikor" was the story of a very young orphan sent to Tbilisi, capital of the modern Republic of Georgia, to work in the shop of a rich merchant. Alone, lonely, miserably poor, overworked, underfed, abused, ill, he yearns for his parents, for somebody to love and protect him, to take care of him. Alas, he has nobody. He dies after an illness, brokenhearted, yearning for his mother. As I read and reread the story, my sister, grandmother, and I wept about the sad fate of Gikor. In reality, we were bemoaning our own fate. We read Hans Christian Andersen's story of Cinderella and the Grimm Brothers' tales, translated into Armenian, with depictions of wicked stepmothers.

The first year of life with our stepmother was bearable, sometimes even pleasant. Rozik was an excellent cook. On several occasions my father took the entire family to some of Tabriz's best private gardens in the early-morning hours to eat fresh mulberries, and just-baked bread, honey, and tea. They were memorable and happy occasions. We ate dinners together and minded our table manners.

The news of Rozik's pregnancy surprised us, but the birth of our brother, Vahé, delighted us. She had a very difficult childbirth at home. A midwife and my grandmother helped with her delivery. She was not a young woman and was shell-shocked. She did not know how to take care of her son. My grandmother took care of our half brother. Unfortunately, Vahé died when he was a year old.

After our brother's death, Rozik's behavior toward us changed dramatically, or at least we thought so. While Vahé was alive, Rozik planted, for good luck, three peach trees in our courtyard. Each one bore our names. Two of them, named for my sister and brother, did not last long. They withered. My tree not only took hold but bore fruit as well. Rozik, who was as superstitious as the rest of my relatives, thought that "my star," my luck, had

cast a shadow or an "evil eye" on her son. Pretty soon, there followed a series of almost regular confrontations between my father and me. I developed a passive-aggressive attitude toward my stepmother and father. The
situation got so bad at home that I began to believe that childhood was a
prison. I prayed to become an adult as soon and as fast as possible. Adulthood, I believed, was the only means of liberation.

A new complication rose to poison the home atmosphere. There developed a tension between Rozik and my grandmother, which was natural and
to be anticipated. Until my father's remarriage, my grandmother had wielded
the moral authority in our home. Even my father called her "Mother." She
had often acted as a mediator between our father and us, her grandchildren.
Now she attempted to assume a similar role between us and our stepmother,
but this time without much luck. She begged us not to anger our stepmother
because she might curse our late mother for having given birth to us.

My grandmother continued to shop, cook, clean the house, and do the
laundry. I came to believe that my stepmother and father treated my grandmother as a hired hand. Whether it was true or not, the perceptions became
reality. I resented it. Soon I developed a paranoia toward my stepmother. I
thought she hated me and was constantly plotting to get us into trouble with
our father. On one occasion, I came home from school to witness an argument between my grandmother and Rozik. Evidently my stepmother was
going through the pockets of my trousers, and my grandmother had admonished her that it was an inappropriate invasion of my privacy. Pretty
soon, tensions mounted in our home to such an extent that my father asked
my grandmother and uncle to leave our home. They moved next door to a
one-room apartment, carrying with them a handful of items, including a bed
and a kilim rug. My sister and I cried. We were devastated. All of a sudden
we had become what today would be called a nuclear family. I felt my
father's action was a great insult to my grandmother and an ungrateful, das-
tardly act as well. The fact that after seven years he had not placed a tomb-
stone on my mother's grave became another bone of contention.

I became a defiant rebel. The punishments became more frequent and severe. I tried to spend as little time as possible at home. At dinnertime, there
was nothing to share except the burden of silence. I spent most of my time
at school, the library, friends' homes, at the movies, and, when I was at
home, reading. By now, my alienation from my father seemed almost complete. Once, I was locked in our basement for coming home late and for dis-
obedience. I went on a hunger strike, refused to come out of the basement,
took off all my clothes, and threw them out of the basement window, shouting at my father, "I don't want to be your son. I never asked to be born." I

must have been there, over the weekend, more than twelve or fourteen hours. My sister and grandmother interceded with my father and me to end my punishment and my self-proclaimed "independence."

My father and I could not get along. I did not have my mother, or my grandmother, to serve as a mediator. My stepmother made no gestures on my behalf. I realized gradually that I could not remain at home. I was miserable and I was making life miserable for everyone. Once I even threatened Rozik with a pair of scissors as she was upbraiding my sister, and was on the verge of hitting her. Naturally, I was severely punished. My father hit me with his belt. I wanted to hit him, too, but I could not. After all, he was my father. Since I had lost my mother, I wanted him to love me. I wanted him to care for me. I even wanted him to stand up for me, at least once, against my stepmother. My anger consumed me. There was a time when I even threatened to go to the police and inform them that my father had a gun, a Browning, hidden in the outlet of our winter woodstove oven. Naturally, I did not. But the very fact that I had thought of it disturbed me and scared me profoundly.

*   *   *

Two outstanding issues continued to poison my relations with my parents. One, my father's inability or unwillingness to pay my school tuition regularly was both irksome and humiliating. Tuition was around ten dollars for the academic year and could be paid in installments. On several occasions, I was even asked to leave the classroom, sent home, and not permitted to return until my father paid the tuition. Then there was the matter of my shoes. They were in tatters. I felt as if the entire population of Tabriz, more specifically, the Armenian community, my classmates, friends, the girls focused their sights on my decaying and tattered shoes.

I wondered whether it was the state of my father's finances or his unwillingness that made him ignore my elementary needs, and I decided that it must be unwillingness. After all, every summer, when my stepmother's relatives stayed with us for their vacation, they were well entertained, served meals, and taken to movies and private restaurants. To boot, we had to baby-sit (without pay) for their children. So I deduced, rightly or wrongly, that my father did not have financial problems. I begged him for a pair of new shoes. He took me to a cobbler who specialized in peasant footwear. I did get my shoes. They were fit for harlequins or circus performers or peasant bridegrooms. I was horrified and mortified. I was afraid of being ridiculed and of being reminded that after decades of residence in urban

Tabriz, I was wearing what looked like a pair of peasant wedding shoes. After wearing them once, I refused to wear them again and continued to wear my decrepit and deteriorating old shoes as a sign of protest. My father and I had arrived at a stalemate. He was too stubborn and I was too proud. I thought he was trying to humiliate me deliberately.

There was no authority to appeal to against my father's real or imagined commission or abuse of his authority. My grandmother had been marginalized. Our family name, reputation, and honor did not permit me to complain to our relatives or acquaintances, not to mention strangers. I could not leave home. It would have meant abandoning my sister and would have brought dishonor to our family name. Under such conditions, my sister and I became confidants, sources of comfort to each other, a relationship of remarkable solidarity that enabled us to endure our fate with dignity.

The library and reading provided me a place of solace, a home elsewhere. I read voraciously. I was fascinated by the works of Alexandre Dumas: *The Three Musketeers, Twenty Years After, Joseph Balsamo, The Queen's Necklace,* but most important, *The Count of Monte Cristo* left an enormous impression on me. I was particularly enamored of historical novels such as those of Sir Walter Scott *(Ivanhoe),* Henryk Sienkiewicz *(Quo Vadis),* and Adam Mickiewicz. In addition, I read Mark Twain's *The Prince and the Pauper,* Harriet Beecher Stowe's *Uncle Tom's Cabin,* and Goethe's *The Sorrows of Young Werther.*

When I was fourteen or fifteen, I read Russian novels and short stories: Tolstoy's *War and Peace* and *Resurrection,* Fyodor Dostoevsky's *Crime and Punishment,* Chekhov's *The Sea Gull,* Ivan Turgenev's *Fathers and Sons,* Nikolay Gogol's *Dead Souls,* Maxim Gorky's *Mother* and *Childhood.* Then I discovered Maurice Maeterlinck and his fantastic work *The Life of the Bee* as well as works on ants and, of course, *The Blue Bird.* Guy de Maupassant was very popular in Iran. I found his short stories captivating and his novel, *A Life,* intriguing. It is full of action and includes murder, adultery, and illegitimate children. Its conclusion, that life is neither as bad nor as good as one thinks, struck a sympathetic note for those of us caught between the limitations and possibilities of our lives. My reading also included the detective stories featuring Arthur Conan Doyle's Sherlock Holmes.

Two works left a profound impression on me: Eugène Sue's *The Wandering Jew* and Franz Werfel's *Forty Days of Musa Dagh.* One dealt with the pernicious and persistent nature of anti-Semitism, and the second with the Armenian Genocide during World War I and the Armenian resistance. What consoled me was that both Jews and Armenians had decided not to be extinguished. They had the will to survive in spite of all the adversities and tragedies visited upon them throughout their long history. Their histories reminded me of the Book of Job.

I read several plays of Shakespeare in Armenian. His works had always been very popular among Armenians. Indeed, many Shakespearian plays were read at Armenian literary societies and performed in Armenian theaters. As I read *Romeo and Juliet* and *Julius Caesar,* I understood the plot and the words, but I never appreciated Shakespeare's poetry, his rich language, his genius, until I read him later in English.

Most of my childhood readings, however, were focused on nineteenth- and twentieth-century Armenian writers. I read such patriotic novels as *Verk Hayastani (Woes of Armenia),* by Khachatur Abovyan (1805–1848), the father of modern Armenian vernacular literature. His patriotic and passionate novel lamented the state of the Armenians under the foreign yoke and advocated the revival of the Armenian language and the reformation of their antiquated educational system. Reviving the historical memory of the Armenians was a major theme of another nineteenth-century novelist, Tzerents (1822–1888), whose historical novels left a vivid impression on me. *Toros Levoni (Toros, Son of Levon)* dealt with the restoration and expansion of Armenian political power in Cilicia, in the eastern Mediterranean, during the twelfth century under the Rubinian dynasty. *Yerkunk T Daru (Ninth-Century Travail)* highlighted the anti-Arab Armenian rebellion in the middle of the ninth century. All these years later I remember that the leader of the rebellion, Hovnan, was beheaded for refusing to abandon Christianity and adopt Islam. *Theodor Rshtouni* was about a valiant seventh-century Armenian prince and commander of the Armenian army. I read Muratsan's (1854–1908) *Gevork Marzpetooni* and Stepan Zorian's (1889–1907) *Pap Takavor (King Pap),* two historical novels that bemoaned divisions and factionalism caused by rival Armenian princes. Because of my name and everybody's celebration of Saint Vartan, I was particularly eager to read Derenik Demirjian's (1877–1956) historical novel, *Vartanank.* I was not disappointed. It presented the history of the Battle of Avarayr in A.D. 451 and showed the determination of the Armenian nobility and the people to die rather than renounce their Christian faith. The battle against the Persians, even though a military debacle for Armenians, led to the nationalization of Christianity.

Novels of Raffi (1835–1888) dealt with the same themes, but in the context of nineteenth-century Armenian history and society. In his novels *Kaytser (Sparks)* and *Khent (The Fool),* he, too, lamented the fact that disunity had been a major factor in the downfall of Armenian statehood. He denounced treachery as a national trait and advocated reform and self-defense as necessary ingredients for reorganizing the Armenian nation. The way from self-defense to national liberation was paved by the passionate novels of Avetis Aharonian (1866–1948), especially his *Azatootian Janaparin (On the Road to Freedom),* which portrayed the nature of a nascent Armenian nationalist, revolutionary movement. In the same vein, Malkhas's *Zartonk (Awakening),* a seven-volume story of the life and times of an idealist Armenian nationalist freedom fighter in the late nineteenth and early twentieth century Ottoman Empire, kept me and my friends spellbound.

Intoxicated with reading, I was fortunate to make the acquaintance of an elderly, very well educated, and well-to-do spinster, Miss Satenik Boodaghian. She lived near the Armenian Prelacy and possessed a wonderful private library that contained many leather-bound books. She opened her library and even lent books to me. The fathers of two well-to-do friends of mine also extended similar courtesies.

I read every evening, sometimes late into the night, with the help of kerosene lamps, often secretly, past my bedtime. The solitude and the silence were for me heavenly gifts that enhanced the joy of reading. The more I read, the more I had to read. One book led to another, one author led to another, one subject led to another. Reading became a compulsion for me. Books freed me from my prison, transported me far away to a wonderful realm of possibilities, to a life of beauty, compassion, generosity, excitement, justice, intense passion, incessant action, and fun. I lived vicariously the lives of such protagonists as Robinson Crusoe, Jean Valjean, the Count of Monte Cristo, the Three Musketeers, Romeo, Werther, Sinbad, Kim, various Armenian princes, kings, and modern-day revolutionaries, and many, many others. I traveled with them, cried with them, laughed with them, fought along with them, undertook dangerous journeys, discovered new lands, fell in love. The protagonists of many books I read became lifetime companions.

During my childhood and early adolescence, I had both "polite" friends and "street friends"; the latter were five tough kids. Two of them were classmates, the others altar boys. The size of the gang expanded in accordance with real or perceived threats or challenges. Most of us had brass knuckles that gave us a sense of power. We were determined, individually and collectively, not to be pushed around by other kids in our neighborhood who were often bigger and stronger. The gang provided a protective shield outside our neighborhood in the public garden, movie houses, soccer stadiums, and the main avenue, where we interacted with Muslim kids and grown-ups. We were particularly worried about the rumored pederasts who made a habit of harassing Armenian schoolboys. Numerous solicitations and intimidations had been reported. Pederasts were known as *ooshagbaz* in Turkish, "those who 'play' with children."

Occasionally, our gang also displayed a symbolic presence. In 1946, when the authorities of the so-called Azerbaijan Autonomous Republic held a youth rally in Tabriz's main stadium, the representatives of many organizations were "invited" to attend. Several Armenian athletic and cultural organizations sent delegations but we were left out. We were affronted and were determined to participate. We secured a white sheet (courtesy of my grandmother) and made a flag, inscribed with "Representatives of the Armenian *Independent* Youth Movement" and marched in the parade to the dismay of the representatives of well-established and well-known organizations. We felt great. We were noticed. We were somebodies. We were important.

To combat our boredom and have fun, the gang embarked upon a series of pranks. As our streets were very narrow, we tied the doorknockers of opposite houses together with a rope and then knocked at both doors. If one attempted to open one's door, his doorknocker knocked his neighbor's door, and so on with each set of neighbors.

We learned that Mr. Njdeh, the owner of probably the first contemporary novelty store in Tabriz, had a fit if you asked him whether he was a "systematic yogurt-selling merchant." We dared each other to visit his store and ask the question. I did so. He became so angry that he left his clients in the store and ran after us shouting unimaginable insults. I was both amused because it was a meaningless question and scared because he had such a wild reaction. I ran for my life. We also harassed one of the best-known fruit merchants in our quarter. He was an Azeri Turk whose shop was full of a rich variety of fruit, beautifully displayed. Every week, invariably, one of us tortured the poor man by asking whether or not he had coconuts. He did not. We made him impatient and angry. He knew we were not actual or potential customers. But one day this exasperated merchant put an end to our harassment when he answered in the affirmative. He did, indeed, have coconuts. "How much do they cost?" we asked. "Give me any price," he said. Since we had no money, we left him alone.

Not all our pranks were so innocent. The most malicious was to draw swastikas on the doors of individuals we happened to dislike. We never thought about the possibility that Soviet authorities might regard them with some interest.

At one stage of our brief existence, we hoped to transform our gang into an "entrepreneurial organization." Pooling our available "capital," we bought one carton of Persian *Ushnu* brand cigarettes wholesale and sold them in the public garden, in single packs or single cigarettes at retail. Naturally, there was not much profit, but it kept us busy. We tried, also, to sell razor blades, a pack of five, or single ones. This was also a failure, for there were no customers. I remember one potential customer who asked me how many times you could shave with the blade I hoped to sell him. I replied, "Three times." He responded that other blades give you six shaves. Naturally, I said. Each side shaves three times. He was not impressed.

We made the Armenian cemetery, at the edge of the city, one of our gathering spots. The cemetery lured us with the most important thing of all, privacy. The trees provided shade. Since there were no public, supervised, clean swimming pools in Tabriz, the reservoir in the cemetery, really more like a swamp, served as a pool. The reservoir was never drained and was full of weeds. Eventually a young man drowned in it, caught in the weeds. As a consequence, we lost our sanctuary. The cemetery and its reservoir became a forbidden land for us.

I also had access to a "polite" world, on the right side of the tracks, and here I found my second set of friends. Five or six well-to-do friends, with bicycles, pianos, violins, private bedrooms, regular allowances, games, books, private tutors who taught them French, English, piano, and mathematics inhabited this other world. This was the world of Varoujan Arakelian, Parouyr Parouyrian, Kajouk Kraskian, Boolik Babayan, Yervant Saponjian, Zarik Gregorian. They were all bright, studious, polite, serious, interesting, and stimulating. I was invited to their homes to study and to dine. They lent me their bicycles and books. They shared their games. They showed me their stamp collections. They made me feel welcome. Their parents talked to me about my studies, my reading, and they all became surrogate families to me.

I remember the owner and manager of the city's oldest flour mill, an engineer-contractor, a merchant, an instructor of piano and violin, and the owner of a small factory. They all had household help. They were Armenian nationalists; some had had parents or grandparents who had perished and others had relatives who had survived the Armenian Genocide during World War I by fleeing the Ottoman Empire to Tabriz. They were the active members of the governing bodies of the local Church and the various Armenian educational and cultural institutions. Some were members or sympathizers of the Armenian Revolutionary Federation, a political party founded by three Armenian university students in 1890, whose objectives were to organize the Armenian nation, modernize its institutions, introduce modern education, improve the plight of the Armenian peasantry in the Ottoman Empire, and protect the civil rights of Armenians within the Ottoman and Russian empires.

Another aim of the party was to stop the depopulation of historical Armenia by securing economic, legal, and administrative reforms for the regions inhabited by Armenians. The party advocated armed self-defense and launched a major propaganda campaign for the Armenian cause in Europe. In 1908, it formed an alliance with the Young Turks to secure administrative reforms for Armenians within a modern, secular Ottoman Empire. The party provided crucial military assistance and direct participation in the ranks of Iranians who sought and fought for a constitutional monarchy in Iran.

My association with some members of the party had a tremendous impact on me. One of them, Hrayr Stepanian, a pharmacist and optometrist and leader of the Armenian community, asked me to distribute several Armenian newspapers to a select number of subscribers. On occasion, I collected the subscription fees on his behalf. I even tried to bring in new subscriptions. This unpaid job gave me yet another wonderful outlet to the world, this time through the Armenian Disapora and its publications. My avid interest in Armenian newspapers and my volunteer job as distributor and collection agent left a favorable impression on Hrayr Stepanian. He became a mentor to me, the first in a series of mentors who played crucial roles in my life.

Since he was the agent of *Alik,* the national Armenian newspaper of Iran, he was the one who encouraged me, at age fourteen, to write articles for the Armenian daily. Sometimes he even arranged for me to deliver eulogies on behalf of the Armenian youth of Tabriz at the funerals of notable Armenian civic and cultural leaders.

It was at his pharmacy that I met Edgar Maloyan. He was a compatriot of Mr. Stepanian's, a survivor from the region of Mush in the former Ottoman Empire, now Turkey. He was tall, imperious, authoritative, and self-assured. All Tabriz was impressed by him. After all, it is not always that the French Republic sends a French Armenian to be vice-consul of France in Tabriz.

A short time after visiting Tabriz to open the French consulate, Mr. Maloyan fell ill with the flu. He was staying at the home of one of my friends, whose father was a well-to-do merchant. Their house had a private bath, private bathrooms, private guest bedrooms, electricity, a radio, and a telephone. I often visited Mr. Maloyan during his convalescence. We had a series of discussions and played chess, which he taught me. Naturally, he won most of the games. During these interesting and uneven encounters, he volunteered: "You are a smart and bright kid. Don't stay in Tabriz. Go to Beirut, le petit Paris, and get a *real* education."

"How can I?" I asked. "I don't speak Arabic or French or English, so how can I pursue my studies there? Even if I could, I have no money and my parents can't afford to send me, nor can they manage to support me in a foreign land."

"Well," he said, "you don't have to worry about *that*. I'll take care of all of *that*. I'll make all the necessary arrangements on your behalf. I will give you three letters: one addressed to Colonel Lahood, the head of the Lebanese Internal Security Agency, who will get you permission to stay in Lebanon. The second to Collège Arménien *(Jemaran),* an Armenian-French lycée with advanced courses in Armenian studies. They'll admit you. The third letter goes to Hotel Luxe, where you can live." I half jokingly asked him, "What will I eat? Where will I eat?" He joked, "Oh, *that!* You don't have to worry about *that*. You don't need much money to survive in Beirut. Lebanon has an ample amount of bananas. They are very cheap. You can eat a banana or two a day and that will sustain you." He concluded with a great burst of laughter. He was pulling my leg, of course, but I believed him. I had never seen a banana. Mr. Stepanian was elated. "You should go to Lebanon," he chimed in. "I'll do my best on your behalf." I was stunned! Here was a Frenchman, a stranger who wanted to be my benefactor, and here also was my pharmacist mentor, ready to support me. The news spread very fast. Overnight, Edgar Maloyan, vice-consul of France in Tabriz, had become my benefactor. *He* was sending me to Lebanon to be educated.

Edgar Maloyan appeared in my life at a critical juncture. I had done very well at school, graduating from the Persian elementary school with honors. In a statewide examination, I had scored sixteen out of a possible twenty points. I had excellent grades in junior high school. I loved my position at the library. It was delightful to be an altar boy in the church. I was proud to have been given an opportunity to write for *Alik,* the Armenian daily newspaper published in Tehran. I cherished my friends on both sides of the tracks. But my relations with my father and stepmother had sunk to a very low point.

When I informed them that Edgar Maloyan had volunteered to send me to Beirut and "take care of" my education, they were surprised—indeed shocked—even though it was the best-kept secret in Tabriz. I thought they would be elated, since following my departure from Tabriz there would inevitably be peace, quiet, and harmony in our home and my parents would not have to concern themselves with my education and its cost for at least several years. I thought my father would congratulate me, and, out of curiosity and gratitude, would invite Mr. Maloyan to our home or go to meet him. He did neither.

I have no explanation for my father's behavior. Maybe he was afraid that the Armenian community might criticize him for not seeing to his son's secondary education, and instead left it to a foreigner. Perhaps he thought it was not a serious offer. I don't know. Instead of congratulations, he told me that if I were able to get an Iranian passport, I *could* go to Beirut. That was a tough proposition. I am sure he knew that was an impossible task. After all, how could any kid aged fourteen obtain a passport? I took up his challenge.

Since the Iranian government issued passports for study abroad only to students who wanted to study subjects not taught in Iran or who intended to obtain postgraduate degrees, I was out of luck. I had to finish an Iranian high school, pass national exams, and get admitted to a foreign accredited college or university in order to obtain a passport and *arz* (government-subsidized foreign currency). I did not qualify under the existing rules.

Under the circumstances, I took a more complicated road. I implored my priest, Ter Karapet, to endorse a petition that requested a passport to enable me to study religion, Christianity, and advanced Armenian studies in Lebanon. He agreed. I took that document, in the form of a petition, to the governor of the province of Azerbaijan and spent hours waiting in front of his office and even his residence. One day, at long last, I was able, as he was walking to his residence, to hand him my petition, which he signed. Now I had an official application but it had yet to be approved by the Education Directorate of the province of Azerbaijan, the Central Police Department of Tabriz, and the Ministries of Education and Interior.

I spent six or seven months going from one agency to another, filing one petition after another, one application after another. Since I had no money to bribe anyone, my application languished. But it was an acknowledged application. It was signed by the governor. It had to be dealt with. After obtaining clearances in Tabriz (no criminal record, no debts, good character, good student, good grades), the matter was referred to ministries in Tehran.

Months passed. Twice I had to go to Tehran. Once my bus fare was paid by my father, the other time by Mr. Stepanian. I stayed with my stepmother's brother and sister-in-law and their children. They had a very modern high-rise apartment. My step-uncle was a taxicab driver, had a garage, and was beginning to manufacture designer iron doors and gates. I had my first shower at their house. Tehran, with its high-rises, paved avenues and streets, major squares, statues, modern shops, fancy showcases, and enormous traffic, overwhelmed me with its wealth.

After several visits to the Education Ministry and the National Police

Headquarters, I became accustomed to the refrain *"Farda"* ("Come tomorrow"). If I had had money to pay, reward, or bribe the *farrash,* the expediters in these ministries, my *farda*s ("tomorrows") would have become *"emrouz"* ("today"). One day, to my great delight, I was told that my documents had been sent to Tabriz. In Tabriz, I needed additional documents, including a property deed that would ensure my return to Iran for military service.

Hrayr Stepanian came with me to the District Police Station in Tabriz with the deed of his house to vouch for me. Since the policeman was rather slow and needed help to register the deed, I "helped" him. Instead of Hrayr Stepanian, I registered it under the name of Stepan Hrayrian and wrote the number of the document in reverse order. My aim was to protect Mr. Stepanian and his property in case something happened to me or I decided not to return to Iran. I waited with great anxiety and impatience for several long weeks and months.

Finally, one day I was informed that my passport was ready and that my father had to come and sign for it. I could not believe it; neither could my father. I had succeeded. My father did sign for the passport. I was one step closer to Beirut.

Now confronted with the stark reality that I was ready to leave Tabriz, my father raised another condition: my grandmother's permission. That was a tough one, particularly because during my quest to obtain a passport, another tragedy had struck my grandmother. My uncle Armenag, a porter, while carrying a heavy load, had an epileptic seizure, resulting in a broken arm and a wound. Although a chiropractor had "fixed" the broken arm, the wound did not heal but developed into gangrene and resulted in blood poisoning. As my dear uncle lay delirious on the bed of the one-room apartment where he and my grandmother lived, I ran for a doctor. By the time Dr. Aftandilian and I arrived in a carriage, he had died. My grandmother could not contain her grief. She was heartbroken and alone. In the span of eight years, she had lost all three of her remaining children. Now she had only us, her two grandchildren, my sister and me.

At my father's request, our close relatives gathered in our guestroom to discuss my wish to go to Beirut. My father and some relatives spoke against my going to Beirut. It was an unknown land full of uncertainties and potential difficulties. He promised that if I stayed at home he would take care of my education and other needs. "Besides," he said, "we need you, especially your grandmother. You must stay in Tabriz." Then there was silence. The air was full of tension. Everybody was waiting for my grandmother's verdict.

"Go, my son, and become a man," Grandmother said. Her voice choked with emotion. I knew it was a very hard decision for her. I was overwhelmed! I began crying with joy, sadness, guilt, regret, gratitude, and love for my grandmother, my mother.

Graham Greene once said: "There is always one moment in childhood when the door opens and lets the future in." That was my moment. I was on my way to Beirut.

Chapter Four

To Beirut, Le Petit Paris

I had obtained an Iranian passport and a Lebanese visa. Now what? How do I get to Beirut? We checked the schedules of the Iranian bus companies that had regular services to Beirut via Baghdad and Damascus. It was a long and expensive trip. A DC-3 IranAir plane was leaving for Beirut early in the fall, a cargo plane with passenger seats. The DC-3s were being withdrawn from circulation, as there had been at least one or two accidents. As a result, I was told, not too many passengers flew on DC-3s and the fare was "very reasonable." Reasonable or not, I did not have the money. I had worked at some odd jobs during the summer, but I had earned a pittance. To obtain a ticket became my next challenge.

Edgar Maloyan and Hrayr Stepanian came to my rescue, as did, to my surprise, my father. All of a sudden, I had a ticket to Beirut, plus fifty dollars in cash. My father purchased a bus ticket to Tehran for me, a pair of new shoes, a couple of shirts, and a necktie or two, as well as a beautiful, warm pashmina blanket. My cousin Bobken's gift was a new suit and some pocket money. Mr. Stepanian, the optometrist, gave me gold-rimmed spectacles. There was excitement on the part of all my friends and relatives who attended an emotional farewell dinner for me. My stepmother had prepared a series of wonderful dishes. There was vodka, wine, and beer. Many toasts and good wishes were delivered, including one by my father. He had tears in his eyes as he wished me a safe journey. He said he was very proud of me. The idea of being separated from his only son all of a sudden was a tough one. Indeed I was the first one in my family's history to embark upon such a long journey, away from our ancestral home. Even my stepmother was concerned. She told me: "You are embarking upon a difficult foreign journey. I am sure you'll be back." I thought this was a sneer.

On my last Sunday in Tabriz, I bid farewell to Ter Karapet and Ter Vartan, the two priests of our church, where I had spent so many happy days as an altar boy and assistant to the deacon. They both blessed me. I treated my street gang to a movie as a farewell gesture. It was hard to leave their company. I thanked my teachers, too. They were very excited. They were very proud of me, they said.

My grandmother took me to church and we lit candles. Then she took me to a mosque in our neighborhood and to a synagogue to pray. She was not taking any chances but was delivering prayers and seeking protection for me through all three Abrahamic faiths, each of which worshipped the same God. The night before my departure, she sewed inside my suit jacket several amulets as well as small, wrapped prayers in Armenian, Persian, Arabic, and Hebrew. "Don't open them," she advised me. "It will result in bad luck." In addition, she gave me some blue beads for protection against the "evil eye."

The day of my departure was hectic. We had to be at the bus station no later than six A.M. There were two new bus services, TCC and Mihantoor. Both had fixed departure hours, like the trains. They did not wait for latecomers. Nor did they wait until the bus was full. In Tabriz this was a revolutionary innovation.

The toughest separation for me was that from my grandmother and my sister, Ojik. She was a beautiful girl, with big eyes, gorgeous hair, a kind heart, and engaging laughter. We were soul mates. In a span of nine years, we had witnessed the deaths of our grandfather, mother, two uncles, and a half brother. We had endured poverty and scarcity and many private and public humiliations. We had cried, suffered, and laughed together.

Edmond Haraucourt (1856–1941), the French poet and writer, in his "Rondel de l'Adieu," wrote: *Partir, c'est mourir un peu* (To part is to die a little). He added: *On laisse un peu de soi-même* (One leaves a little of one's self), and, later in the poem, *En toute heure et dans tout lieu* (In every hour and in every place).

As the bus was ready to leave for Tehran, an emotional Samuel, my father, bid me good-bye. He held me in his arms, followed by my grandmother, stepmother, sister, and many friends. As my journey began, I felt a tremendous sense of guilt, anxiety, and relief: I felt guilty for abandoning my grandmother and sister, I was anxious because I was going to an unknown land, and I was relieved because now I was on my own. At long last, I thought, I was going to have peace, privacy, and even independence.

The six-hour-or-so IranAir flight from Tehran to Beirut was exhilarating. I was excited and scared. The plane reminded me of the flying carpets that captivated us as children in the movies depicting tales from *The Arabian Nights*. At one point, I felt as if I were suspended between heaven and earth. The impact of changing horizons, on the one hand, and a landscape of fast-moving villages, towns, cities, and cultivated fields, along with desert lands, was overwhelming. The view from the plane made everything seem small, even insignificant. My fear of flying gave way to one of utter detachment and liberation. The only drawback to air travel, I noted at the time, was its speed. It did not allow one to reflect on the many thoughts and emotions generated by one's departure. The speed condensed, confined, all of one's emotions within a fixed-time framework. There was not enough time to unwind, even to be nostalgic. Before you were able to conclude your thoughts, suddenly you found yourself in a new world.

Once in Beirut, I had stagefright. My Persian, Armenian, Turkish, even some Russian, proved insufficient as a means of communication. One of my companions on the IranAir flight came to my assistance. He helped me change Iranian rials to Lebanese pounds, negotiated the cab fare for me, and gave the driver the address of my destination in Beirut: Hotel Luxe. "Which one?" the driver asked. I said, "*The* one, the famous one. It is a well-known hotel." The driver shook his head. "I know about the location," he said, "but I have never heard about the Hotel Luxe."

After a wild taxicab ride and an inquiry or two, the driver located the Hotel Luxe. It was in one of the busiest sections of the business district. Buried among a myriad of signs was a discreet, small sign indicating the exact location of the hotel. It was on the fifth floor of a building and was reached by a crude elevator. The hotel had six or seven rooms and a nice, large, airy rooftop terrace. The owner, Mr. Toorigian, and his family lived on the top floor. The kitchen served the family as well as the guests. It was a lively Armenian hotel. In the evenings, it served as a gathering place for several Armenian writers, editors, and politicos, who gathered there to dine, play poker, bridge, or backgammon, and discuss a variety of pressing national and international issues. It was a sort of modern-day salon.

The hotel's rooms were occupied by visiting Armenian writers, teachers, and businessmen from Syria, Egypt, and Iraq. I was the first guest from Iran. I handed Mr. Maloyan's letter to Mr. Toorigian. He extended a warm welcome, gave me a room, and asked me to join him, his family, and guests for breakfast, lunch, and dinner. The guests, all Armenians, spoke the western Armenian dialect. I spoke the eastern one, but we understood each other. My first night in Beirut was depressing. All of a sudden, I felt alone in the world. I was in a faraway place, in a strange city and strange hotel and bed, uprooted and transplanted to follow the unknown. I had neither friends nor acquaintances.

My first two weeks in Beirut were memorable even though I was alone and lonely. I found the city intoxicating. It was my first encounter with a for-eign metropolis, a seaport, and ships. The sight of the Mediterranean was sensational, as were Beirut's lofty palm trees. I experienced, for the first time, the distinctive smell of the sea, and the oppressive, late-summer heat and humidity of the city. This was offset by the clean air and gentle breeze of its beautiful nights.

In Beirut, I experienced for the first time the wonders, the dangers, the excitement, and the frustrations of an automobile culture. The traffic was unbearable, and for a provincial boy from Tabriz, frightening. Fast-moving cars in the narrow streets of Beirut seemed to be participants in a giant ma-cho game or else an intricate acrobatic exercise. The taxicab drivers, de-pending on their religious affiliations, carried a variety of Christian and Muslim religious symbols, amulets, charms, prayers, and slogans on their dashboards, seeking divine protection by these religious and spiritual "in-surance policies." I came to believe that these drivers, especially the kamikaze among them, needed all possible protection.

The fruit markets and fruit stands of Beirut, with their multitude of or-anges, tangerines, apples, apricots, grapes, peas, bananas, and loquats, not only added a pleasant scent but vibrant colors that blended with the red clay tiles adorning the rooftops of many old and new houses, the blue sky, and the greenish sea. The city was a microcosm of the Mediterranean world. The mixture of Arab, Ottoman, French, Italian, and some American architec-tural styles gave Beirut a sense of intimacy and tradition, along with one of comfort and utility. The city was a natural blend of the East and the West, *Le Petit Paris,* and truly beautiful.

In the midst of all the commotion, the Mediterranean had a soothing ef-fect on me. The rhythm of its waves was a welcome and lovely background for dreaming and contemplation. Spectacular sunsets enhanced the sea's dramatic effect. The sight of departing passenger and cargo ships evoked a sense of nostalgia. In the presence of the Mediterranean, suddenly all my geography and history classes and the literature that I had read found a con-text. One could not help thinking of the centrality, the historical dominance of the Mediterranean, its role not as a barrier but as a bridge linking Europe, Africa, and the Middle East, the basin of so many great civilizations.

The Lebanese, like their Phoenician ancestors, are people of the sea, born traders, entrepreneurs, and intermediaries. There was a popular unfair joke about them. Asked what two plus two amounts to, the Lebanese kid responds, "First tell me, are you buying or selling?"

Every ancient and modern Christian Church and denomination was present in Lebanon. On Sundays, the Catholic, Maronite (Uniate), Greek Orthodox, Greek Catholic (Uniate), Syriac, Coptic, Jacobite, Arab Protestant, Armenian Apostolic, Catholic (Uniate), and Protestant Churches competed for God's attention, most of them through their beautiful liturgies, incense, choirs, church bells with different melodies, or plain sermons. On the Muslim side, from the top of their minarets, the muezzins called to prayer, through loudspeakers, the faithful Sunni and Shia Muslims, as well as the Druze and Alawites, three times a day. The Jews worshipped God in the quiet of their synagogue on Saturdays. The church bells and the beautiful melody of the muezzins' call to prayer made me homesick. My first Sunday, I ventured into a Maronite church and almost fell off my seat when I heard the priest officiate the mass in Arabic; I was astonished when I heard the word *Allah* (God). I thought only Muslims called God *Allah*.

Within Beirut, the ethnic mosaic divided itself into neighborhoods. There were the Christian and Armenian neighborhoods, the Jewish quarter, and the Muslim sectors, both Sunni and Shia. There was an international section as well. In addition, on the sidelines, there had emerged a new phenomenon. As you left the airport, on your way to the city, you saw a chain of shantytowns and tents. They housed thousands of Palestinian refugees, caught in the web of history. They were supposed to be "temporary refugees," but they found themselves (and still do) in limbo. They were refused Lebanese citizenship, for if granted citizenship, it was feared, they would upset the delicate historic, religious, confessional, and ethnic balances of Lebanon. In addition, if they were granted citizenship, or given work permits, the Lebanese feared being criticized severely for betraying the Palestinian and Arab causes by absorbing the refugees within the economic, social, and political fabric of Lebanon, thus "solving" the Palestinian "refugee problem."

I was surprised to find out that there was yet another shantytown in Bourj Hamoud, a district of Beirut. This one housed Armenian refugees, the remnants of the World War I Armenian Genocide, and their offspring, who had survived the death march to the Syrian desert and found refuge in hospitable Arab countries, including Syria and Lebanon.

Lebanon of the early 50s stood for tolerance and the peaceful coexistence of a multiplicity of faiths and ethnic groups. It was hailed for turning its ethnic, religious, and cultural diversity into an asset. The architects of this coexistence were several Christian and Muslim political leaders who concluded a National Pact in 1943, according to which the Lebanese Republic would have a Maronite Christian as its president, a Sunni Muslim as prime minister, a Shia Muslim as the speaker of the Parliament, a Druze as its defense minister, a Greek Orthodox as its foreign minister, a Maronite as chief of the Lebanese army staff, and so on. The beauty of this arrangement was that even though it was not written into the Constitution of the Republic, it was faithfully adhered to. The letter and the spirit of the pact were respected, since any deviation from it, or tampering with it, was fraught with potential dangers, including civil war. In some sense, this confessional (religious community) political system was based on proportional representation. Every community had a stake and a share in the government, and in the Parliament.

There was one major flaw in this arrangement: it could not afford the test of a census, which might have revealed that either Christians or Muslims were in the majority or, that within the Christian camp, the Maronites were no longer the majority; or that within the Muslim community, the Shias outnumbered the Sunni. Just in case one faction demanded an official census, the Christians and Muslims alike would argue that it must include all the Lebanese immigrants abroad, especially in Latin America, whose remittances contributed to the well-being of the Lebanese economy and society. Under the circumstances, every political party, including the Communists, that participated in the Lebanese parliamentary elections usually presented itself as part of a bloc, or alliance, of different parties, representing the ethnic and religious mosaic of the country.

Beirut was the banking center of the Middle East and also its commercial hub. The movement of people, goods, and money was unhindered. The country had a free market economy, a rarity in the Middle East, and one of the strongest currencies in the world. It was a haven for the Saudis, Kuwaitis, Iraqis, and Egyptians. It gave asylum to many political refugees. There was an almost absolute freedom of the press. There were numerous newspapers and periodicals published in Arabic. There were two French dailies and an English one, as well as two Armenian dailies. The press represented the voices of many political parties, ranging from the extreme left to the extreme right. The only subject that was taboo was an attack against Christianity, Islam, and/or Judaism (Christ, Muhammad, Abraham). In the bazaars of Beirut, the jewelry shops displayed the hand of Fatima, the Crescent, and the Cross along with the Star of David.

I saw for the first time modern hotels, great European-style restaurants, and varieties of wine and beer, including scotch and bourbon whiskies and gin. Accustomed to fresh food, I was astonished to see the variety of local, European, and American canned foodstuffs. I tasted my first canned sardines and Kraft cheese, my first Coke, first milkshake, first hamburger, and first baklava with pistachios. I saw my first bar and first belly dancing, and heard my first live Arab music.

Beirut of the 50s was also the fashion capital of the region and the center of education. The city and indeed the country were full of first-class universities and high schools: the American University of Beirut, the American College for Women, Saint Joseph University, the Lebanese University, and many French lycées and other public and parochial schools attracted students from all over the region.

Edgar Maloyan's letter to the head of the Internal Security Department of Lebanon worked like magic. I was granted permission to stay and study in Lebanon. My tourist visa was transferred to a student one. The next hurdle and the most important was the question of my admission to Collège Arménien. I had not applied for admission to the Collège. I don't believe that they had even heard of me. All I had was a glowing letter from Edgar Maloyan to Garo Sassouni about my aptitude as a student. Mr. Sassouni, who taught Armenian literature and history at the Collège, and Mr. Maloyan were compatriots.

I went to see Mr. Sassouni at his modest apartment. With his pipe in his mouth, he read Mr. Maloyan's letter and quizzed me about my knowledge of Armenian history and literature. Evidently, Mr. Maloyan had written him an impressive letter, arguing that since the Collège Arménien was founded with the goal of educating the next generation of Armenian intellectuals, teachers, and professionals from the *entire* Armenian Diaspora and not just from Lebanon and Syria, they should welcome me with open arms. A very cordial Mr. Sassouni asked me to meet him the next morning in the main building of the school at precisely eleven A.M. to meet Levon Shant, the director of the Collège Arménien. Don't be late, he cautioned me. Mr. Shant is very punctual.

The next morning, I went to the Collège. Great iron gates led to a beautiful four-story building surrounded by palm trees. The building was the former headquarters of the French Admiralty. Built on high ground, it faced the Mediterranean. At precisely eleven A.M., we were ushered into Mr. Shant's office. An impeccably dressed gentleman with a goatee and a monocle, he fitted the image of a nineteenth-century German professor. Mr. Sassouni introduced me with great gusto. He announced that I was a crane that had arrived from Iran into the fold of the Collège Arménien. After reading Mr. Maloyan's letter, Mr. Shant asked me three devastating questions: "Do you have any money?" "Do you know French?" "Do you know Arabic?" My answer was no to all three. Then he asked me the logical followup question: "What are you doing here?" I had no answer.

All of a sudden, instead of a crane, I had become a kiwi. I had become a big problem, a challenge, and an embarrassment to the Collège. Mr. Sassouni tried to console me: "Don't worry. We'll find a solution." I was devastated. I staggered to the Hotel Luxe to retreat from reality.

The weekend was unending. But another calamity was awaiting me. Mr. Toorigian, the owner of the Hotel Luxe, presented me with a bill for the expenses of my lodging as well as meals. I had thought, naively, that my hotel expenses were covered by Mr. Maloyan, at least until the opening of the school. I did not have enough money to cover the bill. That Sunday, I went to the Armenian church. The liturgy, the incense, the mass reconnected me with my past. As the choir sang "Holy, Holy," tears ran down my cheeks. I remembered my grandmother and her surprising depth of suffering. I did not realize until then that I had a reservoir of will to suffer and endure as well. On Monday morning, I took my beautiful blanket and silver picture frames and gold-rimmed spectacles, my only valuable possessions, to the bazaar to sell.

I searched for Armenian merchants, jewelers, and optometrists who might buy my possessions. Armenian names and, occasionally, even Armenian letters were my only guide in the maze of Beirut's bazaars. I had no notion of the value of my possessions. Anyone I approached immediately knew that I was in desperate need of money. Besides, handmade, ornamental silver frames and beautifully engraved silver teacups and glass-holders were not in fashion in Beirut. As I was going from shop to shop trying to sell my blanket, I ran into one of the teachers of the Collège Arménien, Mr. Mooshegh Ishkhan, a poet and a writer who taught Armenian literature. He was appalled. He alerted Mr. Sassouni, who was shocked, too.

I think everyone who heard of my plight was scandalized that a young Armenian boy from Iran had come all the way to Beirut to study, but before he could even enroll in the Collège, was destitute through no fault of his own. This was due to a major misunderstanding or a snafu, they thought. All of a sudden, my predicament was no longer mine alone, but theirs as well. There were questions in need of answers. Who had sent me to Beirut? On what basis? What promises were made to me? What were my actual and potential sources of financial support? There was a consensus that I needed some protection until my status was clarified and a solution found.

It was at this juncture that I met Lola Sassouni, the wife of Garo Sassouni. She was an extraordinary woman. Born in Turkey (then the Ottoman Empire), she had graduated from the Armenian school in Akn, and from the American College for Women in Istanbul. She was fluent in Armenian, English, Turkish, and French. I was invited to go to the Sassouni residence. Mrs. Sassouni had big eyes and a broad forehead. She had a fierce look but a soothing voice. She asked about my finances. I told her that most of my money had gone to the Hotel Luxe, and that I had been able to sell my pashmina blanket, my gold-rimmed eyeglasses, and two of my silver frames for some twenty dollars, and that I was hoping for, or expecting, another twenty-five dollars from Mr. Maloyan.

"This is outrageous," she said. "You cannot live on expectations. We have to find a place for you to stay and then a restaurant to provide you with meals. Don't worry. We'll take care of you!" she said with great confidence and determination. Within days, she had found, near the college, above a bakery, a small room being rented by an Armenian family. My roommate was an Armenian dentist from Iraq, now a student in Beirut.

Mrs. Sassouni took me to a restaurant called Délice. It was a peculiar eatery. Located on the ground floor of an apartment building, it was operated by two Armenian immigrants from Australia who resembled Laurel and Hardy. The restaurant served only lunch and dinner, at fixed hours. The typical lunch included two thin sliced pieces of bread, a small cube of butter, two small sardines, a slice of ham, or else a small bowl of soup. Dinner included the same thing, in addition to serving, alternately, smoked fish or liver and, occasionally, meat. Everything was served in very small, measured quantities. The monthly charge, per person, was $6.15 (20 Lebanese pounds). Thanks to Mrs. Sassouni, the Armenian Red Cross paid that. Unfortunately, the restaurant did not serve breakfast and was closed on Saturdays and Sundays. They were the difficult days. I had to wait until Monday noon to eat. I took a part-time waiter's job in a dingy Armenian "fast-food" restaurant that served *fool* (fava beans), *hummus* (chick peas with tahini paste), *baba ghanouj* (eggplant), *lahm ajeen* (Lebanese meat "pizza"), and *shawarma* (marinated minced meat). The pay was very little. However, I was able to eat a dish of *hummus* or *fool*.

Now I was ready for the fall term of Collège Arménien. The authorities of the Collège and its director, Levon Shant, decided to allow me to attend school as an auditor only, limiting me to Armenian-taught courses: language, literature, Armenian history, and general history, for at least a year. I assured Mme. Yoland, the stylish and energetic French language and literature teacher, that I could learn enough French in a year to enroll in all the classes taught at the Collège, including mathematics, physics, chemistry, and botany. Mme. Yoland was incredulous. "Do you have money for private tutors in French? How else are you going to learn?" "I'll learn somehow" was my answer. She shrugged. "It is impossible." I assured Mr. Bustani, the teacher of Arabic, that in view of my knowledge of Persian and Turkish, it would be easy for me to learn the level of Arabic taught at the institution. Mr. Boustani gave me the benefit of the doubt.

The Collège Arménien was established in May 1928. Its founders were two notable Armenian intellectuals: Levon Shant, the writer, and Nigol Aghbalian, the literary critic. Mr. Shant had served as the speaker of the Armenian Parliament during the short-lived Independent Armenian Republic (1918–1920). Mr. Aghbalian had held the position of minister of education. The Collège was launched and sustained thanks to the generosity of Armenian-Americans and a handful of Armenian philanthropists from Egypt and Lebanon.

The mission of the Collège was to train Armenian teachers, editors, social workers, a cadre of public intellectuals, political leaders, and Armenologists, as well as prepare Armenian students for professional careers such as lawyer, engineer, doctor, or scientist. The overall goal was to meet the individual and collective need of the Armenian Diaspora. The founders of the Collège had decided to provide their students with an excellent Armenian and French education, thus enabling their graduates to be admitted to French and American universities and fulfill their career aspirations. The faculty of the Collège consisted of some extraordinary individuals, graduates of Russian, French, German, and Czech universities and British and Lebanese teaching institutes. They brought to the Collège both Armenian and broad international perspectives. In many ways, the Collège resembled an intimate, extended family. The student-teacher ratio was ten to one. We got to know all of our teachers and classmates. I was surprised but very pleased that there was no corporal punishment. But there was discipline.

My first academic year was enjoyable and productive. I loved my classes. I read ferociously. I studied several fifth-century A.D. (Golden Age) Armenian classic texts. The Collège's library was for me a trove of treasures. Even though I was only an auditor, I did all the course work and assignments. My teachers encouraged me. I made some friends. But everybody in the Collège, including my teachers and classmates, was aware that I was in a precarious position, not only financially but academically. I knew it too well.

My aptitude for Armenian history, language, and literature was not sufficient to keep me at the Collège. Unless I could learn French, Arabic, and English during my first year at the Collège, I could not be a regular student. I did not want to retain my status as an auditor for another year. Neither did the Collège authorities. I could not afford any more losses of valuable time. Nor did I want to return to Iran to my stepmother and father who, by now, had moved to Tehran.

I did not have money to hire a French-language tutor. Once again, I got lucky. Two strangers volunteered to teach me French for free. One was Vartkes Ter Karapetian, an urban planner, and the other was Vaché Papazian, the son of Vahan Papazian, a former member of the Ottoman Parliament and a leading member of the Armenian Revolutionary Federation. Vaché was the copy editor of *L'Orient,* the leading French newspaper in Beirut. He spent his weekends teaching me French.

Vartkes Ter Karapetian could give me French lessons only in the evenings while he played bridge at the Armenian Club or at the Hotel Luxe, or else during breakaway periods of some political gathering. I remember waiting in the wings during the card games, getting my writing assignments, going to an empty room or the hallway, finishing my homework, presenting it to him, getting the corrections, and then waiting for the next opportunity. It was do or die. I knew that my success or failure to learn French would determine whether I could stay in Lebanon. It was not my pride or reputation that was at stake, it was my survival. Failure was not an option.

I read and reread a dictated letter from my grandmother. She said that God would not allow me to fail, that my star would always guard me from adversity, and that she was praying for me. My grandmother had resumed her supplicant relation to God because of her love for me. Several evenings, walking along the streets of Beirut, I looked up to the sky. It is silly to confess, but I was glad to see that my star, the biggest one, the North Star, was still there. Emily Dickinson's poem was right.

> Hope is the thing with feathers
> That perches in the soul,
> And sings the tune without the words,
> And never stops at all.

After a year, I believed I had learned enough French to be a regular, full-time student. Mme. Yoland was skeptical. She admitted me to her classes with great misgivings and did not give me special treatment. On the contrary, at least that was my impression, she picked on me. She would ask me to read a text, recite a poem by heart. If I missed a line or misplaced a word, Mme. Yoland would inquire whether I was attempting to improve a Victor Hugo or a Lamartine or an Alfred de Musset poem. There were days when I hated her because she never gave me any encouragement or appreciation. I bought an overused copy of *Grammaire Larousse du XXe Siècle,* the ultimate dictionary of the French language and its usage. Each time Mme. Yoland gave grammar lessons or literary illustrations, I raised my hand to cite the exceptions to the rule, my source being the comprehensive standard dictionary. Our exchanges would continue for some three years. In the process, I learned French and passed all my exams. Mme. Yoland did not lower her standards. She forced me to rise to them.

In addition to Mme. Yoland, there were at least four other teachers who greatly influenced my academic interests. Garnik Guzelian was one of them. A graduate of Charles University in Prague, Czechoslovakia, and a noted historian, he instilled in me the love of history. He was a great lecturer, with a sense of humor. In the classroom, he addressed me as "professor." I knew he said it in jest, but I loved it! Mr. Guzelian's mastery of the history of the Middle East and Armenia and his love of social and economic history made a great impression on me.

Antoine Kehyaian, known affectionately as "Sir," taught us English language and literature. A graduate of British schools in Cyprus with a stint at Oxford, Mr. Kehyaian was a devout Catholic. He was fluent in English, French, and Turkish. What was unusual was that he did not know Armenian. His mother tongue was Turkish. There were many Armenians in the Ottoman Empire who had lost their Armenian language while remaining Christian. They read Bibles written in the Turkish language but with the Armenian alphabet.

Over the years, Sir learned how to speak fluent Armenian. He taught us conversational English, insisting that we tell stories in English in our classroom. With his Oxbridge, perfect English accent, he struggled mightily to teach us how to pronounce *th* and differentiate between *v* and *w*. He also made us read Shakespeare's *Macbeth* and English and American short stories and news items from his bible, *Time* magazine.

I was also fortunate to have Kostan Zarian as a teacher. He was a prominent novelist, editor, and intellectual. His lectures were fascinating. He taught history and philosophy of art and introduced me to art and architecture, aesthetics, and philosophy, from Vico to Hegel to Nietzsche to Oswald Spengler; from the Egpytian, Greek, and Roman civilizations to the Renaissance. I loved his lectures on Plotinus and the Neo-Platonic school, Dante, Petrarch, Boccaccio, Donatello, Michelangelo, and Ficino. I still hear echoes of his authoritative voice reminding us that it was Ficino's commentary on Plato's *Symposium* that was the source of the commonly used phrase "Platonic love," and that it was Ficino who brought about the fusion of Platonism and Christianity.

Professor Khoren Gabikian of the Antelias Armenian Seminary was a meticulous scholar and an expert in diplomatic history. In his courses on modern European history, he analyzed the importance of the "Eastern Question," Great Power rivalries, and the Ottoman Empire and introduced me to the evolution of the concepts of nationalism and self-determination and how they had changed the course of Near Eastern history in general and Armenian history in particular.

My school days were long: eight A.M. to four P.M. We had seven different classes a day and one hour for lunch. The course work ranged from Armenian language, literature, and history to Near Eastern history, geography, mathematics, physics, chemistry, botany, and French language and literature, and Arabic and English. There was no recreation. Extracurricular activities were not considered essential for the development of the mind and the discipline of the will. The science courses were tough, partly because they were in French, and I struggled. The courses in humanities and social sciences were easier. I found geography particularly fascinating and helpful, even though it was the names of the rivers and lakes of Europe that were the subjects of many drills. The Arabic language was manageable, and the instruction in English pleasant.

During my first year at the Collège, the weekends were tough. Sometimes a classmate would invite me to his home for Sunday dinner or lunch. But many weekends, even though I was hungry, I considered the rumbles of my greedy, food-craving stomach unreasonable, unfaithful, disloyal, unfair, and selfish. I drank lots of water, took long walks, read passionate romances, and went to bed early in an attempt either to defeat or to forget my hunger. Sundays, I went to church for nostalgia, but also with the ardent hope that one of my classmates or their parents would invite me to lunch or dinner.

When I had money from my wages as a waiter in Lutfiq's fast-food eatery, I bought Lebanese bread and a can of Kraft cheese for the weekend. It was the first time that I saw and ate yellow cheese. I had always thought cheese was white. I remembered Mr. Maloyan's advice about bananas. I bought one kilo of them. I started to eat my first banana while at the store, but without peeling it. The curious looks and the bad taste made me realize my blunder. I peeled it, to the great relief of the spectators. Soon I could not even buy bananas. Whatever money I had, I spent at the post office. Even then, I could not send many first class, airmail letters to my sister, grandmother, friends, and parents. I sent a newspaper, at printed matter rate, to my sister, care of *Alik,* the Armenian newspaper in Tehran. In it, I carefully folded three or four letters, occasionally as many as nine or ten. My sister then forwarded those letters. I had to console myself because here I was in the city of multiple movies with no money to take advantage of them, no means to forget my miseries by being transported to the realms of fantasy. I was very lonely. I had nobody with whom I could share my fears, misery, or anxieties. I certainly could not and did not write home about them. After all, I had become "the exclusive correspondent of *Alik* newspaper in Beirut." I wrote a variety of articles about the Armenian community of Lebanon.

In the fall of 1951, Mr. Shant died. Soon after his death, the leaders of the Hamazkain Cultural Association, the governing board of the Collège, offered the director's position to Simon Vratzian, the last prime minister of the Armenian Republic. Vratzian arrived in Beirut from the United States in December 1951. For me, this development was a fateful one. It changed my life and determined my future. In the meantime, in the fall of 1951, I had caught a very bad cold and a cough and had a high fever as well. As I coughed, I detected blood. I thought I had tuberculosis and, hence, that death was at my doorstep. Having read lots of romantic writers and poets, and knowing that tuberculosis was the "desirable" death for romantics because one expired gradually, and that since the illness was a metaphor endowed with metaphysical qualities, I wrote several melodramatic poems: "Good-bye Moon," "The Autumn Is Wet and Cold," "Good-bye to Sunrises and Sunsets," "Ode to My Grandmother and Sister," "The Heavy Burden of Loneliness," etc.

Two or three classmates and a teacher of mine who visited me would not or could not come into my room. After all, TB was contagious. I told my classmates that I was leaving them my entire legacy, a small collection of books. Dr. Semerjian, the Collège's doctor, who examined me, ordered chest X rays. I had to wait a week for the results. As far as I was concerned, it was the longest recorded week in history. Then came Dr. Semerjian's verdict. The X rays were negative. I had a very bad cold. As to the blood, it was from my gums, due to malnutrition. I destroyed all my self-pitying, sad, bombastic poems.

I met Simon Vratzian with fear and trepidation. I was in awe of his imposing figure, his dominant presence, his status, his reputation, his accomplishments, his fame. After all, he was the last prime minister of the short-lived independent Republic of Armenia. For me, Mr. Vratzian was a living chapter of Armenian history. To my delight, he took great interest in me and my academic work.

Within a very short time, we developed a great rapport. Pretty soon, he became my mentor and, eventually, my benevolent benefactor. A series of events conspired to bring us together. In July 1952, Mr. Vratzian, while on a visit to the United States, was forced to have eye surgery to save his eyesight. He was not able to return until October. Unfortunately, his eyesight had undergone a serious deterioration. This eminent intellectual public figure, who by age seventy had lived a most eventful and productive life of reading and writing, was now losing his eyesight and, hence, his independence. A prodigious and prolific writer, publicist, and now educator, Vratzian needed, in addition to a pair of the thickest possible eyeglasses, a "pair of new eyes," as he put it.

From 1952 until my graduation from the Collège in 1955 and the completion of the program of advanced studies in Armenology (1956), I served as Mr. Vratzian's assistant. I became one of his pair of eyes. I read his confidential, personal mail. He dictated his personal letters to me. When I was not with him, he wrote on small pieces of paper. Because of his failing eyesight, the lines often crossed, but he wrote nevertheless. To decipher his writings was a challenge for me and frustrating to him. To see him struggle with a magnifying glass, to make sense of his crisscrossed sentences, was heartbreaking. I spent four years, including summers, working on several of his projected books and manuscripts, sometimes reading, proofreading, and editing on his behalf, and sometimes doing research in old newspapers, magazines, journals, and yearbooks. In 1961 and 1965 to 1966, when I returned to Lebanon, I continued to work with him. I was fascinated with his encyclopedic mind and amazing memory. With great ease, he could recall small and major events, provide the precise character traits of individuals from many lands and institutions, characterize and categorize a range of complex issues, organizations, ideologies, political factions, and factions within the factions. His energy and work habits were astonishing, his humor enchanting. In addition to my regular classroom work and assignments, I spent considerable and most valuable time with Mr. Vratzian. In doing so, I received an inestimable, rich, percipient, private education, a privileged tutorial. I was given a rare opportunity to get to know him, to participate, albeit vicariously, in a great man's fascinating life and times, in the world of his rich, prolific scholarship, in the world of his intimate and intricate memories.

I have wondered during the past forty years why I was chosen by Mr. Vratzian to be "a pair of his eyes" or his "eyeglasses." Was it due to the fact that I was alone in Beirut? That I had no family obligations, and practically no social life, and hence could spend inordinate hours with him? That I was from Iran and spoke eastern Armenian, his maternal language? That he knew firsthand that I wrote well? That he trusted me and knew that I would never divulge his confidences? That he wanted to help me survive and help educate me? Or was it perhaps that I reminded him occasionally of his late young son, who had died during the 1921 exodus of the anti-Bolshevik Armenians from Armenia to Iran? Maybe it was a combination of *all* these things.

One thing is for sure. Within the span of four years, he had become a surrogate father to me, as well as a teacher, mentor, and friend. Mr. Vratzian was a very private person. He seldom, if ever, discussed his personal feelings, his family, or his various ailments and so he was a lonely man. Most of his close colleagues had died. In Beirut, he had many, many acquaintances but only a handful of close personal friends. Under the circumstances, he drowned himself in work. He had a lot of unfinished work, a lot to say, a lot to write, and he was a man in a hurry. Time was his enemy; he wanted to accomplish as much as possible. He wanted to do justice to the memory of many people he had known and chronicle and analyze events that were important for understanding the history of Armenia and the Armenians.

Notwithstanding his diminishing eyesight, the period between 1952 and 1962 was one of the most productive periods of Mr. Vratzian's life. He wrote a six-volume quasi-memoir, published several scholarly works, and reissued his masterly history of the Armenian Republic.

As the director of the Collège, Mr. Vratzian disabused those who thought he had come to Beirut to retire. He embarked upon the arduous task of visiting North America as well as South America in search of funds for the Collège, and secured major gifts. He built a building to house a new American-style kindergarten, the middle school, and a boarding school. He strengthened the instruction of sciences and the Collège's French baccalaureate program. He increased the salaries of all the employees of the Collège by 15 percent and recruited several nationally prominent figures to join its faculty. Kostan Zarian, a major contemporary Armenian writer, was recruited from Italy to teach art history along with Barsegh Kanachian, a renowned Armenian composer and conductor who taught music and conducted the Collège's choir. I was a member of that choir. The demand for admissions soared. The new boarding facilities attracted students from Iran, Greece, Kuwait, Ethiopia, Iraq, and Syria. The Collège's enrollment by 1954 had doubled to 350 (197 boys and 153 girls).

Mr. Vratzian's energy and the depth and intensity of his commitment to the Collège surprised all of us. We soon realized that our institution had an activist director who, with unparalleled pride, careful deliberation, and steady determination, had undertaken to provide the Collège a long-term strategic plan, which called for additional financial resources. Mr. Vratzian's worldwide network of contacts served him well. During the daytime he worked diligently and with utter dedication and discipline; most evenings and Sundays he dined with select Armenian families who took great pride in having him as an honored guest. His quest for funds and favors was successful most of the time. "Build and expand," he would say. "Don't worry, the Armenian nation will take care of you." There was one fundamental requirement, however: everything the Collège did must be of the highest quality. He believed that if the Collège pursued excellence it would be rewarded.

Most of the gifts for the Collège came from Armenian-Americans. Forty out of fifty-three scholarship funds of the Collège were of U.S. provenance. Mr. Vratzian secured funding for a twenty-thousand volume library, provided naming opportunities for benefactors of the Collège, and energized the Collège's public outreach programs. For me, these were heady days. To read his correspondence alone was a great education; to write diplomatic, caring, candid letters was a great learning experience; to witness the workings of his intricate and brilliant mind was riveting. One thing I did not have to do was help with his speeches. Vratzian never wrote any. On numerous occasions, including cultural, educational, political events, anniversaries, and year-end graduation ceremonies, he would get up, and without a single note deliver a thought-provoking, erudite yet passionate, concise yet incisive speech, a speech that usually overwhelmed the audience. His eulogies were the same, always original, always moving and full of facts, light, and passion.

Even though I made a conscious effort to keep a low profile, my friendship with and easy access to Mr. Vratzian and the amount of time I spent with him was, I am sure, resented by some of my teachers, as well as my fellow students. My role as his unofficial secretary, assistant, and escort placed me in an awkward, yet enviable position. Mr. Vratzian was seen as my protector. I had to work very hard and not take that for granted, study well to prove that I was worthy of his trust, and keep my mouth shut in order not to divulge any of his confidences, or brag about my special status.

The opening of boarding quarters at the Collège freed me from my cell. For the first time, I had a small private room and the joy of a shower. For the first time, I understood why even revolutionaries such as Leon Trotsky, while in New York in 1917, would brag about their private bathtub and bathroom. I was appointed assistant to the director of the boardinghouse. My role was to proctor the study hours, supervise the dining-room rules, oversee the orderly behavior and punctuality of the students, and enforce the cur-few. I had become a petty bureaucrat. But I loved my new job. It provided me with room and board. I was earning my keep. I had time to study and write. I had *privacy,* the most cherished of all the luxuries.

My childhood experiences at home, at the school, and on the street came in handy in my "administration" of the Collège's boardinghouse rules and regulations. As a young boy, I had made a vow that when I grew up I would deal with disciplinary infractions in ways other than by physical punish-ment I had met. One Sunday, I put that vow to the test. I was going to church service and I asked fourteen boarders if they would like to accom-pany me. There were no volunteers. I asked them whether they would like to go to the movies instead. There was a uniform negative answer. What would they like to do? "We want to stay in bed. We want to have a relaxed day," was the response. I went to church but came back early to take them to a popular eatery for a Sunday treat. Every bed was empty. Everyone had disappeared. I did not know that while in bed they were all dressed, waiting for me to leave so that they could attend *their* chosen movie. I don't remem-ber the name of the movie. I felt betrayed. I was angry. I sat on a bench, un-der a huge tree, next to the main gate.

At one P.M., they all returned in taxicabs. As soon as they saw me, they froze. They had planned to be back a half hour before my arrival. I did not say anything. They stood there in front of me for some ten minutes, all silent, with bowed heads. Then, one by one, they went quietly to their dor-mitory. They knew they had lied to me. Therefore, they were full of re-morse. By not exacting any punishment, by not admonishing them, I had, I thought, punished them by teaching them a lesson. Such infractions and de-ceitful acts did not happen again. I asked myself: What would I have done if Samuel, my father, had punished me in a similar fashion?

In addition to my boardinghouse duties and assisting Mr. Vratzian, I had my regular daily classes from eight to four, and during my last three years at the Collège, six days a week, from five to seven in the evening, I took ad-vanced courses in Armenology. Then, of course, there was my membership in the Collège's choir. Thanks to Mr. Vratzian, I received a full scholarship from the Armenian Red Cross of São Paulo, Brazil. At long last, I was a "normal" student. In addition to my room and board, I had a stipend. Now I could send airmail letters to my grandmother, sister, parents, and friends in Iran. I even began saving and sending small amounts of money to my grandmother to help her with her rent. In the land of movies, I could, at long last, see as many of them as my heart desired.

* * *

On my name day (Saint Vartan), February 25, 1954, I received a gift. It was a diary. Accompanying it was a note, both tender and sad. I was afraid it was bad news. The gift and the note were from my first real love, a beautiful slender girl with long black hair, captivating eyes, pleasant demeanor, and tender touch. She was what the French call a *mignonne,* an Armenian student from Iran studying at Beirut College for Women, an American college. I had met her eight months before at an Armenian cultural event. It was love at first sight.

The note read: "My adorable darling. Many years from now, when you have a wife and are surrounded with delightful and handsome children of yours, when you open this diary, I do not know what your reaction to this note will be nor your opinion of me. Maybe you will laugh, or even cry. I only hope that you will find, at long last, peace in your life as well as better luck and happiness to compensate your many hardships and suffering.

"I only beg of you one thing. If we do not reach our destiny, promise never to forget me. Know that I love you with all my heart and soul, and that in my heart I will always keep the flame of love alive."

Was it a farewell note? How could we possibly forget each other when we had professed to each other so many times our mutual love, had assured ourselves that we had become one, that we could never be happy without each other and that even though I had no material possessions, the whole world was at my feet because I had her love.

Three days later, my anxieties were put to rest when we went to the movies. It was a regular Sunday afternoon activity. Movie houses, and a seaside coffeehouse or two, were the only realms of privacy available to us. We held hands, kissed, and talked. Premarital sex was taboo for both of us. You did not have sex with the girl (or woman) you were going to marry. Necking and kissing was tolerated, provided the couple adhered to strict rules of privacy in order not to offend the sensitivities and sensibilities of either relatives or friends. I was elated when she told me, "I will wait. After all, what is time? What is the weight of the years in the presence and power of love! I will wait for you until you finish your education, then we will be together and we'll be happy."

Every week we wrote long letters to each other filled with passion, affection, admiration, and reassurances that the future belonged to us.

The emotional ecstasy was frightening. We reinforced it with romantic literature and movies that portrayed great love stories. We cried for *Romeo and*

Juliet, and *Anna Karenina,* were crushed by the torment of *Camille,* celebrated *April in Paris* and *Rhapsody,* "philosophized" over the relationship of Nero and Messalina, were shocked by *Salomé,* were overcome by the redemptive powers of love in *The Hunchback of Notre Dame* (featuring Charles Laughton), Dostoevsky's *Crime and Punishment* and Tolstoy's *Resurrection,* and we laughed with Fernandel (the French actor). Both of us loved Greta Garbo, Maureen O'Hara, Rita Hayworth, Susan Hayward, Barbara Stanwyck, Anna Magnani, Sylvana Mangano, Sophia Loren, and Greer Garson. We debated about my infatuation with María Félix and her roles in the *French Cancan* (Renoir) and *La Bella Otero* (Pottier). We read Persian poetry, the works of Hafez, Saadi, and Omar Khayyám. They were all about love. I quoted her verses of Baba Taher. One of them said, "Your eyes are arrows, your eyebrows are bows. I don't know anyone in this town who has not been wounded by you," and "Dearest one, I am not crazy! I create a ruckus every night in our town to prevent people from being able to sleep. Because if they sleep they'll dream of you and I will be jealous."

My first romance, which filled my soul with strange, powerful feelings and desires, soon became an obsession. She was my only emotional and spiritual anchor in Beirut. I was starved for love; she filled the void. I was very happy. I could not imagine life without her. Evidently nor could she imagine life without me. My academic work, my administrative duties, my social obligations, and my romance were all in competition. Pretty soon they affected my health. I could not sleep, I lost my appetite, and I lost much weight. I was exhausted. Everybody was worried about my health and my punishing work habits. I kept my romance a secret. Only a handful were privy to it. My loved one was so worried about my health that she wrote a threatening letter to me.

> *You are my life's hope and destiny. Get well! Don't you realize that if something happens to you I will not live for a moment? My darling, if something happens to you I will end my life. I cannot live without you. I cannot be alone. If you don't want me to die of worrying, get well. Don't torture yourself, don't get tired, don't work so hard and don't worry about our future.*
>
> *I have said it before but I would like to reiterate: I will wait for you ten to twenty years. Always remember, I can't live without you. They cannot force me to marry someone else. If they insist or persist and pressure me to do so, I will commit suicide. They'll have to bury me in a white dress. That way I'll wait for you in the next world so that I can meet you in a white dress, my purity intact. My act will be an example, a lesson and proof to*

those parents and families who force their daughters to marry men whom
they don't love. But my parents are not such parents. They will agree with
my choice. I reiterate that I will wait for you as long as necessary, until you
finish your education, find a job, even if it means waiting for twenty years.
. . . Don't worry, I am only yours and I'll always remain yours. Don't
worry about our future. But remember if something happens to you, I'll die.

It was signed, "Yours, only yours, always yours."

I wrote in my diary: "Oh, my God! What is my fate going to be without her? Love is incredible! It is a boundless desire. We must love because time is of short supply. We should and must love because God himself is Love."

In a long letter I reminded her that there was no possibility of my ever forgetting her or abandoning her. After all, I wrote, she was my first love, my true love. How could I forget the fact that some of the most tender, sweetest, most exhilarating moments of my life were spent with her? While our signature song was *There Is No Tomorrow,* I pointed out that for the past eight months we had managed to transform tomorrows into todays and that fate had destined us for each other. Later I wrote in my diary: "Anyone who puts limits to his heart and his feelings does not know what love is or what it means to be in love. It is both an infinite joy and ache. It taxes my heart, my body, my mind, including my education. But I love it. I am so happy! I feel I am in a world of dreams. I am nineteen years old but feel as if life has already revealed to me all its secrets and that I have lived a full life. . . ."

Several months passed. The only times I could see her were early morning, seven A.M., when she walked to school, and on weekends when I was not accompanying Mr. Vratzian to social, cultural, and political events, and occasionally at Armenian cultural events. We worried about the summer recess and her plans to return to Iran. How could we bear not seeing each other for three and a half months? "Why don't you want to come to Iran to see me during the summer?" she complained. I promised to do so.

Then all of a sudden my universe collapsed. While helping my girlfriend pack her papers, a cache of letters and pictures fell into my lap. They were fresh love letters from Iran, along with pictures of her with a handsome man. I was crushed, I was furious, I was livid. I denounced her duplicity in a long letter. How could she talk marriage with me, threaten to commit suicide, assure me of her undying love, and behind my back conduct a long-distance love affair? Worse, I discovered that the man in question was not an ordinary person. He was her fiancé. I thought I was reliving Goethe's *Sorrows of Young Werther,* an impossible love with an engaged woman with no possible positive outcome, no happy ending. I was hopeless. Just a couple of days earlier I had everything and now I had nothing. Suddenly it had all vanished. So I thought.

Her response was amazing. The letters, she explained, were from her "former" lover. Now she loved only me! All she wanted from me was that I study hard "to be somebody," so that I could afford to marry her and take her out of her stifling milieu. I don't want much, she wrote, just a room and us. We'll go to America, start a new life, have a child. We'll dress our child in a fancy Mexican outfit. She noted that since great loves demand great sacrifices she had written a letter to inform her "former love" that it was all over between them and had asked him not to write any letters. Then she invited me to her room and burned all his letters and pictures.

I was determined to return to Iran to visit her. The matter was urgent. Our relationship was at a crossroads. I missed my grandmother and sister desperately. I was homesick. Mr. Vratzian wanted me to spend the summer with him at a summer resort to assist him with his work. Ironically, a discussion about Iran with Mr. Vratzian prompted him to permit me to go to Iran and underwrite the cost of my three-and-a-half-month trip. As a native son of Iran, I felt great pride in the fact that while the first Suez canal was dug between 610 and 595 B.C. during the rule of Necho in Egypt, it was completed by Darius the Great, the Persian conqueror. Mr. Vratzian tested me about my knowledge of Iranian history and found it inadequate. To know Armenian history well, one ought to know intimately Iranian history, Ottoman history, and Russian history, he told me. Go and learn about Iran, its history and culture. My girlfriend and I were on the same flight. She told me that she had informed her parents that she had broken off with her fiancé. But she also intimated that she was afraid that her parents, as well as mine, would never consent to our union. Then one day, I met her "former" fiancé. I knew instantly that it was not over between them. While nurturing that suspicion, I headed for Tabriz to meet my grandmother.

It seemed that everybody in Tabriz from the shopkeepers to friends and relatives were lined up to greet my grandmother and to welcome me. I was treated as the prodigal son. For twenty days every evening there was a reception or dinner in my honor. The variety of dishes and the quantity of meals, all the toasts, the wine, the beer were extraordinary. I visited the public garden, the little square of my childhood days, the church, the movie houses, the Armenian library, a restaurant or two. My "street" friends were in disarray. One of them had become an infamous thief. The others had become artisans. My school friends, on the other hand, had become youth or community leaders.

In the midst of all my activities I was eager to get back to Tehran and be with my love. I wrote her practically every other day. I received only one or two letters. She wrote, "The miracle of love is so great that I am able to endure its tortures with joy."

Upon my return to Tehran, I found no letters. There was silence. Was she all right? I sent her a telegram. I got a devastating letter. The gist of it was that her entire city, rightly or wrongly, believed that she and her "former" fiancé were one, destined for each other; that her parents also loved him. "What can I do? We were in love for eight years. Please give me enough time to dampen his affection and love for me. In the meantime, I beg you, do not write, or send a telegram to me. It upsets my parents. I'll write you a letter every week," she said. "Don't come to our town. I don't want to be embarrassed. It will upset my parents. Otherwise they may not permit me to return to Beirut. My parents have promised my hand to my former fiancé. But I don't love him, though I do respect him. Please defend my honor."

While in Iran I wanted to learn as much as possible about Iranian history and culture, fulfilling one of the obligations of my trip. I decided to travel by bus to all the great cities of Iran, and one of the cities I chose was my girlfriend's city. I thought she was in an untenable situation. I wanted to comfort her. But one way or another I wanted to conclude this fantastic but sad chapter.

Her sister, who was a fan of mine, was astonished to hear that her sister was in difficulty. There was no parental pressure on her to marry her hometown love. She was a mature twenty-five-year-old woman. That was when I learned that she was six years older than I. Her sister also intimated that the person who was upset with my letters was her sister's "former" fiancé, not her parents, and that, contrary to her assertions, she had never broken up with him.

I wrote an angry letter denouncing her as the world's greatest liar, a most deceitful yet talented actress, a person without heart, soul, feelings, or decency. I reminded her of her pledges of love, her promises, her future plans for us. "You introduced me to what true love is and what it ought to be. Are you a mirage? Are you only a magician? How come *you* are not *you*? You once wrote that we were *one*. Please spare me your cascade of tears. I don't believe in them. In your case only God knows what is real and what is not."

To my surprise, I received a letter asking for my understanding, forbearance, and patience. "Please give me six months to discourage him, to find an exit. And please don't pity me! Stars are God's eyes and I hope they will always protect you. . . ." I did not respond. In Beirut, in October, I found several more letters. The news was the same: she still loved me. "I have abandoned my former fiancé. If I cannot be with you I'll sacrifice myself and my future." She cursed her lover for "causing a rift between us."

On November 9, 1954, I received another letter.

Your letters demean me. Even immoral women cannot accept the tenor and content of your remarks. I love you so much that I am ready to give up my father, mother, and sister and everything. For me, there is only you and you. I know that I can be happy only with you.

I am placing my life, my soul, love and aspirations in you. You can accept me or reject me. It is up to you. Think whether you will be happy or miserable with me and then let me know.

Please don't write me more about my falsehoods, lies. I am suffocating. I am going mad. It is enough!

My conscience is clear. I am desperate. Write, write, and give me hope. Have some pity on me. Remember, once you loved me so much. I cannot leave you at any price. I will die if I don't have your love.

I have told my mother categorically I can marry only you or not at all. Otherwise, I will leave home.

There is no place else for me except the grave. It is the earth that will greet me with open arms.

In July 1956, she got engaged, or reengaged. She had given me a ring, which I sent back. Thus ended my first romance. What sustained me was the example of my grandmother, her capacity to suffer and endure, yet always look forward. In addition, I kept myself busy, worked with a vengeance, and consoled myself with one of my favorite Armenian songs, that of the famous Sayat Nova, the troubadour: "The days of adversity come and go like the winter days."

While I was Mr. Vratzian's extra pair of eyes, his personal and confidential secretary, and his companion, I was also his student. I received a first-rate education from him, in the form of tutorials. He assigned me a reading list of some fifth-century Armenian classics. He introduced me to modern Russian history, to nineteenth- and twentieth-century revolutionary movements in Russia, to ideologies and programs of the Social Revolutionary Party, those of the Kadet and Labor parties and that of the Social Democratic Party (including its majority Menshevik and minority Bolshevik wings). He introduced me to the European Socialist movements and their evolution, and to Eduard Bernstein's *Evolutionary Socialism*. I was particularly impressed with Jean Jaurès, the leader of the French Socialist Party, his pragmatism and humanism, his dedication to the cause of peace (he was assassinated in August 1914), his deep humanistic values, his adherence to a nonjingoistic patriotism. That he was also an ardent supporter of the cause of Armenia made him more interesting.

Mr. Vratzian instructed me about the major theoretical divisions among the various socialist parties concerning the issues of colonialism and nationalities and the depiction of a nation. He encouraged me to read about the phenomenon of nationalism, to study the correspondence between Czarist Russian and Soviet nationality policies. In his opinion both of them minimized the divisions between the Russians, Ukrainians, and Belorussians, stressing their Slavic heritage. In the case of the Muslims, they stressed their differences. They both drew the internal administrative lines of their empire in a manner that did not allow any non-Slav ethnic group to achieve ethnic and political cohesion or economic self-sufficiency.

In May 1954, the fall of Dien Bien Phu gave us an opportunity to discuss the importance and persistence of nationalism as a dynamic force and ideology. Mr. Vratzian asserted at the time that nationalism, be it Vietnamese, Chinese, Russian, Polish, or Armenian, would outlast Communism. He predicted the fall of French colonial power and the emergence of a nationalist, unified Vietnam. Mr. Vratzian was wrong, however, in assessing the future of the Armenian Diaspora. In his analysis the Armenian communities of the Middle East were the backbone of the Diaspora; those in Europe and the United States (similar to those in historical Poland and Ukraine who were assimilated) would lose their standing and strength. The reverse happened.

When I graduated from Collège Arménien, Mr. Vratzian gave me two pieces of valuable advice through two stories. One was about an archbishop who was in the habit of giving such lengthy sermons that he often lost track of time. He was oblivious to the fact that his congregation had left the church. One day the archbishop outdid himself. No one was left in the church. The doorman approached him with a message: "When you finish, would you mind locking up the door of the church?" The lesson was clear. Be brief. Respect your audience.

The second story was about a painter, a portraitist, who gave an exhibition. A visitor approached the painter and criticized the artist's portrayal of shoes and shoelaces in a particular painting. "What is your profession, sir?" asked the painter. "I am a shoemaker," the critic answered. Whereupon the painter picked up his brush and fixed the shoelaces. Encouraged, the shoemaker said, "And I don't like the mustache." The painter responded, "Please, sir, do not rise above the shoe." I got the point: Don't discuss subjects about which you are ignorant.

These two parting gifts of Mr. Vratzian have remained with me since my high school days. They have served me well and saved unsuspecting audiences much irritation.

*   *   *

The Collège Arménien gave me an extraordinary education. I learned the Armenian language, literature, and history, as well as the history of the Near East and its various cultures. It opened the doors of European cultures and civilizations through the French language and culture. To be able to read such French classics as François Villon and Rabelais, Jean de la Bruyère, La Rochefoucauld, and Montaigne in their original language was a luxury I had never dreamt of. To be introduced to French and European theater through the plays of Racine, Corneille, and Molière was an added gift. The thinker who most captured my imagination, however, was Pascal (1623–1662). I was fascinated with his life, his mind, and his tragic vision, his attempts to reconcile faith and reason. I read and reread his *Les Pensées* with awe. I am still moved by the spiritual and poetic essence of such lines as "The eternal silence of these infinite spaces terrifies me."

I read and was captured, infatuated, by the works of some of the leading nineteenth-century Romantics: Goethe, Victor Hugo, Alfred de Musset, Lord Byron, George Sand, Chateaubriand, Lamartine, Alfred de Vigny, and others. I agreed wholeheartedly with the Romantics that Reason varies from one age to another, but that Feeling (sentiment) remains constant; that the works of Reason of one age needed commentary to be understood in other ages, but none was needed about works that depicted "the passions of the soul and affection of the heart." Concepts of homelessness, loneliness, endless quests, infinite longing, solitude, pursuit of the unknown, all resonated with me. I was transfixed by the lifestyles of the Romantics and their fascination with the disease of the century: tuberculosis. I was fascinated with their cult of Nature and travel as a means of communion with Nature and as a source of consolation and reflection, as well as an antidote to parochialism.

I read avidly the works of Descartes, Jean-Jacques Rousseau, Voltaire, Diderot, and others of the Age of Enlightenment. I was impressed with their revolutionary ideas about science, education, general will, proper forms of representative government, and fundamental concepts of legal and social justice. I was introduced to the seventeenth- and eighteenth-century salons of France by Mme. Yolande and read several volumes about their historical role in the development of French culture. And finally I read Jules Michelet's (1798–1874) lyrical *History of the French Revolution* and *History of France*.

Michelet reinforced my love of history. He reassured me that history did not have to be dull; it could be passionate, even lyrical.

In 1955, as I rose to receive my diploma from Collège Arménien I faced my teachers, an extraordinary group of individuals and characters. They were colorful exiles, refugees who were intellectuals, public figures, former revolutionaries from Armenia, Europe, Russia, Egypt, the United States, Cyprus, and Lebanon. Almost all of them had advanced degrees from European, Russian, and even Ottoman universities. There were teachers who often forgot that they were teaching in a lycée, an advanced high school, not a university. They treated us as adults. They expected much from us. They gave us a great education. I was full of gratitude for them. I was ready and well prepared for the next phase of my education.

My last academic year in Beirut was challenging and full of uncertainties. I was disillusioned by the debacle of my first romance and anxious about my future. Work became a sedative, a source of solace, and an outlet for my energies, even a means for mental relaxation. My immediate future was still undecided. Would I go to São Paulo as the director of the local Armenian high school, or to the United States as a student? Or would I remain in Beirut and be a teacher at the Collège Arménien? That was the big question! Did I need an advanced college degree to qualify as director of the Armenian school? Did I need to know Portuguese? While my future appeared to be in limbo, I had one important and immediate unfinished task. I had to finish my course work and finish the two-year advanced study in Armenology. Mr. Vratzian decided my fate. I was to go to the United States.

I graduated from Collège Arménien with honors in 1955. It was a great and unbelievable day for me. It had been a long and arduous journey but at long last, against all odds, I was able to graduate, although two to three years later than many of my classmates. I was very conscious of that and indeed defensive about it. I had lost at least three years in transit from an Armenian-Russian, to a Turkish, to a Persian, and then to a Lebanese school. I had been in three different systems that, among other things, required knowledge of Armenian, Russian, Turkish, Persian, Arabic, French, and English. (To differentiate myself from my classmates I had begun in 1954–1955 a correspondence course with the École Universelle de Paris, in the field of journalism. The ceremonial graduation program listed me as a writer, journalist, and a degree candidate in Armenology.)

While I was proud that I had at long last made it, that I was the valedictorian, I was also sad. Unlike my eight classmates, I did not have a single relative present at my graduation. Three of my classmates became elementary

and secondary school teachers, one a bank official, another an airline executive, one a civil engineer who went on to become vice president of a major
French international construction company; three of us eventually became
professors. I had a great relationship with my classmates. They did not mind
my bookishness. They did not treat me like a nerd, but with respect and affection. After all, I was "older and wiser," I was from abroad, I worked for
my education, and I was a "writer," a journalist. I partied, danced, went to
picnics and movies with them. Unlike them, because I was older I could and
did go with some alumni to nightclubs and bars. They were curious about
and sometimes envious of my "mysterious night life," my anonymous "girlfriend," my "love life," my "escapades," the fact that I had even gone to see
the live performance of the celebrated Samia Gamal, the voluptuous Arab
singer and belly dancer, that I was secretary and assistant to the director of
our school, but most important of all, that I was a "writer," who knew and associated with local Armenian poets and novelists, and who as a "journalist"
wrote for the local Armenian newspaper and attended political rallies and
press conferences.

If the United States was my destination, the remaining question was
which university or college. There were two Armenian-American graduate
students at the Collège Arménien, both from the University of California.
Their advice to Mr. Vratzian was to send me to San Francisco State College
or else to begin with San Mateo Junior College. They were worried about
my command of the English language. They were right to worry.

Having learned French, I had believed English would be an easy language
to master. After all, so many words are identical in both languages—
civilization, mobilization, conversation, revolution, protestation, prosperity,
pharmacy, olive, lyric, prose, poem, vagabond, music, nation, village, crayon,
science, nature, equitable, decoration, subordination, humanity, majority, minority, etc., etc., etc. Then there were words with the same origin: grand for
great, vin for wine, bière for beer, arc for arch, esprit for spirit, and on and
on. Then, of course, there are the perennial *savoir faire, maître d'hôtel, concierge,*
and *petits fours.*

Of course, grammar was a problem, but nothing is simple in life. Besides,
I had read Shakespeare's *Macbeth,* and even a chapter or two of Macaulay.
We had lots of "English conversations" in the classroom. Sir, a devotee of
Winston Churchill, occasionally read passages from his famous speeches.
Time magazine was Sir's second Bible. If it was written in *Time,* he believed,
it must be correct. Once in a while he read us a short article or two from
Time. One day I observed his heroic effort to explain unsuccessfully to a

member of the local Armenian community that the Armenian daily *Aztag* did not have the same authoritative status as *Time* did.

Sir's recommendation was that I should apply to at least two major American universities. He was confident that with hard work I could handle the curriculum. Mr. Vratzian had reached the same conclusion: I should apply to two universities on the West Coast of the United States, in particular in California, where there was a major Armenian community. I applied to the University of California at Berkeley and Stanford University. In reality it was Sir who completed my applications. Mr. Vratzian, Sir, and two other teachers wrote laudatory recommendations on my behalf.

The dreaded SAT examination was held at the American University of Beirut. I was both fascinated and scared as to why there were so many questions, and why some of them were so simplistic. I did not understand some. There was a minor earthquake during the exam. I am sure the examiners gave some credit to those of us who did not understand some of the questions. They must have attributed it to our "traumatization" due to the rumblings of Mother Nature. I passed. However, I was not proud of my score, which I have banished from my memory.

The anxious waiting period ended when I received a thick envelope from Stanford University. I was admitted. I ran to Mr. Vratzian's office to give him the good news, then burst into Sir's classroom. A month or two later I received a letter from UC Berkeley. They, too, had accepted me. However, they had sent their letter of admission via surface mail while Stanford had sent its letter airmail. I did not know at the time the difference between private and public institutions of higher education in the United States. One thing was sure: the tuition at the University of California was not high. If I am not mistaken, it was a hundred dollars or so for the academic year. Although Stanford's was $750, I had already accepted their offer.

The application for a student visa to the United States was a complicated, lengthy, and tedious process. I had to get letters from Iran about whether or not I had a police record. They had to be translated into English and notarized. A similar letter had to be obtained from the Interior Ministry of Lebanon. It, too, had to be translated and notarized. The United States required a complete medical examination, chest X rays, and blood, stool, and urine tests. Only the tests administered by the staff of the Hospital of the American University of Beirut were admissible. Notarized official letters were submitted on behalf of Collège Arménien, promising to be responsible for my expenses during my tenure as a student in the United States. Another letter had to be obtained from George Mardikian, the owner of the Omar

Khayyám restaurant in San Francisco, assuring the authorities that he was Collège Arménien's fiscal agent in California, and hence responsible for transmitting the necessary funds to me.

While all this was happening, Mr. Vratzian had decided to accept the Iranian-Armenian community's formal invitation to visit Iran. He had last been there in 1921 when he had fled Armenia along with thousands of refugees after the collapse of an anti-Bolshevik uprising and the Sovietization of the country. He asked me to accompany him as his assistant. I was thrilled. I had just graduated not only from the Collège but from its Armenology program. I was accepted by a great American university, and the visit would give me a chance to see my grandmother, my sister, relatives, and parents and bid farewell to them, my benefactors, and my friends.

I was returning home with a record of achievements. I was the first person from the Gregorian extended family to attend a university. My many publications in Armenian papers had gained me a place of respect as a "promising young scholar." I was assistant to Mr. Vratzian, who took every opportunity to thank the Armenian community of Iran for sending me to Beirut and praised me for my accomplishments. He publicly thanked Edgar Maloyan, Hrayr Stepanian, Dajat Boghossian, and Mrs. Astghik Aftandilian (president of the Armenian Relief Society of Azerbaijan) for having supported me. Mr. Maloyan had "found" me; Stepanian had put up the deed of his house as a guarantee for my passport; Mr. Boghossian, the editor of *Alik*, had supported me as a writer and served as my chief fund-raiser and lobbyist in Iran; Mrs. Aftandilian had joined him in that effort.

While in Tehran, I stayed with my parents and sister in their small apartment. My parents said they were very, very proud of me. My sister felt vindicated in her trust in me. She was a high school senior, a brilliant student, studious and serious, with an excellent academic record and she had great hopes of continuing her education. Unfortunately, during my absence, her relations with my stepmother and father had not improved. She received neither financial nor emotional support to continue her education. This served also to further strain my relations with my parents. For the six years I had received no assistance from them. My father had a good job at the Tehran Airport. Surely they could afford to support my sister's goals and send her to the university. Unfortunately he chose not to. And I never forgave him for that.

Following the example of the Count of Monte Cristo, I decided one day to "punish" all my tormentors and detractors through kindness and generosity. I had brought many fancy gifts for my father and stepmother. I wore a new suit and a new pair of shoes. I had received a watch (my first one), a camera, new shirts, and neckties as graduation gifts. They were the symbols of my independence. Unfortunately I could not resist taking yet another step to demonstrate my "success." I gave my stepmother a small briefcase full of Iranian money, in small denominations, and told her to keep it in a safe place, because it was very valuable. I was certain she would inspect the contents. I told her that during my stay in Tehran, if she needed any household money or wished to buy foodstuffs or anything else she was welcome to use some or all of it. It was my small, shameful way of making the point that I had not failed, that I had not returned as a failure as she predicted, that I had endured all deprivations and hardships but most important of all I did not need their financial or emotional support. I was self-sufficient.

In Tabriz, I stayed with my grandmother in her one-room apartment. We began with a tug of war. She wanted to sleep on the floor and give me her one bed/sofa. I slept on the floor. We spent most of the night talking and reminiscing. We spoke about my mother and uncles, her tough life, my life in Beirut, my failed romance, my forthcoming trip to the United States. I was surprised that she had no animosity toward my father and stepmother. She did not complain about her health nor about the precarious state of her nonexistent finances. She was at peace with herself and the world.

We talked about some of my mischief in the "good old days." She reminded me of the time, at age twelve, when I had hit, "by accident," my school principal with snowballs and had been punished severely. I was slapped and whipped. When I returned home, she noticed my bruises. "Who did this?" she asked. A man, was my answer. "Take me to him," she ordered. I did. We walked to the schoolyard. "There is the man." I pointed him out to her. She approached him. He was pacing. She stopped him. "Have you ever fed this boy?" she asked. No, was his answer. "Have you ever taken care of him?" Again, no. "Then how dare you hit him!" she thundered. She slapped the man twice, very hard. "But madam," responded the man in Turkish, "I am the *modir* (the principal)." "I don't give a damn who you are. Eat shit," she added. I was astonished. That was the first obscenity I heard her utter.

After staying with my grandmother for several days and visiting the graves of my mother and uncles, once again I had to bid farewell to her. Once again she gave me amulets that combined the best protective prayer shields from the three Abrahamic faiths, Judaism, Christianity, and Islam. In addition, I was given blue beads again to protect me from the "evil eye."

I had given my grandmother material for a new dress. It was blue. It was my ardent hope that at long last she would abandon the black that she had been wearing since 1941. She promised to wear blue when my sister or I got married. She did so the next year when my sister and my best friend, Varoujan, got married. While I was in Iran, neither of them told me they were in love. For some reason they were worried that I would be angry, that I might regard it as a betrayal of trust because I had asked my friend when I first left Iran to take care of her.

CHAPTER FIVE

To America

On August 3, 1956, I landed at New York's Idlewild (now JFK) Airport. The flight was long and exhausting and I was anxious. Once again, I was facing the unknown for I really did not know much about the United States. What little I knew was through the prism of Hollywood. My English, to be charitable, was shaky. I was afraid not only of embarrassing myself in America but also the Collège Arménien and its considerable investment in me. I was scared to let down Sir, not to mention the Armenian communities of Tabriz and Beirut—indeed, the entire Armenian nation and my fatherland, Iran, and of course Mr. Vratzian. Like many shy, frightened immigrants, I was too proud to ask questions lest they unmask my ignorance. I pretended to know everything. Behind the façade of my self-assurance, there was a profound fear.

My first test came during my flight from Paris to New York. I was handed a U.S. Customs declaration form. Prior to the flight, I had been given an inventory form by Pan American Airways, to help me make a record of my belongings. I thought there must be a certain connection between the two forms, and therefore I listed everything in my possession in order to satisfy U.S. Customs. I wanted to be both accurate and thorough. After all, I was coming to the "land of laws," of "complete transparency" and "accountability."

After filling in the Customs form ("no purchases, nothing to declare") on a separate sheet of blank paper, I listed the number of socks, evening shirts (I thought any shirt you wore during the evenings was an evening shirt), T-shirts, underwear, handkerchiefs, as well as shoes, gloves, suits, and jackets. I had two or three silver frames. I did not know the word "frame." I asked a passenger across the aisle about it. She told me they were "frames." I heard her say "frabes." So I listed them as "frabes." I am sure the bewildered Customs officer must have thought I was a nut and threw my "inventory" into the garbage can.

As we approached America, my anxiety gained sadness as a companion. Upon the death of my mother, when I was six and a half years old, my younger sister and I were told by our relatives that our mother had gone to America: "a distant but beautiful land." As we were approaching that "beautiful land," my childhood fantasy that my mother was in America came to an abrupt and sad end. I had to catch up with the reality of death.

The dream of going to America had been a fantasy. For me, America itself was a fantasy built and rebuilt in my mind and psyche. I had lived it through scores of cowboy movies. My American heroes, who embodied courage, honor, loyalty, solidarity, integrity, self-sacrifice, patriotism, love of justice, and generosity, had prepared me for a fantasyland and sustained my dreams.

None of the movies prepared me for my first encounter with New York. I was stunned, overwhelmed, intoxicated, "blown away" by it. It was huge, massive, powerful. The varieties of sounds, colors, shades dazzled me. I had never seen or imagined so many cars, buses, ambulances, so many fire engines, police cars, taxis, or so many people in one city! The multitudes, their energy, their fast pace were incredible. All of a sudden, I felt I was in the presence of a microcosm of all humanity, the whole world. Every ethnic group, religion, race, continent was in New York. I had never seen so many tall buildings. Nor had I seen a concentration of so much cement, concrete and, especially, steel and iron. For the first time, I saw water towers and long fire escapes. They seemed to be everywhere. Elevators, escalators, and revolving doors impressed me, as did the number of shops and restaurants, not to mention the multitude of well-dressed people. I got lost in Central Park. It was so huge that I thought it contained all the trees and all the gardens of Tabriz, Tehran, and Beirut combined.

One Sunday, I visited Saint Patrick's Cathedral. It was imposing, majestic, yet open and welcoming. The burning candles, the beautiful music, interspersed with moments of silence and serenity, had a soothing effect on me. The altar boys reminded me of my childhood in Tabriz and my church, where I had spent so many Sundays hearing of and singing for the glory of God. All of a sudden, I felt very sad and nostalgic. My childhood seemed remote.

The sight of the Central Post Office of New York City on Eighth Avenue and 34th Street astonished me. It was a civic monument, rather than a mere post office. It symbolized stability, confidence, and durability. I read with great pride the words inscribed on the lofty entrance: *Neither snow, nor rain, nor heat, nor gloom of night stays these couriers from the swift completion of their appointed rounds.* The quotation, adapted from the Greek historian Herodotus, refers to couriers of the Persian Empire who, in the sixth century B.C., could travel some 1,600 miles in one week.

The Brooklyn Bridge fascinated me. I had never seen such a major, long bridge in my life. It was so powerful and graceful and beautiful! Speaking of beauty and grace, imagine my utter disbelief and enchantment when I saw María Félix, the actress, on Fifth Avenue. I became paralyzed. For a moment, I felt I was in Hollywood! I could not wait to write my friends that I had seen the personification of beauty.

The opulence of Fifth, Madison, and Park Avenues did justice to my Hollywood vision of America. Broadway and Times Square stunned me; I had never thought it was possible for a city not to sleep, or to have so much entertainment, so many bars, theaters, so many nightclubs, so much nudity, so many stations of sin and fantasy. But most impressive of all, I had never imagined seeing so much light and electricity in a single city. I felt as if the entire electric supply of the world was centered in New York, making it the City of Light. These firsthand, fast-moving impressions made me imagine New York as the City of Cities, the embodiment of power and sheer energy. I wrote to my sister that New York was a gigantic magnet. It attracted everything and everyone in the world, every source of power, energy, and scrap metal and every creative idea.

I had seen the Empire State Building in the movie *King Kong,* but nothing prepared me for the experience. I felt as if I were on the top of the world. After observing the range and the depth of the city, its architectural and engineering wonders, I wrote home that in New York I felt like an anonymous ant. If they stepped on me, I wrote, they would not even notice me. "This city will humble anyone and teach everyone humility," I wrote, adding that in New York, while you may be insignificant, at the same time you are just like anybody else, alone yet part of the multitude.

I had brought two letters of introduction from Mr. Vratzian. One was to Edward (Eddy) Sahakian, president of the Broadway-based Pictorial Engraving Company, Ltd., and the other to Martiros Zarifian, director of auxiliary services of the Taft Hotel. Eddy Sahakian was a benefactor of the Collège Arménien. I had lunch with Mr. Sahakian. Mr. Zarifian took me to his home on Long Island.

The reception accorded me by the two Armenian-Americans whom I had never met made me realize the range of all diasporas—whether Jewish, Chinese, Indian, Greek, Lebanese, Irish, Egyptian, Nigerian, Italian, Portuguese, Armenian, Turkish, Kurdish, or Pakistani. I had always thought of diasporas as limited and parochial. In New York, later in California, I discovered that I was utterly wrong. Diasporas tend to be cosmopolitan, international. In any distant region, country, or city, one has an instant link to one's diaspora through one's extended, dispersed family, one's religion, cultural institutions, language, press and, of course, commerce. An immigrant, a student, a visitor finds an easy foothold, a pathway, a bridge to a foreign country.

After bidding farewell to the Zarifians on Long Island, I went to Idlewild to catch my flight to San Francisco. I had sent a wire to those who were instructed by Mr. Vratzian to meet me at San Francisco Airport. I was placed on a waiting list. I did not know that there were more than one or two flights a day from New York to San Francisco, nor did I know that there were several other airlines that had scheduled flights. My message stated that I was arriving in San Francisco on such and such a date with Trans World Airlines.

Then the worst possible thing happened. I lost my airline ticket. I told the ticket agent who had wait-listed me about my "tragedy." "What can I do?" I asked. "Not much," he said. "You have to declare the loss, wait for a certain period of time, and file a claim." "I can't do that," I replied. "Don't you understand? I have to be in San Francisco tomorrow! I must register as a freshman at Stanford University this week. I am desperate, desperate, desperate!" I actually *shouted* at him. Tears of anger, self-pity, and shame and my horrified face must have touched him. He told me, "I have never done what I am about to do. I will stamp this empty envelope, marked *New York to San Francisco,* without a ticket in it. You can board the plane. But you must stay onboard all the way. Do not disembark. Stay on it until you get to San Francisco." Grateful, yet fearful, I boarded the midnight plane. The fourteen-hour flight stopped in Chicago, Kansas City, Phoenix, and Los Angeles, before arriving in San Francisco. At each stop, I told the stewardess that I did not feel well and would rather stay aboard. The generosity of the airline clerk had an impact on me. Even in New York, this massive metropolis, individuals mattered. After all, I was not an insignificant, anonymous ant.

I loved San Francisco. It was one of the most spectacular cities I had ever seen, even in the movies. It was beautiful, open, warm, hospitable, charming, and manageable. You were not overwhelmed by it, you were won over. I felt welcome. Once again, I could see the sky and the stars. In some ways, it reminded me of Beirut and its charm. If the Brooklyn Bridge fascinated me and the George Washington Bridge kept me in awe, San Francisco's Golden Gate Bridge was so beautiful that it sent chills up my spine. I loved to walk in San Francisco. Its steep hills were a great treat. I relished its fog. I found it romantic. Sitting at the Cliff House, my favorite weekend hangout, and watching the great waves of the Pacific Ocean, the clear skies, and the beautiful sunsets gave me joy, peace, even serenity. It was the best spot to reflect and meditate.

The cable car was my favorite pastime. I rode it back and forth, up and down, enjoying the happy sounds of its bell and the sights of San Francisco. In Fisherman's Wharf, I saw an incredible number of species of fish and numerous water creatures that I had neither heard of nor imagined. I thought the wharf was designed to give each visitor an introduction to the ocean and its wonders. I ate my first lobster roll and Shrimp Louis. Later, at Tommy's Joint, I ate the biggest hamburger ever. But what impressed me the most was the décor of the Joint. Its ceiling was full of pots and pans and other assorted utensils. There was even the cover of a toilet seat. I thought, what will they think of next?

Everything in the United States seemed to be very expensive. Hence, I chose to stay at the YMCA. I was mindful of my finances, so much so that I combined my breakfasts and luncheons and chose carefully what I ordered. Prices at restaurants were the most important items on the menu.

My first impressions of Americans during my first two months were many and varied. I wrote in my diary that Americans don't like to be bossed or told what to do by anyone, not their government or their clergy or their employers. They must believe that they are acting of their own volition. Americans are very individualistic. They work hard, they are open, kind, and generous. I wondered how the delicate equilibrium was kept between individual rights and societal interests. The first paperback book that I read in San Francisco was Elmer Davis's *But We Were Born Free*.

The sight of so many dogs in New York and San Francisco surprised me. I had not seen so many dogs and I was shocked to find out that dogs were allowed inside homes and resided there. In Iran and Lebanon they were kept outside in doghouses. Most of all, I was bewildered by the existence of dog food, cat food, animal hospitals, animal shelters, veterinary doctors, and even cemetery plots for animals! I read with great interest the posters of the SPCA offering a one-hundred-dollar reward for the arrest of those who poison dogs and cats or torture them! I had always thought that the expression a "dog's life" meant a wretched life full of hardships. But after seeing all the shelves of special dog foods, dog collars, and dog toys, doctors for dogs, even psychiatrists for dogs, I did not understand what was wrong with a dog's life.

The fundamental culinary challenge of my Americanization was my ability to drink American black coffee. It took me some time to get used to it and to learn that "regular" coffee meant coffee with cream. My first adventure with a cup of black coffee made me lose my appetite for days. At a Zimburger restaurant counter, I ordered a cup of coffee that tasted so bad that I asked for cream. "It is right in front of you," answered the waitress. I had never seen cream in plastic bottles. I saw somebody use it, so in a nonchalant manner, I used it, too. What I did not know, until I drank it, was that I had used the yellow plastic bottle. It was mustard. Having realized my blunder, and aware of the stares of some of the bewildered patrons and the waitress, I pretended that was what I intended to do. After several sips of the horrible stuff, I buried myself and the coffee under a newspaper.

*   *   *

I was under the impression that the United States was so rich that it did not and could not possibly have beggars. Imagine my surprise when someone approached me and said: "Please give me a quarter. I am hungry. I want to eat something." I gave him a coin instantly. I knew what it meant to be hungry.

I arrived in the United States two years after the Supreme Court decided *Brown v. Board of Education* (1954), which ended legal segregation in America. Neither in Iran nor in Lebanon did I have any idea that the United States had a "color" or race problem, that the integration of black Americans, their unmet quests for political equality, dignity, the right to vote, to travel, to be educated, and to use public accommodations posed a major challenge to the democratic fabric of the United States.

As a young boy, I had read Harriet Beecher Stowe's *Uncle Tom's Cabin* and had empathized with the plight of "Negroes." I remembered vividly the slave driver who whipped Uncle Tom to death and how Uncle Tom had accepted his fate and by doing so had proved his dignity and humanity through Christian humility. The idea of "owning" human beings, and their humiliation and degradation created revulsion in me. But I had no idea of the present plight of the blacks in America. I had assumed that all their problems and inequities had been taken care of by Abraham Lincoln and his Emancipation Proclamation, that he had fought a costly, most tragic war to emancipate them. After all, I had seen the epic movie *Gone With the Wind* and its portrayal of the Civil War.

I had read that the United States had entered World War I "to make the world safe for democracy," and World War II to fight against a racist, totalitarian Nazi Germany and a racist, imperialist Japan. I never thought that while fighting for democracy and against racist regimes, the United States would tolerate racism at home. My impressions of U.S. racial and ethnic relations were influenced by World War II movies and their portrayal of how members of different ethnic groups (Italian, Native American, Jewish, Chinese, Polish, Irish, Japanese) had overcome their parochial conflicts and divisions, acted in harmony, and fought to defend the American people and democracy. They were hailed for their sacrifices on behalf of an America that was the champion of democracy and the embodiment of the principles of freedom and equality. They had fought for a country that was the land of immigrants, the land of opportunity for all, in which all citizens had inalienable rights of life, liberty, and the pursuit of happiness. I did not know that African-Americans were invisible Americans who did not enjoy equal rights and equal opportunity. I did not know that while fighting against Nazi Germany, African-Americans fought in segregated U.S. army units and that it was only in 1948 that President Truman integrated the U.S. armed forces.

The invisible Americans were not absent but were present in large numbers in New York, San Francisco, and all over the United States. The knowledge of their history, their struggles, their heritage, and their contributions to the United States became a major interest of mine. For me, the basic question was this: If immigrants can come to the United States to pursue their dreams, why could not African-Americans pursue theirs? Why could not the same opportunities afforded to immigrants be available to them? After all, they were U.S. citizens.

While I was aghast at my ignorance of U.S. history, I was surprised to find out that historical knowledge was not the forte of many Americans either, nor was geography. At several dinner parties, I was asked whether Beirut was in India or South Africa, whether Iran was in Ethiopia. I earnestly hoped to be asked about Armenia and the Armenians, for I had prepared a detailed reply:

The Armenians were the first nation to accept Christianity as a state religion in A.D. 301. We have a long and tragic history. We are three thousand years old. At the present, we have a small country, Soviet Armenia, and a large Diaspora. The first Armenians to travel to North

America were a handful of individuals who settled in the Virginia
Colony in the seventeenth century. Martin the Armenian, who
worked as a butler for George Yardley, the governor of the colony, either from 1618 or 1619, is the first recorded Armenian in the New
World. In 1653, two Armenians were brought to Virginia to begin silk-
worm cultivation in the settlements. Their efforts must have been successful, for one of them, George the Armenian, was awarded four
thousand pounds of tobacco by the Virginia House of Burgesses in
1656. There is a statue dedicated to John Altoon, another Armenian,
for his contribution to Virginia. In 1834, Khachatoor Oskanian was
the first Armenian student from Constantinople to be sent to America
by the American missionaries to attend New York University. He was
followed by another student in 1837 who obtained a medical degree
from Princeton. A third student enrolled in Union Theological School
in 1841, and a fourth student enrolled in Yale University in 1848. During the Civil War, three Armenian medical students served in Union
hospitals. Finally, the bulk of the Armenian population came in the
nineteenth century. They came in three waves: the first one, before the
1890s, came for economic opportunity, the second and third waves
came after the Armenian massacres of the 1890s during the reign of
Sultan Abdul Hamid II, and the third wave consisted of the remnants
of the Armenian Genocide in the aftermath of World War I. They settled primarily in New York, Massachusetts, Connecticut, Rhode Island, Michigan, Pennsylvania, Illinois, and California.

Alas, I was never able to give that narrative perhaps because it was more
than anyone wished to hear. For my interlocutors the important thing was
that I was a Christian and we shared a common bond. Some had heard of
Armenians. Some knew the expression "Finish your meal, remember the
starving Armenians." At Stanford, practically everybody had heard of the
Armenians. After all, the Manoogian brothers, who were great football players for Stanford, were Armenian-Americans. The team was known as the
"shish kebab team."

If the Manoogian brothers had made the name "Armenia" popular at
Stanford, it was William Saroyan (1908–1981), the celebrated author, who
made it part of the American literary mosaic through his writings: *The
Daring Young Man on the Flying Trapeze* (1934), *The Time of Your Life* (1939),
My Name Is Aram (1940), and *The Human Comedy* (1943). He was awarded
the Pulitzer Prize in 1939 but refused to accept it. Two other Armenian-
Americans, Rouben Mamoulian, the Hollywood movie director responsible

for so many major films, and Arlene Francis, the actress, even though they had neither Saroyan's maverick personality or his flamboyance, were well known in their respective fields.

Then, of course, in San Francisco, there was George Mardikian, an Armenian known as the Super American. The owner of Omar Khayyám Restaurant and author of *Song of America* was one of those individuals who was able to reinvent himself, not on occasion but continuously. An orphan who grew up in America, he was a proud Armenian, but a prouder American. He used to celebrate the day he came to America as his birthday. A staunch Republican and a great believer of the virtues of free enterprise, he promoted his restaurant as Armenian, yet it was named after the famous Persian poet Omar Khayyám. The décor consisted of scenes that depicted some poems from his classic *Rubáiyát* in the 1859 translation by Edward Fitzgerald. In one corner, you read on the wall one of the most celebrated passages of the *Rubáiyát: The moving finger writes; and, having writ, moves on. Nor all thy piety nor wit shall lure it back to cancel half a line, nor all thy tears wash out a word of it.*

Mr. Mardikian was a great entrepreneur and showman. The windows of the Omar Khayyám Restaurant, as well as its interior, were adorned with pictures of Mr. Mardikian "breaking bread" with notable Americans or being greeted by him. The UN meeting in San Francisco had provided him with an ample pool of famous people: President Dwight D. Eisenhower, Vice President Richard M. Nixon, Charles Malik, the representative of Lebanon to the UN and president of the UN General Assembly, newsmen Walter Cronkite and Chet Huntley, as well as other notables such as Nelson Rockefeller, Eleanor Roosevelt, and scores of governors, senators, congressmen, generals, actors, and actresses.

It turned out that Mr. Vratzian knew George Mardikian very well. I accompanied Mr. Vratzian to Omar Khayyám for lunch with Mr. Mardikian. Exuberant as ever, overbearing yet gracious, he welcomed us and "broke bread" with us. He promised Mr. Vratzian to keep an eye on me and to assist me in any way he could.

After I graduated from Stanford University, imagine my great surprise to learn that during one of his visits to the president of Stanford, he announced that he had been my benefactor, paying my tuition, room, and board. It was not true, but it must have made him feel great to say so.

*   *   *

After five days in San Francisco's YMCA, I spent a week at the home of yet another set of great friends of Mr. Vratzian: Mr. and Mrs. Avedis

Karageuzian. Anahit Karageuzian was a vivacious, gracious, energetic, driven, middle-aged woman, a pillar of the Armenian community of San Francisco. She was involved in myriad Armenian and American social and educational causes: she was president of the Armenian Relief Society and active in the affairs of the Armenian Church and many cultural institutions and organizations. Her husband had a major grocery market. They had not had any children of their own but had adopted one.

Whenever Mr. Vratzian visited San Francisco he stayed with the Karageuzian family. They were always thrilled to see him. Mrs. Karageuzian greeted me with open arms. She told me that since I had no mother, and was an orphan like her, she was going to be my mother and adopt me. Unfortunately, my newfound second "mother" died unexpectedly. It was a shock to all of us and Mr. Vratzian was crushed. I had to move on. I rented a room for a month at 125 19th Avenue. It was located on the second floor, and was spacious and light, with lace curtains, a great bed with two huge pillows, a chest of drawers, a large closet, a small desk, and a beautiful lamp. I shared a bathroom and shower with two other tenants.

Mrs. Maxwell, my landlady, was an eighty-year-old widow. With great pride, enthusiasm, and a touch of sadness, she informed me that her daughter had been stricken with polio at a young age; nevertheless, with great determination and hard work, she had managed to finish school, attend and graduate from a university, and earn a law degree. Unfortunately, she had not lived long enough to enjoy the benefits of her hard work and courage. I admired Mrs. Maxwell. She was self-sufficient. She cooked, drove her own car, supervised the repairs of her house, did her own accounting, and acted as her own real estate agent. After spending a month as her tenant, I realized that I had never seen any Hollywood movie that depicted the lives, solitude, boredom, struggles, problems, anxieties, and aspirations of elderly Americans.

It was in San Francisco that for the first time I also learned about the evolving structure of America's nuclear family. I was surprised that parents, instead of living with their children and grandchildren, were often placed in retirement communities, nursing homes, or "old age" establishments. I could not understand it. It appeared to me to be a callous and insensitive act. I thought all grandchildren had to be with their grandparents and vice versa; they had to be given an opportunity to enjoy their extended families. I had no idea of the socioeconomic forces that had brought about the fragmentation of extended families.

Mrs. Maxwell had a good heart and a good mind but loneliness oppressed her. I felt sorry for her. I am sure she felt sorry for my loneliness as well. Since I was a good listener, Mrs. Maxwell latched on to me. She loved to talk. She reminisced about "the good old days." My sympathy was boundless. I was only annoyed when she began to repeat herself, over and over again. I should not have told her that I was staying in San Francisco to practice my English. She thought she was helping me do just that.

In San Francisco, I felt free, liberated, and independent for the first time in my life. I came to cherish privacy and even seclusion. No one supervised me, there were no curfews, no peer pressures. I was in charge of my own time. I could sleep as late as I wished and return to my room whenever I desired. I could see several movies a day, or none at all. I could go to nightclubs, I could dance, I could eat an "unbalanced" or a "balanced" meal.

It was at Mrs. Maxwell's that I performed one of the most stupid deeds of my life. I knew I had total freedom and I knew I had strong willpower and discipline. But there were so many attractions, so many distractions, so many temptations, and yet so little time that I wanted to invent an insurance, actually a reinsurance, policy to back up my willpower so that I would not socialize. I had to read and to study. I had to practice my English. There was only one month left before the beginning of classes at Stanford. So I decided to shave my head. I went to a barber. I was shocked by the price tag. With that kind of money, I could have had two or three haircuts in Beirut. (In Beirut it was cheaper to shave one's head than get a haircut.)

I decided that my solution to the temptations of the city was to shave my own head. I had very thick and tough hair. It did not occur to me that to begin with, I must cut my hair, then shave off the stubble. Instead, I put my shaving cream all over my head and started shaving my hair with a regular razor. It was a disaster. I cut myself in many places. I was bleeding and I did not know what to do. By then, I had two alternatives: to cover my head, go to the barbershop, and ask the barber to end my agony, or finish the miserable task. I was too ashamed to go to a barbershop, so I chose the alternative. It took me many hours to finish. In the process I ruined several towels and made a mess of my head. I did not know how to stop the bleeding. Suddenly I remembered, rightly or wrongly, that in Tabriz, during the Ashura, when Shiite Muslims commemorate the martyrdom of Ali (Prophet Muhammad's son-in-law and his grandchildren Hasan and Hussein), occasionally, self-flagellation resulted in profusely bleeding scalp wounds. To stop it, they used egg yolk. I used several of them. For whatever reason, the bleeding stopped. I had to apply many cotton balls to cover my wounds, along with a beret, to hide my stupidity. For days, I smelled of egg yolk and for some time I could not bear the sight of eggs.

My head prevented me from attending any public events, including church service. I could not and would not remove my beret. It would have revealed a great disaster. So I spent most of my time reading English newspapers, listening to the radio, reading books, and watching television. I watched both the Democratic and the Republican conventions. They were extraordinary, bewildering and loud. I did not understand the speeches. Nor did I figure out the differences between the platforms of the two parties. My favorite part of both conventions was the roll call of the states for nominating their presidential candidates. I loved the self-promotion of each state by their delegates. They did it with so much joy, emotion, and self-importance. They were simply amazing.

What astonished me more than anything were the symbols of the two parties. The Republicans had chosen the elephant. I understood this because the elephant stood for power. But why had the Democrats chosen the donkey? What did they see in the donkey? What did the donkey represent? (So many Middle Eastern stories feature a donkey as a metaphor for the lowest common denominator that this was inexplicable to me.) One outcome of the 1956 convention was that I became addicted to conventions. Since then, I have never missed a single one.

I bade an emotional farewell to Mr. Vratzian who left for Beirut. He had rescued me, taught me, and protected me. Now I was on my own. I had to fly with my own wings and at my own speed. Vratzian's parting words were: "Study hard, but don't be a monk. Have a social life, take advantage of the cultural, educational, and intellectual richness of the United States. Get involved in the life of the community."

I was on my way to Stanford.

CHAPTER SIX

Stanford University: A New World

1956 was the year of the Suez Crisis, the Hungarian Revolution, the advent of the second Eisenhower administration, and the emergence of Elvis Presley. For me, however, it was important because it marked my transfer from the Old to New World, the beginning of a new life, a life of learning and adventure, a life full of possibilities and uncertainties, one of struggle and joy.

Stanford, founded in 1885, was huge. Like a small city, it was well designed, beautiful, self-contained, open, and welcoming. The road to the campus, Palm Drive, lined with trees, was most dramatic and led to the Quad, at the center of which, facing Palm Drive, was the Stanford Chapel, a Byzantine-style church. Its façade was decorated with beautiful mosaics. The Quad with its arcades resembled a well-built, ornate, spacious, and airy monastery.

I arrived on campus with three fellow foreign students, two from Japan and one from India. Their self-confidence and poise frightened me. I was certain all of us were hiding our anxieties.

Two weeks before the formal beginning of classes, all the freshman gathered on campus for registration, orientation, and yet another physical examination. Once again there was a parade of naked men, this time young men; one thing differentiated this set of naked men from the ones I saw in New York's YMCA—no wrinkles. The color was almost exclusively white.

There were maybe four or five African-Americans, maybe a few more Africans and a dozen or so Asians, and many Europeans, primarily from the Nordic countries. While we were lined up for our physical examinations, an American student inquired where I was from. I answered Iran. He asked whether it was in Ethiopia! My retort was "Do I look like a Utopian?" It provoked a great deal of laughter and was considered a cute joke.

Stanford's student body was homogeneous, healthy, well-to-do, eager, cheerful, and energetic. Women were well dressed, beautiful, and stylish. I had never seen so many young, attractive women in one place. I was surprised that so many students had their own cars—the parking lots were full of them. I was also surprised that some male students had Jr. as part of their names. I was astonished that others used numbers as part of their names: Watkins IV, Butler II, Firestone III. I had always assumed that only the popes and royalty had the right to bear numbers. I did not realize that it was a common practice in the United States. When, for the first time, someone introduced himself to me as Mr. McIntosh IV, I introduced myself as Gregorian XI. I don't think he found it amusing.

Classes began at Stanford on September 26. The campus resembled a beehive. There were 8,047 students, undergraduate and graduate, along with some 350 or so faculty and many teaching assistants and busy administrators. There were cars and traffic jams everywhere. The weather was beautiful; you could feel tremendous energy all over the campus. Students were rushing from one class to another, to the bookstore, to the library, to dining rooms, to dormitories. There were signs everywhere, as well as numerous mimeographed sheets of information about every conceivable subject, from room rentals to bicycle rentals to neighborhood restaurants.

Unfortunately I did not get a room on campus. I was assigned, along with some other foreign students and some graduate students, to Stanford Village, a euphemism for some World War II temporary army barracks. Its address was simple: Building No. 121, Unit 119, Room B. I skipped breakfasts to save money, ate my lunch on campus, had my dinners either on or off campus. At a Chinese restaurant in Palo Alto right off the Stanford campus one could have a complete meal consisting of soup and liver and tea for 95 cents. If you got bored with liver you could always order noodles. After all these years, I still remember that the tough part of the liver was always covered with parsley. Stanford Village rooms, even though they were barracks, were comfortable. However, you did not have a private bathroom or shower, unless you were a married couple. Nevertheless, I was happy to be there. I had my own room!

I attended my first history class. Since I was three or four years older than most freshmen and unfortunately conspicuous, I wore a jacket and tie, hoping to pass for a graduate student. In Beirut and Iran, I always stood up when my teachers entered the classroom. At Stanford, as the professor entered I stood up as a sign of respect. Nobody else did. Some chuckled. The professor smiled. I had to shed my old habits, because now I was in America and among adults and grown-ups. I had to follow their example. After all, when in Rome . . .

My courses were great. But I found myself in the position of a thirsty person who wants to drink water from a fountain and is given a hydrant. This was the case with my courses as well as with the Stanford library. The library was a mecca for me. I spent long days there in awe of the collection of books, like a little kid jumping from one toy to another. An interesting item led me to another and on and on. Even at the end of the day, I still felt intoxicated. At long last I had a *personal* library, open, accessible, and always there.

*   *   *

The courses that I took at Stanford both as an undergraduate and as a graduate student concentrated on history and the humanities. I began with a two-year survey of courses on Western civilization, affectionately known as "West Civ." The purpose of the survey was to provide a common vocabulary to all the students at Stanford, a foundation, a historical context, a synopsis of Western civilization, from antiquity through the Middle Ages and the Renaissance to the modern world. The survey textbooks that gave continuity and context were buttressed with additional texts or excerpts from the classics of Western civilization: Homer, Plato, Aristotle, the Greek tragedies and comedies, Saint Augustine, Saint Thomas Aquinas, Dante, Luther, Calvin, Erasmus, Cervantes, Shakespeare, all the way to modern "isms": Liberalism, Conservatism, Socialism, Fascism, Communism.

In the late 1950s, teaching large survey courses was considered a status symbol. Some professors even campaigned to get such assignments. Leadership in survey courses meant one was recognized as an outstanding scholar and expert. It introduced the professor to hundreds of freshmen and sophomores who easily drifted into his other courses. It also led some professors into the lucrative field of required textbooks. What was attractive about the West Civ courses was that there was curricular hierarchy. They were not simply survey courses for "non-majors" but were prerequisites for all majors, in the sciences as well as social sciences and the humanities. The academic major itself had cohesion. It did not consist of mere clusters of unrelated courses.

I appreciated the structure of the West Civ courses. They filled many voids in my education and stimulated me to read individual works and texts of many cultures. At the time there was no major dissent about the purpose and scope of West Civ courses. There was no criticism for attempting to achieve historical and cultural synthesis. There were no "new linguists," or deconstructionists, or a Foucaultian "archeology of knowledge," or dissenters representing ethnic or racial or feminist minorities criticizing the absence of the legacies of non-Western civilizations, or their important contributions within Western civilization and other courses as well.

The Stanford curriculum was attractive not only for the myriad courses it offered but also for the introductory, junior, and senior humanities honors seminars as well. In addition to the West Civ courses, I took many lecture courses and seminars in subjects ranging from Indian civilization to Europe since 1914, the Muslim world, the Near East, the diplomatic history of the Far East, the histories of Russia, the Balkans, Byzantium, the Ottoman Empire, the Chinese revolution, and Latin America, from Plato's *Dialogues* to Goethe's *Faust,* world literature (classical, medieval, and modern), comparative studies of the French, Russian, and Chinese revolutions, ideological and literary currents in the nineteenth and twentieth centuries, the role of the individual and personality in history, anthropology, the history of architecture, art history, and Latin.

I finished my B.A. in two years (two academic years and two summer sessions). My senior thesis for the Humanities Honors Program was on "Toynbee and Islam." It had to be read and approved by three professors from history and the humanities. Everybody was pleased that I received my B.A. with honors and that I finished the Humanities Honors Program with distinction. Even the Iranian embassy in Washington was pleased enough to send a laudatory letter to my father in Iran, congratulating him for having such "a talented, hardworking son."

I could not have done what I did at Stanford without the support of my professors. Every professor of mine encouraged me and challenged me, but more important, made me feel welcome. I was invited to the homes of each one of my professors, either for dinner or holiday festivities. For me these professors were an amazing group. They reinforced my faith not only in humanity but in the academic profession.

My professors came in all different sizes and shapes and accents; some came from California, some from the South, the East, and the Midwest, others from Europe. The president of Stanford himself was a Canadian.

One of my great teachers was Professor Frederic Spiegelberg (1897–1994). He was born in Germany and had earned a doctorate from Tübingen

University and a theological degree from the German Lutheran Church. He was appointed in 1933 to the professorship at the University of Dresden vacated by Paul Tillich. In 1937, Tillich helped Spiegelberg and his wife escape Nazi Germany. After teaching at various U.S. universities and the C. G. Jung Institute in Zurich, Spiegelberg joined the ranks of the Stanford faculty as professor of Indian civilization.

Dr. Spiegelberg was the ideal professor, completely absorbed in his teaching and scholarship and he loved it. That he knew Latin, Greek, and Hebrew was not surprising but that he had also learned Sanskrit and Pali was amazing. I took several courses of his, the two most memorable being on Indian civilization and the *Bhagavadgita*. I was fortunate enough to be asked to be one of his graders for his large classes. He then secured two books for me to review for professional journals. As his assistant, one of my pleasant duties was to meet the Indian and sometimes Vietnamese monks who visited Stanford to lecture in his classes or to the general public. I had to be sure to keep females away from them, to prevent any contact prohibited by their religion. I remember even drawing a circle around one of the monks on the stage of the auditorium before his lecture.

Professor Spiegelberg was famous for his Tibetan "ghost traps," which he had found in Tibet in 1948. These ghost traps usually consisted of structures up to ten feet high, consisting of wooden masts and struts strung with yards of multicolored yarn and dotted with tufts of wool. There were some sixteen types of traps. These traps were mounted on top of Tibetan houses to catch malevolent demons causing illness and misfortune. The ghosts were conceived to be liquid and thought to become entangled in the trap, making the tufts damp. If that happened, the trap was to be destroyed. He used to have some difficulties with U.S. customs agents when he came back to America with these traps.

Professor Spiegelberg taught us about the culture and the social structure of ancient India. In addition to the *Bhagavad Gita,* we read excerpts from the *Upanishads* (600 to 300 B.C.), *Purānas* (A.D. 500 to A.D. 1000) and, of course, translations from the enormous corpus of *Māhābārata,* the Sanskrit epic (assembled between 500 B.C. and A.D. 500). Dr. Spiegelberg informed us, who were "the parochial followers of the Judeo-Christian and classical Western traditions," that the *Māhābārata* was more than three times as long as the Bible and at least seven times as long as *The Iliad* and *The Odyssey* combined. We were duly impressed.

Gordon Wright, professor of French and modern European history, was another favorite teacher of mine. Quiet and dignified, highly respected by all, soft-spoken, serious yet occasionally sardonic, passionate yet private, highly intense, meticulous in his scholarship, extremely conscientious in his teaching, fair, and judicious in his dealings with colleagues and students alike, he was the ultimate professional. His ambition as a teacher and a scholar was to stimulate his students to read carefully, to think, to reflect, to challenge, and to argue some major issues in history, in general, and modern history, in particular.

Even at Stanford, strangers changed my life. By luck, I was assigned to Professor Wayne S. Vucinich as my freshman academic advisor. He taught history of the Balkans, Eastern Europe, Byzantium, and the Ottoman Empire. He advised me to major in history. To his students Professor Vucinich stood for many things. He was a scholar who organized and contributed to major conferences and publications on topics as wide-ranging as Russia and Asia, contemporary Yugoslavia, and the peasant in nineteenth-century Russia. He was a vigorous champion of Balkan, Slavic, East European, and Near Eastern studies. Moreover, to many who had grown accustomed to thinking of scholarship and teaching as conflicting choices in an academic career, Professor Vucinich was living proof that it need not be that way. My first dinner at his home, when I was a freshman, almost turned into a disaster. After a wonderful meal, as I was ready to leave I thanked him and his wonderful wife, Sally, for their hospitality. "What do you mean, thank you? Why don't you slip us a five-dollar bill?" Professor Vucinich asked in a serious tone. I was aghast; I did not have five dollars. Sally chastised him for teasing me, to my great relief. It was the beginning of a series of dinners at the Vucinich home, a hospitality also extended by his late brother, Professor Alex Vucinich, and his wife, Dorothy. Alex was a prominent scholar of the history of science in Russia and the Soviet Union, including the history of the Soviet Academy of Sciences. (This relationship turned into a forty-five-year friendship. Alex Vucinich became a colleague of mine at the University of Texas at Austin and the University of Pennsylvania. He died in 2002. He was a wonderful man, a great teacher, and an outstanding scholar.)

In 1958, I was officially accepted as a Ph.D. candidate in history as well as in the graduate Humanities Program and became a research and teaching assistant to Professor Vucinich. The department awarded me its Wilbur Fellowship.

My graduate courses and seminars leading toward a Ph.D. degree in history and the humanities were rewarding. The seminars I took were: Social Darwinism in European Thought; European Socialism: The Second International and the Problem of Colonialism; Russian Foreign Policy; The Role of the Peasantry in the French, Russian, and Chinese Revolutions; Soul and Body in Renaissance Thought; The Role of Education and the Function of the University; The Philosophy of Education; Marxism in America; Western Traditions (the Renaissance, seventeenth and eighteenth centuries, nineteenth and twentieth centuries); and Intellectual History of Europe, the Balkans, and the Near East.

Paul H. Kocher, professor of English and the humanities, was an extraordinary scholar, sometimes brilliant, sometimes pedantic, sometimes provocative, once in a while humorous, but always engaged and focused. He set high standards for his students. Getting an A from Professor Kocher was one of the great moments in one's career as a graduate student.

The most charismatic undergraduate teacher I had at Stanford was Professor Henry Blauth. I did not and still don't know much about him. He taught in the German department. His course on Goethe's *Faust* had an emotional and intellectual impact on me. His lectures were informative and passionate. He described, in detail, Faust's loves, his ordeals, his quests, his longings for the infinite, and his desire for immortality. He made Faust's dilemmas, defiance, and struggles our dilemmas and struggles. Faust became one of my main intellectual preoccupations and has remained so after all these years. I don't know why but Faust's defiant obstinacy reminded me of the Book of Job. Here, too, I was fascinated more by Job's defiance than by his patience and endurance and his capacity to cope with so many tragedies, punishments, and misfortunes. I was always impressed by Job's integrity and his assertion of individuality in the face of what seemed to be an arbitrary divine power. I came to accept Goethe's Faust as a symbol of the greatness and, at the same time, tragedy of modern man.

John L. Mothershead Jr., professor of philosophy, was an extraordinary teacher. His was one of the first courses that I took, an introduction to philosophy that was given with a historical context and included an extensive discussion of Plato's *Dialogues*. It was in his class that I encountered the generous spirit of some Stanford students, strangers again. I remember with great affection one particular student in my philosophy class: Roxanne Witke, who later became a professor of Chinese history and the biographer of Mao Zedong's last wife, Jiang Ching. She was very smart, kind, and beautiful. She arrived on her bicycle, sat in the front row, and kept a seat for me next to her. I sat on her right and copied some of her lecture notes.

Professor Mothershead's book, *Ethics: Modern Conceptions of the Principles of Right* (1955), was a gem. For me his class marked a formal break from the traditional education systems of Iran and Lebanon. It was a departure from an *arbiter dicta* system, away from memorizing, to one that forced students to think, to provoke, to challenge, to ask questions, to engage in a dialogue.

David Harris, professor of history, was a Texan with an Oxbridge accent, a true gentleman with great poise. He had studied in Paris, Berlin, and Vienna and had served in the State Department. After joining the Stanford faculty he taught European history, international diplomacy, and later European intellectual history. I took several courses from him in European history and intellectual history. He was an eloquent lecturer, a good listener, very pro-student with an open-door policy that extended from his office to his home. His wife, Christine Harris, taught the history of the Middle East. The Harrises epitomized Southern hospitality. They, too, "adopted" me. I served as a teaching assistant to Professor David Harris.

*   *   *

In 1956, I participated in my first political rally in San Francisco. It was against the Soviet Union, and it was about the Hungarian Revolution. The protest was against the visit of Anastas Mikoyan, vice premier of the Soviet Union. Mikoyan happened to be Armenian. I was interviewed about the event by a radio station, and lo and behold, when I heard myself later, I found out that I had an accent, a thick one. Mikoyan proved to be a very crafty character. When asked what Chairman Khrushchev's advice to him was as he headed for America, he was supposed to have responded: "Not to defect and stay in America." This remark had elicited surprise and laughter and had charmed and disarmed the reporter.

In the 1950s, training for a teaching career at Stanford University and anywhere else, for that matter, was minimal. As teaching assistants, we were not given any instruction. Some of us knew about various theories of teaching and pedagogy, but we had to learn our craft by observing and learning from great teachers, practitioners at hand. Professors who allowed their students to lecture in their classes were rare. Professors David Harris and Wayne S. Vucinich were two faculty members who gave me an opportunity to lecture in their classes. I was terrified as I walked into my first classroom. I wanted to be casual and "cool" yet authoritative. Everything I said during my lecture, students wrote down. Realizing this created within me a sense of awe and respect for the art of teaching and for teachers. It inspired me to try to do right, "to know it all," and to transmit it with integrity. When I told professors Harris and Vucinich that I was scared to get up and lecture to the class, they said, "The day you stop being scared you should stop teaching."

John W. Dodds, professor of English and one-time dean of the School of Humanities at Stanford, and the founding director of the Humanities Special Programs, was a towering yet kind and soft-spoken individual, a well-known scholar. He interviewed me for admission to the Humanities Honors Program and served as the principal supervisor for my senior thesis on Toynbee and Islam. In subsequent years, he was a great intellectual mentor of mine.

Several other professors played an active role in my education: George Knoles, John J. Johnson, Anatole Mazour, Arthur Wright, Mary Wright, Lawrence Ryan, Albert Guerrard Sr., and, of course, Kingsley Price.

George Knoles, professor of American history, a Californian (born in 1907), a holder of a Ph.D. degree from Stanford, was an extraordinary teacher. He was tough yet kind, had a wonderful sense of humor and a laugh that engulfed and enchanted everyone. My sole anchor to U.S. history was Professor Knoles's colonial history course and later David Potter's antebellum history. I took a course in the history of the Middle Ages from William Bark and was astonished to find practically the entire Stanford football team in that class, plus their female admirers. I was impressed to find that so many scholar-athletes were eager to know about the structure of medieval societies and institutions. Only later I found out that Professor Bark was an avid football fan. And that he never flunked a football player.

Professor John J. Johnson was the history department's main Latin America expert. He was the author of several important scholarly works. His main survey course was my only exposure to Latin American history. Full of zest, tall and vigorous, an effective lecturer and a patient listener, Professor Johnson gave thought-provoking and demanding midterms and final exams, but unfortunately multiple-choice identification tests accompanied the essay questions. One day he burst into the classroom and announced in his husky, masculine, robust voice: "We have an intellectual snob among us." We all looked around to identify this individual. He told the class it was Mr. Gregorian. "He has written a great essay but has refused as a protest to answer the multiple-choice questions." The fact was that I did not know the answers. His attributing an act of snobbishness to me helped me. Had it been mere ignorance, he would have reduced my grade.

Later he asked what my difficulty was with his questions. I said I did not know the answers because all the names sounded alike—López, Gomez, Martínez, etc. All the z's confused me. He roared with laughter. "How about all the Abduls, ibn this, ibn that, in Middle East history?" he asked. From then we called each other, affectionately, López and Gomez.

Anatole Mazour, professor of Russian history, had an interesting and unusual background. Born in Kiev, he was a veteran of the White Russian army during World War I. He had come to the United States in 1923, received his B.A. from the University of Nebraska, and Ph.D. from UC Berkeley. He was a prolific writer and great lecturer.

Professors Mary and Arthur Wright were an extraordinary couple.

Arthur Wright taught the history of ancient China, and Mary taught the history of modern China. Both were brilliant scholars and great teachers. Professor Arthur Wright was impeccably dressed, very formal. His office was elegantly decorated with fine antique Chinese porcelain and books lined up in an orderly manner, according to author and subject. His desk was neat. Professor Mary Wright dressed casually and was disorganized. Her office was a labyrinth. There were pamphlets, Chinese posters, books, and papers all over. I was fortunate enough to know both of them. Professor Arthur Wright was my senior thesis advisor. As the subject was Toynbee and Islam, I had read most of Toynbee's writings, including *A Study of History*. I had lengthy and fascinating discussions with Professor Wright about his historiography. What fascinated me was that experts like Professor Wright dismissed his interpretation of Chinese history but praised another portion of his study; Jewish historians dismissed his treatment of Jewish history but praised Toynbee's treatment of Greek history; and so on. My study was about Toynbee's views and account of Islam.

Professor Mary Wright taught a seminar on a comparative study of the French, Russian, and Chinese revolutions. It was one of the most stimulating courses I took at Stanford. One of my vivid memories of that seminar was of a guest scholar who came in to discuss the Bolshevik Revolution. This was none other than Alexander Kerensky, the last democratically elected leader of Russia. Following the 1917 March Revolution, he was ousted by the Bolshevik Revolution, or "coup d'état" as he called it. He was short and old, wore spectacles, and walked with a cane. Even though I had already met him (thanks to an introductory letter from Mr. Vratzian), I was nevertheless excited by his spending two hours in class with us to discuss the Russian Revolution.

It was all serious talk. While the answers he gave were concise, he sometimes wandered off into the past, citing names of individuals, documents, obscure pamphlets, and so on. It was as if he were in another world. We were awed because we were in the presence of history.

There were lighter moments, too. A gentleman of the old school, Kerensky stood up to hold a chair for Professor Wright before she sat down. Each time she got up to write a name or two on the blackboard or a date or a concept, Kerensky interrupted the flow of his thoughts to get up and hold her chair. Each time Professor Wright wanted to smoke a cigarette Kerensky got up to light it for her.

My experiences with Albert Guerrard Sr., professor of French and humanities, were joyous. He inspired, encouraged, helped, admonished, and counseled all of us in a fatherly manner without offending anyone. Then, of course, there was Professor Lawrence Ryan, professor of English and humanities, again a marvelous teacher, caring administrator, and a great lecturer, as well as a first-rate scholar. I still remember his lectures on Chaucer.

The most unusual teacher I had at Stanford was Professor Kingsley Price, a visiting professor of philosophy and education from Johns Hopkins University. He was unusual because he was born blind. I could never have imagined that a blind boy could not only survive in society but could receive an education, go to a university, obtain an advanced degree, publish scholarly articles and books, and get promoted to full professorship. I was stunned. I had never encountered a blind scholar before. I thought my difficulties and hardships could hardly compare with this man's struggles, efforts, and ordeals. I admired him very much. The course he taught was extraordinary. It was a seminar on Plato and education. In reality it turned out to be something more because it dealt with the definition of definition.

The most unusual seminar I took at Stanford was with Professor William Langer, the prominent diplomatic historian from Harvard. His topic was the role of potatoes in history. It was a fascinating subject, and his analyses of the economic and social impact of the potato on the course of European history were illuminating. I still remember his vivid description of Frederick the Great of Prussia eating a potato in public to assure his citizens that it was not poisonous, and his assertion that more poems were written about the potato than any other staple.

I cannot finish this section on my professors, however, without talking about David Levin and my ignorance of English. David was a wonderful professor of English, and I was in one of his seminars. Even though I was a graduate student, I still was unfamiliar with the meaning of certain English words. One day I missed one of Professor Levin's seminars because I had a terrible sore throat. I thought that the English technical term for a bad sore throat was "mononucleosis," so that's what I told him I had. Of course, you can imagine his shock when he saw me on the dance floor only a few days later! He must have thought I was taking him for a ride. I was too ashamed of my mistake and too proud to tell him that I did not know what mononucleosis meant. Since much of our grade was based on class participation, that brought my grade down, and he gave me the only C+ I ever received. The C+ was actually very generous of him. David Levin passed away several years ago, and unfortunately it was not until very recently that I was able to confess this to his wife.

I have dedicated so much time, space, and attention to my principal professors at Stanford because they were an unusual group of people, from a different era, when students and teaching were the central preoccupation of the professors and the university, when the central mission of the university was education, when undergraduate education was the core of the university and the quality of graduate education the ultimate goal.

While defensive about being admitted to Stanford as a freshman at age twenty-one, I soon realized that it was an asset. I learned more because my education at the Collège Arménien had been invaluable, especially in history and European literature. My familiarity with several languages came in handy. I also came to believe that being a foreign student was itself an advantage for I could be in two or more places simultaneously: I could compare my experiences, see things from different perspectives, and be both observer and participant. While I met with many obstacles and difficulties in the United States—financial, social, psychological, and academic—all of them combined could not match my ordeals in Iran and in Lebanon. In the United States I saw hope. I perceived the United States as a place where dreams did not die, and one did not have to live off the flesh of dead dreams.

*   *   *

I wrote several long essays for my graduate seminar courses in history as well as for the Humanities Honors Program. I have kept most of them. I list several to give an idea of the range of the topics:

"Socialism and the First World War"
"Marxism in the United States"
"Social Darwinism in Russia"
"Song of Roland, Its Social and Artistic Values"
"Voltaire as a Historian"
"Russian Foreign Policy in the Middle East"
"The Failure of the Little Entente"
"The Last Days of Constantinople, May 20–29, 1453"

I also wrote one long, heavily footnoted, pedantic, occasionally moving research paper for Professor Albert Guerrard's graduate seminar in the humanities. The topic was the role of the individual in history. I chose Karl Marx as my subject. I was most impressed by Moses Hesse's description of him: "Imagine Rousseau, Voltaire, Holbach, Lessing, Heine, and Hegel—united in one person . . . and you have Dr. Marx." I decided to study the impact of various social, economic, cultural, and political factors that helped shape his personality and his worldview, which in turn influenced his work and his career. I had read the philosopher Bertrand Russell's verdict that "the circumstances of men's lives do much to determine their philosophy

but, conversely, their philosophy does much to determine their circumstances." This was my first foray into psychohistory, my attempt to join historical materialism and psychology. After reading several biographies of Marx, I focused on five factors in his life: his persistent ill health; his position as a firstborn child; Romantic and religious influences; his Jewish origin; and the impact of poverty.

I wrote about his many health problems, his liver troubles (and his fear of cancer of the liver), his gastric and intestinal disorders, his hemorrhoids, and other ailments. I attempted to analyze the causes of his virulent anti-Semitism. When Marx was six years old, his father, confronted with the choice of changing his Jewish faith or leaving the legal profession, embraced Christianity, and had himself and his family baptized. He told his son that he had forsaken Judaism and become a Christian as a matter of conviction. Marx had a strong devotion, respect, and admiration for his father. I tried to link his vicious attacks against Jews and Judaism as a defense of his father's religious conversion.

I asserted with conviction that persons with digestive disorders are depressed, capricious, spiteful, discontented, and full of suspicion, and find it hard to enter into sympathetic relationships with others. They are isolated and embittered. They eat little and irregularly. I even quoted from Otto Ruhl's biography of Karl Marx that Marx had "a bad relation to his work and to his fellow men," that "bad eaters are bad workers and bad comrades." Then I proceeded to outline the impact of Romantic literature on Marx.

I was astonished to find out that Marx had written three volumes of poetry, dedicated to Jenny, his love. I "analyzed" (now they call it "deconstructed") the contents of several of these poems. They were very tender, very romantic, and very lyrical. Then I surveyed his letters describing the hardships and indignities suffered by him and Jenny, his fiancée and later his wife. Here are a couple of samples: "I have been engaged now for more than seven years and my fiancée has had to fight the hardest battles for my sake, shattering her health in the process, partly due to her bigoted, aristocratic relations, whose twin objects of worship are the 'Lord in Heaven' and the 'Lord in Berlin.' "

Describing their extreme poverty, Marx noted: "The situation is very gloomy. It will be the end of my wife, if it goes on much longer . . . the never-ending worries of the petty, paltry bourgeois struggle are a terrible strain on her." Or ". . . to pound and grind dry bones and make soup of them, as paupers do in the workhouse, that is the sum total of the political work to which one is generously condemned in such society." Poverty forced Marx to sell

his library and go into debt. He pawned everything. While in London, his family moved to Soho, where most poverty-stricken people lived. This was also the neighborhood where epidemic after epidemic raged. In 1854, cholera struck. Three of Marx's children died. When his one-year-old daughter died, Marx was forced to borrow money from a French émigré to pay for the coffin.

He wrote, "My wife is ill. Little Jenny is ill. Lenchen has a sort of nervous fever, and I cannot call in the doctor because I have no money to pay him. For about eight to ten days we have all been living on bread and potatoes, and it is now doubtful whether we shall be able to get even that. . . . How am I to get out of this devilish mess? During the past week or so I have borrowed a few shillings and even pence from workers. It was terrible but it was absolutely necessary or we should have starved." In February 1852, Marx could not go out because his coat was in the pawnshop. The family could no longer eat meat because he could no longer get any credit. He was almost arrested when a London pawnbroker suspected him of being a burglar. This happened when he attempted to sell some valuable antique silver belonging to his wife.

"Faced with the crude realities of the material world, suffering from his failure to provide his beloved wife and children a comfortable life and living, Marx the disillusioned Romantic," I wrote, "turned into a rebel against the 'revolting slavery of mankind.' . . . Hurt in his pride, stricken with misery, infuriated by renewed political persecution, full of contempt for his 'reactionary fatherland,' jealous, suspicious, intolerant, Marx rebelled against the bourgeois society." Meanwhile, one thing was certain: Marx had emerged from Romanticism as a strong individualist. This manifested itself in the fact that Marx believed in dueling. He wrote, "Within the biased limitations of bourgeois society, it might be necessary to justify one's individuality in this feudal manner." Indeed he fought a duel in 1836 and received a thrust scar over his left eye.

When a German paper, published in London, slandered him about the excellent relations of the "red revolutionary" with Prussia's interior minister (his wife's brother), Marx, who granted the press the right to insult politicians, comedians, and other public figures, lost patience and challenged the editor to a duel. He rejected as "bestial" the idea of communalization of women, characterizing it as "utterly crude and unintelligent communism," which "denied personality." He considered marriage sacred. Arnold Ruge's ideas on marriage were characterized as "inhuman" and "philistine." Marx believed that the immediate duty of man was to serve mankind.

In his observations of a "Young Man Before Choosing His Career," he

wrote: "If we chose the career in which we can do humanity the most good, burdens cannot overwhelm us, since they are nothing but sacrifices for the benefit of all. . . . Experience rates him as the happiest who has made the greatest number happy, and religion itself teaches us the ideal for which we should all strive, to sacrifice oneself for humanity." However, he wrote later, man should not depend upon religion because after nineteen centuries this religion (Christianity) that claims to be the most social in its teachings has not even demanded, much less achieved, social justice for all. Religion, for Marx, was "the fantastic materialization of the human entity." What humanity needed was not escapism, or new interpretations of human nature; "the philosophers had only interpreted the world differently." "The task is," Marx wrote, "to change it."

Notwithstanding Marx's agreement with Ludwig Feuerbach's *The Essence of Christianity* (that man is the highest being, that the supernatural is pure fantasy, that the invention of God impoverishes life on Earth), I was determined to find the impact of Romantic and religious thought on his philosophy. I found the answer in Lucien Goldmann's extraordinary book *Le Dieu Caché (The Hidden God),* published in Paris in 1955. I read it in 1958 because of my fascination with Pascal and his writings.

In his book, Goldmann, a Marxist, made a very interesting, debatable comparison between Pascal and Marx, presenting Pascal as the predecessor of Marx. I had read about Pascal's views on human nature in high school. According to Goldmann, Pascal had a "tragic vision" of the human condition. Everything that is not of God is devalued to nothingness *(néant).* He appealed to God with all his existence, but God remained "hidden" because neither the world, nor the mind, nor reason could prove His existence. For Pascal there was either All or Nothing. Considering the "totality" of human aspirations, he wanted to see Man simultaneously as Reason and Heart, Angel and Beast, Body and Soul: *un moi ouvert à tous et en communion avec tout.* Since the reconciliation of these opposites was impossible in this world, Pascal transcended them.

According to Goldmann, Marx took what was positive in Pascal—he, too, had the Pascalian Demand—but instead of wanting God to resolve it in Eternity, he expected Man to surpass himself in Time and realize it through his effort and action, without God, the synthesis of the opposites. Hence, Marx, too, according to Goldmann, attempted to unite Reason and the Heart, the Body and the Soul, the Individual and Society, Man and the World. If religion is "faith in total values which transcend the individual," Marx believed that "Man can find God, which is synonymous to Community and the Universe." Hence, there will be religion without God, the religion of Humanity: *Religion sans Dieu, religion de l'homme et de l'humanité est néanmoins, religion quand même.* According to Goldmann, the Marxist faith, which is in the historical future, resembles Pascal's "Bet," but this bet is about the eventual success of humanity and its actions here on earth. It envisions the disappearance of "the enslaved subordination of the individual under the division of labor" and with it the "opposition between manual and intellectual labor; in the future labor was to become not only a means of life, but also the highest want in life." It anticipated a new Society. Inscribed on its banner would be the following: "From everyone according to his faculties, to everyone according to his needs." This new society was to be built through the will of men and the use of their intelligence. God could not explain anything in these matters, because God Himself needed an explanation.

Marx's determinism asserted that there is a purpose and a law in the Universe with which man can cooperate and, in cooperation with inevitable Destiny, attain the fullness of being. What fascinated me was the issue of predestination, another legacy of religion. I found R. H. Tawney's *Religion and the Rise of Capitalism* most interesting, specifically when he draws parallels between Calvin and Marx: "It is not wholly fanciful to say that on a narrower stage but with not less formidable weapons, Calvin did for the bourgeoisie of the sixteenth century, what Marx did for the proletariat of the nineteenth century, or that the doctrine of predestination satisfied the same hunger for an assurance that the forces of the Universe are on the side of the Elect as was to be assuaged in a different age by the theory of Historical Materialism. He . . . taught them to feel that they were a chosen people, made them conscious of their great destiny in the Providential plan and resolute to realize it. . . ."

I concluded my essay on Marx by asserting that his work was a compensation for his life. Poor, in ill health, subject to social discrimination and political persecution, repeatedly in debt, a "master of unsociability," Marx developed an elaborate economic and social philosophy to emancipate man from economic bondage in order to provide *everyone* with a share of the world's material goods. Marx, who proclaimed the universal brotherhood of men, founded an economic and social system in which everyone would be able to do what he himself could not, and all men were to have what he did not.

This crude attempt at psychohistory was apparently well received, for I got an A. But the praise from Albert Guerrard Sr. was devastating: "Friedrich Engels, Marx's close ally, did not have any of Marx's handicaps yet he wrote about and believed in the same vision. . . ." Thus ended my "bold adventure" in psychohistory.

My foray into psychohistory was a beguiling but temporary intellectual curiosity. My research paper "Jean Bodin: State, Sovereignty, Law, or Natural Law as a Basis for Political Theory" proved to be far more rewarding. Bodin (1530–1596) was the first one to conceive a theory of sovereign state power. Bodin's works introduced me to the fertile fields of natural law, political theory, and the history of ideas. For Bodin, knowledge of the history of human societies was the surest path to guide us in the "labyrinth of politics." In his analysis of history and human societies, he wanted to work out the rules of a practical political philosophy.

I developed a deep interest in the theories of natural law and in evolution from Bodin to Johannes Althusius (1557–1638) to Hugo Grotius (1583–1645) (perhaps the first major theorist of international law), to Thomas Hobbes (1588–1679), to John Locke (1632–1704), to Montesquieu (1689–1755), culminating in two great documents embodying the aspirations of two major eighteenth-century revolutions: the American and the French revolutions. I am referring, of course, to the Declaration of Independence of the United States, which refers to the Laws of Nature and the "inalienable rights" of life, liberty, and the pursuit of happiness as "self-evident." The French Declaration of the Rights of Man and of the Citizen also affirms liberty, property, security, and resistance to oppression as "imprescriptable natural rights."

*   *   *

My hectic academic life was gradually matched by a fast-paced social life, underwritten by various part-time jobs that covered my out-of-pocket expenses. Here again my sojourn at Stanford was made easier thanks to yet another stranger: Peter Kirianoff, one of only three Armenians at Stanford. His parents had emigrated from Iran to the United States. His father had been a prominent dentist in Tehran. Peter took me under his wing. He was suave, thoroughly Americanized, knew the university well, was very social, likeable, well-to-do, very polite, popular with the girls, and respected by the university administration. He was the president of the Cosmos Club, which had mostly foreign students but also many Americans who were interested in international affairs or else had lived in foreign countries.

Peter, who was a junior and had a car, was well known on campus for his ability to organize great, popular parties for the international community at two nearby famous French restaurants, L'Omelette and Chez Yvonne. He introduced me to the campus social scene, its etiquette, the rule of hospitality, and, of course, the dating system. Peter also introduced me to the Big Game, the football game between Stanford and UC Berkeley, two traditional rivals. As a result, I came to love the game of football. He worked very hard under the leadership of Dr. Werner Warmbrunn, the foreign student advisor, to secure a space for foreign students that would serve as their social base on campus.

Since he was about to graduate, Peter groomed me to succeed him. He made me assistant program chairman of the International Center, thus launching my career as a "student leader." We had a couple of hundred undergraduate and graduate foreign students. I could not campaign on my own behalf, so Peter did it for me. So did others. I was elected president of the International Center. The other candidate was a fun-loving, humorous, and attractive Pakistani student. There were only three votes cast on his behalf; Peter had been an effective "campaign manager." In his "concession speech," my opponent joked, "I know I voted for myself, my girlfriend voted for me because I forced her to, but who cast the third vote?" "I did," I said. I was brought up in a tradition and belief that you did not vote for yourself. It would have been immodest to do so. Everybody laughed.

Our parties, now organized by me, were great hits on campus and gave me an opportunity to meet many foreign and American students. The staff of the International Center adopted me and became part of my extended family. Community board members acted as friends of the International Center and of foreign students. They invited students to their homes for dinners and holidays. They helped organize visits to local institutions. They helped Stanford acculturate its foreign students and gradually become an international university.

Their ranks included Mrs. Dorothy Steere (the wife of the graduate dean), Mrs. Carl Spaeth (the wife of the Law School dean), Mrs. Lowell Clucas (the wife of the vice president of the Crown Zellerbach Company), Mrs. Wallace Stegner (the wife of the famous American writer and novelist), the wives of many prominent Stanford faculty members, such as Mrs. Henry Keyes, and Inez Richardson, the head of International Studies. All of them became friends. They provided remarkable hospitality to countless foreign students, including me. It was a great manifestation of American openness, generosity, and the volunteer spirit. This was apparent also among the students: many young women students volunteered to teach dancing to foreign students.

By chance, the International Center also launched my career as a speaker. In 1956, the show that followed the annual international dinner to which all the faculty and administrators were invited along with the "student leaders" was delayed because the MC did not show up. I had never heard of an MC, did not know what the letters stood for, and had never managed a public event. Somebody told me that MC was the Master of Ceremonies, who read the program and introduced the guests. Either they asked or I volunteered to do the job. Once I got up, they told me I had to say a few jokes and/or make funny remarks.

The organizers told me, "Don't worry. We'll tell you the lines, and you just repeat them." I agreed. I was asked to welcome the "top brass" of the university. I had heard of "brass tacks" but not "top brass," so I welcomed the "brass tacks" of Stanford University. The audience was very amused. I told them of my encounter with naked Stanford students when one of them had asked whether Iran was in Ethiopia, and whether I was an Ethiopian, to which I had replied, "Do I look like a Utopian?" and on and on. The crowd roared with laughter.

Someone told me it's the year of the dog. I repeated it was a dog of a year. They thought I was a born comedian and had a mastery of the English language, understood its nuances and ambiguities, and was making fun of them and ourselves. From then on I started getting invitations to Rotary Clubs and churches for MC jobs. The pay was most welcome, ten to fifteen dollars, plus free lunches and dinners. My other part-time jobs included that of a ticket controller at Cubberly auditorium, where classic movies were shown. I was admonished for letting people in without tickets. "But there are plenty of vacant seats" was my response. "You are being paid to let only people with tickets in and prevent those who don't have tickets from coming in," my supervisor told me with a stern voice.

I also worked at the Engineering Library from five to seven P.M. This was thanks to Mr. Priddle, the deputy librarian of Stanford, who was our varsity soccer coach along with Professor Weinstein of the French department. Those hours were great; the usage was at its minimum. I had time to do my homework.

For a brief period, I worked at Stanford's famous Cellar, the only nonresidential dining room open to students, faculty, and visitors. There I learned a fundamental lesson about America: working for one's education was not shameful, it was a badge of honor. Work was respected, especially since everybody knew that it was only the means to a lofty goal.

When I learned to love black coffee, I knew that the first step of my Americanization had been completed. The second step was to buy and use deodorant. In the Middle East during my childhood and youth, deodorant was very expensive and was considered something for women. Men could use after-shave lotion but not deodorant. The third step was to buy a used car. Yes, I was told by Peter, in America you can bargain for a used car. I bought a third-hand Ford and that purchase changed my life. Sometimes I did not have enough money to buy gas, so pretty soon my car became a public accommodation vehicle. When one of the many foreign students borrowed it for an evening naturally he was obliged to return it with a full tank of gasoline. It was a fair exchange. Thank God, I never thought of the legal liabilities that I assumed by lending my car. The most definitive act of autonomy was to obtain a single room off campus. Of all things, I cherished privacy and occasional solitude most of all. Most of my earnings went to cover the cost of this single room with bath, and the car. I studied hard, I partied hard, and I worked hard. I needed time and space to recuperate. My landlady, Mrs. Lake, had one rule: no female visitors and no guests. That was fine with me.

Although I was able to adjust well to my classes, academic culture, campus life, and my assorted part-time jobs, the highly evolved and intricate American ritual of "dating" was an unknown phenomenon. It turned out this was true for scores of other foreign students from around the world. Dating seemed to have complex and rigid rules. You had to ask someone out at least a week in advance. Under no circumstances would a girl accept a Saturday date after Wednesday. Female students would not go out alone or in the company of another female student on Friday and Saturday evenings, as that would have revealed that they had no dates. Perhaps a rumor might start that they were lesbians. Middle-class women's social life and freedom was tightly structured. Many college kids, especially foreign students, were intimidated by the fear of being turned down for a date and everybody on campus knowing about it.

Once you had successfully asked someone out, you had to be on time, get out of your car, go inside the dormitory, and ring for your date. You had to open the car door for her. Even if you had no place to park, under no circumstances could you honk to let your date know that you had arrived and were waiting for her. Naturally you had to know the person before you asked her out. If she gave you her phone number, it was an indication of her willingness to be asked out. American college students dated in search of mates, or to have fun. Sexual relationships were taboo, rare, or discreet and unheralded. The pill had not been invented yet. If there was off-campus sexual activity, it was kept secret for fear of the gossip that might ruin a reputation. The story was that male students were free to have sex with anybody but as a rule married only virgins. There were unwritten rules. If somebody went out with you three times and had a dinner date but did not kiss you and neck with you, that was a sign that your relationship was not going any-

where. Some students as early as their freshman year got "pinned" to fraternity boys, thus establishing an exclusive relationship. "Going steady" meant
a female and a male student had decided to be a couple and go out only
with each other. Senior year was one for clearing the deck. Many girls and
boys got engaged or married or else dissolved their longstanding relationships and became "just good friends" or left each other quietly.

There were strict curfew rules for female students. During the weekends
they had to be back no later than midnight if they were freshmen and by two
A.M. if they were seniors. There were limited numbers of overnights for un-
derclassmen. The female students had to sign in. If they were late, they received demerits; if they exceeded the allowable points they had to see a
dean. If a male student caused the tardiness, he had to send one rose for
each minute exceeding the curfew time. Then there was a "tradition," I am
sure manufactured by male students, that in order to become a true Stanford
woman you had to be kissed under one of the arches of the Stanford Quad.
One other oddity was to see lines of cars parked in front of female students'
dormitories with couples or two couples necking, awaiting the curfew hour.
This ritual, I was told, had another purpose: transparency. It was a signal
that all the relations were in the open and aboveboard.

Some couples preferred double dating. This was especially important for
those who did not have a car, and also for girls who were intrigued by boys
but not certain yet whether they wanted to go out with them alone. Double
dates were sometimes exploratory dates: "to see how they got along." The
male students were always supposed to pay the expenses of the evening.
The male also had to drive the car. The dating system was freighted with
high expectations. The greatest challenge or difficulty on both "dating" parties was to prevent a prematurely declared romantic interest.

I had many encounters with Stanford's dating system. During my second
week at Stanford I asked a classmate whether she would like to go out for a
cup of coffee. She told me, "I am sorry, but I am pinned." "I am sorry" was
my reply. I did not know what she was talking about! My friend Peter Kirianoff filled me in. Until my arrival in the United States I was accustomed to
going to movies or dinners or bars with a bunch of friends as a group. Stanford's rules dealt primarily with a couple or two couples dating each other.

My first date was almost a disaster. I took a very nice girl to the movies
and for a hamburger. We enjoyed the movie and we talked. At the end of the
evening I drove her to her dormitory, jumped out of the car, and opened her
door. She burst into tears. "Didn't we have a good time?" she asked. "Of
course, we did," I replied. "Then why are you taking me home so early?
People may think we had a lousy date." She nodded at tens of cars parked in

front of Lagunita Hall. In each car there was a couple or two necking. It was awkward. I hardly knew her. We talked for an hour. Then I accompanied her to her dorm. It was a respectable time span. I did not make that mistake again.

It was very difficult to date those you were not properly introduced to. I thought I had found a clever technique to deal with that problem. There was a very beautiful girl. I made a bet with my friends that I would take her out on a date. I approached her directly and said I didn't know anyone who knew both of us, so I had decided to skip the middleman and ask directly for a date. It worked.

I went out with many nice girls on weekends. To alter my daily routine (no breakfast, ham and cheese sandwich and V8 juice for lunch, a hamburger or a piece of pizza—a new discovery—for dinner, work, or study), I decided once a month or every other month to treat myself. I took a date to the Venetian Room of the Fairmont Hotel, ordered a nice meal, saw a show (Ted Williams, Jimmy Durante, José Uturbi), even left a tip (sometimes worth three or four times my hourly wage).

If I went dancing at a nightclub I usually took my dates to Bimbo's 365 in San Francisco. It was a great club, but it was only years later that I learned what Bimbo meant. Sometimes carried away by exuberance and challenged by my other Armenian friend from Iran, Leon Koochayan, we drove with our dates all the way to Los Angeles to have a "great pizza" and returned to San Francisco via Palo Alto. On one occasion I had taken a date to a nightclub where they sang great songs from various operas. It was her birthday and she was very well dressed and had a fancy purse. We drank, we ate, we danced. When the time came to pay the bill I realized that I was short twelve dollars or so. I asked whether she had any money, but she had only a couple of dollars. It was late. Remember this was the pre–credit card, pre-ATM era. I did not know what to do. I left the nightclub, drove to my friend Leon's apartment, awakened him, grabbed his money, and went back to the nightclub. My date was in tears. It was a close shave.

Then there was my "bizarre" behavior. We had a great International Center party at Chez Yvonne's restaurant and everybody wanted to come. I asked one European and two American girls to the dance. They had a great time, but when the time came to take them home, they were all outraged. They did not want to be taken back together. Each one insisted she was my "date." I had to drive each of them separately to her dormitory.

There were some very nice, beautiful, tall girls who were not asked for a date. Some of us assumed that they were out all the time and would therefore turn down any offers. As a result, these girls thought that there must be something wrong with them. Evidently this was not a new problem. The chaplain of Stanford had a discretionary fund to help alleviate these kinds of heartaches or misunderstandings, money presumably designated by a donor who had similar experiences. He first flattered me, saying that I was a very popular young man on campus, and would I mind taking out beautiful girl X to the movies, dinner, or dance. He would help to defray "reasonable costs." I called the girl and she was thrilled. I took her out to Bimbo's 365. We had a great time. While dancing with her I realized what the problem was: she was six feet tall. All the songs were about "put your head on my shoulder . . ." As we came out of the nightclub, a car full of fraternity boys shouted out: "Hey, shorty, what are you doing with that tall girl!" It ruined our evening. I was glad, however, that I had taken her out. We became friends. She married a tall Texan.

The other tall girl was European. I tried to build her a great reputation, an aura of mystery. I called many times from different locations and left messages on behalf of fictitious European counts and gentlemen, even a Japanese and an Arab from New York, expressing regret that due to a snow-storm they would miss their date in San Francisco, or Los Angeles, or I left messages to meet a given gentleman at Ricky's Hotel in Palo Alto on such and such a date. All those messages were posted on her dormitory door, boosting her reputation. She was elated. She knew I was behind that cam-paign. She married a short man. "I am not an American," she said with cer-tain satisfaction. "Love is what counts, not height."

I graduated from Stanford in 1958. I also received my first public award: Stanford's Institute for International Relations Award "for the student who has contributed most to international understanding." It was given for my role as president of the International Center, for the scores of parties, festi-vals, and international dinners and programs that the center had organized. I thought I deserved it mainly for one major contribution: the social orienta-tion of incoming foreign students. It was the hardest task—to cross so many cultural realms, to try to bridge them to avoid misunderstandings, disap-pointments, heartbreaks, and breakdowns. The gist of the orientation was simple: when you are invited to dinner by an American family, be on time, especially if it is Thanksgiving dinner. Several students from Latin America, the Middle East, and some even from Europe, thought that showing up on time was impolite, for it may indicate eagerness to eat dinner. The second advice was also clear: if you are served dinner and they ask if you want sec-onds, say yes. Many foreign students who declined second servings and took very little at the initial serving came back from American homes hungry. They were used to hosts and hostesses who insisted that they take second or third servings. That did not happen in American homes. Italian, Greek, Armenian, and Jewish households were the exceptions.

I witnessed two manifestations of racism. In 1957, the International Center organized a trip for foreign students to Las Vegas and Lake Tahoe to give them firsthand knowledge of America's gambling industry and its casinos. Several of our African students, who wore their national costumes to underscore that they were not American blacks, were not allowed to enter the casinos. It was an upsetting and degrading experience for all of us.

In 1959, Amlak Makonnen, an Ethiopian graduate student in engineering, was unable to rent an apartment on Princeton Street in Palo Alto, adjacent to Stanford's campus, because he was colored. I rented a two-bedroom apartment on the same street and sublet one of the rooms to Amlak. The landlord was outraged but could not do much. Amlak, thoroughly Americanized, loved his pipe and Paul Harvey broadcasts. After returning home, he set up an engineering company. He was shot during the reign of Colonel Mengistu, the "Little Stalin" of Ethiopia.

For me, the most difficult part was to explain the American dating system, especially that when a girl or boy kissed you, even "necked" with you, he or she did not necessarily love you. That was completely incomprehensible to many foreign students. That misunderstanding usually led to accusations of unfaithfulness, lack of morality, being fickle, superficial, and insincere. "How can someone kiss you, be in your arms, and not love you?" asked an Argentinian.

On Sundays I drove to San Francisco to sing in the Armenian Church choir and to attend occasional Armenian cultural events held in San Francisco, a round-trip of seventy-five miles. I had to work part-time. I needed the income. I had to cope with organizational issues involving the International Center, including opening a sidewalk café, the first of its kind at Stanford. (My partner in this venture was Bridgit Dobson, a smart, exuberant, vivacious student with a great imagination and organizational talent. She later became a writer and producer of *General Hospital, Santa Barbara,* and other television shows.) I had to play club soccer (I was a lousy player, no match for my friends from Ghana and Ethiopia) and study. Thank God, I was healthy. I did not need more than four or five hours of sleep.

I had once again fallen in love, this time with an American girl from Winnetka, Illinois. She was beautiful and funny, spoke French, loved to dance, laughed heartily, was energetic and a sports enthusiast, and studious. My life was very hectic. To fall in love was exhilarating but also often painful. It is easy to fall in love within an idyllic university setting, when all the cultural, social, economic, and political differences can easily be dismissed, minimized, and overlooked, rationalized, or made irrelevant. But the iron rules of reality always catch up. We who thought we were inseparable, we who thought we had pledged our futures to each other through numerous love letters and phone calls, found ourselves not at a crossroads but at a dead end. I realized that when at the end of the summer of 1958 I drove to Illinois to see her.

I drove with minimum stops and at maximum speeds. I slept in the car to save money for gasoline. During the last lap, I checked into a motel to shave, bathe, and dress properly, since I was to meet her parents. I stayed two or three days at her home. I knew our relationship had been derailed. Her parents, who were nice, had other plans for her. From their sympathetic yet direct questioning, it was clear that her entire clan was there to dissuade her from linking her fate to a poor, strange, or rather exotic, soon to be first-year graduate student, without a clear future and very little security.

What are your future plans? her father asked me. I am on my way to New York to seek a job as a foreign correspondent with the Hearst newspapers, I said. And, indeed, after my visit to Illinois, I drove to New York to seek employment. Having seen the movie *Dateline U.S.A.* and, I am sure, been influenced by it, I visited the Hearst Corporation headquarters, and asked to see Randolph Hearst. What about? I would like to be a foreign correspondent. They asked, did I have an appointment with him? I said no. Why don't you write him a letter? I did. I wrote about my background, my education, my familiarity with the Middle East, stating that I could be an asset. Several years ago, when I got to know Randolph Hearst very well, and became a friend of his, I reminded him in jest that he had missed an opportunity to exploit me. He agreed and laughed heartily.

On my return to Stanford, the letters and calls from Winnetka became sporadic and then stopped completely. My girlfriend's parents had sent her on a grand tour of Europe and registered her at Columbia University. She was hoping to join the Foreign Service. Needless to say, I was devastated, heartbroken. Subsequent correspondence did not help the matter. "I hope we can still be friends" is not always soothing. Sometimes it is like salt poured into an open wound. After all, the shift from passion to Platonic friendship, while sounding mature and civilized, is not an easy transition. I thought it was a cover meant to relieve oneself of guilt. Only time and space proved to be the best remedy.

I assumed that two devastating experiences in the realm of love, within the span of four years, was too much. I declared a moratorium on love. I dated a young Scandinavian actress, whom I met at the San Francisco airport (her main worry was always whether any given restaurant was expensive or classy); a zestful Norwegian "free spirit"; a brilliant, complicated Ph.D. candidate in psychology/psychiatry (who had just broken off her engagement); a delightful, beautiful, tall sophomore who spoke impeccable French, had a great education, and had seen most of the world. One woman volunteered to teach me Portuguese (I thought I better look into it just in case I decided after all to go to Brazil to assume the directorship of the Armenian high school in São Paulo). I found out, however, that she was more interested in me than in my competence in Portuguese. Then France came to my rescue.

A young French exchange student came to Stanford. She was smart, charming, and beautiful. Everybody wanted to date her. We became instant friends (we still are). Our relationship was strictly platonic but people were unbelieving. How can a French girl go out with you every week, dance with you, come home so late without any romantic attachment on your or her part? I guess it was incredible. But sometimes truth is incredible. We both loved to dance and enjoyed each other's company. She lived in Durand Hall. One day, as I was waiting for her in the parlor, I was immensely attracted to a tall, blond young woman who was playing an entrancing Joplin ragtime on the piano.

Her name was Clare Russell. She was from Tenafly, New Jersey, a long way from home. She was an undergraduate, a major in U.S. and Ottoman history. As luck would have it, she was enrolled in two of Professor Wayne Vucinich's classes on the Balkans and the Ottoman Empire and I just happened to be the teaching assistant for both courses. I was fascinated with the clarity of her thought and writing, as well as the depth of her knowledge of the subject matter. She was a very serious student, both intelligent and beautiful. As they say, she was a class act. To get her attention or a smile from her was extremely hard. She had utter self-confidence, great poise, and an elegant walk. Although I remember the first time I met her, all she remembers is that she was in Vucinich's classes where I was the teaching assistant and as far as she was concerned I was a one-man swarm. I started going out with her and, yes, once again I fell in love.

I informed Professor Vucinich that as I was going out with one of his students, I thought it was improper for me to correct her exams. He agreed. He could not resist teasing her, however, that while *he* thought she was an A student, I had tried to convince him that she was a B or B+ student. For what I thought was six months (Clare informed me it was only six weeks), Clare and I had great fun together, frequenting all of Stanford's favorite watering holes: the Oasis, Rosotti's, Mama Garcia's, some International Center parties at Chez Yvonne, a variety of restaurants, frequent visits to San Francisco restaurants, and such operatic nightclubs as Bocci Ball, or the Venetian Room and, of course, even Bimbo's 365.

We drove to Big Sur and Carmel. We even attended Spring Sing. Prior to that event, she was upset with me because I was late picking her up. I told her, don't worry, we'll find the best parking spot. She was incredulous. When we arrived at the police barricade, I honked at Lester, the campus security guard. He cheerfully removed the barrier, and we parked next to the Stanford president's car. She was stunned. "You are parking illegally," she told me. When the event ended and we came back, there was a traffic ticket on my car's windshield. "This is a country of laws," she said, pleased I had gotten my just deserts. I opened the envelope. It was empty, so she accused me of corrupting Stanford's police force.

The fact is that almost all Stanford policemen liked me, my car was well known to them, and they almost always overlooked my parking infractions. Some evenings when it was too late or when I thought I'd had too much to drink, I just slept in my car, in front of Clare's dormitory, without being bothered by the police. Of course, there is always an exception. There was one policeman who rode a fancy motorcycle. His beat was Palm Drive. He wore a silk scarf with a tie clip in the design of a gun. He was known as Captain Midnight and usually stopped drivers of fancy cars and/or beautiful girls. It was rumored that he even asked women whom he ticketed for dates.

After going out together for some six months (or Clare's six weeks), I was frantic. Clare was a senior. She was going to graduate in June 1959, had already secured a job with the CIA, and would be leaving for Washington. I dreaded the end. Then something spectacular happened to help me. Majid Rahnema, the Sorbonne-educated, suave, and sophisticated consul general of Iran in San Francisco, invited me to represent Stanford University at a plush gala to celebrate the hundredth anniversary of the publication of Edward Fitzgerald's classic translation of the *Rubáiyát* of the celebrated Persian poet, Omar Khayyám. I rented a tuxedo and invited Clare, the most serious, elegant, beautiful, and smartest woman, to accompany me as my date.

The celebration took place at the California Palace of the Legion of Honor. Darius Milhaud had composed a piece for the occasion; Edward Teller gave a brilliant speech on the atomic theory of Omar Khayyám, reminding us that he was a great scientist and an algebraist; Stephen Spender, from London, gave a speech on the life and times of Edward Fitzgerald. There was Iranian music, caviar, champagne, great food, and an open bar. The entire diplomatic corps was there along with California's "beautiful people," the famous and literati. Mr. and Mrs. Rahnema had not overlooked

anything. It was a grand party. We had a great time, dancing, rubbing el-
bows with important figures, eating caviar, sipping our champagne. The
party was one of the most elegant ones for both of us. The evening was beautiful: there were shining stars in the sky along with a full moon.

As we were getting ready to leave, Mr. Rahnema thanked us for coming,
then he asked in Persian, "Who is this beautiful blond with you?" I told him,
in Persian, "She is wonderful, I love her. Who knows, one of these days I
may even marry her." We both laughed. Then he turned to Clare and said,
"Congratulations! When are you getting married?" That was certainly unexpected. Both of us sobered up very fast. Then came the long silent drive to
Stanford. It seemed to be an immense journey. We talked about the party.
Then silence. Suddenly Clare asked, "What was that talk about marriage?"

"Well," I said, practically trying to get out of my car, "one of these days,
when I finish my Ph.D. exams, and the dissertation, and get a job, I may ask
you to marry me." To my great surprise and delight, her answer was "If you
ask, the answer is yes." My reply was "I already did." We got engaged that
night. It was May 28, 1959. It was Armenian Independence Day.

Ten or eleven days later, Clare was to graduate from Stanford. Her parents and family were on their way to her graduation. They had never heard
of me and certainly did not know we were engaged. The next day, Clare
called her parents to tell them that she was engaged. It was a bad connection. "Guess what, Ma? I got engaged," Clare said. The phone line crackled
and hissed. "You are in jail, dear?" her mother responded. "He's Armenian," Clare said. "An Indian?" came the response. Her mother's final question was whether I was Christian.

I met her parents at the Oakland train station, full of anxiety. I had
washed my car, gotten a haircut and shoeshine, and was ready for them.
They were happy to see their maverick daughter and pleased to meet me.
After dinner at Ernie's in San Francisco, we drove Mr. and Mrs. Henry Russell from San Francisco to Palo Alto. It was a wild drive. I was so nervous
that I took the wrong street, a one-way street going the wrong direction. Her
parents were petrified but the hair-raising experience bonded us. They became my new family.

Clare's parents were very smart. Here was their daughter, an indepen-
dent-minded woman, who had decided to get engaged to a first-year graduate student. Was it an adventure or infatuation? To be sure, they insisted that
Clare move back east, find a job, and wait until I had finished my Ph.D.
exams and had gotten a job before we got married. When Clare told the
CIA she was marrying a foreigner, her job disappeared.

Bloomingdale's first branch, in Paramus, New Jersey, was hiring and

Clare went to work there for a few months before our wedding. She came to California to visit me at Thanksgiving and I visited her in New Jersey at Christmas. We kept in touch with each other almost on a daily basis through letters and also the dreadful telephone—long distance calls were so easy to make and so hard to pay for.

I was deeply moved that Clare decided also to learn Armenian, and was able to read and speak the western Armenian dialect after taking private lessons. We were married on March 25, 1960, in Tenafly, New Jersey. I thought I would have to wait for a year or two to earn some money to pay for the cost of the wedding. I did not know that in the United States it was the bride's parents who pay.

It was a great wedding party that Mr. and Mrs. Russell gave for us. They even ordered, in my honor, Armenian delicacies as hors d'oeuvres. The only sad part was that Clare was recovering from pneumonia and that I did not have a single relative present at my wedding. Clare's brother acted as my best man.

The next important official date that changed my life—and the course of my academic career—was April 15, 1960. It was the official date for the announcement of the list of Ph.D. candidates who had received the much coveted Ford Foreign Area Training Fellowships.

In the meantime, I had to pass my Ph.D. written exams (in five fields, including history and the humanities) and my oral exams as well (in the same five fields) during the hottest day in California history. The last question was asked by Professor Gordon Wright: What is the Treaty of Finkenstein? My answer: the 1807 treaty between the Shah of Persia and Napoleon. Anybody who knows the answer does not deserve to pass his exams, joked Professor Wright. I did not know that it was one of those cute questions that was asked to humble a student for being ignorant about at least one question.

The president of Stanford had nominated me as a suitable candidate for a Ford Foreign Area Training Fellowship, with endorsement letters from all of my professors. I had been interviewed by several selection committees. Even though the official announcement of the fellowship was April 15, I knew at least a month and a half earlier that I was one of the recipients, thanks to the generosity and compassion of Dorothy E. Soderlund. She was the program assistant in charge of the administration of Ford Foundation's Training in Research Fellowship.

On an impulse, I called Ms. Soderlund on March 1. I implored her to tell me if I was among those who had won a Ford Foreign Area Training Fellowship. I informed her that I was getting married on March 25. I was anxious enough and I did not want another anxiety to compound that one while

I waited for an announcement on April 15. I told her that practically the entire Armenian history was full of moral victories only; that I could take the bad news, but naturally I'd be overjoyed with good news and that she could consider a happy announcement as a wedding gift. She told me, with a great deal of caution and trepidation, that I had received an eleven-thousand-dollar grant. She warned me that I could not share the news of my good fortune with anyone, except perhaps my future wife. By telling me in advance of the official date, Ms. Soderlund had broken all the rules of the foundation; if it was divulged she would lose her job. Once again I pondered my luck. Here was another stranger who had reached out to help me, even if it meant taking a big risk.

Several years later, when Ms. Soderlund paid us a visit in San Francisco, I invited her for dinner at Aliotto's Restaurant at Fisherman's Wharf. We had a good time and a good meal. We drank many toasts. When the time came to pay, I almost fainted from shame for I had left my wallet at home. A radiant Ms. Soderlund roared with laughter. She paid the bill with a Ford Foundation credit card.

                            *   *   *

In the past forty years, I have reflected many times on the impact of Stanford on me, my education, and my career. In 1990, I had an opportunity to express publicly these reflections when I gave the following convocation speech on the occasion of Stanford's Centennial:

> "When I matriculated at Stanford, my command of the English language was both poor and inadequate. I found the USA, California, and Stanford fascinating, frustrating, bewildering, and exciting.
>
> The New World, with its dynamism, its freedoms, its optimism, its egalitarianism, its variety, its diversity and intensity was exhilarating; the social mores, the dating system bewildering; manifestations of discrimination and vestiges of racism appalling.
>
> Stanford became my gateway to the USA, my gateway to knowledge, to individualism and to citizenship. Stanford adopted me. The International Center became my home, and a cohort of professionals and community volunteers my extended family. And I married a Stanford graduate . . . I am therefore grateful to my alma mater.
>
> I am indebted to Stanford for giving me an opportunity to receive a broad and excellent education from scores of great teachers and scholars. It is they, the faculty, who make Stanford a great national and in-

ternational university. Thanks to its robust and rich curriculum I was privileged to have many intellectual encounters:

- The Old Testament, a book sacred to three major religions, and the New Testament, provided a distillation of human experience, for good and ill.
- The *Iliad* fascinated me for its fundamental modalities: the meaning of life, the importance of friendship, learning, and the realization of death.
- I read with awe the Nibelungen and the Norse myths: I was impressed with the power of Thor, the wisdom of Odin, the beauty of Idunn and the malice of Loki.
- *The Peloponnesian War* of Thucydides instructed me about human nature and history. I was moved by Pericles's funeral oration and later on by Lincoln's Gettysburg address.
- I recited *La Chanson de Roland,* mourned the death of Roland, traveled with Dante into the depths of human deprivation, devoured Hamlet and Macbeth, debated with Calvin and Luther, appreciated Erasmus, laughed with Cervantes, bore witness to the tragedy of Faust with Marlowe and Goethe, struggled with the Glorious Revolution, the American, the French, the Russian and Chinese Revolutions.
- I had encounters with liberalism, conservatism, socialism, anarchism, feminism, Marxism, fascism. I cried with the romantics, was uplifted by the symbolists, enthralled with existentialists. I agonized with W.E.B. Du Bois and later was enlightened by Martin Luther King's "Letter from the Birmingham Jail."
- My learning was not confined to the Western traditions alone, but I immersed myself in the fascinating world of Islam and the Islamic civilizations: I read the Quran, the works of al-Ghazali, Avicenna, Averroës, the *Shahnama* of Firdawsī, the poetry of Hafez, Saadi, Omar Khayyám, Bābā Tāher, Iqbāl, and Abu-Shabaki.
- I was fortunate to read the *Bhagavad Gita* and delve into the rich history and culture of India and the Indian subcontinent. Gandhi's philosophy and teachings inspired me. I was fortunate to study the histories of China and Japan, to read about Buddhism, Confucius, and Sun Tzu, to study Byzantium, the

Ottoman Empire and the Balkans, the Middle East, East
Europe and Russia, Latin America, and North Africa.

At Stanford I learned a fundamental lesson: that we cannot and
must not lose our sense of history and our memory for they constitute
our identity. We cannot be prisoners of the present and wander out of
history. For a society without a deep historical memory, the future
ceases to exist and the present becomes a meaningless cacophony.

While I immersed myself in the humanities, arts, and social sciences, I cheated myself. Burdened with an inadequate background in
the sciences and a handicap with the English language, fearful of not
getting good grades, I sacrificed a fundamental ingredient of a solid
liberal education: I did not take courses in the physical and life sciences. One course I dared to take was geology, which I had to drop,
for I thought it was a mystical séance."*

That day I did not confess about one of my most embarrassing experiences
at Stanford. I did not want to take a course in physics, which was required. In
Beirut I had taken physics and chemistry in French and passed with difficulty.
Botany and mathematics were all right. Since it was freshman physics and it
was in English, I did not want to take it. I was afraid it would lower my grade
point average. I was told I had to take it and that the only way I could avoid
doing so was with the approval of the freshman physics advisor.

I went to see him. I explained that I was a graduate of the Collège Arménien, that I had taken two years of physics and chemistry, and, therefore,
I did not wish to repeat it. He asked me what my textbook was. I told him it
was a coauthored book, and I knew one of the names but had forgotten the
other. So I made up the second name. "Funny," my interlocutor said, "I have
not heard of that one." I said, "If you want to test me on any aspects of freshman physics, I'll be happy to comply." And, I don't know why, but I added,
"even the law of relativity." "Tell me about it," he said. I responded, "Inertial
frameworks are equivalent for the descriptions of all physical phenomenon
and that the speed of light in empty space is constant for every observer." After a pause, I added, "If everything in the universe was multiplied ten times,
nothing would change." Thank God he did not ask me what it meant because I had read it in *Reader's Digest* and memorized it.

"Ok, you don't have to take freshman physics," he said. I took the form
and was ready to leave his office when I saw the freshman physics' advisor's

* "A Convocation Address Commemorating 100 Years at Stanford University" (1990).

picture with Albert Einstein. My knees buckled, I practically crawled out of his office. I was full of shame. The freshman physics advisor was Professor Richard Hofstadter, who later received the Nobel Prize. It took me a year or so to go see him and apologize. I am sure the only reason he did not want me to take freshman physics was to spare his colleagues from a real bore.

I also did not tell those gathered at Stanford's Centennial Convocation that I had witten to my friends and to Vratzian that, while everyone had to take freshman English (I think it was called English 1 or 5), I was taking Speech and Drama 101. I was so proud of that, until I realized that all the students in my class were also foreign students and that the instructor, a Lieutenant Colonel Maxwell from Hamilton Air Force Base, was a speech pathologist!

He tried desperately to have us differentiate pronunciations of "the" and "d," "w" and "v," and asked us to go around the campus to pick up unfamiliar English words or expressions and make a list of interesting euphemisms. My list included the expression, "It's cool, man," which I found very confusing. I understood when boys and men called each other "hey, guys," but did not know why some women called other women "guys." Many of us were puzzled by the expressions "funeral homes" and "funeral parlors." We had heard of ice cream parlors but "funeral parlors"? We had not heard the expressions "passed on" or "passed away" in lieu of "dying" or "deceased" in lieu of "dead." Nor had we heard the expression that somebody had "kicked the bucket," meaning a person had died. Why "kick the bucket"? What kind of bucket?

Another mystery was "the die is cast," which I later frouund out referred to an ancient backgammon-type game governed by dice.† When the dice were rolled, it meant there was no turning back. Perhaps the most perplexing to me personally was that I did not understand why Good Friday was called Good Friday. "Because Christ died," Mr. Maxwell told me. "Why is that good?" I asked. "Because if he had not died, he would not have been resurrected," Mr. Maxwell replied. That did not satisfy me. After all, in the Armenian Church, the entire week leading to Easter is known as Senior— Senior Monday to Senior Friday. After some research in ancient dictionaries, I triumphantly announced to the class that during the Middle Ages Good Friday meant "pious" Friday.

I soon realized that not having a native-born American's familiarity with nursery ryhmes, Sunday school references to the Bible, comic strips, and cartoon characters, national sports like baseball and football, and countless

---

† Shakespeare's *Julius Caesar* made the expression famous; it is what Caesar said on crossing the river Rubicon to invade Italy in 49 B.C.

other aspects of American culture prevents one from appreciating many literary allusions and other references in the English language. I also discovered the dangerous impact of headlines in this country, which were devious allies in prompting me to skip prepositions and definite articles.

*   *   *

During the Centennial Celebration, as I delivered my convocation address, I looked at the audience and I became very emotional, for there in the audience were most of my professors, many friends, and, of course, my wife. It was an overwhelming occasion for me as I realized how far I had come, how much I had learned while at Stanford and from Stanford, how much I had done since I left Stanford, how much I owed Stanford, and how so many generous strangers had helped me. In the process, Stanford had taught me not only a new language but also opened up many doors to a fascinating future.

*   *   *

The news of my marriage surprised everyone, friends and relatives alike. The fact that I had married a non-Armenian, an *odar* (foreigner), raised the ire of some Armenians in San Francisco, Beirut, and Tehran. They were dismayed, disappointed, and angry. I was asked time and time again—why did I not fall in love with and marry a nice Armenian girl? Rumors began to circulate that Mrs. Russell, my mother-in-law, had Armenian blood, and therefore Clare must have some Armenian blood too.

In early August 1960, Clare and I sailed aboard the SS *New Amsterdam* to England, where I would begin my research on Afghanistan in the British Museum and Public Records Office. Even though I had been in Beirut for some six years and occasionally visited the port to see major passenger and cargo ships, I had never been on one. The prospect of crossing the Atlantic Ocean on a ship was very exciting. While getting ready to leave for Europe, Clare learned that she was pregnant. We were very surprised, daunted, and excited. We had to revise our schedule and cut short most of our travel plans. The ship was huge, multilevel, and extensive. Its dining rooms, movie houses, athletic facilities, educational and entertainment programs, and the cuisine were most impressive. There was dancing, chamber music, lectures, and, to my great amazement, gambling. We enjoyed the trip very much. What made it even more special was the fact that Professor Wayne Vucinich, our teacher and my mentor, was also on board. He was headed to England and from there to the Balkans.

Clare and the entire Russell family had spent a month in London in 1950.

This was my second trip. I had stopped there on my way to the United States in 1956, but I had not seen much of it. I had read a lot about England. I was in awe of the courage of its citizens during World War II, especially during the Battle of Britain. As a historian, I was always curious about how the United Kingdom, a small country, and its people, through their military power, economy, financial acumen, effective bureaucracy, and diplomacy were able to conquer and rule vast chunks of the world, affecting the collective and individual lives of millions and millions of people around the globe.

Not unlike many tourists, we visited all the major historical and cultural sites of London. We saw the Royal Guards. We witnessed many impressive parades and a great deal of pageantry. The traffic, the order, the queues, the temperament of the English people, their manners were all impressive. For me, the most important institution was the world-famous British Museum. It embodied the power and the majesty of Great Britain and was the repository of humanity. I was there every morning before its doors opened and was the last one to leave.

The museum's great reading room had a humbling effect on everyone. As you looked around, you saw hundreds of scholars, journalists, government officials, students, businessmen, and artists working. It seemed as if the British Museum was the United Nations of the Republic of Knowledge. The "readers" came in all shapes, sizes, and colors, as well as accents. While sitting in the magnificent reading room, you could not help wondering about these individuals—what are they reading and writing? How many conservative, radical, and liberal documents were being written? What inventions and philosophical and scientific treatises were soon to emanate from there? Who had occupied my chair in the nineteenth century? Marx, Darwin, Lenin? Who among a legion of British and expatriate writers, poets, statesmen, politicians, intellectuals, revolutionaries, and artists had labored at the museum?

As you looked up, you saw row after row of books, hundreds of thousands of volumes that surrounded you. Suddenly, an uneasy feeling gripped you. You asked yourself: What are you going to contribute to the World of Knowledge that has not been already done? Is there even a place left in the library to accommodate one's very slim volume? One thing I knew right away was how to spot an American at the museum. Between ten and ten-thirty every day there was a great commotion in the reading room. Americans were getting ready for their coffee breaks. I felt guilty about taking any breaks. Time was too scarce.

While in London, we saw many movies and theater performances and went to nightclubs. I was surprised to find out that nightclubs were considered exclusive. One had to be a "member" to get in. I took Clare to

Murray's Club, only to find out that not only were we probably the only married couple in the place but that she was the sole seven-months' pregnant woman on the dance floor. Later we learned that Murray's Club was one of the places where War Minister John Profumo's scandalous affair with call girl Christine Keeler took place.

While I spent six days a week at the British Museum and the Public Record Office, Clare visited all the museums and watched all the parades. Sundays were spent going to the movies and listening to Radio Luxemburg. We did not have a TV. November 1960 was Clare's first election to vote in and we stayed up all night waiting for the final results of the Nixon-Kennedy election contest. It was a huge relief when Kennedy won. It is a cliché that it usually rains in London, but in 1960 it seemed as if it *was* raining every day and night. It was often dark and gloomy. I was surprised that each movie program was preceded by the British national anthem. Our rented studio apartment in Holland Park was a disaster. We had no heat, no curtains, a wet bed, and discontinued electricity. When I complained, our Romanian landlady responded, "I do not want to partake in an Oriental bazaar." Having paid two months of rent in advance, I had to go to the local police, only to find out that that studio had been condemned as an unfit dwelling and that the landlady had no right to rent it to us. It was not a pleasant encounter.

The holidays presented another difficulty. Thanksgiving was (and still is) my wife's most cherished holiday and Thanksgiving 1960 was her second away from her home. Besides, she was in a foreign country, pregnant, and very isolated. As we had only a gas ring for cooking, we arranged with Antoine's, a French restaurant in Chelsea, to make us a Thanksgiving dinner, carefully explaining every part of the traditional meal. We invited Dr. and Mrs. Hart and a colleague of his and his wife's to join us for dinner there. (Dr. Hart was a physician whom we had met through one of Clare's relatives.) It was a great dinner, but it did not approximate the American Thanksgiving. The Harts and their friends were enormously relieved when we told them Thanksgiving had absolutely no connection with the Revolution.

After the holidays, we traveled from London to Paris. It was one of the worst and scariest trips I've ever been on. The weather was stormy, so the nighttime crossing was rough. Clare had to be tied to a bunk so that she didn't fall off. She actually appreciated this safety measure after initial resistance. I was seasick. That trip wiped out all the romance that I had associated with crossing the Channel. The novelists had been kind to it.

In 1956, I had spent two weeks in Paris and had fallen in love with it. It is an incredible city, a city of cities, many cities bundled into one. For me it was a city of nostalgia. It was as if I had been there many times, albeit vicariously, through literature and history. I knew the monuments, the streets, the institutions, even some of the restaurants, through the novels of Victor Hugo, Alexander Dumas, Honoré de Balzac, and Emile Zola. I was familiar with the Left Bank, the favorite restaurants frequented by such existentialist luminaries as Jean-Paul Sartre, Simone de Beauvoir, and Albert Camus. I am sure each visitor has his or her own Paris!

We were enchanted with Paris and Clare found it a far more congenial place than London. Although I spent my days at the Bibliothèque Nationale, I found occasions to hear my favorite French singers, Edith Piaf and Jacqueline Françoise. We went to the famous Père Lachaise cemetery. What fascinated me was not that so many famous historical, artistic, and literary figures were buried there but that there was a section for dogs.

There was a robust Armenian community in Paris. There were Armenian bookstores, libraries, newspapers, periodicals, and, of course, a church. Clare and I visited the Armenian church on a beautiful Sunday morning. The church, near the Arc de Triomphe, was stunning, the choir spectacular, the service intimate. I was very energized; the liturgy reminded me of my childhood days when I was an altar boy and of many of my friends.

After our month in Paris, we went on to Beirut. During the flight, I could not help wondering about how my life had changed in the past ten years. On my first trip to Beirut, I had arrived with nothing but three letters of recommendation and fifty dollars. I was alone, anxious, and scared. Now, I was arriving from Paris, married and, thanks to the Ford Foundation, with plenty of money. Yet I was anxious once again, this time about the impending birth of a child. How would my wife, with our soon-to-be-born child, cope with the difficulties of a foreign country? Would she be welcomed by the Armenian community, my teachers, my friends, and, in particular, by Mr. Vratzian?

I had managed to finish high school and college. Now that I was ready to finish the last phase of my Ph.D. degree, I was worried about my research in Afghanistan. Would I be able to succeed? What would be the consequences of my being an Iranian citizen and permanent resident of the United States? But what worried me most of all was that for health and safety reasons I would not be able to take Clare and a brand-new baby with me on this part of my trip. How would my wife and child fare in Beirut without me?

We landed in the city on December 30, 1960. We stayed at the Hotel

Rivoli, in the center of Beirut, above the Rivoli movie house. I had chosen that hotel in the mistaken belief that it was one of the best hotels in Beirut. It was, however, neither comfortable nor elegant nor clean.

New Year's Eve was remarkable. We watched from the hotel as several hundred cars drove around the square, honking their horns to celebrate the arrival of a new year. Inside the hotel we were witnesses to a squad of king-size cockroaches in the bathtub and shower, doing their own celebration. Clare was horrified. She had never seen such gigantic night creatures, in fact had never seen a cockroach before, ever.

The first thing I did was to visit the Collège Arménien. I entered the Collège with great fear and anxiety, intent on paying a courtesy call on my teachers and Mr. Vratzian. I knew Mr. Vratzian was unhappy, indeed angry, with me, not because I married a non-Armenian (after all, he had married one also, a Russian Jew), but because to him my marriage was an early indication that I would not be settling in Beirut.

He had been reluctant to see me pursue the goal of a Ph.D. degree for the same reason but was persuaded about the desirability of my quest based on several factors, one of which was that the Collège had supported me for two years instead of four. During that short period I had obtained my B.A. with honors. Subsequently, I was awarded a Stanford University Graduate Fellowship to continue my education. I was self-supporting and not dependent on the Collège Arménien. He had written to me to the effect that when I first came to Beirut, I was a small fish in a big pond. From now on, he concluded, I would be a big fish in a small pond. It is fair to say that our relations were strained. Indeed, we had exchanged angry letters. All kinds of individuals from America and Beirut had begun to poison our relationship and friendship. I was distraught and felt guilty. The last thing I desired was to hurt Mr. Vratzian's feelings. After all, he was my surrogate father, teacher, and mentor. I loved him. Everything I had accomplished during the past ten years I owed primarily to him. Having served as his private secretary for several years, I knew that Mr. Vratzian kept grudges for a lifetime. Once he crossed you off his list, that was it!

As I entered his office, there was an awkward silence, then we embraced each other. We both became very emotional. I actually cried, but my tears were of joy. I had not lost Mr. Vratzian. Once again I began to help him with his memoirs and scholarly work. We resumed our close relationship. Mr. Vratzian extended a very cordial reception to Clare. He became very fond of her, admiring her courage, tenacity, and independence. He was touched by the fact that out of her love for me and interest in Armenian culture she had learned Armenian and continued to take Armenian lessons.

Having rented a furnished apartment behind the Bristol Hotel, I had hoped to evade the presence of dancing and flying cockroaches. Unfortunately that was not to be. Every night I attacked a new batch of them with an umbrella, "massacred" them, but each night a new squadron arrived. As we were expecting a newborn, we wanted to be sure that the apartment was clean.

Our son Vahé was born in Beirut on January 28, 1961, at Dr. Sahakian's private maternity ward. (Dr. Sahakian was a professor at the American University of Beirut.) It was very hard for Clare. She was in a foreign country, separated from her parents, and without female friends. The night Vahé was born I was in seventh heaven. I was overwhelmed with joy. When I first saw him, I wept. He was a handsome, even beautiful baby with beautiful eyes. I could not believe it. I could not imagine myself as a father! I had had no role model. The idea of having a child, a son, a family was extraordinary, joyful, and intoxicating. That joy almost turned into a nightmare. The night Vahé was born, I almost died. I took a taxicab to go home, but it turned out the driver was a kamikaze. Challenged by another taxicab driver, he began a drag race with him. On a two-way street, they were racing side by side. I was so petrified I was shaking. I asked my driver to stop, but he ignored me. I begged him, attempted to bribe him if he stopped, all to no avail. I told myself that maybe God has a plan for me—as soon as I had a son, I would die. One life in, one life out.

Clare's stamina, courage, adaptability, comportment, and bravery in a foreign land became the subject of much admiration within the Armenian community of Beirut. An American-Armenian woman, Mary Dakoozlian, from Chicago, Illinois, who resided in Beirut, adopted Clare, appearing one day at the maternity clinic to introduce herself. So did Sir, my English teacher, my high school classmate, Sahag Baghdassarian, and his extended family, three surrogate families from the time I attended Collège Arménien, as well as two members of the board of directors of the Collège, Dr. and Mrs. Konyalian and Vahé Setian, and scores of others, including Antoine Bustani, my Arabic teacher.

Mr. Vratzian visited Clare in the hospital and gave Vahé a small golden spoon as a token of his affection. To cheer Clare, Mr. Vratzian, my friends, and some of my former teachers sent flowers. I felt great. My wife had been accepted by my friends and my community! The Collège heralded my return to Beirut by organizing two public lectures under the auspices of Mr. Vratzian.

After Vahé's birth, I took some time to reacquaint myself with Beirut, and with Lebanon. On the surface not much had changed during my five-year absence, but in reality, there were many changes. Arab nationalism was in full swing. There was great emphasis on the instruction of the Arabic language. A new Lebanese Arab university was founded to serve as a countervailing force vis-à-vis the American University of Beirut and Saint Joseph University. The city was still beautiful and the living conditions were much improved, except for those in the Palestinian refugee camps. Lebanon was prosperous. I was happy that unlike in the past I could now afford to be independent, go to restaurants, seaside cafés, and as many movies as our time and circumstances permitted. I could afford to be charitable and even give contributions to the Armenian Relief Society and Collège Arménien and invite my teachers and friends to be our guests for a change.

I saw that multitudes of newspapers were not the only outlets for public opinion and opinion makers. The movie theaters occasionally provided yet another venue. I remember vividly the showing of *The Crusaders*. When Saladdin entered Jerusalem, all the Muslims in the audience applauded vigorously. When Richard the Lionheart conquered Jerusalem, the Christians responded with a greater energy. Even the movies had become "battlefields."

A month after Vahé's birth, I left Clare and him in Beirut and headed for Tehran, Karachi, New Delhi, Amritsar, Peshawar, and Kabul. The Ford Foundation Foreign Area Training Fellowship had given me a unique opportunity to visit all these cities to study all the available historical literature that pertained to Afghanistan. Because I had to leave Clare and Vahé, it was gratifying to see how friends of mine and family contacts of hers all banded together to assist and protect them during my absence. They took Clare out for dinners, movies, and family gatherings. A few months later, Sir even found a part-time teaching position for her at the Armenian Sisters Hripsimiantz school. She taught English. According to the principal, she was a very good, conscientious, hardworking teacher, but there were no textbooks and she had to rely on material Sir would create for her. Sometimes, however, languages play tricks on one, and Clare was no exception. When she attempted to make the class be quiet and pay attention she said, "Shush." Invariably the class would laugh. To the students, *"sha'sh"* meant cross-eyed.

CHAPTER SEVEN

The Long Road to Kabul

On the way to Kabul, I stopped in Tehran. I had not seen my grandmother, my sister and her family, or my parents and friends for five years. My father, who was working for the Iranian National Oil Company at the airport, greeted me with a warm embrace. All my relatives, including some from my stepmother's side, my cousin Bobken and his family, and many of my friends were there.

From what I could see from the car window as we traveled through the city streets, Tehran, cold and crisp, looked prosperous. You could see snow on Alborz Mountain. People were well dressed and fashionable. The pace of the city was incredible, as was the traffic. I stayed with my parents in their small apartment. They offered me their bed, which I declined. One had to preserve the etiquette. One stayed with one's family. One did not stay in a hotel.

Visiting Iran was an ordeal if you were a student. You had to receive permission from the Ministry of Education—in my case, permission to extend my passport for one more year because I was working on my dissertation. You needed an entry visa and an exit visa, even if you had a valid passport. My permission from the ministry was granted early. They were proud of me, although perplexed as to why I would want to study Afghanistan and not Iran.

My passport, however, had not been delivered from the airport to the Ministry of Education. (They collect your passport at the airport and when you want to leave you have to go and fetch it). It was irritating. You come to your country with great joy, but then meet bureaucratic hurdles. "When can I get my passport?" I inquired. "*Inshallah* (God willing), tomorrow" was the reply. Twelve Inshallahs later, I went to see Ahmad Eghbal, an old acquaintance, the former consul general of Iran in San Francisco, who was now deputy foreign minister. It was purely a social call, though I hoped he would ask about my impending trip to Afghanistan and the difficulties I had encountered. He did and I retrieved my passport. There was a catch, however. I had one exit and one transit visa, which meant that I could not return to Iran from Afghanistan unless I was determined to start the formalities all over again. I wrote to Clare that, miracle of miracles, I had managed to get my passport without bribery.

While I was polite, I could no longer stand those who bent their entire body in a servile manner or use flattery of the highest order just to obtain what is their right as an Iranian, Lebanese, or American. I could not bear to describe myself as "your humble and most obedient subject." I could not bend. America had "corrupted" me. My attitude did not bother Mr. Eghbal. He wrote three recommendations on my behalf: one to the librarian of the Iranian parliament, the others to the Iranian ambassadors in Pakistan and Afghanistan.

There was a bright spot among all the encounters with the bureaucracy, proving that life does have its ironies. In Beirut, a couple of officials of the Iranian embassy in Lebanon had given me grief over my entry visa to Iran. The day I went to see Mr. Eghbal, the two were waiting to see him. Mr. Eghbal kept me for an hour. As I left, his assistant told the bureaucrats that the boss was busy and that they should come back tomorrow. I looked at them with studied satisfaction.

Returning home, while exciting, has its many disappointing moments, too. I realized that I had forgotten many distant relatives over the past decade and felt negligent. In Tehran, I received a warm reception by the leaders as well as the rank-and-file members of the Armenian community. Sako, the official photographer of the Royal Palace, took my picture but refused any payment. "You are our nation's lighthouse," he said. The remark reminded me of British prime minister Lloyd George's description of Marshal Haig during World War I, comparing his mind to a lighthouse: "Once in a while there was a light beam, followed by prolonged periods of darkness."

I took the train to Tabriz to see my grandmother, a journey of eighteen hours. She was so moved, so thrilled, that her voice failed for a couple of minutes. She was completely paralyzed. There were tears of joy. I celebrated my first wedding anniversary with my grandmother. She had Clare's and Vahé's pictures. She kissed them and put them on her heart. Her eyes were shining and she was smiling. I was smiling and crying tears of happiness.

But the sight of the city saddened me. It seemed as if nothing had changed in a decade, as if the entire city had come to a standstill—same shops, same shopkeepers, same products, same décors, same arrangement of fruits and vegetables, same unshaven grocer. As in the good old times, life stopped at seven P.M. in Tabriz.

My formerly great city seemed to me a great village. I felt sad and anxious, as if the entire place was decaying and nobody was noticing. It seemed to have been abandoned not only by the government but by its own people. I wrote to Clare that Iran was like a rich head with a naked body. I thought that maybe having seen Beirut, London, Paris, New York, San Francisco, and Chicago had changed my parochial perspective.

My emotional reunion with my grandmother turned out to be the last. On the eve of my departure, we went to the cemetery to burn incense and to bid good-bye to the graves of my mother, grandfather, uncles, and brothers. I discovered that my grandmother did not believe that while it was daytime in Tabriz, it was night in San Francisco. I told her there were parts of the Earth where there was constant light for months. She did not believe a word of it. She thought I was pulling her leg. Maybe she was pulling mine.

All my relatives were upset that I had left Clare and Vahé in Beirut instead of bringing them along. I told them that the problem was that they had to obtain Iranian passports and citizenship. But the real reason was that I did not want my father and stepmother to boss my family around in a strange land, since Clare would have to rely on them in my absence.

On April 1, 1961, I left for Kabul on an Ariana Afghan Airline DC-4. Along with Soviet Aeroflot and Air India, that was Afghanistan's only link with the outside world. The plane was late and it took four hours to reach Kandahar airport. We had to stay overnight; planes could not fly at night, as they did not have radar nor did the airport have any guiding lights.

The hotel where I stayed was so dirty and cold that I decided to sleep in my clothes with a blanket and overcoat. While hotel amenities were lousy or nonexistent, the cuisine was great. My companions included Mr. Krugger, the representative of the Krupp industries (he was traveling to Kabul to set up a factory as part of a billion-dollar German investment earmarked for underdeveloped countries); Dr. Taraki, an Afghan, the holder of a Ph.D.

from the University of Chicago and the director of the Afghan Institute of Education, and his American wife; a Greek-Australian salesman arriving from England (he was a sales representative of Imperial Carbon Paper, who was determined to sell carbon paper for Afghanistan's typewriters); Professor and Mrs. Charles Stewart from the University of Illinois, who were arriving to advise the U.S. embassy as agricultural experts; and Hal Cooper, from Long Island, who represented an American pharmaceutical company with the mission of opening a market for the sale of drugs, primarily penicillin.

After we had eaten a breakfast of bread, boiled eggs, yogurt, and honey, a Mercedes-Benz bus picked us up for the journey to Kabul. Unfortunately, the driver got lost and then got stuck in the mud. All of us, except the women and children, two Egyptian religious scholars, and an Afghan "nobleman," got out and pushed the bus. The Afghan nobleman was a bore, as he told his spellbound audience about his "experiences" with women in Europe, Istanbul, and elsewhere. Then we encountered a flooded road and had to get out again. We did so at least six times. Toward the end, a U.S. navy truck picked us up and we managed to cross the road. Professor Stewart and his wife started singing, "Merrily we roll along . . ." But nobody was in the mood to join in even if they knew the words.

In Kabul, we had to retrieve our luggage and go through customs. There was a long line that was not moving. There was one supervisor and one clerk trying to sort out all kinds of complicated documents. I knew instantly what was wrong. The clerk was trying to register passports and needed information on expiration dates but could not find them. I asked him gently if I could be of some help. He said no, but it was not a firm no, so I started reading passports and giving the dates to him in Persian. Pretty soon I was sitting next to him, assisting him and directing traffic, checking out ordinary and diplomatic passports. I managed to clear all the luggage without its being searched. Then I managed to get porters to carry the Americans' baggage, always under the watchful eyes of Soviet citizens who had been waiting for an hour or so. Then I helped register all the passports of my companions with the Afghan police within the same day. The next day, when I went to the U.S. embassy, the U.S. consul greeted me warmly in Persian. He thought I was an Afghan customs official!

Hotel Kabul, the main hotel of the Afghan capital, was paradise compared to the one in Kandahar. It was solid, clean, airy, and cheap. The first-class rooms with private baths were 450 afghanis ($11.50) a day, the second-class, 300 afghanis. A complete breakfast was 20 afghanis (50 cents); lunch and dinner were each 40 afghanis ($1).

1

The author on the occasion of his appointment (1981) as president of the New York Public Library, with Patience, one of the Library's two lions.

Clockwise, from left: The author, nine months old, and his mother, Shoushik; the author, nine months old; the author, three years old.

2

3

4

Clockwise, from left: The author's grandmother Voski Mirzaian (1882–1964); his mother, Shoushik Gregorian (1915–1941); his father, Samuel B. Gregorian (1908–1995); his sister, Ojik Gregorian, in 1955.

5

6

8

7

9

Picture of the author in 1954 (Beirut) sent to his grandmother.

Below: The author and his grandmother and Simon Vratzian in Tabriz (1956).

10

11

The author, Ter Karapet, the vicar of St. Sarkis Armenian Apostolic Church of Tabriz, and Simon Vratzian (Tabriz, 1956). In 1966, Ter Karapet baptized the Gregorians' sons, Vahé and Raffi, in the same church where the author's parents were married and he was baptized.

Simon Vratzian (1882–1969), the last prime minister of the Independent Armenian Republic (Tabriz, 1921). He served as the director of the Collège Arménien from 1951 to 1969.

12

Simon Vratzian, director of the Collège Arménien, surrounded by nine graduates of the class of 1955 and by principal teachers of the Collège. The author is in the third row, fourth from the left.

The author, his car, and Peter Kirianoff (1957).

Below: The author and his wife, Clare Russell Gregorian, on their wedding day (March 25, 1960).

Model United Nations Security Council panel discussion on the Suez Crisis (Stanford University, October 1956). Bernard Lourier, representing France, Professor Christine Phelps Harris, the moderator, and the author, representing Iran.

John Silber, dean of the College of Arts and Sciences, University of Texas at Austin (1970).

Above, left: The Honorable Walter H. Annenberg (1908–2002) and the author in "Sunnylands" (Palm Springs, California, 2000). Mr. Annenberg was the publisher of Triangle Publications, Inc., which included the *Philadelphia Inquirer, TV Guide, Philadelphia Daily News,* and many others. He served as U.S. ambassador to Great Britain. He was a life trustee of the University of Pennsylvania, its greatest benefactor, and, for more than three decades, a wonderful personal friend.

Above, right: Martin Meyerson, president of the University of Pennsylvania (1970–1981).

Facing page: The Honorable Thomas S. Gates Jr. (1906–1983) and the author. He was a life trustee of the University of Pennsylvania (where his father was president from 1930 to 1944). Mr. Gates Jr. served as secretary of the navy and secretary of defense in the Eisenhower Administration. In 1976, he was appointed by President Gerald Ford as the head of the U.S. Liaison Office of the People's Republic of China. He served as chairman of the board and CEO of J. P. Morgan. He was a good friend and mentor during the author's tenure as dean of the Faculty of Arts and Sciences and provost of the University of Pennsylvania.

The author, dean of the Faculty
of Arts and Sciences, University of
Pennsylvania (1974–1978).

Below: President Meyerson and
Provost Gregorian (1979).

21

22

20

23

Brooke Astor (Mrs. Vincent Astor) and the author (1982). Mrs. Astor was the honorary chairman of the Board of Trustees of the New York Public Library and one of its major benefactors.

Jacqueline Kennedy Onassis, Brooke Astor, Clare Gregorian, and the author (1982).

Literary Lions dinner (1983). *From left:* The author, Clare Gregorian, Andrew Heiskell, Marian Heiskell, Richard Salomon, and Edna Salomon.

Literary Lions (1983). *Front row from left:* Joseph Alsop, James Baldwin, Ruth Prawer Jhabvala, Sumner Locke Elliot, James Thomas Flexner, Laura Hobson, Chaim Potok. *Second row:* Philip Roth, Swan Mary Alsop, Ved Mehta, Elizabeth Hardwick, Ann Beattie, Herman Wouk. *Third row:* Peter Matthiessen, George Plimpton, Frances FitzGerald, Elie Wiesel, William Manchester, William Styron, Harrison Salisbury. *Fourth row:* John Kenneth Galbraith, Susan Sontag, Arthur Miller.

Providence Sunday Journal Magazine article introducing the new president of Brown University to the people of Rhode Island (December 1989).

The formal installation of the author as president of Brown University (April 1989). Chancellor Alva O. Way *(left)* and Charles Tillinghast, senior fellow and chancellor emeritus *(right)*.

The author and his sons *(from left):* Vahé, Raffi, and Dareh Ardashes.

First Ladies *(clockwise, from left):* Barbara Bush and the author; Laura Bush and the author; Hillary Rodham Clinton and the author.

30

31

32

The author and his sons *(from left):* Raffi, Dareh Ardashes, and Vahé.

The author and his wife, Clare Russell Gregorian.

The most interesting character I met during my entire stay in Afghanistan was the Greek-Australian salesman of the carbon paper company. He had a row at the hotel, asserting that he had a reservation. "You don't, sir," said the manager. "What kind of outfit is this?" he raised his voice. "Don't you receive any telegrams? I sent one from London confirming my reservation." But the hotel was full. So I volunteered to give him one of my two bedrooms. He was grateful. But most important, so was the hotel director. I learned from my new friend that his real occupation was that of an antiques dealer and that he was traveling under the auspices of the carbon paper company in order to defray his costs. His advice to me: If you carry American Express Travelers Cheques, and if you are in a "Godforsaken" country such as Afghanistan, cash them and declare the cheques stolen. Then get them replaced at your next stop. Companies don't investigate small sums in exotic lands. I pointed out that that was unethical as well as illegal. "No wonder you are poor, and you will always remain poor," he replied with great sympathy.

He also advised me not to carry a heavy briefcase, as that signifies that you work for somebody else. Have a thin attaché case and never, never begin sentences with "Excuse me." It puts you in the position of a supplicant. He asked for my help in the Kabul bazaar. We made inquiries at the hotel for the proprietor of the biggest stationery store in Kabul and we went to see him in his shop, a humble establishment.

"Good morning, Haji Mustapha," he greeted the shop owner. "How did you know my name?" asked the merchant. "I am from London. Everybody knows about your being the owner of the most important stationery shop in Kabul. Did you not get my telegram? Pity." Within half an hour, he had sold fifty pounds sterling worth of carbon paper and made the merchant the official representative of his company in the kingdom of Afghanistan. The next stop was the Ministry of Foreign Affairs, which had the largest number of typewriters in Afghanistan. Again he claimed that he had sent a telegram from London. He succeeded in selling carbon paper to the Ministry of Foreign Affairs.

When it came time for him to leave, he took hundreds of afghanis from his pockets and placed them all before me. "Take all this dirty money. I am leaving. Pay my share of the hotel bill, keep the rest or give it to the hotel staff." "No, no," I said. "I can't take advantage of you. Let us check out, then I'll reregister. Each of us should pay his own bill." We did just that. In the process I found out that he had charged all his expenses to me. When confronted with that, he replied that he wanted to check whether Armenians are as smart as they are thought to be. I have never forgotten him.

My days in Afghanistan were pretty regular and monotonous. After breakfast, I spent my entire day at the headquarters of the Délégation Archéologique Française, going through their rich collection of European literature on Afghanistan. Occasionally, on Sundays, I visited the Italian church located at the Italian embassy. It was the only official church in the entire kingdom.

The social life of Americans in Kabul consisted of visiting each other's houses and attending formal receptions given by the U.S. embassy and other foreign missions. The dominant discussion during these social gatherings was the "servant problem" and "housing costs." (Houses were rented for 5,000 afghanis a month [$120], a "sumptious mansion" for 10,000 afghanis [$240].) A competent cook could be hired for 1,500 afghanis a month ($35) and a *bacha* (boy) who cleaned the house and did odd jobs was paid $12.50 a month, plus food. I was told, "There was nothing servile about an Afghan servant." "Good ones are hard to find; honest ones are practically impossible to find." "It is impossible to get along *without* servants and sometimes impossible to get along *with* them." Most Americans in Afghanistan had never had any servants. They had no clue about how to treat them, and they often either spoiled them or offended them. There was constant friction. There were no female servants.

Afghans were referred to as locals or natives, and every once in a while, nonwhites. Even the U.S. embassy gave two separate parties: one for local drivers and the other for American drivers. Americans were discouraged from riding local buses or even in taxis. The embassy used up to twenty minibuses to circulate in Kabul and pick up Americans.

Most foreigners in Afghanistan, especially those from Europe, frequented the International Club of Kabul. It had tennis courts, a swimming pool, a dining room, a bar, and a lounge. Membership was about five dollars a month. It was not much but it was the only joint in the entire kingdom of Afghanistan, other than the embassies, where there was an open bar. It was a sad place, where Germans, French, Englishmen, and Swiss sat separately. The Americans too. Soviet citizens did not frequent the club but when they came, they had one drink and left. There was no dancing. Lonely people sat around, until a married couple or a single woman showed up, at which point they all drifted toward them. All the talk at the club was about sex, boredom, and what to do without women. Most of the patrons were married men. They told each other that Afghan women (gradually becoming visible) were beautiful but you could not pursue them, as your throat would be cut.

The International Club was home to many alcoholics. People drank from eight to eleven P.M., waiting for a female to walk in. They talked about their mistresses (wives of other colleagues or members of a foreign contingent).

They whispered about a clandestine house of prostitution: "A well-kept secret and well guarded." The penalty for being caught there was three years in prison. The others were envious of Americans who had cocktail parties and dinners every night.

One evening, I met a Soviet official, a Russian. Already high, he asked me to join him. It was a big mistake. After several drinks we began a discussion about freedom and its meaning. Our "discussion" turned into a nasty argument. The more he drank, the angrier he became. I realized that the Cuban missile crisis and the Cold War had found a new front at the International Club of Kabul. The Soviet was denouncing America, the Americans, our institutions, and our record as a "colonial power." At first I tried to joke by telling him the first Cold War joke I had heard in Tabriz in 1946: An American soldier tells a Soviet soldier that America is so free that he could go and stand in front of the White House and yell, "I hate Truman's guts." The Soviet soldier replies, "Big deal. I can go stand in front of the Kremlin and yell, 'I hate Truman's guts, too.' "

My companion was not amused. I told him that I could express any opinion about any subject I wanted even if I was wrong and that in itself was a gift of freedom. "If I wanted to be provocative I could state openly that I hate Stalin and I hate Kennedy, or anybody else for that matter. Whereas you, comrade, you can only like somebody until 1929, or until 1937, or 1949, or 1951. After each purge, you are required to hate people you liked or forget about them. Is there anybody you dislike in the U.S.S.R.? Can you tell me about it, here and now?" My Soviet colleague was silent. I felt sorry for him, and guilty. I had lost track of the number of drinks I had. The next morning I had a terrible hangover. I rationalized that it was for a worthy cause, for "freedom."

The Afghan official attitude, outwardly cordial, was deeply suspicious. Afghans had good reason to be suspicious of foreigners after a century of wars, invasions, and self-imposed isolation had made them distrustful of neighbors and strangers and I was no exception. I was staying in the Hotel Kabul where no Afghans were allowed and where only a very few were permitted to be entertained socially. Although I used no U.S. facilities or privileges except for the United States Information Service (USIS) and did not frequent American parties, I was suspect and was followed everywhere. They found it difficult to believe that I could leave San Francisco, spend so much money, and come fifteen to eighteen thousand miles just to study the modernization of Afghanistan. Finally, I was an Iranian citizen who was in Kabul to write about a touchy subject, a politically incorrect one. After all, I had to deal with such issues as traditionalism, the role of the religious establishment, social, economic, and judiciary reforms, the status and rights of women, the relationship of *sharia* (religious law) and tribal laws, and the impact of the reign of King Amanullah (1919–1929) and his reforms, a taboo topic. (His reforms had triggered a rebellion that ended his reign and that of his dynasty, along with his reforms.)

During my first week at the Hotel Kabul, three unexpected visitors provided the Afghan authorities ample reason to be suspicious of me. The first was Captain Burch, the U.S. military attaché, whom I had never met. Having learned that I was working on the history of modern Afghanistan, he called on me to ask for my assistance. He was working on his master's thesis on Pashtoonistan and needed bibliographical data. I explained this carefully to a suspicious Afghan hotel manager.

My second visitor was the commercial attaché of Iran. He had learned from the Iranian ambassador to Afghanistan that I was in Kabul and was a native of Tabriz. He implored me, as a compatriot, to accept his invitation to dine with him and his wife and family. He felt he was in Siberia and was counting the days and hours when he could return home. We drank two bottles of vodka and wine and sang old Tabrizi songs in Turkish, including one dedicated to Tamara, a famous prostitute. The attaché informed me that all his servants were Afghan spies. He told them to be sure they got the facts right. We had drunk two bottles of vodka, not one.

My third visitor was Rashidi Haeri, the Iranian ambassador, who expressed disappointment that I had not paid a formal visit. I explained that as well to the hotel manager. By now the hotel management was sure that I was too important to be merely a student of history and that therefore I must have a different purpose for being in Afghanistan. I confounded the daytime and nighttime managers by teasing them, whispering that perhaps I was a spy! I enjoyed the joke. They were not amused. Throughout my stay I had a constant companion. At first I thought I was imagining things. Later I realized that somebody was trailing me all the time. One day I approached the poor chap and asked him: "May I help you? You seem to be lost." I don't think he liked it but I certainly did. . . .

After attempting the proper and diplomatic way of obtaining permission from Afghan authorities to use Afghan libraries and archives, and having failed, I decided to do it the Iranian way. I assumed I had the necessary permission. I walked into various libraries, with great authority and determination. I asked in Persian for the materials I needed. I received them. I called it the process of self-authorization. Nobody objected.

In Kabul I made the acquaintance of a brilliant young man. Of Iranian extraction, he was the recipient of a Harvard University Shaw Travel Fellowship. Subsequently, he embarked upon his pursuit of a Ph.D. under the auspices of Sir Hamilton Gibb, a great scholar of Islam. The young man was Roy Mottahedeh, currently Gurney Professor of History at Harvard University. At the time, Roy was studying Persian. We became friends and travel companions. Two of our adventures remain with me. As we were getting ready to leave Kabul for Beirut, via Karachi, diplomatic relations between Pakistan and Afghanistan were severed. We could reach Pakistan only through the Khyber Pass. Both Roy and I saw a window of opportunity. The value of the Pakistani rupee had plummeted in Kabul to eighteen rupees per dollar, while in Pakistan the official rate was still eight per dollar. We decided to cash in our tickets, which were in dollars, buy Pakistani rupees in Kabul, and buy two new tickets for Beirut in Karachi, using Pakistani rupees.

Just to be on the safe side, we went to the Pakistani Mission in Kabul. The embassy personnel were packing their belongings. We asked them if we could buy everything in Pakistan with Pakistani rupees. Of course, it is our national currency was the answer. I wished we had asked if we could buy tickets from Pakistani National Airlines with Pakistani rupees.

Before I left for Beirut, I wanted to have clean clothes, so I sent two of my suits to the dry cleaner. I discovered that Kabul dry cleaners' method of cleaning was to dip clothes in Russian gasoline.

Our passage through the Khyber Pass was uneventful. I thought about how many conquerors had passed through there on their way to subjugate the Indian subcontinent. How many were successful, how many lost their armies? In Peshawar, Pakistan, we stayed at Dean's Hotel, famous in the annals of British colonial history. So many generals, governors, British and Indian officials, and agents had stayed there. We lived in style. After all, we had "lots" of Pakistani rupees. At the Peshawar offices of Pakistani International Airways, we ordered two one-way tickets to Beirut. As we were about to pay them in rupees, the ticket agent told us with great disdain that foreign citizens could buy tickets only with dollars. However, Pakistani citizens could purchase their tickets with rupees. We don't have that many dollars, we said. No dollars, no tickets was the answer. Who can help us? I asked. Only the director of the Peshawar branch of the Pakistan National Bank.

We went to see Amjad Ali and he received us politely. I explained that I was an Iranian citizen and a resident of the United States and that Roy Mottahedeh was a U.S. citizen of Iranian extraction. We were offered tea. We found out the bank manager was a poet and a lover of Persian poetry. We discussed the merits of various Persian poets, including Saadi and Hafez. We disagreed about the poet Iqbal. I claimed that he belonged to the Iranian pantheon and Mr. Ali replied he was Pakistani. He was so impressed by my appreciation of Iqbal and my attempt to expropriate him for Iran that he decided to stamp our passports, giving us permission to purchase our tickets with rupees. Besides, he said, Iran, Pakistan, and Turkey were allies, members of the CENTO pact. We were gratified by Mr. Ali's decision, naturally, especially that his love for poetry was so intense that he would make business decisions based on his literary convictions. I was puzzled, nevertheless, about Iqbal. After we left him, I realized that I was talking about Iqbal the Persian poet, whereas he was talking about Iqbal (1877–1938) the intellectual idol of nineteenth- and twentieth-century Pakistan.

Roy and I had a wonderful time in Lahore, a magnificent, colorful city, full of history and historical monuments. In the twelfth century, it was the capital of the Ghaznavid dynasty. During the sixteenth through the eighteenth centuries, it was a major center of the Mughal emperors from the rule of Babur (1483–1530) to that of Shah Jahan (1628–1657) and the death of Aurangzeb (1707).

We enjoyed the great monuments of Lahore: the Mosque of Wazir Khan (1634); the eighteenth-century Badshahi Masjid (Imperial Mosque), built by Emperor Aurangzeb; Runjit Singh's mausoleum; the Shahdara Gardens, containing the tomb of Mughal emperor Jahangir; and the famous Shalimar Gardens, laid out in 1641 by Emperor Shah Jahan. We were not able to visit the University of Punjab, the oldest university in Pakistan, founded in 1882. The sheer number of people, their distinctive colorful clothes, the variety of scents, the fragrance of the gardens, the soothing sound of water fountains, the muezzin's call to prayer, the site of minarets, all of them captivated us.

Happy that we were not insolvent, Roy decided to treat me to a great meal at one of the best restaurants of Lahore. The food was fabulous, the décor imposing, and the service great. The presentation of the bill was equally impressive. Roy handed the headwaiter a Carte Blanche credit card, then a great innovation. "What is this?" asked the waiter. "It is a credit card," Roy answered. "In lieu of payments?" the waiter asked with amazement and some agitation. "Yes," replied Roy. "No way!" was the headwaiter's retort. "But you have a credit card advertisement displayed on your restaurant's door," Roy pointed out. "Oh, that!" said the waiter. "That is for decoration."

After our great trip to Lahore, we arrived safely in Beirut. Roy, who stayed at the Bristol Hotel next door to us, had been attacked by exotic bugs and had a bad case of dysentery. I was happy to be home. Roy was happy, too: he was on his way to the United States. His Harvard Shaw Travel Fellowship had been a success.

After two months in Beirut, I returned to Afghanistan. It took me ten days to get there. The first leg of my trip was to Karachi. To access Afghanistan via the Khyber Pass was problematic and downright risky. There was a weekly flight from Karachi to Kabul. The big problem was obtaining an Afghan visa. The Afghan interests in Pakistan were represented by the United Arab Republic. The chance of getting a visa from them, I was told, was less than 30 percent.

September was monsoon season in Karachi. Temperatures varied between 92 and 110 degrees. I stayed in the Palace Hotel, a "luxury" hotel, which had no air-conditioning, just a big fan. Between the bedbugs and the heat, it was impossible to sleep. The plumbing was erratic. There were uninvited guests: three lizards and a rat or two. They had eaten portions of the bathroom rug. Then there were the ever-present, stubborn, demanding flies of Karachi. To cope with all of these I took three showers a day. The rates of the hotel, ranked as the third best hotel in Karachi, were reasonable: eight dollars a night. In late September, Ayoub Khan, president of Pakistan, inaugurated the Karachi International, a new air-conditioned hotel. The movie theaters that were air-conditioned were expensive (50 cents) by Pakistani standards, but provided welcome relief against the heat. The only drawback was the advertising, which lasted from a half hour to forty-five minutes.

In the 1960s, the city of Karachi was one of the busiest ports east of the Suez. It was the terminus of the country's freight and passenger center. Its airport had become a major hub of international traffic. Half of the city's estimated 4.5 to 5 million people were migrants and their descendants, who had settled in the city following the 1947 division of the Indian subcontinent into India and Pakistan.

I had seen poverty in Iran, in Lebanon, even in the United States, but nothing prepared me for the scale of misery, poverty, and subhuman conditions I witnessed in parts of Karachi. On a Sunday tour of the city, on a mini Vespa "taxicab," I faced one of the greatest shocks of my life. The cabdriver, having been informed that I was an Iranian citizen, assumed that I was a fellow Muslim and took me to the local bazaars and slums. What shocked me and disgusted me was the prostitute bazaar, where semi-clad females, young and old, were lined up behind a huge straw partition. The driver told me that they were fourth-class prostitutes, destitutes good only for other destitutes, who provided sex for pennies.

I was horrified to see that their "rooms" and "beds" were makeshift huts, covered with small straw "curtains." Women were sitting in front of these holes, soliciting clients. Others were lined up behind the huge straw partition. They had no holes. They performed sexual acts while standing behind that screen. Scores of street sweepers, beggars, and destitutes were lined up for sex. Some women even had children on their laps. They were begging for business, advertising themselves and bargaining. In this context, the ideas and ideals of love and sex as ennobling acts seemed vacuous, the concept of human dignity empty. My inability to help made me angry.

I saw thousands of homeless people—children, women, and men—lying on the streets, some with one bed for the whole family. Millions of flies gathered on cheap, rotten, stinking fast food that was being prepared for sale by downtrodden food vendors. On September 24, I wrote to Clare of my disgust and revulsion at everything, including sex, that debased human beings, their dignity, the meaning of life, the indifference of people to such a vast sea of misery. I fulminated against the world, especially the "free world." If this is part of the free world, then down with the free world where people are nothing but slaves of subsistence. They must have something to die for besides wretched misery. For the first time in my life, I wanted to be rich, rich as Croesus to be able to build lodgings for 100,000 people in Karachi. I wrote that U.S. aid should concentrate mainly on giving people shelter. Military aid is nothing compared to human aid; people should be given hope to cling to life.

I left Karachi for Delhi with great anticipation. I had long been fascinated by the rich history, religions, and cultures of India, especially those of its capital, Delhi. I don't believe any city in India has as many historical monuments. In Delhi, you are in the presence of three thousand years of history. Delhi has some of the best examples of Indo-Muslim architecture. I visited the Qutb Minar (Qutb Tower), Jama Masjid (Principal Mosque), and Lāl Qa'lah (Red Fort) with its seventy-five-foot-high massive red sandstone walls and palaces and gardens. I saw the Emperor Humayun's elegant tomb and the Birla Temple. Delhi had endured many invasions; some came to loot, others to settle and build. Old Delhi was full of gardens and trees. It was a green city and, unlike many old Eastern cities, appeared to have been well planned. My first impression was that it was an Eastern city with Western clothes. I was under the incorrect assumption that everyone in India, especially in Delhi, spoke English, I was disabused of that. Delhi presented great contrasts. Its well-stocked bazaars, its interminable rows of jewelry stores, resplendent with gold, silver, and diamonds, the vast numbers of stores with colorful silk and Kashmir scarves, hundreds of shops with spices—it seemed as if the entire wealth of Asia, all its gold, silk, and ivory was there. The scent of exotic spices was overwhelming and intoxicating.

Then there were the slums, which could easily compete with those in Karachi. The face of poverty and misery was manifest in hordes of half-naked men, women, and children. They looked like walking shadows or skeletons lying on the pavement. Little boys and girls with their big eyes, unwashed clothes and hair, were scavengers along with the dogs. These slums were inhabited by hundreds of thousands of individuals whose homes were the streets, their beds, the pavements.

In the 1960s, India was a Cold War cultural battleground, fought over by the Soviet Union, the United States, and Great Britain. There were numerous Marxist and Russian works in translation. Marx's *Das Kapital* sold for twenty-five cents. Not to be outdone, though not on the same scale, there were competing paperback works of Abraham Lincoln, Mark Twain, Justice Douglas, *The Federalist Papers,* and many others, which were equally cheap. The Great Powers had chosen a fertile field for their competition, for Indians were a reading nation.

I was amazed to read personal and matrimonial ads announcing one's income, sex, sexual preference, height, occupation, habits, education, and caste, and expressing an interest in mates with matching qualities and rich dowries. It shocked me because while reading about religion in India, we learned about the spirituality of Indian culture and society, while Americans were criticized by Indians for being materialistic.

My quest to return to Afghanistan took me to the Afghan embassy in Delhi. After a three-hour session, which turned out to be an examination of my background, the scope of my research project, and the duration of my previous stay in Kabul, two cautious Afghan officials gave me their decision. They could not give me an entry visa for Afghanistan because all reentry visas must be authorized by the authorities in Kabul. "How about a transit visa?" I asked. "I am leaving for Beirut via Kabul." They gave me one good for only five days. It did not matter. Once in Kabul, I knew I could manage to change its provisions.

Kabul had undergone many changes during the past few months. There were many new buildings and trees, and the airport had customs officers with uniforms. I was given a royal reception at Kabul Hotel. I got my old room back. Everybody from the manager to the director to the cooks and waiters were delighted to see me. Prices of the rooms had increased from 200 to 300 to 400 afghanis a day, and meals from 20 to 40 afghanis. The Afghans were much more relaxed. After all, since I had been allowed to return to Kabul, they presumed I must be all right.

Once again the Iranian commercial attaché, my Tabrizi compatriot, and the Iranian ambassador visited me. So did the Italian ambassador. I met former King Amanullah's brother-in-law and niece, the first woman to be divorced from an Afghan and to marry a foreigner. I also met a daughter of King Habibullah (1901–1919) and several Afghan intellectuals. With the exception of Dr. Javid, who taught Persian literature at Kabul University, none of the Afghans were willing to be entertained at Hotel Kabul. It was for foreigners only. I assumed that they were discouraged by the authorities from visiting the hotel. Afghan intellectuals and public figures such as former King Amanullah's brother, King Habibullah's daughter, the sons of Mahmud Tarzi (the reformer and former foreign minister), who helped me with facts, documents, or advice, begged me not to thank them publicly or even to mention them.

My work was progressing smoothly when I became ill and had to leave for Pakistan, where it was found that instead of the suspected ulcer, I was the victim of no more than acute dysentery, coupled with a fever. (The Americans had a doctor who took care of diplomatic personnel only, except in cases of emergency. The British embassy had an excellent doctor who had just left. While in Kabul, he took private patients at a very reasonable fee, I was told. The Soviet embassy had a doctor, too. As for dentists there was only one German dentist who people recommended with confidence.) I went to Beirut where my illness was compounded by a throat infection and a cold. After a month-long rest and recovery period, I returned to Afghanistan.

By 1962, through my research at the United Nations, the British Museum, the Library of Congress, the New York Public Library, the Bibliothèque Nationale, the Library of the Majliss in Tehran, and libraries in Kabul, Karachi, Lahore, and Delhi, I had gathered some seven thousand 5 x 8 cards of handwritten notes, had met scores of competent authorities, and gained much insight into Afghan society and history. In the process, I had collected an enormous corpus of research material on Afghanistan, from every conceivable source. The easy part was done. Now I had to return to the United States and finish my Ph.D. dissertation. Unfortunately, twenty-five to thirty rare books that I had purchased in Peshawar, Pakistan, and shipped to Beirut via Pakistan International Airlines never reached their destination.

CHAPTER EIGHT

San Francisco State College

Before I left for Afghanistan, during the spring semester of the 1959–1960 academic year, San Francisco State College's history department sent urgent letters to the Stanford and UC Berkeley history departments asking them to recommend a Ph.D. candidate who was willing to step in immediately and teach the history of modern Europe. There was a catch. The class was to be taught at eight A.M. on Mondays, Wednesdays, and Fridays and there were not many eager candidates. San Francisco State College was in a bind: Professor David Hoggan, who had taught the course, was in the hospital. David L. Hoggan (1923–1988) was a graduate of Reed College and received his Ph.D. from Harvard in 1948. His dissertation was on German-Polish relations in 1938–1939. His revisionist work was entitled *The Forced War.* He set forth the thesis that World War II was imposed on Nazi Germany, not initiated by it and that the "oppression" of Poland's ethnic German minority was an important factor in Hitler's decision to go to war against the Polish state. Most of David Hoggan's historical writings appeared in German. He wrote *The Myth of the Six Million* (1969) under a pen name, Anonymous, denying the Holocaust. He had several nervous breakdowns. There were more than one hundred students in his class who needed to finish the course. Even though the pay per course (actually half a course) was very little, and the hour ungodly, I volunteered for the job, which started just after our honeymoon.

I stayed up all night preparing my first lecture. I rehearsed it and timed it. As I entered the classroom I was anxious. As a result, I finished the lecture in forty minutes rather than fifty. I did not know what to do, so I asked if there were any questions, hoping that there would be none. Unfortunately there were two. I did not know one of the answers. It was hard for me to acknowledge that. I thought it would undermine my authority. Therefore, I told the class that it was a good question and the next lecture would deal with it. Those were a long ten minutes.

My part-time teaching at San Francisco State had major consequences for my future academic career. It gave me a chance to get to know some of the members of the history department, but most of all, it gave me the chance to get to know its chairman, Professor Gerald (Jerry) White. A soft-spoken, amiable, and gentle man, the holder of a Ph.D. degree from UC Berkeley, Professor White was a highly respected scholar. His specialty was business history and his major study was the history of the Standard Oil Company.

A year later when Professor Hoggan resigned, SF State launched a search process to replace him. Professor White was determined to recruit me to his department. He had revised the job description in such a way that only a handful of people could qualify. In a sense he had fashioned it for me: "We can't think of anyone we should prefer half as much to see with us than the most able young historian who helped us last spring. The question is, Are you interested? We certainly hope you are! The man we are seeking ideally would have European intellectual history and the Middle East as twin specialties, and you fit that like a *hand to a glove*."

I declined the offer. I wanted to finish my research and my dissertation. White was disappointed but did not give up. The job was given for one year to Dr. Jerome Kuehl, who taught intellectual as well as German history at Stanford. He was an Isaiah Berlin student who had tutored for a couple of years at Oxford.

A year later White wrote again. "Would you consider coming back to us?"

By January 1962, I had to decide about my academic future. The American University of Beirut did not have any vacancies. I had an offer from Stanford University to be an instructor of Western civilization. The pay was $2,900 for three quarters (two semesters). The other offer was from San Francisco State. Professor White notified me of the "unanimous decision of the department . . . that we would be delighted to have you with us," that I "was accorded very impressive support by George Knoles, Wayne Vucinich, Gordon Wright, and David Harris, which, plus your own fine record . . ." had put me "above the masses." The one concern that the department had was to be sure that the man it hired would stay at least three to four years and "not be a bird of passage." I consulted with my mentors at Stanford. Professors Gordon Wright and Wayne Vucinich gave me the best advice: you have a family and you cannot eat prestige, you have to take the San Francisco State offer. After all, they would pay me $6,516 for nine months. Once again, a stranger, this time Professor Gerald White, had taken upon himself the task of being my protector and benefactor.

In 1962, we returned from Beirut to Menlo Park, California. We wanted to be near Stanford and close to good public schools. California, in general, and northern California, in particular, had some of the best public schools. We had no money to buy an apartment or a house. We had no furniture. Professor Wayne Vucinich found a small furnished house with a yard in a cul de sac in Menlo Park. The rent was $150 a month. My monthly net pay was $400. We became minimalists. Diaper service was a luxury. "Beef" Stroganoff was made of hot dogs. Ernie's half-gallon red wine was $1.90, toys were a luxury, and the car a necessity. After we'd been there a year, the owner had to sell the furnished house.

John Lilly sold us the entire contents of the house for some three hundred dollars. Ignorant of the price of furniture and household goods, I had the temerity to tell him that a small black table was missing. He returned it. I did not realize that he had given us all the furniture for a token amount. Years later I met a John Lilly at Stanford and soon realized he was our former landlord. By now he was a successful businessman and chairman of Stanford University's board of trustees. I thanked him for his generosity and apologized about the small black table. After John Lilly's house we moved into a nearby unfurnished smaller duplex for the same amount of rent. Between these moves we spent summer in the vast, sprawling Vucinich home in Los Altos Hills, "house-sitting" for them while the family was in Europe. Our only obligation was to do the watering for their new garden and small orchard.

San Francisco State College was transformed in the aftermath of World War II into an outstanding college. It was primarily a teaching institution. Because of its location, it attracted good faculty and many native Californians and immigrants and/or children of immigrants. The veterans of World War II, beneficiaries of the GI Bill, teachers who wanted to get their teaching certificates or master's degrees, and employees of various governmental agencies and private organizations who were interested in professional development flocked to the college. It was primarily a college for commuters, located conveniently in the southwest corner of San Francisco at 1600 Holloway Avenue, right across from the streetcar and bus stops.

San Francisco State College imposed a heavy teaching load. I taught

Twentieth-Century Europe: Europe Since World War I on Mondays, Wednesdays, and Fridays, another section of that course on Tuesday nights, and European Intellectual History on Tuesdays and Thursdays, with each class being one and a half hours. I also taught the Middle East in the Nineteenth and Twentieth Centuries on Mondays, Wednesdays, and Fridays. Preparing and teaching three different courses, commuting from Menlo Park to San Francisco State College (seventy miles round-trip), doing research on Saturdays at the Hoover Institution on War, Revolution, and Peace at Stanford University, trying to write my dissertation at night, and meeting my family and social obligations overwhelmed me. To supplement my salary, I taught three nights a week at the Extension Division of the college, as well as at the Presidio army base in San Francisco and the Hamilton Air Force base in Marin County. In addition, I taught two consecutive summer sessions at the college.

*   *   *

While teaching at San Francisco State I learned much about the United States, its institutions, its politics, and its constituents. In 1956, when I had landed in New York, I knew nothing about the U.S. political system. I knew and I was told repeatedly that the United States was the land of freedom, equality, religious tolerance, and opportunity, that its Constitution protected the individual's rights against arbitrary power, that freedoms of speech, assembly, and press were sacrosanct, that the country had a representative form of government and an independent judiciary, that there were checks and balances between the legislative, executive, and judicial branches of the government, and that there was a complex federal system consisting of forty-nine states and the District of Columbia.

I knew nothing about the history of American political parties. I knew about President Woodrow Wilson, but even that knowledge was limited and based primarily on a parochial Armenian perspective: namely, that during World War I, Woodrow Wilson had promulgated his Fourteen Points, which included the right of national self-determination, that he had seriously entertained the prospects of an American mandate for an independent and large Armenian state, that in the Treaty of Sèvres (1920), he had envisaged an extensive Armenian Republic in order to make it economically viable, that the treaty also envisaged and made provisions for a Kurdistan. I knew that he was a Democrat. I had no knowledge of the Republican Party, except that Abraham Lincoln, "the great Emancipator," was a Republican and that Senator Lodge of the State of Massachusetts, also a Republican, had successfully opposed President Wilson's efforts to secure the ratification of the Versailles settlements and treaties by the U.S. Senate.

I did not understand the context of the 1956 U.S. presidential elections by which I had been so intrigued, nor the contest between the Republican Dwight D. Eisenhower and Adlai Stevenson, the Democratic candidate. I had heard of Eisenhower, even in Tabriz, and I had a picture of him and of General Omar Bradley. I had never heard of Adlai Stevenson. Under the circumstances when I was given an "I like Ike" button in September 1956, I wore it. I even joined the refrain: "A general who has seen war can keep us out of war." I remember a classmate challenging me about Eisenhower's views. My answer, which infuriated him, was, I don't know but I like Ike. Stanford students appeared to be mostly from upper- or middle-class families. The campus mood was mostly conservative and Republican. With an "I like Ike" button, I was in good company. (By 1960, I was exposed to Adlai Stevenson's writings and speeches, I had heard Eleanor Roosevelt give an eloquent speech on his behalf at Stanford, and I also was overwhelmed by Eugene McCarthy's speech nominating Stevenson at the Democratic National Convention—in short I had become an Adlai Stevenson, and later a JFK, fan.)

In October 1956, a few foreign students had been invited by KPIX television station in San Francisco to view a presidential debate and give our reactions. I made an outrageous comment to the effect that the existing election system gives an unfair advantage to the incumbent, that the campaign was between a president and a candidate for the presidency. The latter had none of the cachet or instruments of power at his disposal. An incumbent president was able to use the might and the prestige of his office in his campaign; the opposition therefore was at a great disadvantage. Ergo, the arrangement was not fair.

My proposed "solution" to this supposed dilemma was that if an incumbent president decided to run for a second term, he should step down three months before the presidential election to let the vice president assume the post. During that interval, the two candidates would run against each other. This, I concluded, would provide a fair election and spare a sitting president from being defeated and making him a lame duck for two months. My comments elicited laughter.

During my Stanford years, I was introduced to the history, theories, and practices of American democracy. Two books offered invaluable insights: *The Federalist Papers* and Alexis de Tocqueville's *Democracy in America*. They gave me a good introduction to U.S. democracy, its institutions and its challenges. I read various surveys of American history. In order to have some sense of "youth culture," I read Jack Kerouac's *On the Road,* reread J. D. Salinger's *The Catcher in the Rye,* Henry Miller's *Tropic of Cancer,* Norman Mailer's *The Naked and the Dead,* and, most important of all, David Riesman's *The Lonely Crowd.* I read Paul Goodman's *Growing Up Absurd,* C. Wright Mills's *The Power Elite,* and Ralph Ellison's *The Invisible Man.* Nothing had prepared me for the advent of a vast student movement and its major political and social goals.

In 1960, when we left the United States for England, there were scattered student demonstrations in San Francisco against HUAC (The House Un-American Activities Committee) and against the execution of Caryl Chessman. When we returned in 1962 and I was teaching at San Francisco State College, there was no indication that soon a student movement would sweep the nation's campuses and have a lasting impact on many universities, their leaders, faculties, curricula, and governance.

More than the antinuclear movement, initially it was the civil rights movement, led by the Reverend Martin Luther King Jr., that captured the imagination of most Americans. His philosophy of nonviolence and his willingness to pay the price for his actions and convictions gave him great moral authority. His championship of equal rights for African-Americans and people of color rested its case not only on the Bill of Rights and the Constitution of the United States but on the very precepts of Christianity. His was a moral appeal that touched the soul of America. It evoked guilt and shame. It inspired his supporters and stunned his opponents. There were sit-ins, demonstrations, boycotts, marches, and freedom rides in the South. The civil rights movement built bridges of moral and political solidarity between blacks and whites not only in the South but also in the North, Midwest, and West. Universities and colleges became natural centers and sources for such solidarity. Students were awed by the presence of those who had been "witnesses for justice and righteousness" often at the expense of their physical well-being and safety, by being prey to police dogs, being clubbed or even killed. In 1963, I used Martin Luther King Jr.'s "Letter from Birmingham Jail" as required reading.

The assassination of President John F. Kennedy in 1963 shocked the nation into numbness. Everything stopped. The promise of a bright future for the United States, an era of idealism, action, and compassion, both at home and abroad, disappeared. As the radio announced the president's death, we faculty members who were in the dining hall staggered out in silence, dejected and depressed. Many were weeping. Then a young man, who had climbed onto the roof of one of the college's low-rise buildings, played taps with a horn, as we all froze.

I think President Kennedy's assassination was yet another factor in encouraging the youth of America, especially those in the nation's universities and colleges, to be involved in the business of American society, democracy, and such unfinished agendas as civil rights and social justice. Throughout 1964, there were demonstrations in San Francisco and the Bay Area, staged as acts of solidarity with the Birmingham, Alabama, protests. While such acts were gaining momentum in the nation's major residential and research universities and colleges, including even Quaker ones, students at the state colleges (which were nonresidential colleges for commuters) were not major players.

What galvanized the students was the growing U.S. involvement in Vietnam. It began in 1963 when some twenty thousand U.S. combat troops arrived in Vietnam and gained momentum after the 1964 "retaliatory bombing" of North Vietnam and the 1965 landing of U.S. forces in Da Nang. For the next eight years, as U.S. involvement in the Vietnam War grew, so did antiwar sentiment and the student movement. In 1965, when Students for a Democratic Society issued its call to protest the war in a march to Washington, D.C., some twenty-five thousand people participated. By 1967, hundreds of thousands marched in Washington, D.C., and New York. (In 1967, there was a peace march in San Francisco as well that Clare went to.) The military draft came under attack for its bias against black and poor white youths. It was pointed out that while the latter were drafted, white students from upper- and middle-class families received college deferrals or ROTC shelters.

The year 1965–1966 was a turning point for the antiwar movement. King came out against the war in Vietnam. Shortly before his assassination, Malcolm X denounced the war as an assault against people of color. They were joined by many black activists and organizations. The Student Nonviolent Coordinating Committee also took a stand against the war. The Mississippi Democratic Party called on African-Americans not to participate in the Vietnam War.

The activism of the student movement was not confined to civil rights and the war in Vietnam. Student activists focused their attention on American higher education, its mission, its institutions, its professors, and the status of students. In 1963, Clark Kerr, president of the University of California system, delivered the Godkin lectures at Harvard, entitled "The Uses of the University." He discussed the evolution of American universities, especially research universities, from the 1862 Morrell Act to World War II and the postwar period. He described the present state of the university as a "multiversity." By that he meant that American universities were offering education, research, and service to a myriad of constituencies—to undergraduates, graduate students, the professional schools (law, medicine, engineering, and business), and hospital patients, while trying to meet the research demands of corporations such as IBM, organizations such as the AFL-CIO, and the U.S. government and its agencies.

Kerr's "multiversity" became the focus of student activists. None other than the president of the prestigious University of California, in the first major "public confession," was admitting that the modern American university was serving primarily the interests of capitalism and the U.S. government and its military, *not* the students nor our nation's and the world's social underclass. Activists claimed that profit, not virtue, was the university's main objective. Large class sizes and overcrowding were characterized as manifestations of exploitation of students prompted by profit motives. It was asserted that college teaching had been downgraded in favor of research enterprises that served the interests of corporations and the defense industries. Kerr had asserted that the pluralism of America's institutions of higher education corresponded to the pluralism of American society. This generalization prompted student activists to argue that presidents of universities and colleges had overlooked racial, ethnic, and gender pluralism. According to this critique, the university had become a corporation, its president the general manager, and the students "the cogs" or the raw material of the system. The California Board of Regents was criticized for acting as if it was the Board of Directors of a for-profit corporation. The membership of the board, consisting mostly of rich people, was considered the symbol of corporate America.

The universities and their presidents were characterized as hypocrites. While they advocated adherence to and protection of American democratic values, including the First Amendment, while they preached and encouraged student participation in the civic life of American society and their communities, their policies subverted their sermons. Universities were accused of complicity or active collaboration with the FBI, Army Intelligence, and other agencies for a "Communist-free" campus.

Student radicals criticized the faculty, especially its liberal members, for dereliction of their moral, academic, and social responsibilities. The faculty encouraged students to get involved as they sat on the sidelines while university administrators enforced "trustee-imposed" rules that forbade using the university grounds for partisan political activities or free speech. For student activists, political debate and action were not antithetical to the educational process; they were an integral part of education.

The student movements—usually placed under the umbrella designated as the New Left—were merciless in their criticism of the Old Left, as well as the Communist Party and even the Socialists, but ironically not the Trotskyites or anarchists. They claimed that both the Communist system and its antidote, the American form of representative government, had failed. Radical students accused liberals of enacting a system of dependency based on a welfare state and its ally, the warfare state. They attacked the "liberal establishment" for promoting the cause of a technocratic mass society based on uniformity, a system that reduced its citizens to clients and consumers, a system that was a source of alienation and dehumanization of its citizens.

In 1964, the intellectual epicenter of the student movement was at UC Berkeley. Known as the Free Speech Movement, it captured the attention of academic communities and universities throughout the country. It raised many important issues but the crucial one centered on the concept and the right of freedom of speech and advocacy. It defied university rules that prohibited the use of campus grounds for partisan political activity and the exclusion of controversial speeches. The movement was not about the rights of the students alone. It challenged the faculty to defend its individual and collective rights and the autonomy of the university vis-à-vis the regents' rules that required monitoring the loyalty of each faculty member through an oath. The university was accused of violating the intellectual freedom of its faculty during the McCarthy era. At UC Berkeley, the Free Speech Movement managed to enlist the formal support of the faculty. It voted for free speech by a margin of more than seven to one.

Universities were not ready for the student movement; they were not ready for conflict from within and they certainly were not ready or able to engage in an ideological battle with their students outside the classroom. Faculty members taught about revolution, provided critical analysis, discussed existentialism, issues of autonomy, authenticity, integrity, and conflict management, never imagining that they themselves would be subjected to the test of intellectual integrity and authenticity or be questioned as to whether they practiced their beliefs or merely preached about them. They were asked to provide students with the means to close the gaps between concepts, ideas, beliefs, process, and action.

Unlike UC Berkeley, whose faculty, in the aftermath of the Free Speech Movement, played a major role in initiating and ushering in institutional reforms, much of the faculty at San Francisco State College stayed out (or tried to), considering the conflict one between the students and the "administration." But events and developments made that kind of withdrawal or ratio-nalization very hard. The fact was that the entire educational system, its phi-losophy, governance, and curricula were being challenged. Every faculty member was under pressure to become a public intellectual, whether or not he was knowledgeable or ready temperamentally, ideologically, or politi-cally, whether or not he or she was willing.

Students at San Francisco State College were impressed by the develop-ments at UC Berkeley. While they, too, championed "free speech," their main focus was at first on civil rights and then more and more on the antiwar movement. The makeup of its Students for a Democratic Society (SDS) was different, as were their tactics. There was a fierce debate and competition among radical students concerning the nature of American society and its future, how to organize, how to lead its transformation, what kind of move-ment would be able to achieve that, with what kind of ideological platform, and using what strategies and what tactics. At San Francisco State, SDS had lots of competition from representatives of the Old Left (some Communists, Socialists, and Trotskyites) and primarily the membership of one of its fac-tions, the Progressive Labor Party, which was influenced by the Cultural Revolution and teachings of Chairman Mao. Some were influenced by the revolutionary roles of Che Guevara and Fidel Castro. Old-line Communists were held in contempt. For a person to be called a CP (a member of the Communist Party) was pejorative.

I know all of this because, for two years, 1966–1968, I was assigned as faculty advisor to the Progressive Labor Party. Without a faculty advisor, you could not register as a campus organization. Denial of registration would have created free speech and advocacy issues on campus, similar to those of UC Berkeley. I was persuaded by the administration of the college to assume the advisor task, because, I assume, nobody else wanted to be involved with the group. Moreover, I was teaching European intellectual history, which among other things discussed the eighteenth-century Enlightenment and nineteenth- and twentieth-century ideologies—liberalism, conservatism, so-cialism, Marxism, anarchism, Communism, Fascism, and Nazism, subjects of hot student debates. I had representatives of all the radical factions in my class, including many in my history of the Middle East and modern Euro-pean history classes.

Members of the Progressive Labor Party did not know how to cope with me and vice versa. I was their faculty advisor. To them, that did not mean much. It was a mere bureaucratic requirement, a formality. I felt I was their faculty advisor and therefore I was responsible for their behavior and ac-tions. I attended one meeting. They had nothing to discuss. If there were sit-ins, I had to be there in case there was a police action. I had a thankless job. I told them I did not agree with their positions but I was in favor of their exercising their First Amendment rights. One thing was evident. They did not want me around. They did not trust anyone. I did not realize that being a faculty advisor to the San Francisco State–based Progressive Labor Party was a hazardous occupation. (SDS had assumed that I was the major obstacle, the reason why the Progressive Labor Party had decided not to form an alliance with them. After all, wasn't I their academic advisor? Weren't many of them my students?)

One day, the leader of the party called me at home with an urgent message: "Notify your local police, take your family, and get out of town. Some Argentine radicals are heading to Menlo Park 'to take care of you.' We don't want innocent people to die; it would result in bad publicity for us and for the cause." The caller, a savvy guy and a "serious ideologue and tactician" who held the reins of his party at San Francisco State, was not known for hyperbole. His call was chilling because he did not express any doubts. We called the police. They advised us to leave our home. We spent one night with our neighbors, the Willises, then went to Berkeley and spent a couple of days at the home of our friends Elaine and Reginald Zelnik. Professor Zelnik, a historian of the Soviet Union and Russia at UC Berkeley, was one of the Berkeley faculty members who played a crucial role in the history of the Free Speech Movement. Before leaving Menlo Park, together with a couple of neighbors (we had notified all of them), we changed the street signs to sabotage the mission of the "Argentine guerillas." Thank God, nothing happened. But it was not an empty threat. The office of Professor John Bunzel was bombed. My office was on the same floor.

As a teacher with a profound faith in education, as a rationalist and a historian, I was eager to understand "the student movement" and my students. I wanted to know the nature of various forces, both moral and political, economic and social, that were affecting America's youth in general and those in California and the Bay Area in particular. I read periodicals, pamphlets, and position papers published by groups both of the Left (Old and New) and the Right (Conservative). I read Democratic and Republican positions on various issues to understand the Young Republicans, Young Americans for Freedom, and the Young Democrats. I read publications of the John Birch Society to understand the logic of their conspiratorial theories.

I challenged the students as they challenged me. For those who belonged to various organized groups, I used their own publications as points of reference. I challenged their lack of knowledge, the inadequacy of their preparations, their theses. The students were at the university to learn. I was their teacher and they were my students. Many students were both surprised and "impressed" by my knowledge of what was going on, as well as my interest in them. I told my students that they had to know the facts. Slogans and platitudes are not sufficient. Even if you are a revolutionary you have to be an educated one.

When the Soviets invaded Czechoslovakia in 1968, the Progressive Labor Party was at a loss. What should their stand be? Delivery of the *Beijing Review,* which provided a theoretical framework for some of their positions on different issues, had been delayed. My advice was that logic, previous stands, and, hence, consistency required them to denounce the Soviet invasion. They did. When the latest *Beijing Review* arrived, it denounced the Soviet decision. My reputation was saved. The Progressive Labor Party was desperate to "revolutionize the classroom" and to reach the working class, the blue-collar workers. Their attempts were not successful. Two or three of them, including Brenda Goodman, one of the student leaders and one of my students, came to my European history class and asked me, politely, if they could address the students. At first, I said no, but then I said, "Why don't I ask the entire class if they would like to hear Brenda Goodman speak or not? Perhaps for ten minutes? Five minutes? One minute?" No one raised a hand. I told Ms. Goodman, "Student power does it again. Please leave." On another occasion, they came to address the students in my Middle East class. This time the leaders were two or three Iranian "Maoist" students. They apologized profusely, in Persian, for their intrusion, handed me a red book of quotations of Chairman Mao, in Persian, shouted several slogans and left. It did not leave a great impression on the class.

The years 1966 to 1968 were difficult ones at San Francisco State. In addition to antiwar protests, demonstrations against ROTC and the CIA, and solidarity rallies on behalf of the civil rights movement, two other issues became subjects of great contention: the 1967 Arab-Israeli war and the emergence of the Black Panther Party and other black organizations. Members of the New Left coalition, especially the Jewish ones, who had defended the rights of Palestinians and Arabs, found themselves torn between their ideological positions and personal and family commitments to the survival of Israel. The war created severe family and generational conflicts.

The inability of the New Left, and even the Old Left, to incorporate the black organizations and hence the black leadership and their followers into a single, integrated organization soon became apparent. While the blacks welcomed the solidarity of the whites, they were determined not to give up their independence, their authority, their leadership, or their freedom of action. They welcomed cooperation, but on their terms.

"Black Is Beautiful" insisted on a separate social and economic agenda. Blacks wanted to be in charge of their own destinies. They wanted equality but they also wanted jobs. They wanted integration and more black students in the nation's universities. They wanted their history and legacy not only to be recognized but studied and taught. At first, they wanted courses, then a program, and finally a department. What upset the faculty and college administrators was their insistence that students would control the curricula and the faculty appointments. That was a nonstarter.

The faculty did not know how to respond to "nonnegotiable" demands. They wanted to control their autonomy and authority in academic matters. The black militants and their white allies were interested in outcomes; they did not want to compromise on their nonnegotiable demands. They were not interested in face-saving, symbolic, academic "solutions." The president of the college, John Henry Summerskill, a liberal, was caught between the regents, faculty, students, and the militants. He tried the old technique of telling each group what it wanted to hear: he was against the war, but he opposed sit-ins; he was sympathetic with minority demands but he had a stubborn conservative faculty. To the faculty, he said he was with them, and they should uphold the standards. He called in the San Francisco police to establish his authority on campus. He apologized for inviting the police.

When the faculty, students, administrators, and regents discovered that he was with each one at any given time, President Summerskill lost his moral authority. I remember the general faculty meeting when the president asked for the faculty's help. Someone, maybe me, asked which president was asking for our support, the liberal, the conservative, the radical, the pro-student, or the pro-faculty president. That night the president resigned and left for Ethiopia.

For the faculty it was easier to deal with antiwar issues than the ethnic ones. The antiwar issues put the students against the administration and the State, whereas the ethnic issues put the students against the faculty. Matters were not made better when President Robert R. Smith, Summerskill's successor, was presented with ten nonnegotiable demands and told it did not matter whether the demands were met or not, as the students intended to strike and shut down the campus. For some students, the campus was a means to organize society; ethnic groups and ethnic studies, a much neglected subject, were a means to create ethnic alliances.

The Black Panther Party sought "Black Power." One of its basic tenets was: "We start with the basic definition that black people in America are a colonized people in every sense of the term and that white America is an organized imperialist force holding black people in colonial bondage." My class was one of the first to be "invaded" by the Black Panthers. I was teaching in the first classroom on the first floor of the first college building near the street. I was so "bourgeois" that I was upset that the "visitors" did not knock before entering the classroom. And I was scared.

"What do you teach?" the leader asked. "European history," I replied. "Europe should not exist!" was the retort. "Good luck!" was my answer. "We demand that you dismiss your class." "I cannot dismiss my class. I am paid to teach. I still have twenty minutes left." The leader repeated his demand. I repeated my answer. I explained that my students were sympathetic to the plight of the minorities. The students, which included many radicals, raised their hands, but that did not impress them. They insisted that I dismiss my class. I refused.

I told the leader of the Black Panthers, "You have to give me a real reason why I should dismiss my class." "Well," he said. "There is a strike. We want to shut down the campus. The police are coming and there is going to be trouble on campus." I don't know what possessed me, whether it was fear, courage, or humor, but I shook his hand with great vigor and exclaimed, "Ah! Thank you very much. You have come to protect us from the police, haven't you?" Shaking his head, he looked at me, exasperated, and uttered: "You've got the whole thing wrong, man, wrong!" They left my classroom to continue their rounds. They were surprised to meet a "dumb" white man who was oblivious that he was being intimidated.

I was relieved when they left. I was shaking. I was apprehensive. There were still ten minutes left. I did not want to be courageous at the expense of my students. I told the class to leave. A student, Carolyn Johnson (I remember her name, a Trotskyite, if I am not mistaken), asked me whether I intended to leave, too. I said no. So, no one left. It was an act of solidarity I will never forget.

The campus was beset by rallies, sit-ins, and strikes. President Smith once again asked for police intervention. There was a tense confrontation followed by more arrests, apologies, and finally by the resignation of President Smith, another liberal who attempted to rally the faculty behind him and failed.

There were fundamental differences between the Free Speech Movement at Berkeley and the student movement (SDS and the Progressive Labor Party) at San Francisco State. At Berkeley, the student and faculty leaders managed to focus on free speech not only as an exclusive student right but also as a fundamental faculty right, indeed as the symbol of its authority and autonomy. At San Francisco State, a factionalized faculty and a fractured student movement with competing agendas (between the Old and the New

Left and the New Left and the Black Panthers) and the emergence within the New Left itself of various competing factions did not allow for the formation of a common agenda or a common will.

After the resignation of President Smith, the trustees of the California state college system made an unusual appointment. They named Professor Samuel Ichiye Hayakawa, a Japanese-American and noted semanticist, as president. His primary task was to establish law and order at San Francisco State. Whereas presidents Summerskill and Smith and other administrators had attempted to rally the faculty behind them in order to "legitimize" their actions and had relied on such time-honored methods as mediation, accommodation, and due process, President Hayakawa ignored the faculty. He believed he had full moral and legal authority to act; he did not need any "legitimization." He believed the trustees, and through them the State of California, had already given him all the legitimacy he needed. Whereas his predecessors had agonized and apologized that they had no choice but to call the police to campus, President Hayakawa did not hesitate. Since he was an Asian-American, those with an ethnic agenda were at a loss as to how to deal with him. He confounded and disappointed both the activist students and liberal faculty. Overnight he became a folk hero for many Californians who clamored for law and order, including Ronald Reagan, then governor of California.

The events at San Francisco State, especially during 1964–1968, had a major impact. On the positive side, it created a campus-wide and nation-wide discussion on American foreign policy, national priorities, the civil rights of African-Americans and other minorities, free speech, the mission of American universities, and the autonomy of faculty and the curriculum. On the negative side, it factionalized the faculty and resulted in the breakup of many friendships and even marriages. The inability of university administrators to cope with conflicts within their domains unleashed the open and aggressive intervention of the regents and state governments. It resulted in the decline of the authority of the presidents of many colleges and universities and the increased intervention and activism of the governing boards.

*   *   *

In 1964, when Clare was admitted to Sequoia Hospital in Redwood City to deliver Raffi, our second son, I was teaching a class at the Presidio army base. An army sergeant came to the classroom and handed me a note. I finished my lecture, jumped into the car, and drove—no, flew—to the hospital. The hours that passed seemed to be interminable. Thank God, both Clare and the baby were fine. It was one of the most joyful days of our lives to have another son. Clare called her mother to announce the good news. Then she passed the phone to me. When I gave the receiver back to her, suddenly Clare shouted at her mother, "But Ma, I'm the one who had the baby!" "What was that about?" I asked. Her mother had told her, "Why, Clare, Vartan sounds so tired. . . ." My mother-in-law was very fond of me.

1964 was a banner year. Not only had Raffi been born but I also finished my dissertation. I was astonished that it took me four years to get my B.A. degree and complete all my course requirements and exams for a Ph.D. degree and that it had taken me four years to finish my dissertation. The history department promoted me and gave me a salary raise, as well. Our financial burdens eased a bit. The last days of the month, when we would run out of cash and go through our red couch in search of coins or investigate which grocer or business deposited their checks on Mondays rather than Fridays were over. I did not have to give lectures to local churches or the Rotary or Lions Club for extra income.

1964 was a sad year, too, because my grandmother died. I was heartbroken. I felt guilty for not being with her during her last days. I cried like a baby, in sorrow and in gratitude for all of her care, devotion, sacrifice, suffering, hard work, unconditional and unalloyed love, for her faith in me, for her prayers, and for all the amulets she gave me for my protection. I cried that she did not live long enough to see Clare, who took our children to Tabriz a year later to be baptized in the same church by the same priest, Ter Karapet, who had married my parents and baptized my brothers, my sister, and me.

I think about my grandmother all the time. Several years later, I read the following poem, "My Grandmother," by the Armenian poet Hamo Sahian, translated by Diana Der-Hovanessian, which captures some of my sentiments:

> She is the mother continent
> in the universe of my memory;
> the novel from which
> not one line has been written;
> the legend that lives and breathes
> but has not been told.
> My grandmother is the mother
> continent waiting in my memory.

CHAPTER NINE

To Armenia: Land of Ararat

Now that I'd finished my dissertation, I applied for and received an ACLS-SSRC (American Council of Learned Societies/Social Science Research Council) fellowship to undertake a study of Soviet nationality policies, specifically a case study of Soviet Armenia from 1920 to 1960. In contrast to Afghanistan, the history and literature of Armenia, as well as Soviet history and literature, were accessible and I was in touch with many Armenian, Soviet, European, and American experts. I wanted to write a comprehensive study of Armenia's history and culture, as well as the Armenian Diaspora. My research base was to be Beirut and Yerevan, the capital of Soviet Armenia, with trips to Boston (the archives of the Armenian Revolutionary Federation), the Russian Research Center at Harvard University, the New York Public Library, and the Library of Congress in Washington, D.C. I would go to Venice and Vienna, where the Mekhitarists, an order of Catholic Armenian monks, had established two monasteries (in Venice in 1711 and in Vienna in 1811).

We arrived in Beirut in 1965, happy to be back, rented a furnished house, and had a wonderful time with our many friends. I could do my research and work again with Mr. Vratzian on his memoirs and benefit from his profound knowledge of modern Armenian history. It was also a relief to be out of San Francisco. I needed a reprieve from the turmoil at San Francisco

State. After several months, Clare took our children to Iran to meet my parents and my sister and her family, and to baptize the children in Tabriz. I went to Yerevan in Soviet Armenia, a couple of hours from Tabriz. I did not accompany Clare because the Iranians insisted that my wife and children were Iranian citizens and could travel only with Iranian passports and I was not willing once again to spend months securing an exit visa.

Clare was received with open arms and a great deal of affection by everyone. That she did not stay in a hotel but in my parents' two rooms, that she did not mind sleeping on the floor, that she had learned how to cook Armenian food and speak Armenian astonished everyone. Most of all, my family and friends were impressed that she had brought the children all the way to Tabriz to be baptized.

I could not believe I was in Yerevan. After so many years, so many books, songs, so much fantasy, emotion, and nostalgia, I was looking at Mount Ararat, the symbol of Armenian steadfastness and continuity. Yerevan is Armenia's thirteenth capital in its long history. It was celebrating its 2,750th anniversary. Forebears of the Armenian people had lived on the Anatolian Plateau since 1300 B.C. Among the first tribes to inhabit it were the Hayasa and Nayris, who merged to form the kingdom of Urartu with its capital in Tushba (present-day Van). The Yerevan region was known as Erebuni and the Armenians called themselves Hais. According to legend, the founding father of Armenia was Haik, the great-grandson of the biblical Noah. Haik had defied Bel, the Babylonian ruler, who wanted him and his descendants to settle in the lands of Babylon. Haik, who preferred independence and freedom to Babylon's security and comfort, left for Armenia, the land of Ararat. In an ensuing battle with Bel, he won and his wishes were fulfilled. He had chosen a land of mountains and rocks. Armenia became not only Hayastan (land of Hais) but also Karastan (land of rocks). Today, only 38 percent of the territory of the Republic (the size of the state of Maryland) is arable or habitable.

The Hotel Armenia, Yerevan's main hotel, had modern accommodations, but more important, it was right in Lenin Square, a great place with a fountain as well as a statue of Lenin that was the biggest in the U.S.S.R. It was a showplace for both natives and foreigners. There were many government buildings nearby, housing some of the ministries as well as Armenia's Historic Museum and the National Gallery. Buildings around the square were designed to reflect some features of ancient Armenian architecture. In addition to the buildings around Lenin Square, there was the Opera House (for the use of the Armenian Opera, choral groups, and the symphony orchestra). Perhaps by design, the most imposing building in Yerevan was the

Matenadaran, a library and museum that housed more than thirteen-thousand ancient Armenian manuscripts and incunabula.

At the main entrance of the building (situated on a hill), there was an enormous stone statue of Mesrob Mashtoz, the father of the thirty-six letter Armenian alphabet. Statues of various prominent Armenian cultural icons from the past representing historiography, philosophy, and the arts and sciences stood guard along the front arches of the building. With the exception of those buildings and some predating 1918 that bore a touch of elegance, originality, and nostalgia, most of the buildings in Yerevan were oppressively monotonous. Stalinist tastes and policies had arrested the development of the architectural imagination of Armenians, though you could see, here and there, some attempts to humanize and even give a national character to some of these buildings through ornamental stone carvings.

My trip was arranged by the Soviet State Agency Intourist, which handled tourism and took care of foreign visitors' needs and programs. They were proud that my first visit as a historian was to Matenadaran and it was an extraordinary experience. To see so many rare relics of Armenian culture assembled in one place itself was amazing, but what was moving was that these manuscripts, which had been dispersed all over the globe like the Armenians themselves, had at long last been gathered together in one place. I had one of the great surprises of my life. Onnik Yeganian, my elementary school teacher, who had instilled in me the love of reading, was there. We had an emotional reunion. There were also several experts on Iranian and Ottoman manuscripts from Iran. Some of the great illuminated Armenian manuscripts were here, and also some Iranian and Ottoman imperial edicts pertaining to Armenia or Armenians. It was a rare treat to see the works of ancient Greek philosophers, including Plato and Aristotle, and ancient Greek texts that had survived only in their Armenian translation.

Naturally, I had to visit my cousins (descendants of my father's uncle Tevan), the four brothers, their parents, and their families, who had immigrated to Soviet Armenia in the late 1940s. I remembered the one who had told me when they left Iran, "If one day we find each other on different barricades, don't think you'll be spared just because you are a relative."

I called Petros, one of my cousins, and in a perfect east Armenian dialect, inquired: "Comrade Petros Grigory Grigorian?" "Yes?" "Do you have a close family relative by the name of Vartan Samveli Gregorian in the United States of America?" There was dead silence on the other end. I could "see" and sense that he was trembling out of fear. My stern official tone and my precise language must have frightened him. "Answer yes or no," I said. All he could say was "I can hear you!" He did not dare ask me who was calling, who was asking. I repeated my question feigning impatience. Once again, "I can hear you" was the response. "That is not an answer," I said. "Give me a yes or a no." At this point, Shahen, my favorite cousin, took the phone. He, too, was anxious. "Who is this?" he asked. "Vartan" was my reply. "Your American cousin." They could not believe it. They'd had no idea I was coming to Armenia.

The entire Grigorian family rushed to the Hotel Armenia. I had not seen them for some seventeen years, nor had we kept up with each other. I was afraid to get them into trouble. Now I told them, "Don't worry. I am here with the approval of the Soviet authorities." No, I had not told the Soviet officialdom that I had relatives in Soviet Armenia. But once in Armenia I told them, "Miracle of miracles. Guess what? I have discovered some distant cousins in Armenia." Two of my cousins were tailors, one a house painter, and the fourth the manager of construction projects. They had a great dinner party for me, to which they invited all their friends.

The brothers and their families had a comfortable life. But it came at a cost. In the evenings, while they were having a reception or dinner, strangers would come calling, with bundles under their arms. My cousins, the tailors, were moonlighting by making custom-made suits for private clients. The European fashion magazines that I brought for my cousins were a great hit. Some citizens were very fashion conscious. Each of the brothers had an illegal extra business on the side. They were not alone. Many individuals had at least two jobs.

One day when five of us rode the streetcar, I told them it would be my treat. I paid for five tickets but received only three. As to the other two, my cousins explained, one belongs to the conductor and the other to the ticket taker. These were other venues for corruption, too, including the lottery. First prize was a Volga car; second prize was two weeks' vacation in Sochi on the Black Sea. I had thought the lottery was a capitalist phenomenon. Who are typical winners? I asked. We don't know, they said. Sometimes it takes five or six months before individuals step forward to accept their prizes. But why? I asked. The answer made sense. Those who have lots of cash through embezzlement or illegal moonlighting buy the ticket from the winner for *lots* of cash, enabling them to launder their money. At another dinner party, an engineer was astonished that I paid utility bills in America. He said he would be happy to provide me with a magnet that stops or turns back the meter.

My days were spent at the Miasnikian State Library (the National Library of Armenia), which was endowed with major collections on Armenian history and culture, especially that of the Soviet era, and also housed one of the best collections of Armenian periodicals. I was impressed by the librarians and researchers, fervent missionaries dedicated to the preservation and dissemination of Armenian heritage and its national memory. They were flattered that I had come to the motherland to study its history. Even though they were very cooperative, I faced predictable difficulties in acquiring certain historical texts, studies, and monographs that belonged to "complicated periods" of Soviet Armenian history: the 1920s, the 1934–1937 purges, and 1949–1952. I was able to get almost everything on World War II, but I could not obtain the works of those who had been purged or accused of being allies of Trotsky. I was particularly interested in the archival materials and a periodical issued by the archives with a limited circulation of only three hundred copies. It contained the texts of some extraordinary, rare, and sensitive materials, such as a telegram from Lenin to Bolshevik party leaders of the Transcaucasus, urging them to take advantage of ethnic strife in order to promote the cause of the Revolution.

In order to meet many intellectuals and writers without getting either myself or them in trouble, I decided to lunch at two P.M. at the Hotel Armenia's dining room. I had discovered that that was when several of Armenia's prominent writers, artists, and poets gathered. Once they asked me to join them, it became a routine, daily occurrence. I was thrilled. After all, I had read most of their works. They were pleased that someone from the United States was familiar with their work, able to discuss their literary merits, historical context, and symbolism.

The many writers with whom I dined included Soghomon Tarontsi (1905–1971), Hovhannes Shiraz (1915–1984), Khachig Dashtents (1900–1974), Gegham Sarian (1902–1976), Hovhannes Ghukassian (1919–), and others. What fascinated me was the attitude of these nationalist poets and writers toward Nairi Zarian (1900–1969), a "Stalinist" writer who was scorned for his attacks on fellow writers during the 1930s purges and the postwar period. They never asked him to join them. They also snubbed the writer Kostan Zarian (1885–1969), my former history and philosophy of art teacher at Collège Arménien, not because he had immigrated to Soviet Armenia but because he had changed portions of his great novel *Nawe Leran Vra (The Ship on the Mountain)* to accommodate Soviet Armenia's Communist literary authorities. I was particularly pleased to meet Arto Yeghiazarian, an expert on Soviet nationality policies, a former minister of education, and a Communist who had spent some time in exile.

May First was a great day in Lenin Square. As I descended to the dining room to have breakfast, I saw scores of generals and Red Army top brass who were having breakfast and drinking brandy. As I sat down, they asked me to join them (Russians and Armenians can't stand to see people alone).

After several drinks they offered a toast to my country. I got up and thanked them on behalf of the people of the United States. They were astonished! I am sure they thought I was either a citizen of the Middle East or of an eastern Mediterranean country, such as Cyprus or Greece.

I visited Etchmiadzin, the oldest church in Armenia. Legend has it that Jesus Christ came down from Heaven to point to the site where the first Armenian church should be built, hence, the name Etchmiadzin (meaning "where the only Begotten Son descended"). The church had been the center of Armenian Christendom for many centuries. It had been subject to the vicissitudes of history: Persians, Byzantines, Arabs, Mongols, Uzbeks, Turks, Russians, all these conquerors had passed through there. I pondered how many millions of prayers were uttered in this small cathedral, begging for God's mercy and grace. I wondered how many people had died for this church.

Outside the church, my Intourist guide offered me the standard story. Armenians are proud of their biblical origin and consider Armenia the cradle of civilization, because, in the aftermath of the Great Flood, Noah's Ark came to rest upon Mount Ararat; the Armenians were the first nation to accept Christianity as a state religion (A.D. 301); etc., etc. Inside the cathedral, the wonderful choir and the liturgy moved me to tears. I remembered my early years, when I sang the same hymns to God from the altar of our Saint Sarkis Church in Tabriz. I thought of my wife and our two sons being baptized there . . . and I remembered my grandmother and all my relatives who had died. I remembered my childhood friends. The incense and candles added to the solemnity and beauty. The Catholicos, the spiritual leader of the Armenian Church, was presiding over the Sunday mass. All the bishops and priests were resplendent in their gold-embroidered church vestments. In the midst of their splendid surroundings, I became agitated and angry. Many members of the congregation were talking to each other, several of them in loud voices about mundane daily affairs and some even transacting business. I chastised them for their rude behavior and the noise: "Many of us have traveled tens of thousands of miles to be here in this extraordinary cathedral to partake in a unique aesthetic religious experience. Don't you have any shame? Why can't you be quiet?" Some apologized, "Brother, please forgive us. We have not been in a church for a long time. Frankly we do not know how to pray or behave." At the end of the mass there were many couples and families who were pressing, pushing their children toward the altar. They were there to be baptized. It was the nationalist thing to do and many, who in the past had been oblivious, or frightened, to do it, did it now with much fanfare.

Standing in the crowded and noisy church, I wondered about the role of Christianity and the Church in shaping the national identity and consciousness of Armenians; to be an Armenian and Christian had become inseparable. As I listened to the beautiful liturgy in Grapar (classical Armenian), I reflected on the invention of the Armenian alphabet at the beginning of the fifth century A.D., the translation of the Bible into Armenian in 412, and their impact on developing a national Armenian culture.

Standing in the courtyard of the Etchmiadzin Cathedral after the service, and watching the congregation, I was struck by how diverse it was. There were native Armenians from different regions of the country, and immigrants from Egypt, Iran, Greece, Lebanon, Syria, and France. There were visitors from Russia and other republics of the Soviet Union. Then there were those of us who were from the United States, Ethiopia, France, and Lebanon, visiting Armenia. All kinds of languages were spoken in that courtyard and I wondered what it was that had brought all of us together. Faith and religion? Cultural and moral ties to past generations? A commitment to tradition as an anchor of stability? Craving for individual and collective historical community immortality? Paying homage to our national heritage? I did not have clear answers to those questions and to many others. I asked myself what I had in common with these Armenians and all the others I had met in Armenia. History, language, culture, and religion? Race, ethnicity, nationality, common genes, national consciousness, intellectual and moral ties to the dead, the past? Collective suffering? Discrimination, massacres, and genocide? How about the fact that I was also an Iranian and an American?

How does one reconcile these legacies and realities and still retain one's individuality and the integrity of one's commitments? I realized that in each of us in such circumstances, the whole is more than the parts; the multiple heritages are not liabilities, they are assets, they provide one with a critical distance from ideological straitjackets and frozen orthodoxies. I realized then and there that my multiple legacies had played a major role in my teaching philosophy; that they had given me a healthy perspective toward all orthodoxies, a belief that they were all to be tested; that I had an obligation as a teacher to help my students develop the critical thinking and discernment that would allow them to make a conscious commitment to develop a capacity for perspective. I realized that as a teacher I had to provide my students with an intellectual compass for their travels from one culture to another, yet at the same time strengthen their knowledge of their own cultural legacies to prevent deracination and alienation, to provide them a moral, cultural, and intellectual base.

Armenia, which had a rare ethnic homogeneity (94 percent), owed its diversity to the Armenian Diaspora, to the Soviet Union, to the presence of small communities of Russians, Ukrainians, Greeks, Kurds, Jews, and Yazidis. Modern Armenian culture had been exposed from the eighteenth century on to Russian, French, Italian, German, English, Ottoman and Persian cultures. Their influences were readily discernible within Armenian culture. I was amazed that Armenia had over 95 percent literacy, and that many Armenians were familiar with Russian, Persian, French, English, Arabic, Turkic, and Georgian languages and literatures. There was an astounding respect for the book, for writers, poets, and artists. In a land in need of living heroes, the writers and artists, and even the scientists, were a pantheon for the Armenian nation. The greatest gift one could give an Armenian intellectual or a graduate student were foreign literary and art books.

In 1966, when I arrived in Moscow, I had brought with me three books requested by the poet Abraham Alikian, a graduate of the Collège Arménien, who had emigrated to the Soviet Union. The books, literary works of Sartre, Camus, and Céline, were gifts from none other than Mme. Yoland, my French teacher. At Soviet customs, I told the officer in charge that I was reading these books and asked him if I could keep them. "Do you engage in any censorship?" I asked. "No, by all means, keep your books" was the response. I was so pleased that I was able to hand those books to Mr. Alikian. I have never seen so much happiness on the face of a man living in a small, miserable room with his wife, who was in the grip of cancer. When I handed him the books, it was as if I had brought him medicine and gold combined.

On weekends, I visited historical sites. The entire country seemed a vast museum. Wherever I went I heard the same proud refrain: We are an oasis of civilization; we cannot live without culture; we were the ones who established the first printing house in the Middle East in 1638 (in Isfahan); Armenia is too small for Armenians. They bragged that half a million Armenians had fought for the Soviet Union during World War II, and at least half had died; some 100,000 were decorated for bravery. They expressed gratitude to Russia and the Soviet Union for providing career opportunities to Armenians throughout the Soviet Union in the realms of education, culture, science, politics, and the military, and for protecting the Armenian republic.

If, in addition to security and opportunity, the Soviets would provide freedom and equity, then everything would be great. They complained that Soviet nationality policies were unjust, that such ethnically mixed regions as Nakhichevan (where Armenians were in the minority) and even historical regions such as Nagorno-Karabakh (where Armenians were in the majority) were made autonomous zones and placed under Azerbaijani control. The republics of Georgia and Azerbaijan were given control of such "autonomous" regions but not Armenia. They were adamant that the people of Nagorno-Karabakh had a right to self-determination and should be allowed to join the Armenian republic. After all, they argued, hadn't Armenians lost more soldiers in defense of the Soviet Union than Georgians, Azeris, and peoples of some other republics combined? Did not the Soviet constitution grant the right of self-determination, even cessation?

During my lunch hour and at dinner, I met writers, historians, and public figures. They recounted with great excitement the events of 1965. In Yerevan, they said, the month of April was full of tension, agitation, and anticipation. Everybody was anxious about April 24, 1965, which marked the fiftieth anniversary of the Armenian Genocide. How to commemorate the event, what was to be the official stance of the Communist Party and Soviet authorities in Armenia were subjects of speculation. On April 24, thousands of Armenians gathered in front of the Opera House. Inside, the Soviet authorities had organized a solemn, dignified, but quiet official commemoration. Pretty soon, the gathering became a mass demonstration, which was at first peaceful and orderly, then gradually got out of hand. There were fiery nationalist speeches demanding that the Soviet Union formally recognize the Armenian Genocide and seek to retrieve the "lost Armenian lands from Turkey."

Such an outburst of Armenian nationalism placed a heavy burden on the government of Soviet Armenia and the Communist Party. There were arrests. Strenuous efforts were made to calm the unruly crowds and to convince them to disperse. To avert a disaster, the Communist authorities asked for the intervention of Vazken I, the Catholicos of All Armenians, the spiritual leader of the Armenian Church. However, even the Catholicos could not restore law and order. Promises were made to build a national memorial to commemorate the victims of the Armenian Genocide. The demonstration sent shock waves throughout Armenia. Everybody was relieved, however, that there was no military crackdown and no mass arrests. A few years later the Soviet government built a grandiose and imaginative memorial and gave its official sanction to the annual Genocide commemoration ceremonies.

Armenians were right to worry. Several writers and historians told me in confidence, and in hushed tones, about their forty-year ordeal due to ever-changing, contradictory, arbitrary Soviet literary and cultural policies that landed some of them in jail and sent some to exile in Siberia or to execution. Armenia had lost three generations of its intellectual and political elite. The first was its prerevolutionary elite (left, moderate, and conservative), which was forced into exile in 1920. The second generation was decimated during the Great Purges (1936–1938) and the third during World War II and later (1949–1952).

The Communists, I was told, encouraged nationalism, mobilized it as a potent force against the Nazis during World War II and then in the aftermath, accused the writers and artists and scholars of having "harbored nationalist sentiments." We discussed the personality cult of Stalin. The poets too had been guilty. The most outlandish praise of Stalin was that of Shiraz, who had written that there is dawn because the sun is ashamed to rise every morning since on earth there is another sun, the Real Sun, Stalin. I asked him how he could have written that. His answer astonished me: "Everybody did it but I overpraised him so that people would know I didn't mean it. . . ."

I learned how the writers hibernated during periods of repression and persecution, protecting themselves by translating Shakespeare. The Great Bard was considered a safe bet since Marx, Lenin, and Stalin all considered him to be a part of the great humanistic patrimony of mankind. Those who did not know English translated Shakespeare from Russian. By examining the publication dates of translations of Shakespeare's works, one can detect periods of special political persecution in Armenia and I am sure elsewhere in the Soviet Union as well (Pasternak, for example). Armenians named their sons Hamlet and their daughters Ophelia and Desdemona. There were many Romiks (Romeos) and lots of Juliets. The national obsession for Shakespeare was matched only by chess and soccer.

The most amazing evening I had in Armenia was with a writer who came to see me at the hotel. We had, as was the norm, several drinks. He read to me from his prose and his poems, and at the end of the evening, dedicated his manuscript to me: "Take it, do what you wish to do with it. It is yours." I was aware that he wanted me to smuggle his manuscript and publish it abroad. I declined. I was being "supervised," and I didn't want either of us in trouble.

The most depressing evening was at the home of an Armenian engineer from Alexandria, Egypt, a Communist and an Armenian nationalist who had immigrated to Soviet Armenia. He was disillusioned. He had begged me to have dinner with his wife and two teenage children. Their small apartment was full of cultural icons. During the dinner he broke down. "Please get us out of this hell. The rulers of the country have no ideals and no principles; they are ruthless opportunists. Our life is one of misery. Our meals are the only occasions of civility, manners, and decorum; we play Mozart, Bach, and Beethoven to reclaim our humanity and dignity in the sea of bar-

barism where everything is ugly, corrupt, and decadent." Then he wept openly, as did his wife. They wanted to return to Egypt. I could not do anything to help them and the sight of this disillusioned idealist, drowning in misery, haunted me for many years.

I spent another depressing evening at the home of Hovhannes Ghukassian. He had written an extraordinary novel entitled *Voskan Yerevantsi,* about the life of an Armenian monk from Yerevan who had gone to Amsterdam and in 1660 printed the first Armenian bible. The novel became a best-seller. The author, who was also from Tabriz, was the son of the secretary of the Armenian Prelacy of Azerbaijan whom I knew. Mr. Ghukassian, too, after several drinks, broke down. "I have written this novel. It is set in Amsterdam. I have never seen that city. I want to visit it but the authorities do not permit me. They fear, because I am an immigrant, that I may not return. Who do they think I am? Would I leave, abandon my wife and children? I simply want to see Amsterdam. Please help!"

The most moving, extraordinary evening was the night of a concert of the Armenian Philharmonic Orchestra. As the concert was about to begin, there was a great commotion. His Holiness Vazken I, the Catholicos, and several bishops and seminarians arrived and took their seats in the balcony. We visitors stood as a sign of respect. Most of the audience remained seated. Some asked, in Russian and Armenian, "Hey, isn't that Vazken?" I was taken aback by the crude behavior of the audience. At the end of the concert, however, when the time came for encores, the audience began to shout in unison, demanding that the orchestra play *"Sourp, Sourp"* (Holy, Holy), one of the most moving hymns in the Armenian Church liturgy. The conductor demurred, then played an excerpt from Handel's *Messiah.* The audience kept shouting, *"Sourp, Sourp."* At the end, the frightened conductor, fearing a riot, played the hymn. Grinning with satisfaction, the audience turned towards the balcony.

I continued to wonder about the tenacity of the Armenian Church and its hold on Armenians. After forty-six years of Soviet assault against the foundations of religion, massive atheist campaigns, closures of almost all the churches of the country, persecution of the clergy, and the suffocation of Khoren I, the Armenian Catholicos, the Church was still there, as was its leader and his audience, who had forced a state orchestra to pay homage to the spiritual leader of a church that still existed after 1,650 years, and still claimed their loyalty.

The desk manager of the hotel, an immigrant from Tabriz, would ask me about my work and my family. I told him that I was worried about my wife and children: "I know my wife writes me regularly but I have not received any letters for two to three weeks. I have sent telegrams and have received responses that they are all right, but something must be wrong. I better cut short my stay and return to Beirut." "Don't rush, don't worry," he said. "You never know, you may get some mail tomorrow." The next day I received a bundle of some seven to ten letters. . . .

The Soviet writers and intellectuals that I met were curious about the Vietnam War and the American involvement. "What is the attitude of the American intelligentsia toward that war?" I told them that it was unpopular. Then they would ask, "Is it true that the Vietnamese have shot down American planes and destroyed American tanks?" "Yes," I said. "My goodness, do you mean the Communist propaganda is so strong that they have even convinced the smart Americans of such outlandish tales?" they would respond with laughter. Soviet propagandists had lied so often that when they were actually reporting facts, citizens took it with a grain of salt. I was asked repeatedly about my salary, if I had a car, how many bedrooms we had, and if we had a private bathroom. They asked whether, when I went from California to New York, I needed a visa or police permit. My response was received with skepticism.

When it was time to leave, I was given a great send-off by my cousins and their families, as well as by the librarians and the writers and scholars with whom I had established cordial relations. That last meal was memorable because of its length and the number of toasts and the amount of liquor we consumed. I don't remember whether it was the poet Shiraz or Dashtents who offered the assurance that the Armenians are trees of civilization: we have been crushed many times, leveled by heavy bulldozers not so long ago, but as long as the roots remain, and, thank God, they do, we will continue to rise like the Phoenix.

My months in Yerevan were productive as I had gathered volumes of research material, but I was unable to get some of the sensitive and rare literary and scholarly works of authors who had been purged and not yet rehabilitated. Months later when I arrived back in the United States, I received ten to fifteen packages of books from the National Library. On the cover was stamped "Complete Works of Lenin." When I opened the packages, I found all the Armenian periodicals that I had asked for from the dedicated librarians of the National Library.

Before my departure, I paid a visit to Catholicos Vazken I in his residence in Etchmiadzin. He spoke about culture and civilization. He spoke French. He reminisced about his youth and education in Romania. He, too, stressed that as long as the roots remain intact Armenia will endure. As I rose to leave, he pinned on my lapel a golden medallion that depicts Etchmiadzin.

He was a sad, beleagured man. He considered himself a witness for God, the Christian faith, and the Armenian Church. I wished him good luck. I thought of Mr. Vratzian. I felt sad that he, who had left Armenia in 1921, was not with me. It was his ardent hope one day to return to his beloved country. I gathered the Soviet authorities had suggested that he go there as a tourist. He was too proud, had too much dignity, to do that. If he had been invited as a writer, I am sure he would have gone.

I returned to Vienna via Moscow. At the Moscow airport, I was strip-searched. They asked me about papers and manuscripts. I had none. They confiscated ten rubles. It was illegal to export Soviet currency. It was my intention to give it to the porters, I said, but I was told that tips are not permitted. A receipt was given, and I was informed that when I returned to the Soviet Union, I could reclaim my ten rubles. I had with me four bottles of Armenian cognac as gifts. I was told that I could take only one or two. Fine, was my answer, then on behalf of the people of the United States I would like to present them to the two porters. . . . And so it went.

In Vienna, I had a quiet meal with the Mekhitarist monks at their monastery. Most were old, some very old. One read a long passage from the Bible. Meals were a time of reflection and contemplation. During the luncheon, I thought of their brethren in Venice and their monastery on the Island of San Lazzaro. The differences were stark. After some three centuries in Italy, the monks of Venice had taken on some of the characteristics of the Italians—they were warm, hospitable, full of gesture and laughter. Those in Vienna were reserved, correct, measured, quiet, businesslike, yet courteous. With the Venetians, you could be ambiguous; with the Viennese, you had to be precise. In Venice, it was clear to me why Lord Byron, the Romantic poet, chose the Armenian monastery as his refuge (and struggled to learn the Armenian language). Then again I compared these Armenians to those I had known in Iran, Lebanon, and the United States with those in Armenia. What was our common bond? Were we a virtual nation, held together by memory, language, and faith? Had we become the first transcendental nation? How about the Jews? I spent some time reading and rereading William Saroyan's observation on Armenia and the Armenians:

I should like to see any power of the world destroy this race, this small tribe of unimportant people, whose wars have all been fought and lost, whose structures have crumbled, literature is unread, music is unheard, and prayers are no more answered.

Go ahead, destroy Armenia. See if you can do it. Send them into the desert without bread and water. Burn their homes and churches.

Then see if they will not laugh, sing and pray again. For when two of them meet anywhere in the world, see if they will not create a new Armenia.

Once again we bid farewell to beautiful Beirut and to our friends. Once again, I bid farewell to my former teachers, to Sir, and, of course, to Mr. Vratzian. I was particularly happy that my relations with him were solid and our friendship intimate, as it had been in the past. He gave me several of his books with a written instruction: "Read." It was clear to both of us that teaching at the Collège was not a realistic option for me. The ideal arrangement would have been to obtain a teaching position at the American University of Beirut and then teach a course or two at the Collège without pay. Unfortunately, there were no available positions at AUB.

Thanks to Mr. Vratzian's guardianship, I had become a historian. I had finished a project on Afghanistan and now I was working on another one on Soviet Armenia. He had a drawer where he kept over one hundred articles, short and long, scholarly and popular, that I had written on various aspects of Armenian history and literature. He was particularly pleased by my "discovery" of the writings of President Theodore Roosevelt on the Armenian Question, which I had summarized in an article I published in 1959 outlining Roosevelt's merciless criticism of President Woodrow Wilson and the United States for failing to declare war immediately both against Germany and the Ottoman Empire in 1915 because of German deportations of Belgians and the Ottoman deportation and subsequent "murder of the Armenian nation."

When I left Mr. Vratzian, I did not know that this was to be our last farewell. We corresponded for the next three years. He died in 1969 and was given a national funeral. He never saw Armenia again. I hoped that Soviet Armenia would welcome the remains of the last prime minister of Independent Armenia (1918–1920) to Armenia, but they did not. I hope the government of the newly independent Armenia will do that someday in the near future, for Mr. Vratzian belongs to Armenia. And without him, I would not be where I am and remain who I am.

In Soviet Armenia, many people had advised me not to give any interviews because one way or another my remarks would be misconstrued. Before I left, I was interviewed by a Soviet magazine. They asked about my impressions of Soviet Armenia and the Soviet Union. I answered, "It's amazing. What can I say?" Several months later, a magazine article appeared. It said, "As Gregorian so aptly summed it up, 'What can I say!' "

*   *   *

Back in California, I resumed my teaching at San Francisco State and served as faculty advisor to the Progressive Labor Party.

In 1966, upon our return, I was promoted to the rank of associate professor with tenure. As we celebrated, I felt happy and content. I had reached a safe, secure harbor in my life. I was ready to spend the rest of my life at San Francisco State College. Clare, who had endured so many hardships without much ado, astonished me. Do you mean after all your suffering, all your hard work, you are content to be where you are? Is this your ultimate ambition? she asked me. I was taken aback. I began to think, once again, about possibilities. I began to dream about teaching at a university. It was at this juncture that I met two extraordinary strangers, who, once again, played pivotal roles in my professional life: professors Eugen Weber and David Riesman. Eugen Weber was chairman of the history department at UCLA. He was a celebrated scholar; I had read his seminal work, *Action Française,* on the French rightist movement. He taught a seminar at Stanford University on fascism. A weekly seminar brought together members of Stanford's history department as well as professors from neighboring state colleges. I was delighted to be invited to be a member. By the end of the seminar, Professor Weber had adopted me. He asked me whether I would teach his major lecture course on European history in 1968, as he was to be in France. To teach a prominent professor's celebrated lecture course at UCLA was scary but exciting. I accepted with trepidation and hope. And Professor Weber's encouragement did not stop there. It inaugurated three decades of an enduring friendship as he became one of my scholarly guides.

David Riesman, a member of the Harvard faculty, appeared suddenly in my life in 1968. He was a visiting Fellow at the Center for Advanced Study in the Behavioral Sciences at Stanford. He had dedicated himself to the study of American higher education (since the mid-1950s). A leading member of the Carnegie Commission on Higher Education, he was very interested in the student movement. I had read *The Lonely Crowd,* whose central thesis is that the dominant features of the social character of Americans had undergone a dramatic shift since the nineteenth century due, among other things, to the emergence of a service- and consumption-based economy. The change, according to Riesman, was from "inner-directed" personality types (self-reliant, determined, independent, purposeful) to "other-directed" types, who looked for guidance to their peer groups, and to mass media for their worth and place in society.

We had debated those classifications in my classes, questioning some of the conclusions of *The Lonely Crowd,* especially "the idea that men are created free and equal is both true and misleading; men are created different;

they lose their social freedom and their individual autonomy in seeking to become like each other." We debated the dangers of a centralized, homogenized, pasteurized, bureaucratized society, inhabited by oversocialized, anxious "personality mongers," mindless and helpless consumers, glad-hands and salesmen, isolated and lonely individuals who are empty, clueless, and devoid of independent meaning and purpose, easily malleable and subjects of manipulation and social engineering.

I went to Stanford to meet Riesman and what was supposed to be a courtesy visit became a substantive, lengthy discussion about American higher education. Professor Riesman had a deep interest in ideology and politics. I was surprised by his distaste for nationalism and amazed by his advocacy of rights for women, long before feminism became fashionable in academic circles. It is fair to say that he was not one for small talk. Shortly after that he asked me to read two manuscripts on higher education and comment on them. I was flattered and worked hard to make "a meaningful contribution." I sent him a nine-page, single-spaced commentary.

Now, all of a sudden, a man I stood in awe of had become not only a friend but also a busy champion of mine. More than anyone, it was Riesman who instilled in me the self-confidence that I needed to enter the domain of the university. For thirty years, he was an enthusiastic interlocutor, intellectual gadfly, tutor, mentor, booster, and friend.

As 1968 drew to a close, San Francisco was the focus of yet another new phenomenon: white students, mostly from upper- or middle-class families, were dropping out. Their mantra was "do your own thing." Calling themselves hippies, they were in rebellion against a "sterile society," the corporate state, and "dehumanizing technology." They advocated a return to Nature and experiments in "true communities." They described themselves as conscientious nonconformists in matters of religion, drugs, sex, art forms, all amplified by rock music. They promoted Eastern religions and sects—Hinduism, Shamanism, Zen Buddhism, Sufism. Eclectic, exotic clothing and long hair became their symbols of authenticity and nonconformity. San Francisco, already known for the Beat literary movement, became a center of the counterculture, celebrated through love-ins, live-ins, and be-ins. Hippies soon became a matter of national and international curiosity. The Haight-Ashbury district became a tourist site.

Hippies were criticized or caricatured as being "hollow," "spoiled," "self-indulgent drop-outs," "aimless rebels," or "rebels without a cause," "anti-rational," "selfish and self-centered," reactionary, narcissistic and hedonistic, or cultists of youth culture. Their critics were usually members of an older generation. Some elements of the Old and New Left criticized them as irresponsible "escapists" and "decadents" who, through their lifestyle and use of drugs, had harmed "the movement." Others, such as Abbie Hoffman, the activist, and Allen Ginsberg, the poet, attempted, with some success, to recruit and politicize the hippies and to use them against the war in Vietnam, to show its "absurdity" through a "theater of the absurd."

While white students had the "luxury" to "drop out" and "do their own thing," the black, Chicano, and Asian students considered themselves representatives of their communities, asserting *group rights* rather than individual ones. Black militant students looked with suspicion, even disdain, on such "white exports" as consciousness-expanding through drugs or mysticism, "liberation through decadence," and a "return to Nature." Blacks already possessed "soul." They considered "dropping out" an unaffordable privilege. "Individualism" outside the realm of artistic creativity was also deemed a luxury. They emphasized organization, discipline, and community. They saw universities not as tools of the corporate state but as sources of education, leadership, and power, necessary for the emancipation and reconstruction of their communities. Black students by and large were interested in identity politics.

The Students for a Democratic Society, whose original mission was to serve as the northern partner of the southern civil rights movement, did not know how to cope with Black Power and its exclusion of whites. It did not know how to deal with identity politics. It was involved in the antiwar movement and was also interested in the creation of a national and international "movement for the poor." SDS was a movement, not a party. It did not have a single, coherent ideology and had no effective central control. SDS and the New Left, in general, spoke of the poor and class struggle, while the black students, the Black Panther Party, and others talked about quotas, courses, programs, and departments of ethnic studies.

The New Left's eventual alliance with blacks and the Black Panthers proved to be one of convenience rather than of ideology. To blacks, ideology and rhetoric were organizing tools. They had no space for "deviationism," "factionalism," and ideological consistencies. They were interested in power, they were pragmatists, they could change their strategies, tactics, and even alliances. White radicals did not have that flexibility. Some were puritans; they believed moral values were absolute. They engaged in intense ideological and theoretical disputes. They were dealing not only with issues of racism but also those of the war, the nuclear threat, capitalism and poverty, the structure of universities, gender.

By 1968, SDS broke into competing, warring factions. One wing, the Old and New Left, led by the Progressive Labor Party, advocated a Maoist brand of Marxism-Leninism. A second faction consisted of the Weather Underground, and the third was the Revolutionary Youth Movement. The tactics of the Weather Underground and its campaign of terrorism created further divisions within the SDS. Soon the Progressive Labor Party found itself at odds with the Black Panther Party. While both of them were against "the Establishment," one wanted to build a Marxist labor movement, and the other was interested not in universal working-class solidarity but in specific issues such as Black Power and black control. Prompted by the Progressive Labor Party, SDS made unsuccessful attempts to reach out and organize the rank and file of U.S. labor. In 1968, I even saw leaflets and booklets put out by student activists, or "revolutionaries," on "how to talk like a worker" and "how to pass as a worker." Needless to say, the AFL-CIO did not welcome any such effort.

During 1967–68, my last academic year at San Francisco State, two developments that galvanized the campus had major consequences for the future of the college and the politics of the State of California. On November 6, 1967, a group of nine black students beat up the editor of *The Gater,* the campus student newspaper, and ransacked its offices. The group included a part-time English instructor who was the minister of education of the Black Panther Party, and who said that the attack was prompted by alleged "racist writings" and the "racist attitudes" of the editor. The faculty of the journalism department asked the American Federation of Teachers and the college's Academic Senate to take a stand on behalf of the editor and *The Gater.* They passed. As the nine black students were arrested for assault, the campus erupted.

On December 6, fifty classes were disrupted. San Francisco police arrested one hundred students. This incident did not overshadow the fifteen nonnegotiable demands of the black students and of the Third World Liberation Front, which wanted, among other things, the creation of a Black Studies department and automatic admission of any black student who wanted to attend the college. The academic leadership of the college, attempting to deal with these challenges, had to deal with a new crisis—the demand of student revolutionaries to evict the air force ROTC. There were sit-ins, threats, disruptions, and demonstrations. Once again the police were called to campus. Once again they used force and arrested many protesters.

The governing board of the California state college system had instructed President Robert Smith to relieve George Murray, the Black Panther minister of education, from all teaching duties. The president demurred until the trustees ordered him to do so. The students ordered a strike. They wanted to shut down the campus. The American Federation of Teachers, which represented 120 of 1,300 faculty, decided to support the strike in the name of faculty autonomy. Student revolutionaries hailed the federation's support though in the long run it weakened their position. The AFL-CIO Council had approved the AFT strike for its "economic objectives" or platform but not its political agenda. Some radical students found themselves saddled with a "reformist" ally not in line with their revolutionary platform. Having obtained AFT support, the students could not openly reject that alliance without weakening their cause in the eyes of the public and the students. It would have been perceived that SDS was unable to make an effective alliance with labor.

The student movement, its antiwar activism, its stance against nuclear weapons, and its defense of civil rights appealed to many members of San Francisco State's faculty, especially the liberal ones. The students' attempts, however, to have a major voice in the curriculum, hiring, the promotion of faculty, and faculty governance was met with resistance, if not hostility. Student and some faculty support of the Black Panther Party and its platform and tactics caused further discord within the ranks of the faculty.

In the shadow of the San Francisco State crisis were Mayor Joseph Alioto of San Francisco, a potential Democratic gubernatorial candidate, and Governor Ronald Reagan. Reagan was eager to send the National Guard to the college (which would have bolstered his law and order image and hurt Mayor Alioto's image by dramatizing his inability to cope with the breakdown of law and order in his own city). Alioto was eager to preempt Reagan's position. He sent the police to the college and, as a former top labor negotiator, mobilized religious, civic, and ethnic leaders and political organizations to try to end the strike by mediation.

In *The Liberal Imagination,* Lionel Trilling had defined some of the essential features of liberalism: "imagination of variousness and possibility" or complexity and difficulty. At San Francisco State and elsewhere, liberals attempted to grapple with major challenges through novel, university-wide forums or "teach-ins." It was their attempt to create a rational forum, a means to educate their activist community and to affirm one of their basic premises: that every problem can be solved through reason, that problems and challenges by their very nature require reflection, deliberation, tolerance, and compromise—in short, rational solutions. Some liberal faculty members were shocked when radical, especially black radical students, were not satisfied with such public testimonials and demanded specific actions and timetables. Faculty members' agonizing over means and ends, long-term implications, whether actions were democratic or unconstitutional were usually met by suspicion that they were rationalizations for faculty inaction.

My last course at San Francisco State was an advanced seminar. Both inside and outside the classroom, I had an ongoing debate with many white, radical, revolutionary students about Dr. Martin Luther King Jr. Some of them did not think much of him and considered him to be an "Uncle Tom," "a tool of the Establishment," provider of religion as an "opiate" to the masses. Several of his harshest critics were in my seminar, including a conservative who considered King to be a demagogue.

On April 4, 1968, Martin Luther King was assassinated and all hell broke loose. I had been won over by Dr. King's writings and actions. His death shocked me. I was outraged but I didn't know what to do. That evening Professor Reginald Zelnik drove me from Berkeley to San Francisco for my seminar. I could have canceled it by phone but I did not. All my students were there, quiet, including King's critics. I wrote on the blackboard: "I refuse to teach tonight" and left.

As we were getting ready to leave for UCLA, there was one farewell dinner I never anticipated. Having enlisted my wife's cooperation, some students of mine, past and present, had organized a surprise party. I entered the room and witnessed a rare sight. There were many familiar faces—Young Democrats, Young Americans for Freedom, Republicans, Socialists, Trotskyites, Jews, Arabs, Iranians, Armenians, an anarchist or two, several members of the Progressive Labor Party, a Saudi prince, several Zionists, and two members of the Black Student Union. They had declared their own temporary, unilateral moratorium. Some of them had even cooked the meal together. For a change I was speechless. As I shook everyone's hand, I was in such an emotional state that I shook Clare's. "Hey, wake up!" she said.

It was one of the most gratifying days of my life. As a teacher, I felt vindicated and hugely rewarded. There was goodwill, a warm atmosphere, and many toasts and speeches. I was in such a trance that I don't recall any of the remarks. The sheer presence of such a mix of people and causes was enough for me. I felt hopeful, I was convinced that teaching actually matters.

The night before we left for UCLA, President S. I. Hayakawa called to ask me a simple question. What does SDS stand for? After all the years, and all the turmoil, he had not had sufficient curiosity to learn about a national organization that, by the end of 1968, had an estimated national membership of 100,000. My advice to him was to read their literature.*

---

* For the context and chronology of facts and figures in this chapter I am indebted to Robert Cohen and Reginald E. Zelnik, editors, *The Free Speech Movement* (Berkeley: University of California Press, 2002).

CHAPTER TEN

To Texas

While there was high academic drama unfolding at San Francisco State College, 1968 became an important landmark for me. To my great surprise and joy, I was one of ten faculty members in the nation chosen to receive a ten-thousand-dollar tax-free E. H. Harbison Award for Distinguished Teaching given by the Danforth Foundation. The news was conveyed to me by my wife, who was crying with joy. Professor Vucinich, my Stanford mentor, had called her. It changed our lives.

A couple of months earlier, I had been invited by the University of Texas at Austin's Center for Middle Eastern Studies to give a talk. They were paying my expenses as well as an honorarium. I was surprised that there were only ten or fifteen people in attendance. I didn't know that the "talk" was a subterfuge to get me to Texas and to interest me in a job. Professors Roger Shattuck and William Arrowsmith of the University of Texas were members of the Danforth Foundation's Harbison Award selection committee or its advisors. They had seen my file, as had John Silber, the dean of the College of Arts and Sciences. They had enlisted the support of the university's Middle East Center, and it needed the support of the history department. It was Silber's plan to recruit recipients of the Harbison Award. He himself was one of the winners, as was Arrowsmith. The fact that my manuscript *The Emergence of Modern Afghanistan: Politics of Reform and Modernization, 1880–*

1946, was accepted by the Stanford University Press and was to be published in spring 1969 came in handy, as did many letters of recommendation the university had sought from scores of my professors, along with David Riesman and Eugen Weber. Texas offered me an associate professorship with tenure, a salary (eighteen thousand dollars) double what I was getting at San Francisco State, and a research sabbatical.

When I went to Texas for my interview, the university was in turmoil. They were still recovering from a tragedy—a sniper firing from the University of Texas Tower had killed and wounded many students. As I met with members of appropriate faculty committees and was given a tour of the city, I realized how parochial a Californian I was. I had no knowledge of Texas in general, Austin in particular, or the university. My impression of the state was based entirely on Hollywood movies. I phoned Clare to tell her of my surprise that the city of Austin had lots of hills, water, trees, and great houses.

On Sunday, November 3, 1968, the University of Texas announced my appointment. I was overwhelmed by the headlines. The *Austin-American* wrote, "One member of the Harbison selection committee, in his final assessment on the teacher, reported that Dr. Gregorian 'stands high on an absolute scale but is clearly an isolated peak of excellence, a Mt. Everest, among state college professors in the land.' " That became the subject of many jokes, as height is not my long suit, but I was pleased and embarrassed. There were many flattering quotes from students. They sounded like eulogies. I tried to be blasé but without success, however, as my wife told me, without her, my head would be the size of a large watermelon and one of my professors told me, "You're not that great to be that modest."

Some of my friends had teased me about my accent. "How the hell are you going to be able to teach European intellectual history and the history of the Middle East to Texans? They will not understand you." "Don't worry," I said. "They will." My first class in Garrison Hall was very exciting. I had a large class, full of well-dressed male students and beautiful, well-coiffed females. The class was preponderantly white. If I am not mistaken there were two or three Mexican-Americans and one black student. I began by telling them a few basic things about me. Then I said, "I understand you have a problem with your accent. I'll try to do my best to understand you." After a few moments of silence, the class roared with laughter. Then I gave them my "rules of conduct" in the classroom. Even in the 60s, I had managed to sell my "bourgeois rules" to my students. I listed them in order of importance:

Don't eat in the classroom or chew. I already have a problem with
   my English and the rhythm of your chewing hypnotizes me.
Don't read the newspaper during my lecture. It is rude. But if you do,
   interrupt me to let us all know about any important news.
If you intend to leave the classroom early, please sit next to the door,
   in order not to cause a commotion in the classroom. Otherwise
   your classmates may be under the false impression that you are
   walking out as a sign of protest.

I told the students that my ambition was to teach them to know the facts;
to understand the nature and the impact of historical data and the role of individuals and ideas in shaping historical trends and social forces; to understand all the orthodoxies and be able to challenge them; to navigate through
many cultures; to go beyond identity politics; and to learn how to reconcile
the unique and the universal. In short, I wanted them to be able to think. I
told them that the university was giving them a treasury and a guide to help
them develop an informed, open mind and a receptive and experienced
heart. When asked about my personal philosophy of life, I told them I was a
rationalist, as well as a Pascalian. Occasionally, there is room for promoting
the heart's reasons over those of reason itself.

Texas was huge! It was an endless frontier. To me, it stood for motion,
commotion, momentum, and power. It was a proud, self-confident, opti-
mistic state. It was the land of "why not?" and "can do." Whether you knew
it or not, while in Texas you had to think big. With size went a swaggering
boastfulness. "It's the biggest state in the Union." "It's the best state." There
was speculation that Texas attempted to block Alaskan statehood in order to
remain the biggest state. Texas had the biggest horizons, the biggest skies,
and the largest number of stars. In Texas, you never felt confined, you never
felt claustrophobic. It seemed as if the whole state was restless and on the
move.

Thanks to cowboy movies, I had come to know Texas not only as the
land of cowboys, but also as the land of individuals, where justice always
prevailed, where the good guys always won, where individuals did matter
and were not lost in the multitude. I found out that Texas was not a neat cat-
egory. It defied any categorization. Indeed, Texas had many maverick individuals. The word maverick originated in Texas. I met numerous original
characters in Texas, proud, assertive, and active. Texas was also the land of
great raconteurs and adventurers who told tall tales. Texans were hospitable, generous, direct, stubborn, opinionated, proud of their land, proud

of their heritage, their localities, and their peculiarities. They were proud that Texas had joined the Union as a *sovereign state* and not as a *territory.*

Texans always talked about size. Among the hundreds of jokes, I remember two. The subject of the elephant was given as a dissertation topic to a group of international students. The Italian wrote about "the vocal capacities of the elephant," the Frenchman about "sex in the life of elephants," the Japanese about "elephants and politeness," the Indian about the "passive resistance of the elephants," the German about "the term elephant, a linguistic and metaphysical analysis." When the time came for the American, who happened to be a Texan, he wrote, "How to produce bigger and better elephants."

Then there was a joke about a Texan who was visiting his friend in Vermont. He was given a tour of his friend's four-hundred-acre farm. Is that all? asks the Texan. Yes, replies the friend. First of all, where I come from, says the Texan, we don't call our lands farms. We call them ranches. Secondly, mine is so big that when I get into my car in the morning, by nightfall I am still in my car. I used to have a car like that, too, the Vermonter responds.

There were some peculiarities that were not ficticious. At one time there were congressmen from Texas named Pickle, Onion, and Herring and one of the major foundations was named Hogg.

It always astonished me that I, a Tabrizi boy from Iran, felt so much at home in Texas. My family and I adjusted immediately. We loved Austin and Texas. I loved the university. Unlike some who had come to Texas from other parts of the country, Clare and I did not feel in exile. We bought our first house in Austin. We celebrated the birth of Dareh Ardashes, our third son. We enjoyed the company of Shelly (our first dog, acquired at UCLA). I became a chauvinist about Texas and a booster of the strengths, the qualities, and the potential of the University of Texas.

The city of Austin was beautiful, full of charm. I saw my first country music festival there and heard many renditions of country tunes. We went to our first and last live bullfight in Mexico, and we were horrified. I also saw my first rodeo and liked it. Sure, summers were very hot, humid, and often horrible, but air-conditioning made them bearable. Then, of course, there was the car. It was a vehicle of escape and discovery, a means of independence and freedom from the limitations of geography, not just a vehicle of transportation.

I was surprised by the ethnic diversity, the presence of large numbers of Mexican-Americans, African-Americans, and Latin Americans, Protestants of every brand, Catholics, Jews, and even some Muslims. What astonished me, however, were the thriving German communities in Texas, some of them dating back to the 1840s. I attended several Oktoberfest celebrations and was surprised that German linguists were visiting the region to record the "pure German dialects" that were preserved in Texas.

Besides size and progress, another dominant theme in Texas was land and oil. I was intrigued by the preoccupation with land. To have social standing in Texas you had to have land or a ranch. Oil money was not enough. Land symbolized the pioneering spirit of those who made their money the old-fashioned way—in cattle. Land was the bridge between old and new money.

I loved seeing Texans with their ten-gallon cowboy hats. They reminded me of good old cowboy movies. Texans loved their history, but they did not often advertise the fact that they had sided with the Confederacy, that at one time they had passed Jim Crow laws and even had the presence of the Ku Klux Klan. Once these laws were outlawed, they acted as if nothing of the sort had happened.

The University of Texas, not unlike the state, was huge. It was founded in 1883 with one building and forty acres of land, thirteen instructors, and two departments: academic and law. When I arrived in 1968, it had one hundred buildings, 440 acres, 1,600 professors, 1,200 teaching assistants, fifty-three departments, fifty research units, and sixty degree programs. It granted seven thousand degrees a year and had thirty-five thousand students. Like everything else in Texas, the University's buildings were big and solid. In addition to Austin, there were six other universities in the UT system.

In 1968, the university was a vibrant, dynamic place, an institution on the move, aspiring to be great, to achieve excellence. At the helm was Chancellor Harry Ransom, the moving spirit, the architect of its renaissance. A Texan with a Ph.D. from Yale, Ransom had joined the faculty of Texas in 1935 as professor of English. He moved from the deanship of the College of Arts and Sciences to the position of vice president and provost and president and then finally to chancellor.

Ransom was a soft-spoken, chain-smoking, courteous gentleman, with deep, sad eyes. He was a good, patient, responsive listener. His interests were bibliography, literature, liberal arts, and the history of Texas. He was determined to make the university a major national institution. He believed he could accomplish that not only by attracting a great faculty and building major laboratories but also, more important, by establishing a major national and international research center with a great library. He built an Academic Center (with an open-shelf library) for the undergraduates. He built the Humanities Research Center, with nine million items, one of the best of its kind in the nation. It had a Gutenberg Bible and the first book published in English; thirty-six copies of the first edition of Joyce's *Ulysses;* the papers of Evelyn Waugh and Arthur Conan Doyle, and on and on. Ransom was a man in a hurry. He wanted accelerated change. He surrounded himself with a group of Young Turks (John Silber, Bill Arrowsmith, Roger Shattuck, and Donald Weismann), who were known as "Harry's Boys." They were "young men in a hurry." They were for a progressive Texas. Dr. Norman Hackerman, the president of UT Austin, a prominent scientist, was not in a hurry. He did not believe the university needed "all that reform." He wanted steady, incremental, time-proven changes only. There was a clash of expectations.

The University of Texas had a good faculty and a serious student body. The students were there to get degrees, to get educated, to enjoy their four-year sojourn, to get jobs. There were some who were there to change the world. At the end of my first academic year at UT, the student activist anti-war movement became very visible in Texas. Following the U.S. bombing (and "incursion") of Cambodia, the faculty of UT voted by a two-to-one margin to suspend classes. Several students, having learned that I was a "veteran of San Francisco State," came to seek my advice. In retrospect, I am certain one or two of them were government agents, or agents provocateurs, eager to know the plans of radical students. I was asked whether they should occupy the offices of Walt Rostow, who had been in the Johnson Administration, and thus cause a national uproar. I advised against it. I told them, either quoting or making up a quote, that you leave the fallen angels of the Establishment alone. I don't know what it meant. To my great surprise, they heeded my advice.

At San Francisco State I had learned about the intricacies of student movement politics, competing ideologies, with their personalities, and agendas. In Texas I learned about the academic politics of higher education, faculty politics, the politics of the State of Texas, the rules of university governance, the role of the regents, and, most important, the acquisition and exercise of power.

There was a three-way struggle at UT Austin. One pitted Dean John Silber, the ambitious reformist, against President Norman Hackerman, the cautious administrator. The second placed President Hackerman on a collision course with Chancellor Ransom and the third one, off and on, pitted Frank Erwin, the chairman of the Board of Trustees, against all three.

Dean John Silber, a native Texan with a Ph.D. from Yale, was an expert on the philosophy of Immanuel Kant and a very complex man of enormous energy. He was a great teacher, an original mind, passionate and driven, studious and hardworking. He was eager to make the College of Arts and Sciences one of the best not only in Texas but also in the entire United States. After all, Texas had the vision, the resources, and the will to make it so. He was ambitious, determined, and impatient, with a dose of misplaced temper.

Silber fascinated me for another reason. He had fought for the integration of UT at a time when such a call was not only unpopular but also costly to one's career. He had come out against the death penalty in a state that was comfortable with it. I noted—there was no way to avoid it—that one of Silber's arms had not grown. Instead of treating it as a handicap, he had through sheer willpower and patience marginalized its impact: he drove a car, he painted, he played the trumpet, he sailed, he played the piano, he typed. He did not hide his short arm. His brisk walk, his authoritative voice, his impatience, all conveyed determination and action. He thought and acted as a teacher and believed that everything worth doing was worth doing well. He believed great teaching was equivalent to publication, or was at least one form of it. He fought for high-quality teaching at UT, encouraged the instruction of foreign languages, established area studies research centers, changed twenty-two of the twenty-eight department chairs, and vetoed one-third of salary recommendations.

Silber, like Ransom, was a man in a hurry. LBJ's presidency, Ransom's chancellorship, the resources of Texas; all of these, he believed, had provided him with a unique opportunity to transform the College of Arts and Sciences (the largest unit in the university) and through it, the entire university. But there were obstacles. The antiwar stance of the faculty made the university a target of the Texas legislature and put the university's leaders in a tight spot. They had to be tough without losing the respect and the support of the faculty and students. President Hackerman, instead of taking credit for the many educational reforms initiated by Silber, either opposed or sabotaged them by benign neglect or passive resistance. He did not want to be upstaged by Silber before a watchful Board of Regents.

Ransom, the visionary leader, gradually lost his authority. The rumor was that either overexpenditures of vast sums of money or malfeasance allowed the chairman of the Board of Regents or the president to blackmail him. He became inactive and ineffective, the symbol of what might have been. He was unceremoniously replaced by Dr. Charles LeMaistre, a medical administrator, rumored to be the doctor of the late Mrs. Erwin, the wife of the chairman of the Board of Regents. Erwin played a great chess game with the ambitions and anxieties of the major leaders of the UT administration, pitting them against each other while remaining the sole arbiter.

Silber was not a devious man. As the Texas journalist Ronnie Dugger put it, he did not know "how to be honest gently." You knew where you stood with him. When he thought someone was mediocre, he told him so. He must have forgotten the injunction of Thomas Hobbes that people think they are equal, and that whether or not this is accurate is irrelevant. It is a political factor that has to be taken into consideration. Silber was also utterly loyal to his friends. Some deserved that loyalty, some abused it.

In addition to full-time teaching, during my second year in Texas I was appointed by Silber as director of Plan II, Junior Fellows, Independent Studies, and chairman of the Departmental Honors Council—in short, the Special Programs of the College of Arts and Sciences. Plan II, which was an honors B.A., was the incarnation of the idea of building an excellent honors program. It was to bring together some of the best professors of UT with some of the best and brightest students. It allowed a couple of hundred students with outstanding academic records (very high SAT scores) to study philosophy, classics, English, literature, biology, and European and American history in classes and seminars that ranged from eight to twenty students. This was a big deal in a university of thirty-five thousand students.

I had magnificent, smart, engaged students. I was responsible for advising them and for the quality of their academic programs. Plan II was my first academic administrative position. As a result, I found myself in the thick of university politics: in the middle of conflicts between Dean Silber and President Hackerman, departmental chairmen and the dean, student activists and faculty, minority faculty and students and their request for ethnic studies. I was amused by David Riesman's gentle admonition: "I don't see how you get through the day when you are on so many committees. You are like a girl freshman at Radcliffe who doesn't know better and is elected to everything in sight! I think it is great, so long as you can last at it."

I could not say no to Silber. He was counting on me to revitalize Plan II and to do so expeditiously. I had no budget but I had the authority to recruit the best of the faculty from throughout the university. I recruited the dean of the law school to teach a freshman seminar. Since in Texas personalities transcended the issues, I was seen as "John Silber's man," "his Trojan Horse." It took some time for opponents and friends of Silber to find out that I was my own man.

In the midst of all these happenings, in 1969, Stanford University Press published my book *The Emergence of Modern Afghanistan: Politics of Reform and Modernization, 1880–1946*. It has been said that a book not reviewed is a dead book. I was extremely happy and proud that my nine-years' work on Afghanistan was recognized and well received by many scholars and scholarly publications. I was particularly flattered by one extraordinary review. It simply stated that: "In the past, all books written about Afghanistan had to be measured alongside Elphinstone's 1815 classic. We now have another yardstick—Gregorian, 1969."

In March 1970, I received a phone call and a letter. My old friend Professor Gerald White of San Francisco State, who had moved to the University of California at Irvine, was at it again. He was building a new history department there. Dean Hazard Adam's letter offered me a Step IV full professorship at the University of California and a higher salary. To my great surprise, the history department of the University of Texas voted unanimously to recommend my appointment as full professor. The dean, the president, and the chancellor decided to match the offer, the rank, and the salary.

Professor Riesman, who had written on my behalf both to Irvine and Texas, advised me to stay in Texas. So did my family. I was a full professor at the age of thirty-five. I was on a fast track. Clare felt vindicated. That year I was also awarded the University of Texas's Cactus Teaching Excellence Award.

Another development in 1970 had an impact on my professional career. Professor David Potter (1910–1971), one of the most distinguished historians of America and the American South, who had taught at Yale and then at Stanford, was chosen to be the president of the American Historical Association, the highest professional recognition awarded to a historian. He surprised me by asking me to chair the 1971 AHA annual program. This was an unexpected and undeserved honor that entailed a lot of work. We received 1,300 suggestions and proposals. The annual program was a great success, thanks to many prominent historians who served on the committee. Attempts were made to include nonhistorians (political scientists, economists, artists, and critics) in the program. Included were some thirty organizations that held joint meetings. One of the highlights of the meeting was the session about "The Historian and the Pentagon Papers." It attracted more than 1,400 scholars.

The success of the AHA program brought many kudos. J. Anthony Lukas featured it in the *New York Times Magazine*. David Potter's generosity had come at the right juncture in my career. It gave me further visibility. It was time to enjoy the fruits of my labors. But that was not to be. All of a sudden I found myself in the middle of one of the biggest academic battles, between the faculty and the regents, or, more specifically, Frank Erwin, the chairman of the Board of Regents, and his submissive cohorts within the University of Texas administration.

In Texas, three individuals wielded enormous political power: the lieutenant governor, the head of the Railroad Commission (an innocuous title for the person who was, among other things, in charge of oil and gas leases), and the chairman of the Board of Regents of the University of Texas system, who had authority to set spending priorities for the University of Texas through the use of the "available fund," the oil and gas revenues owned by the higher education system of Texas, which could be used for capital projects. Erwin wanted the University of Texas at Austin to increase the enrollment of students from thirty-five thousand to forty thousand. There were many construction companies and real estate interests who wanted that. The faculty of the College of Arts and Sciences, presided over by Silber, voted by a margin of 245 to 8 against it, recommending that the regents should limit the enrollment of the University of Texas at Austin to thirty-five thousand. Right after that vote, I told Silber he would be fired. He had just advertised how independent and how incorruptible he was. I was right. Frank Erwin's reaction was as anticipated.

In the aftermath of that vote, Erwin told President Hackerman, "It is time to break up the college and get rid of its dean." Next to the dean of the law school, Silber was the most powerful dean at the University of Texas. Outside the university he was popular in some political circles. He was ambitious and he was considered dangerous by his opponents. Frank Erwin exploited the Hackerman-Silber rivalry in order to get rid of both of them. Silber was accused of allocating too much money for undergraduate education, to the detriment of graduate education.

Those who wanted to get rid of Silber planned to do so by abolishing his job, by getting rid of a unified College of Arts and Sciences. The Arts and Sciences faculty, on the other hand, wanted a unified college. It confirmed that by a vote of four hundred to one hundred. Twenty-three of the twenty-eight departments were for a unified college.

Along with David DeLaura of the English department, Paul English of geography, and Erwin Spear of biology, I became a fierce opponent of the division of the college. I attended meetings, organized the faculty, wrote letters and articles, and gave scores of speeches. My public stance was clear: If you want to get rid of Silber, why don't you just do it? Why do you have to resort to the gimmickry of dividing the College of Arts and Sciences in order to force him out? The unity of the college was too important, from an educational point of view. The sciences were needed to balance the humanities and the social sciences, to protect them in a state such as Texas, where any "undesirable" politically incorrect speech or activity by a member of the humanities faculty would be used as an excuse to punish, to starve that faculty. President Hackerman sided with the majority of faculty. But then in the midst of all that, he resigned and left for Rice University to become its president.

The university established a presidential search committee. Along with five other faculty members, I was elected by the faculty to be a member of that selection committee. Everyone expected me to nominate John Silber for president. I confounded them by nominating Page Keeton, the dean of the law school. Some six hundred faculty members supported that nomination. I thought Keeton would preserve the integrity and the autonomy of the university. (Dean Silber, incidentally, was nominated by a Frank Erwin, a lieutenant in Vietnam and a former student of Silber's.) Keeton and Silber were on a short list and I fought to include their names on our final recommendation. It was very clear that they would be unacceptable to Frank Erwin and his regents. Silber's opponents wanted him to be turned down by the regents. That way they could claim that the process had worked, that not only Frank Erwin but the entire board did not want him. Silber confounded them by withdrawing his candidacy. That left Page Keeton.

I then nominated Mrs. Lyndon B. Johnson as a candidate for the presidency of the University of Texas. Many thought it was a cynical act or a joke. Actually I was dead serious. The university needed a national figure, a person of high integrity and visibility, a person who had national standards, was a proud Texan, and had a reputation to protect. She would be the first female president of the university. She would bring visibility and presence and national connections. Above all else, she would resist the interference on the part of Frank Erwin and others. Even Ronnie Dugger, the editor of the *Texas Observer,* thought I was joking. I was not. Either Dean Keeton or Mrs. Johnson would have been powerful presidents and would have led UT to greatness.

The regents chose Stephen Spurr from the University of Michigan. As far as Mrs. Johnson was concerned, they appointed her, a year or two later, as a regent. Many at the university and throughout the state were offended that Page Keeton had not been chosen. Incidentally, the announcement of Stephen Spurr's selection was made while I was in New York interviewing Dr. Robert Lumiansky, the president of the American Council of Learned Societies, for the presidency of UT Austin.

Hackerman, Silber, Ransom; all had lost their power. Dr. Charles LeMaistre was appointed the new chancellor. I used to visit Chancellor Ransom regularly, in the hope that he would stand up and defend what he had built, but to no avail. "Bless you, my son, bless you, my boy" was his only retort. Bryce Jordan of the music department was named acting president with the task of dividing up the college and getting rid of Silber. Once again the faculty and eleven deans opposed it.

In July, I was going to Iran to visit my sister and relatives. As I said good-bye to Chancellor LeMaistre he told me, "Have a nice time. Nothing will happen while you are gone. . . ." He also promised "a bright future for me, in his administration, where I would rise to the top of the power structure." Well, a lot happened! Frank Erwin met with Silber and told him, "The war is over. I am going to make you famous. I am going to fire you." He offered him a gracious exit if he agreed to resign. Silber refused. "You don't ever want to take another administrative job when you are not top man" was Frank Erwin's advice to John Silber.

The only success we had within the presidential search committee was our ability to block the candidates we did not want, including Bryce Jordan, interim president. (He was ultimately appointed president of UT Dallas.)

After Silber was fired, I handed in my resignation as director of Plan II and Special Programs of the College of Arts and Sciences as an act of protest against arbitrary decision making at UT Austin. Meanwhile, there was a move on campus, propelled by Frank Erwin again, to get rid of his bête noire—the *Daily Texan,* the student newspaper, which had a large circulation. They wanted to make it a nonuniversity publication.

That sent me into yet another organizing spree: to garner faculty, student, and community support for the *Daily Texan.* We worked for two months. We gathered eighteen thousand student signatures, the support of the university's Faculty Senate, the University Council, the Student Association, even the Senate of the State of Texas. We organized a testimonial dinner for the *Daily Texan.* It brought out some 350 people, including various influential members of the Texas establishment. At my urging, right smack in the middle of the auditorium, we set up a special table for the regents. Naturally none of them showed up. Soon after that we had to work against a twelve-hour teaching load, conceived by the regents as a punitive measure against the faculty. There was never a dull moment. Meanwhile, John Silber was named president of Boston University.

I was told by a close associate of Erwin's that I was on his "enemies list," that he had told his minions that there are three sons of bitches, and that he was going to get rid of them even if he had to plant marijuana on them. "One is Professor George Schatzki of UT Austin Law School. One is Gregorian, and one is Andy Yemma, the editor of the *Daily Texan.* Gregorian, that smart son of a bitch—he's never made a mistake."

Erwin was right. I taught full time. I served as director of Special Programs of the College of Arts and Sciences, with no additional stipend. I corrected my own exams. I had many advisees. I did not criticize Texas or America; I idealized them. I had taken their pronounced principles at face value, and no one had the heart to tell me that I was wrong, that there were vast gaps between ideals and aspirations and reality. They did not know how to deal with me. I had no skeletons in my closet and I had no ambitions for a job within the UT administration.

I attended a General Faculty meeting after Silber was fired. I was fascinated by the range of recriminations and ad hominem attacks against him. I quoted an Albanian saying that "When the cow falls, all the butchers appear." At one moment the tempers ran very high. To calm them down I got up and said the words: *Ich bin ein Berliner*. It added a surreal moment. People were stunned but it succeeded in calming everyone down.

During my four years at Austin, I met a lot of interesting mavericks. One of the most memorable was the late Professor Oliver Radkey. A proud Texan of old German immigrant heritage, he was a prominent scholar of Russian history and a great, conscientious teacher. To be invited to lunch with him was a great honor, an occasion, a happening. I'll meet you at 12:17, he would say. That was the exact time that the sun was ready to remove the shade from his car. He had a phobia about germs. He seldom shook hands, but if he did, he washed his hands immediately with rubbing alcohol, a large bottle of which he kept in his office. Professor Radkey, like all good Texans, believed in the value of land. He had properties in Texas as well as in Palo Alto, where he spent his summers at Stanford doing research at the Hoover Institution. In Texas, he would invite friends to walk with him on his rattlesnake-infested land. To watch this Russian scholar with his ten-gallon hat was quite a sight. He was my barometer of the Texas faculty. He was politically conservative but had liberal positions on some social issues, such as abortion. All his communications were formal. He was proud of the University of Texas but frustrated by the political meddling of the regents, especially its chairman, Frank Erwin. Whenever the university was ready to soar, they clipped its wings, Radkey said. He told me once that the University of Texas reminded him of Czar Alexander III, "strong but dumb."

In 1972, Representative Francis (Sissy) Farenthold, after serving two terms in the Texas House, decided to run for the Texas governor's office. She was another maverick Texan. I worked on her position paper on higher education and on a resolution to censure Frank C. Erwin Jr., collected some 550 faculty endorsements on her behalf, and raised ten thousand dollars. Had she won, I am sure she would have had a salutory effect on UT, as well as on the politics of the State of Texas. Unfortunately, she lost by some 150,000 votes out of about 3 million cast.

Sissy Farenthold's nomination had shaken the Texas Democratic machine. She defeated the incumbent lieutenant governor, Ben Barnes, who was supported by the entire Texas media and Texas "establishment" for the nomination. She made higher education and the University of Texas the central issue in her campaign, and that in itself, I believe, may have had some positive effect on the future of UT, by making the regents controversial and, in some circles, a political liability. Everybody was astonished to see Professor Radkey's name endorsing Sissy Farenthold. He also contributed to the campaign fund. He told me he did not want people to know about it because he had never contributed or voted for a "maverick politician."

While working on Farenthold's campaign, I came to know and appreciate Ronnie Dugger, another maverick Texan, very well. The editor-at-large and publisher of the *Texas Observer* and a UT alumnus, he had profound affection and deep concern for UT and its future. He decided to write a book about UT, the Harry Ransom era, and the aftermath. I read his manuscript, commented on it, and corrected some facts. Since I was told that the manuscript had been put to bed, I described candidly and in a somewhat indelicate manner some of my impressions of UT, its administrators and faculty. When the book, *Our Invaded Universities,* was published, I was astonished to see that Dugger had added a whole chapter about me, incorporating all my remarks, some accurately and a few not so.

Dugger described me in the following terms: "Although he is Dickensian, Dickens could have known no such man, a wild Persian, escapee from some anonymous Armenian mortality, laughing all the time and full of genius, enjoying all the lies and foibles of the American powerful, but caring mightily for the human beings whose endeavors he became a part of. He was one of the most hypnotic tipsters of my journalistic career. . . . In a play, Gregorian would be the one who releases everyone's worst suspicions by saying them out loud. Since everyone's worst suspicions more or less materialized, he was, in general, right. Talking fast, laughing headily, he had a faith in the country and the freedom of the mind, qualified by a devilishly penetrating and mainly accurate knowledge of the workings of selfish power. Unfailingly earnest, he struggled against the weltering currents of self-interests and deceits, and when the cause was lost, he left sadly."

I was fascinated by the centrality of athletics at UT, especially the role of football. Darrell Royal was the successful and, therefore, untouchable coach of the Longhorns. He invited me to spend a day or two with the team to watch them exercise, train, eat tremendous portions of steak, to witness a strategy session, all that in order to persuade me that football was not just a sheer clash of bodies but that it was also a smart game, a "brainy game." I was impressed. I came to love football even more than I had before and went to the Cotton Bowl. One of my early shocks had been the Texan's hook-'em horns hand sign. My first reaction was one of shock; I thought it was an obscene sign. Imagine my surprise to see some eighty thousand people giving the hand sign! I thought they had gone mad. Darrell Royal's office, salary, perks, even office furnishings outclassed those of the president and chancellor. The fact that I knew him and that he and his wife came to visit us impressed our sons and their friends, not to mention our neighbors.

My Plan II duties, on several occasions, had placed me in delicate, and sometimes potentially dangerous, situations. There was the case of an advisee of mine, let us call her Elizabeth. Her parents came to inform me that their daughter was pregnant. She was a devout Catholic and did not believe in abortion. She was on her way to a "home for unwed mothers." The parents asked me to help them with a cover-up story: Elizabeth was studying abroad. They asked me to send her final exams to the home for unwed mothers. I did. I received a very emotional letter from Elizabeth. She informed me that she had decided to name her child Vartan in my honor. I panicked. I wrote immediately, "Please, please don't! Name him anything but Vartan!"

One Sunday morning, I received an urgent call. One of my students, who was brilliant and had a black belt in karate, had taken LSD and had become violent. His roommates were afraid to call the police so they had called me instead; they believed that I was the only one who could calm him down. For two hours, we sat together. He pulled my beard. I pulled his. We watched Captain Kangaroo on television. Later I accompanied him to the hospital. I lay next to him until the doctors gave the necessary medications to calm him down.

Having lost the battle for the unity of the College of Arts and Sciences and having failed to elect Dean Page Keeton as president of UT Austin, I found myself in an untenable position, cast in the role of permanent opposition. The faculty of the university, having elected me as a member of the presidential search committee, kept electing me to other committees as well: Vice President and Provost Search committees and the Dean of the Humanities and Social Sciences Search committees. I was hailed as "the conscience of the faculty." I hated it. I did not want to be a caricature of myself. Moreover, I did not and could not serve people I did not respect, especially those who were political hacks, men without integrity, mission or vision, empty suits.

I decided to leave Texas after finding out that I loved its politics, especially the academic politics of UT. While detesting manipulation, I had become good at it, always rationalizing that since my cause, our cause, was the right one, my actions could be justified. I realized also that while I abhorred the exercise of arbitrary power by others, I exercised it, rationalizing that all I was doing was preventing the "wrong" individuals from fulfilling their goals and ambitions, and that was not necessarily power. The fact that I shrouded all my activities with righteousness frightened me. I told my friends I did not want to be a Don Quixote or worse, a Sancho Panza. I wanted to be an honest professor; I wanted to teach.

Meanwhile, elsewhere, David Riesman was busy on my behalf. He had nominated me for many presidencies and deanships, including the presidency of the University of Nebraska and the deanship of Arts and Sciences at Northwestern University. Then, on April 15, 1971, President Martin Meyerson of the University of Pennsylvania called to offer me a job in the history department. The department, under the leadership of Professor Alfred Rieber, another E. H. Harbison Distinguished Teaching Awardee, had voted unanimously to extend me an invitation to be a member of the faculty of the University of Pennsylvania.

It was very hard to leave Texas. Naturally, there were many farewell parties. One of the most memorable days in my life was the farewell party that the faculty and our friends gave for us. It was a very colorful party, a couple of hundred people. There was a band, lots of food and drinks, lots of fun, many speeches, many humorous remarks. What pleased me no end was the presence of not only my friends, our friends, but also many of my opponents in the battle over whether UT's College of Arts and Sciences should be divided or not, whether Dean Page Keeton or Dean John Silber should be president of UT Austin or not, whether the size of the student body should be increased or not, whether we should oppose Frank Erwin or not, whether our only recourse was to elect Sissy Farenthold as governor (and she, in turn, name new regents or not).

Ann Richards, later elected governor of Texas, was one of the central organizers of the party. She brought humor, biting political criticism, and satire. Governor Preston Smith gave honorary Texas citizenship to my family members and made me an Admiral of the Texas Navy. Among the gifts were the "autographed" and framed portraits of Frank Erwin and Charles LeMaistre. One of my leading opponents gave a gracious toast bemoaning that after my departure "Texas wouldn't be the same. There won't be as much fun. . . ." Ann Richards read a humorous scroll.

Black-bearded Bushytailed Armenian Muckraker
(Protestus Incessantus)

(commonly called Headline Bird)

FIELD MARKS: Appearance and actions much like the Doomsday Bird *(Billigramus)* but darker in color, this small acrobatic bird is somewhat sluggish in fall, building to a crescendo of frenzied activity and noise by spring. Easily identifiable by a profuse hairy drizzle surrounding a constantly moving beak and conspicuous crest of black. Wing tips are clasped in back. The droopy underparts conceal rapidly moving legs and feet that run to and fro in circular motion causing the bushtail to tip upward and downward for balance. This bird is a spectacular performer, capable of tail wagging but not perch straddling. A fine game bird. Potshots may be taken year round with regental license.

VOICE: The call is a rapid "what-what-what" followed by a "when-when-when," "where-where-where," and in agitation a screaming "no-no-no." When joined by birds not of the muckraker species he cries "tory-tory-tory" in warning.

WHERE FOUND: Migrant feeding on pistachios from Mideast to West Coast to Southwest to East. Generally happy muckraking anywhere.

HABITAT: Choice watering spots, soap boxes. Often sighted scratching through blue books.

NEST: Lines nest with grape leaves and kirman or sarouk fibers.

SIMILAR SPECIES: a) The Common Muckraker does not have the sparkling eye orb so appealing to the female. Do not mistake either for Fly by Night or Flash in the Pan. b) The Frankee Erwee is similar in combativeness and tenacity but the Erwee belly is streaked with yellow.

CHAPTER ELEVEN

The City of Brotherly Love

When we left Texas for Philadelphia, it felt as if we had left an open, often boisterous, assertive, proud, fast-moving society for a completely different one. Philadelphia seemed quiet, private, nonostentatious. It had a self-confident restraint, polite and self-satisfied. Its high society was present yet invisible. Bragging was considered bourgeois.

In Philadelphia, you are always in the presence of history and I was excited to be in the City of Brotherly Love, where the nation's destiny was forged, the First Continental Congress was held in 1774, the Second Continental Congress in 1776 adopted the Declaration of Independence, and the Constitutional Convention met in 1787.

I was in awe—when I visited Independence Hall, and I still am—of the depth and range of the intellects of our Founding Fathers. I was equally impressed by the vision of English Quaker William Penn who founded a welcoming and pacific commonwealth with ethnic and religious diversity, separation of church and state, political, judicial, and journalistic freedom.

Arriving from California and Texas to Philadelphia one can't help but feel claustrophobic. Lancaster Pike looked like a major Texas street, houses were small, so were the gardens and shops. Somehow, you were not overwhelmed by cars. Trains and public transportation were welcome features.

When in Philadelphia, you do not feel you are in a city of immigrants. You are, however, definitely in a city of neighborhoods.

One could not help being impressed by the number, quantity, and the wealth of so many educational and cultural institutions within a fifty-mile radius, as well as numerous scholarly and artistic professional organizations. But I was surprised that this great metropolis, once one of the largest cities not only in America but within the British Empire, where hundreds of inventions and institutions began, gradually became marginalized. Was it because the city became fragmented, that the autonomy and discreet charm of local communities, their isolationism, detracted from the overall power and influence of Philadelphia? The concept of a Greater Philadelphia never materialized. Bryn Mawr, Swarthmore, Haverford, Ardmore, Gladwyn, Wynnewood, Upper Darby, Lower Merion—all of them remained viable communities, stations either on the Main Line or Media Local. Most people at Penn commuted to Philadelphia and worked there, but did not live there. Unlike the imperialist San Francisco that laid claim to everything around it, Berkeley, Stanford, and Marin County, often under the umbrella of the "Bay Area," Philadelphia did not claim Bryn Mawr, Haverford, Swarthmore, Villanova, Lincoln, or other educational institutions, not to mention the many cultural ones.

*   *   *

I approached the University of Pennsylvania with a certain trepidation and excitement. After all, not only was it one of the oldest institutions of higher learning in the United States but it was founded by the amazing Benjamin Franklin. Here are just four exemplary contributions of Benjamin Franklin: The Library Company of Philadelphia (1731), a public library; the University of Pennsylvania (1740), the fifth oldest college in the United States and the first nondenominational institution; the American Philosophical Society (1743); Pennsylvania Hospital (1751). His statue, College Hall, and the many old and quaint buildings of the University of Pennsylvania were in marked contrast to the tall, soaring, massive buildings of the University of Texas. The University of Pennsylvania, not unlike Philadelphia, did not need such buildings to assert itself. It was comfortable with its history. It knew who it was and was pleased about it. There was no identity crisis in Philadelphia or at the University of Pennsylvania.

After a brief residence in Ardmore, we, too, discovered the charm of a small college town, with a good public school, quiet neighborhood, and good neighbors. We bought a house in Swarthmore. I became a commuter, a captive of the Media Local. Commuting by train was a new culture for me.

You got to know your fellow commuters: the slow readers who spent a week on the same paperback, the crossword puzzle addicts. You even had some idea about the politics of some of them from the magazines and newspapers they read, even the economic status of some. There were those who carried their lunch bags and others who did not. If you are interested in people, commuting is never dull.

I have always been lucky in universities where I have taught, thanks to friendly chairmen of the various history departments, who can make one's teaching experience pleasant: Jerry White (San Francisco State); Eugen Weber (UCLA); Robert Divine and especially William Goetzman (University of Texas, Austin). At Penn it was Professor Al Rieber who became my shepherd. A professor of Russian and Soviet history, a fantastic teacher and an eminent scholar, Rieber was chairman of the history department. He assigned me a large office to accommodate most of my books. My new colleagues, all impressive scholars, extended me a cordial welcome. I was an "add on," a new position that was added to the department. I was not taking any of the vacant positions within the department that might have created an "imbalance" between various fields and subfields.

My position was funded by a distinguished trustee of Penn, Sarkes Tarzian, a 1937 graduate of the Moore School of the University. An eminent scientist, engineer, and entrepreneur, Mr. Tarzian, an Armenian-American, had pledged $2 million, provided the university could find an appropriate scholar who would teach Armenian history and culture. I was coming to Penn "with a dowry."

Since I did not want to be marginalized within the department nor in the university as an ethnic in charge of a highly specialized field, it was agreed that I would be appointed as professor of history, professor of South Asian history, and Tarzian Professor of Armenian and Caucasian History. I was very amused when one of my students once asked whether I was teaching about the Caucasians, as in whites.

It was a great job. I was to teach European intellectual history, history of the Middle East, *and* Armenian history and Caucasian history. Harvard and Columbia had chairs of Armenian studies. So did the University of Michigan and UCLA. I was joining a select group of scholars of Armenian history and culture. In Swarthmore, we were in the proximity of a viable, well-established, old Armenian-American community with its churches, many cultural, athletic, and political organizations, and schools. The Armenian-American community was ecstatic about my joining the faculty of the alma mater of so many of them.

We enrolled our youngest son in the Armenian Sisters Academy, a

Montessori school in Radnor, Pennsylvania, operated by Armenian Catholic nuns (Sisters) under the aegis of a nondenominational, secular board. The school's high standards, its rigor, the quality of its teachers and teaching, its robust curriculum, and the record of its academic achievements were such that there were even some Irish- and Italian-American children in the ranks of the student body. To see them learn, read, write, and speak Armenian was amazing. Their parents' reaction was very normal: "Why not? Armenian is just another language."

Sarkes Tarzian, my benefactor, was the CEO of Sarkes Tarzian, Inc., of Bloomington, Indiana. He was a major inventor. His firm manufactured radios, and he owned TV and radio stations and newspapers. The son of immigrants, Mr. Tarzian was a proud American. A conservative businessman, he was very influential in Indiana. To celebrate my appointment as Tarzian Professor, he gave a reception in my honor in Indianapolis. The governor of the state, the mayor of the city (Richard Lugar), Eli Lilly, publishers, broadcasters, editors, public officials, and leaders of the Armenian community of Indiana were in attendance. Naturally, TV and radio stations and newspapers owned by Mr. Tarzian gave great coverage of the event.

Mr. Tarzian visited our family in Swarthmore several times. We talked frequently and dined occasionally. He never interfered in my activities as Tarzian Professor. He gave us our first new car, one of his company's leased cars, and payed for its insurance. Every two or three years it was replaced.

President Martin Meyerson greeted me with warmth. I thought he was an extraordinary person. He was well educated, well read, cultivated and cultured. A serious man with boundless energy and curiosity, Meyerson was one of a handful of intellectuals who was heading a major university. He had been acting chancellor at UC Berkeley, where he strove to reestablish order and restore confidence and trust among students, faculty, and administration in a post–Free Speech Movement Berkeley. He appointed a handful of great administrators to crucial and sensitive academic and administrative posts. When he was not appointed as permanent chancellor, he accepted the presidency of the State University of New York at Buffalo and attempted, with some success, to transform it into an outstanding public university. Soon after, he assumed the presidency of the University of Pennsylvania. Well connected nationally and internationally, Meyerson had inherited a university on the mend, revitalized by the hard work of a great team: President Gaylord Harnwell and Provost David Goddard.

Meyerson had big plans for the University of Pennsylvania. He needed the support of the trustees. More important, he needed the leadership of an effective provost. The provost and the president needed strong deans, who, in turn, needed the cooperation of the chairmen of the departments in order to enlist the support of the faculty. Any plans that envisaged change, whether curriculum, research facilities, the appointment of new faculty, the quality of undergraduate and graduate education, or even the physical plant, needed the support of the faculty. Meyerson was mindful of President Woodrow Wilson's cautionary note, when he was president of Princeton University, that it was easier to transplant an entire cemetery than to undertake curriculum reform.

Meyerson was an academic leader, not a manager or a bureaucrat. He presided over the university. He did not micromanage. His style was one of delegation. However, he was torn between process and outcome. We had several private meetings. I found him curious, interesting, and provocative. Pretty soon we established great personal and intellectual rapport. He asked for my candid views on a variety of issues. Naturally, I was flattered. It became obvious to me that Meyerson had plans to involve me, one way or another, in his administration. He spoke frequently of the importance of U.S. higher education and the need to recruit and prepare future leaders to manage U.S. universities and colleges. Whether he was influenced by David Riesman or not, I do not know. Having arrived from Texas, I saw only possibilities at Penn, rather than limitations; the "can do," "let us begin," "why not?" Texan attitude of mine must have appealed to the optimist in Meyerson. When I asked him about the university's plans for the celebration of the Bicentennial of the American Revolution and how the administration intended to take advantage of this unique historical occasion and opportunity to advance the university's national and international visibility, along with securing new funds for the university, he appointed me coordinator of the Bicentennial Programs of Greater Philadelphia–based consortium of colleges and universities. He subsequently appointed me as a faculty member of the Provost Search Committee. That was an unusual appointment. I was a newcomer; I did not know the university or its faculty that well. We recommended the appointment of Eliot Stellar, an eminent scientist, as provost. He was appointed.

Next came my appointment as an American Council of Education Fellow. I became faculty assistant to the president and the provost. That led to my appointment to a faculty search committee, chaired by Professor Robert Schrieffer, Nobel Laureate, to recommend candidates for the deanship of the yet-to-be-formed Faculty of Arts and Sciences. One thing led to another.

The committee recommended my candidacy to the provost and the president. This, too, was unusual. Within a year and a half, I am sure thanks to Meyerson's maneuverings, I was pushed to center stage.

The reaction on campus was one of surprise. Most faculty members did not know me. Other than my past administrative role as the director of special programs of the College of Arts and Sciences at Austin, I had no major administrative or managerial experience. I had never headed a department or a division. There was suspicion that all along I was "Dr. Meyerson's man," that I had been brought to Penn ostensibly as a professor but in reality for the specific purpose of heading the new Faculty of Arts and Sciences. Various internal candidates who were well qualified but not chosen were angry, not at me but at the president. It all looked too cozy. I was a member of the Provost Search Committee. Eliot Stellar became provost, and then he recommended me to be dean of the Faculty of Arts and Sciences. One candidate, Professor Irving Kravis, a great faculty leader and chairman of the economics department, who had promoted the formation of the Faculty of Arts and Sciences, was incensed: "The job was mine. I had earned it. The president has betrayed me. I have nothing against you but don't expect me to lift a finger to help you!"

The student reaction was positive. The *Daily Pennsylvanian* pointed out that I was teaching two courses a semester and that I had 175 students in my European intellectual history class alone. I had twenty advisees, had written some sixty recommendation letters on behalf of seniors, and was correcting my own exams, while doing additional administrative chores on behalf of the president. My dedication to undergraduate education was singled out.

The president's and provost's joint statement announcing my appointment, which spoke about "an extensive search inside and outside the university for the best scholar-teacher-administrator," did not assuage the feelings of disappointed candidates, critics of the president, or suspicious faculty. The usual suspects came forth, thank God, to stress my integrity and independence. Many generous statements were made by David Riesman, Harry Ransom (chancellor emeritus of the University of Texas system), Lewis Spitz (dean of the humanities at Stanford), and Richard Lyman (president of Stanford University). But the one that had the biggest impact was the outlandish, most generous statement of John Silber, the new president of Boston University: "Vartan Gregorian is one of the most imaginative and learned men I know. Although he is a superb teacher and a renowned historian, his most revealing quality is his unpredictable and compelling sense of humor—a magic carpet that carries his ideas and purposes to fruition with remarkable frequency and minimal opposition. He has the innocence of a baby, the integrity and dedication of a saint, and the political skills of a Talleyrand. A marvel of energy, wit, determination, winsome laughter and high idealism is now dean of arts and sciences at Pennsylvania. How fortunate you are!"

The assurances gave weight and credibility to my appointment, but what pleased the faculty were the widespread rumors, reported by the *Daily Pennsylvanian,* that I had presented to the president and the provost "some forty demands" (not true) and that it was only upon their acceptance of those demands that I had agreed to accept the deanship. In reality, what had transpired was my insistence, based on lessons learned in Texas, to get clear assurances from the university about its commitments to the new Faculty of Arts and Sciences. The needed assurances centered around several major subjects:

Significant aid to arts and sciences

Full budgetary authority both over the existing funds and
    development of new resources

Free hand to create "coherence in curricular planning, space
    utilization and efficient use of financial, physical, and human
    resources"

Central planning authority for the curriculum and the structure of the
    faculty

When possible, close ties with professional schools

Full responsibility for faculty recruitment

Authority to coordinate undergraduate and graduate education

Establish and enhance a new continuing education program

Strengthen ties with educational, religious, artistic, civic, professional,
    and ethnic constituencies of Philadelphia

Control of affirmative action programs for women and minorities

Establish a Board of Overseers for the Faculty of Arts and Sciences

The president and the provost pledged their full support. I accepted the deanship. It was the beginning of a major task to create a Faculty of Arts and Sciences for the University of Pennsylvania. The *Daily Pennsylvanian* wrote in an editorial: "It remains to be seen whether Gregorian can overcome the roadblocks that have stymied many an able reform-minded administrator before him."

Prior to 1974, education in the arts and sciences at the University of Pennsylvania was conducted in several separate entities:

The Graduate School of Arts and Sciences, which consisted of some
  sixty-three "Graduate Groups" (the master's and Ph.D. degree–
  granting units); thirty-three of them were in the arts and sciences.
  The Graduate School also housed five departments (Oriental
  Studies, American Civilization, South Asia Regional Studies,
  History and Sociology of Science, Folklore, and Folklife) as well as
  some interdisciplinary centers. The dean of the graduate school
  had overall responsibility for the quality and administration of all
  the above units, but no overall budgeting authority.
The College of Arts and Sciences, the undergraduate school for men.
  It consisted of eighteen departments. It was responsible for the
  undergraduate liberal arts degree programs. The college faculty
  was divided into two categories: those who were members of the
  graduate faculty and those who were not.
The College of Liberal Arts for Women. While it supervised the
  Bachelor of Science Program in Elementary Education and
  was responsible for a Program in Women's Studies, it was an
  administrative rather than an academic unit. Its dean had no
  budgetary authority. Students in the College of Liberal Arts for
  Women shared the same liberal arts program as their male
  counterparts in the College of Arts and Sciences. However, their
  degree requirements differed slightly.
The Wharton School housed the social science departments:
  sociology, economics, political science, and regional studies.
The College of General Studies, which supervised some of the
  university's evening, summer, continuing, and part-time education
  programs. It was headed by a director.

While such decentralization had certain virtues, it had brought about serious fragmentation. Each of these autonomous organizational units, with their separate administrative degree requirements and goals, made effective academic planning and development nearly impossible. The conception of an organic, integrated arts and sciences was lacking.

In the early 1970s, two major studies on the structure and goals of the university had addressed the fundamental problem of the fragmentation of education in the arts and sciences. Their conclusions were obvious: "When decentralization approaches complete autonomy, its virtues become less certain. The whole becomes no more than the sum of its parts, the dangers of parochialism become real, and the sense of *universitas* becomes lost." They recommended the integration of undergraduate and nonprofessional graduate education under the aegis of a new faculty, the Faculty of Arts and Sciences. The formation of a unified and strengthened Faculty of Arts and Sciences was considered essential to the future of the university. It was to serve as the intellectual core of the university, which in turn was to promote increased intellectual and academic interaction among the professional schools and the arts and sciences. That was the objective. That was my mandate and that was my job. I was scared by the magnitude of the challenge but excited about its promise and potential.

The Faculty of Arts and Sciences (FAS) brought together twenty-eight departments, thirty-three graduate groups, eight special programs and offices, 528 faculty members, some 5,500 undergraduates, and 2,500 graduate students. It formed the largest single component of the university, consisting of one-third of the standing faculty of the university (and if one includes the biomedical faculty affiliated with the Faculty of Arts and Sciences, then FAS constituted almost 50 percent of the standing faculty), and an original budget of approximately $42 million.

Efforts to integrate such major yet diverse units into a cohesive educational and administrative structure faced many obstacles and problems, but perhaps the most immediate and pressing of these was the need to resolve reservations and concerns that were the by-product of decades of suspicion and misperception. The former social science departments of the Wharton School had to be assured that joining FAS would not harm their economic well-being, affect their sources of auxiliary support, or diminish their reputation. They needed assurance that the new faculty would bring them new intellectual and educational opportunities and benefits. The faculty and graduate groups of the Graduate School of Arts and Sciences, particularly the five departments located within that school, had to be convinced that the creation of the Faculty of Arts and Sciences did not mean an eclipse of graduate education nor the decline of interdisciplinary programs and research in favor of undergraduate education.

The faculty members of the College of Arts and Sciences, concerned about the possible ramifications of a massive infusion of interdisciplinary and semiprofessional programs into the more traditional liberal arts, had to be persuaded that the new Faculty of Arts and Sciences would not become a service school with the burden of teaching undergraduates mainly on their shoulders. They had to be persuaded that the Faculty would be based on the liberal arts disciplines and traditions found in the College. The College for

Women and its alumnae, who took pride in the flexibility of their requirements and in their sound academic advising, had to be convinced that the new school would continue to be sensitive to the needs of women while offering them broader opportunities. And the university community had to agree to placing the College of General Studies in the Faculty of Arts and Sciences in order to fulfill the objectives and recommendations of the Development Commission concerning continuing education. The faculty in FAS had to be equally persuaded that the programs of the College of General Studies would not diminish the reputation of FAS and that they would neither drain the existing resources of the new faculty nor deny it new sources of income.

There were questions about the size of the new Faculty of Arts and Sciences, about how to achieve efficiency without a costly and cumbersome bureaucracy, and about how to forge the unity of the new faculty without neglecting the particular needs of various disciplines of the new faculty. Should the new Faculty of Arts and Sciences divide itself organizationally into quadrants—humanities, social sciences, life sciences, and physical sciences—each being headed by a full or associate dean reporting to the dean of Faculty of Arts and Sciences? There was overwhelming concern as to how the new Faculty of Arts and Science, with an endowment as minuscule as its dependence on tuition revenues was great, would survive the decade of recession and the rival needs and claims of its twenty-eight departments.

Within the framework of the university's budgeting system, might not each unit claim its share of revenues on the basis of student enrollments and research monies it had generated rather than on the basis of excellence or the centrality of the unit within the general needs of the new Faculty of Arts and Sciences? And with all these problems, did the new faculty have the capacity, leadership, and ready plans to participate in the university's Campaign for the Eighties, which was to be launched immediately? Would we be left behind?

The challenges were many and enormous. A new school had to be formed and given its own identity, cohesion, unity, and self-confidence; it was to be provided with an effective administration functioning on a sound financial basis; and most important, it was to possess a distinct educational vision and intellectual mission.

The process of unifying the Faculty of Arts and Sciences required a new administrative structure and a strategic fiscal and academic plan of action. I was fortunate in being able to recruit a group of highly respected, outstanding faculty members, who served as associate deans for Budget and Planning, Graduate Studies, Instruction and Curricular Development, Undergraduate Studies, and Special Programs. Donald M. Stewart was named associate dean for Continuing Education and director of the College of General Studies. Twenty-eight new departmental chairs were appointed. As dean I met with every department to discuss its needs and aspirations. A council of chairmen was formed to deal with ongoing academic, administrative, and budgetary problems. An Educational Policy Committee dealt with short- and long-range academic plans and issues of the new faculty.

We created the Society of the College: Alumni and Alumnae of Arts and Sciences. We also revamped the entire undergraduate advising system and formulated uniform requirements for the Bachelor of Arts degree. A Development Advisory Board was set up to prepare a long-range development plan that would enable Arts and Sciences to take part in the university's $255 million capital campaign. The plan envisaged the external reviews and evaluations of all twenty-eight departments of the Faculty of Arts and Sciences, to determine the comparative strengths, advantages, and disadvantages of each of the departments. The external reviews were headed by prominent and knowledgable academic experts from across the country.

The financial performance of the FAS was very positive. We managed to balance its budgets every year and pay off its major inherited deficits.

The successful integration, functioning, and performance of the Faculty of Arts and Sciences surprised everyone. It required tact, humor, compassion. My cultural background was of great help. I did not mind visiting faculty members in their offices and asking for their assistance. Once their egos were satisfied they lent their help. I even went to see Professor Irving Kravis to ask for his help. He relented. He said, "You have to compensate me for all the work I did for FAS. It will cost you ten thousand dollars. It should be put in my retirement fund." I did it.

The 1975 commencement at Penn was unusual. The speaker was President Gerald Ford, who was in Philadelphia to pay tribute to the Bicentennial of the American Revolution. Ford was the first president to appear at Penn since Franklin D. Roosevelt. I was excited to meet my first U.S. president. There were several hundred protesters whose placards read "Power to the People" and "Hands off Cambodia." In his commencement address, President Ford alluded to the difficult economic conditions of the country. "Almost a million young Americans who are graduating from institutions of higher learning this year are faced, through no fault of their own, with economic difficulties greater than any since the period of my own commencement in 1935," he said. The president announced that his main objective was to solve the nation's economic dilemmas and achieve the goal of "jobs for all who want to work." The nation's economy (and the university's finances) were in bad shape. In the fall of 1975, Penn launched a $255 million campaign, the Campaign for the Eighties, to maintain its fiscal stability and physical infrastructure and to implement some of its ambitious academic goals. The university had to convince the trustees as well as the alumni, not to mention national corporations and foundations, that the campaign was not designed to cover the university's budget deficits but rather to advance new ideas, challenges, research, and excellence. So, while the university was seeking major gifts, it was also attempting to demonstrate that it had fiscal discipline and, most important of all, that it had its priorities right.

The Campaign for the Eighties was launched with great fanfare. There was a university-wide campaign cabinet that included the president, the chairman of the campaign, several deans, the vice president for development, and several members of his team. There was a great deal of competition among the deans over the names of potential prospects. Pretty soon I realized that if someone was operated on in the university's hospital, whether or not he survived, his name would be assigned to our medical school. People with dental problems went to the dean of the dental school. If somebody had his pet taken care of by our veterinary science school, she was referred to the school as a "live prospect." Businessmen went to Wharton, engineers to the engineering school, architects to the architecture school, beneficiaries of the lawyers to the law school, and so on. Once I asked in a pleading tone, "If there are any mental cases, please refer them to me as prospects for the Arts and Sciences." The chairman of the campaign committee, Robert Dunlop, CEO of Sun Oil Company, the chair of the medical school campaign, was not amused.

As the campaign cabinet was setting goals for each school, I was asked what our target was. I told them, "The same as the medical school's." We were given a $25 million target. We were able to raise it. That was a lot of money then. (I had asked for $40 million.) This was my initiation into the art of fund-raising. To understand the significance of this sum, one has to remember that FAS, the largest faculty at Penn, had the smallest endowment. It yielded an income of $1,150,000 in 1974 and $1,030,000 in 1979. Of the latter, only $491,000 was unrestricted. Total graduate fellowship support had declined from $3 million in 1960 to $500,000 in 1977 (versus Harvard's $4.5 million, Yale's $4.9 million, and Stanford's $2.5 million).

I discovered that not only did I not mind fund-raising but that I enjoyed it. I particularly liked the opportunities to solicit from foundations. We received major grants from the National Endowment for the Humanities, the Andrew W. Mellon Foundation, the Ford Foundation, the Sloan Foundation, the Rockefeller Foundation, the Lilly Endowment, the Hewlett Packard

Foundation, and the Glenmede Trust. We were awarded three endowed professorships by Ambassador Walter Annenberg and five others from Penn trustees or alumni. I was pleased that Thomas S. Gates Jr., the CEO of J. P. Morgan, designated his endowed chair to the humanities rather than the Wharton School. In fact, he insisted on it.

My greatest pride as dean was our ability to recruit outstanding faculty members* from across the nation and our ability to launch several new interdisciplinary centers and programs, such as Italian Studies, Dutch Studies, the Center for the Study of Art and Symbolic Behavior, the Center for Medieval Studies, and the Philadelphia Center for Early American Studies.

The formation and integration of the Faculty of Arts and Sciences took four years, much effort, and lots of struggle. It happened at a time when the university adopted a system of Financial Responsibility Centers. The idea was imported from Harvard and commonly referred to as "each tub on its own bottom." It envisaged that each school would be charged to match, as nearly as possible, its expenses to its income. An inevitable result of this budgetary device, without adequate safeguards, was fraught with the danger of organizing the university around the schools and departments with saleable skills, each competing to maximize tuition and grant income.

President Meyerson's vision was to realize the concept of "One University," where faculties, students, and schools would interact, reinforce their academic programs, and facilitate interdisciplinary collaboration. Unfortunately, the university had installed a system of Financial Responsibility Centers *before* the full development of an overall academic plan. The financial system was to be the instrument to help implement that academic plan. The system was to be a budgetary and planning blueprint, and there were fears that, if abused, it could become instead a budgetary straitjacket. The system of decentralized decisions stressing fiscal responsibility could also prompt schools to undertake actions detrimental to the university's overall goals and

---

* Among them were Houston Baker (University of Virginia); John Cebra (Johns Hopkins); Stuart Curran (Wisconsin); David DeLaura (University of Texas, Austin); Carlos Fuentes; Henry Glassie (Indiana and Yale); Judah Goldin (Yale); John Graham (University of Manchester); Michael Katz (York University); Moshe Lewin; Ezekiel Mphahlele; Daniel Poirion (Sorbonne); David Premack (University of California, Santa Barbara); Samuel Preston (United Nations); Philip Roth; Gillian Sankoff (University of Montreal); Nathan Sivin (MIT); Barbara Herrinstein Smith (Bennington); Brian Sutton-Smith (York University); Rosemary Stephens (Tulane and Yale); Alexander Vucinich (University of Texas, Austin, and the University of Illinois); Sigfried Wenzel (North Carolina); and Larzer Ziff (Oxford University and the University of California at Berkeley). Finally, two new Benjamin Franklin Professors were named: Leonard Meyer of the University of Chicago as Benjamin Franklin Professor of Music and Humanities, and Leo Steinberg of Hunter College as Benjamin Franklin Professor of History of Art.

mission for financial reasons. In the competition for course enrollments, marketability and excellence did not have to go hand in hand. There were fears that the new fiscal system would usher in an era of social Darwinism, which might result in the attrition, decline, and even disappearance of nationally and internationally renowned programs and departments that could never be "profitable." Possible replacement of "content" for "popularity" as the chief criterion for the structuring of courses and programs was another cause for anxiety. The overall question on the part of the faculty was: What happens to the university's obligations and mission to support scholarship and research except that for which immediate external funding could be secured?

The Financial Responsibility Center system placed the Faculty of Arts and Sciences in a tough spot. It was a new faculty with practically no endowment to speak of. Eighty to 90 percent of the members of the Board of Trustees of the University of Pennsylvania were graduates of the professional schools. Notwithstanding President Meyerson's desire to make the Arts and Sciences the central achievement of his presidency, and given the state of the economy in the 1970s, there were no major resources to be allocated to Arts and Sciences. The system had limited even the president's ability to "tamper" with it. Under the circumstances, the university taxed the revenues, mostly tuition, of the Arts and Sciences and then gave back most of it as "subvention." For example, in 1978, FAS tuition revenue was $30 million, out of which it contributed to the university a tuition tax of $6 million; in 1979, out of $33 million, $6.5 million. In addition, FAS had to allocate $12.2 million for student aid in 1978 and $13.8 million in 1979.

Faculty members and departments in the Arts and Sciences thought they were paying too much to other university schools. Wharton and the schools of medicine and engineering especially thought FAS was getting a free ride. There began an open "warfare": advocacy, passive resistance, and sometimes unregulated competition. I had had good training in Texas in matters of academic politics and advocacy. I knew that my strength lay in the fact that I headed the largest academic unit of the university and the largest number of faculty members; if one added the biomedical faculty, it was almost 50 percent of the entire faculty. In FAS the university had created a giant. I realized that as long as I enjoyed the trust and solid support of the faculty, sooner or later, FAS would prevail.

My fierce advocacy on behalf of the Arts and Sciences, public confrontation on its behalf with other deans and the Budget Office and even the provost and the president, earned me the faculty's trust and support, not to mention a legion of undergraduate and graduate students. The situation became tense when the biomedical faculty petitioned the president, requesting that it report to me, and that, at the minimum, the dean of FAS should grant their Ph.D. degrees because the medical school granted M.D. degrees, which were professional degrees rather than basic science degrees.

The situation even became comical when I discovered that the Budget Office was carrying the costs of the university library as "a subvention" to FAS. When asked why, they responded that FAS was its preponderant client. I threatened to "save" millions of dollars for FAS by asking faculty and students to declare a one-year moratorium on the library. I was happy that the university did not let me do it. The library became a university Financial Responsibility Center.

All of a sudden, I was thrust into the position of identifying the interests of the Faculty of Arts and Sciences as identical with the university's overall mission to have "One University," by advancing the view that if the schools of "One University" are to be mutually supportive, then the policies of each must transcend "parochial interest."

To protect the interests of FAS within the university and, vis-à-vis the Board of Trustees, provide external visibility, as well as serve as a sounding board for the FAS administration, we established a Board of Overseers that included some Penn trustees, as well as many prominent national figures.

President Meyerson was in an untenable situation. Having set the budget responsibility centers into motion, he had unleashed a fierce competition among the schools. Any gifts, grants, or tuition revenues generated by the schools were considered the fruits of their labor and the credit went to the school and its dean. The university's general operations and expenditures were being criticized along with its taxation of the schools' revenues. The Campaign for the Eighties, organized under the rubric of "One University," was aimed at eliminating the barriers between different schools, in order to foster interdisciplinary programs but, since the fund-raising was centered around the different schools and their alums, it was a struggle. There was no significant unrestricted component that gave the provost and the president the money to act on their priorities. They were in the uncomfortable position of negotiating with the deans to facilitate cooperation, interdisciplinary learning, joint degree programs, the cost of libraries, etc. At Penn, as everywhere, victory had many parents, and defeat was an orphan. The schools took credit for everything good that happened; shortcomings and failures knocked on the door of the president and the central administration.

In my capacity as dean of the Faculty of Arts and Sciences, I was prohibited from meeting or contacting Robert Smith, the head of Glenmede Trust (Pew Charitable Trusts). That source was earmarked, I was told, as the exclusive preserve of medicine. After all, Bob Dunlop, our eminent trustee, was chairman of its board, and he headed the medical school's campaign.

Notwithstanding the competition, several deans managed to work out arrangements for joint B.A. degrees between the Arts and Sciences and Wharton, B.S. degrees between the Arts and Sciences and engineering, and a joint B.A./M.A. degree. The provost launched the Benjamin Franklin Scholars Program to attract excellent students, and the University Scholars Program. The latter admitted pre-med and pre-law freshmen to the college as well as to the medical or law schools. All of our schools attempted to internationalize their student bodies and to establish links with foreign universities.

My first crisis at Penn was the case of I. F. Stone, the great radical, maverick activist, the publisher of *I. F. Stone's Weekly,* and the author of numerous books. He had dropped out of Penn during his last semester. For many years, some faculty and students had kept nominating him for an honorary degree. Penn trustees, even the liberals, were not enthusiastic about it. In 1974, the president asked me to handle the Stone situation. Instead of an honorary degree, I decided to grant him his B.A. To do so, I needed the recommendation of the philosophy department. When they approved, I walked twice with I. F. Stone around College Hall. That, in my opinion, satisfied the physical education requirement for graduation that he had never met. We held a private graduation ceremony for him at the library. Then I signed my first diploma as dean of the Schools of Arts and Sciences and I. F. Stone became an alumnus of Penn. He delivered a public lecture at the Irvine Auditorium, which was packed with students and faculty. They were there to hear Stone give a provocative speech. He disappointed everyone. He gave a talk about several mistranslations of key words and sentences from the original Greek texts of Aristotle into German and English. He wanted, he said, to impress everyone with his erudition. After all, he was now a college graduate. He added that from now on he would, of course, be demanding much bigger honoraria for his speeches.

I kept in touch with I. F. Stone for many years. We disagreed about his book on Socrates. We agreed that it would be great to reenact periodically the Trial of Socrates in our colleges. A department of classics and philosophy would act as his prosecution and his defense team. A randomly chosen jury of five hundred would be chosen from the ranks of the college student body. They would read Plato's *Apology,* hear both the case for the prosecution and that for the defense, and issue their verdict. Unfortunately, when I. F. Stone died in 1989, so did our joint project.

I thought the Bicentennial of U.S. independence gave Philadelphia and the University of Pennsylvania a singular opportunity to reaffirm their historical roles and generate vast investments in Philadelphia and the university. I don't know why, but I thought, selfishly, that the best way various foreign countries could participate in our celebration was to make investments in the form of endowed chairs, lectures, fellowships, and visiting professorships. I had proposals for prominent East European and Asian immigrants, the National Endowment for the Humanities, and even the Catholic Church. One of my proposals was to have a Nordic chair, endowed by Norway, Sweden, Finland, Denmark, and Iceland. My visit to Iceland's mission in Washington was very educational. I rang the embassy's bell. The door was answered by Iceland's ambassador, who served also as its cultural attaché and its consular officer. He heard my case for an endowed chair as a gift to the University of Pennsylvania in honor of the Bicentennial of the American Revolution. His polite answer was: "Mr. Gregorian, Iceland celebrated the one-thousand-year anniversary of its constitution and independence. No one sent us any gifts."

John Cardinal Krol, who liked me because I was an Armenian and an immigrant, heard about my plea for a Catholic studies chair. Why should all the great Catholic scholars' teaching be confined to Catholic universities and colleges? I asked. Why not, each year, bring one of them to teach at Penn as a visiting scholar? Cardinal Krol's retort was: "It was not Catholics who discriminated against the University of Pennsylvania; it was the latter who had pursued exclusionary policies vis-à-vis Catholics. By the way, who would be the first theologian that you would invite to Penn if such a chair was available?" My answer stunned him. "Hans Küng," I said. "But he is not even a Christian" was the cardinal's response to this distinguished priest-theologian. Needless to say, I did not get the chair.

Having seen firsthand the familiarity of bus and cabdrivers in Edinburgh, Scotland, with Shakespeare, I had the crazy idea of educating Philadelphia's bus and cabdrivers, and the policemen, about the history of U.S. independence and the Constitution, the Bill of Rights, and the history of Philadelphia. I had lined up several professors to do this. We had even gotten money to celebrate their graduation with a picnic in Franklin Field. My hopes were dashed when the unions asked for overtime pay for their participation. They thought of it as extra work.

My plans for an endowed chair in Polish and East European history did not materialize either. Ed Piszek, the owner of the Mrs. Paul's Company, promised me a chair. He had also agreed to underwrite the cost of the Philadelphia-area universities and colleges joint exhibition. As we were ready to inaugurate the exhibition, the former retired head of the local FBI, who was employed by Mr. Piszek, visited the exhibition and informed me that it was not what Mr. Piszek had in mind. I had to raise $127,000 for the exhibition, but Mr. Piszek sent me a real chair.

The only success we had was our application with the National Endowment for the Humanities. It gave us a Bicentennial College, bringing together the expertise of all the scholars from Philadelphia area colleges and universities in the fields of colonial and revolutionary history.

Then there were two "high society" events that ended in disaster. The City of Philadelphia had invited Queen Elizabeth II to visit Philadelphia in 1976. During her visit, Mayor Frank Rizzo took his revenge on those who had attacked him, or snubbed him as a coarse or embarrassing person and who had excluded him from their events. Since I had always invited Mayor Rizzo to come to the University of Pennsylvania commencements—even though he never came—evidently he was grateful. Clare and I were invited to a reception in honor of the queen, a very big deal in Philadelphia. It was a very hot day. There were lots of drinks and very little food. They ran out of ice. The queen was running late. On the orders of the protocol officers, the waiters and guards collected all the glasses, advised people not to smoke, and lined them up behind the red carpet. Then the doors opened and there was the queen. It was very exciting.

I was apprehensive that Her Majesty would stop and ask for my name. So, in order not to be verbose, I had rehearsed our entire dialogue. I assumed the queen would say: "How do you do? What is your name?" My response: Vartan Gregorian. Then she would ask, "What is your current position?" My answer: I am the dean of the Faculty of Arts and Sciences at the University of Pennsylvania. She would then ask: "Do you teach?" "Yes, of course, I teach a course on European intellectual history and one about the history of Armenia and the Caucasus." "How interesting," she would reply. Fortunately, that did not happen. The queen, before she reached us, stopped to talk to someone who simply said: "Hi, Queen. How are you doing?" She responded graciously by asking him where he was from. Lancaster, Pennsylvania, was his answer. I was relieved that the queen did not talk to me. Only Ambassador Walter Annenberg stopped to say hello. Then out of the blue, Prince Philip came straight to me and asked: "What keeps you busy?" My answer: "Vartan Gregorian." I thought he was asking for my name. He walked on, bewildered! I got a clue as to how royalty moves so fast; they never ask how you are, only where you are from.

During the Bicentennial, I was invited to speak at the Lower Merion Cricket Club by the Welcome Society of Pennsylvania. I sought the advice of President Meyerson about whether I should accept, and he said it was a great honor and therefore I should. I gave what I thought was a "brilliant" speech, extolling the virtues of Philadelphia and the importance of the American Revolution to an attentive audience. I distinctly remember saying that eighteenth-century Philadelphia was the last British city in America and the last discreet city where a woman's name would appear in print only three times—at birth, marriage, and death—and where nobody would be caught dead in one of Ruth Seltzer's columns (she was the society editor of the *Philadelphia Inquirer*).

When I finished, I expected a rousing, patriotic reception, but there was only a handful of scattered applause. I was stunned. Lo and behold, I found out after my speech that I had been mistaken about the purpose of the Welcome Society of Pennsylvania, which I thought was a Chamber of Commerce outfit, organized to welcome individuals and families who had just arrived in Philadelphia, similar to Welcome Wagon events organized by local merchants and neighbors that welcomed the newcomers in their respective communities. With great horror I discovered the truth: the Welcome Society of Pennsylvania consisted of the descendants of William Penn, the founder of Pennsylvania. I was an immigrant preaching to the choir, an all-white, nonethnic, bewildered choir. That episode taught me one lesson. I made a rule that I would always read the history of an institution, an organization, or a society before accepting their invitation. There was one immediate repercussion from my speech. Ruth Seltzer, the society columnist of the *Philadelphia Inquirer,* was in the audience. As a matter of fact, she was sitting in the front row. She did not take my remarks about her to be complimentary; as a result, after my speech, I seldom, if ever, was mentioned in her column.

But something extraordinary happened to me in the aftermath of the Bicentennial. There were two or three prominent "old Philadelphians" who were jealous guardians of WASP institutions and traditions of America and Philadelphia, such as the Colonial Society of Pennsylvania, the Daughters of the American Revolution, and the Society of the Cincinnati, among others. I gathered they liked me and respected me. They must have felt sorry that I was not a WASP, and they were determined, somehow, to repair that damage. That effort was led by Clifford Lewis III, the head of the Colonial Society. He was a wonderful, gentle man with a soft voice and pleasant laughter, an avid reader and an amateur historian. Unfortunately, he stuttered.

He would call me practically every other Sunday, after church services, to discuss a Bicentennial-related issue. He informed me one day that he had managed to get me elected to the prestigious and exclusive Rittenhouse Club. To his great horror, I declined with deep gratitude. I had no time to come down and have lunch or dinner at the club. I did not realize at the time that club membership was not about food, it was about status. Subsequently, there were several lengthy calls from Mr. Lewis. And one day, with great excitement, he called to notify me that I, along with the French ambassador to the United States, was made an honorary member of the Society of the Cincinnati; its members are the descendants of George Washington's officer corps. I was now a Son of Cincinnati. With a solemn voice, he cautioned me that my membership was not a hereditary one.

I attended my investiture meeting of the society. I was the only non-WASP at the meeting. I was expected to say a few words about the honor. Naturally, I expressed my gratitude. I had wondered for some time, I told them, about my selection. If you have chosen me in the belief that there were some Armenian officers in George Washington's army, I am here to disabuse you of that notion. There were not even Armenian soldiers. If you have chosen me because of the quality of my black beard, I will be the first to admit that it is no match to your forefathers' beards (I was the only one at the meeting who had a beard). But I soon realized, I said, why you have chosen me. Noah's Ark landed on Mount Ararat. I come from that region; as a matter of fact, my origins are in the Caucasus. I have sad news for you I told them—you don't look Caucasian to me. They were good sports and laughed.

While most of my fund-raising endeavors failed, the spectacular celebration of the Bicentennial, both in New York and in Philadelphia, had an emotional impact on me, my family, and, I am sure, millions of Americans. As a historian, as well as an immigrant, I appreciated the historical and symbolic significance of the American Revolution and the fact that I, along with a multitude of others, had been a major beneficiary of the United States. I owed my education, my family, and my career to the opportunities afforded me by America and its institutions. I had both gratitude and love for America. The sight of the tall ships in New York, the Statue of Liberty, the fireworks, the singing of "The Star-Spangled Banner" and "America the Beautiful" were exhilarating. I realized that my ties to America were not legal ones alone, but spiritual ones as well. After all, America was my home, my country, the home and the country of my wife and three sons, all of whom were U.S. citizens. I was the dean of the Faculty of Arts and Sciences of the University of Pennsylvania. I taught my students about the importance of history, memory, democracy, justice, service to one's society, mankind, and engaged citizenry. I felt I was teaching them all those values, yet somehow, I had remained on the sidelines by not becoming a citizen.

In 1975, I had a great opportunity to pay tribute to my birthplace, Iran, and its heritage. The occasion was the twentieth anniversary of the collabo-

ration between the University of Pennsylvania and Pahlavi University in
Shiraz. To mark the occasion, the University of Pennsylvania honored Mr.
Assadollah Alam (who at the time was minister of the Court and one of the
most influential individuals in Iran), chancellor emeritus of that university,
and its then-chancellor Farhang Mehr, by awarding them honorary degrees.* It was my privilege to address the distinguished audience. I confined
my remarks to the multiethnic and multicultural character of the Ar-
chaemenid Empire of Persia under the aegis of Cyrus II (585–529 B.C.) and
Darius I (550–486 B.C.). I reminded my audience that the genius of Iranian
culture is also manifested in the fact that under Darius the Persian Empire
cast off polytheism in favor of Zoroastrianism and its one god, Ahura
Mazda. Later through Manichaeism, Persia influenced both Christianity and
Islam. Furthermore, Islamic Persia, through the Shiite form of Islam,
changed drastically the course of the Muslim Middle East and made major
contributions to the realm of Islamic thought and culture. Through Sufism,
Persia provided yet another singular manifestation of its legacy. As the noted
scholar C. M. Wickens pointed out once, "Through Persia there flowed the
principal channel irrigating the somewhat arid field of Islam with the rich al-
luvial flood of ancient culture." In doing so, Persia raised up within Islam
those ideas, practices, and personalities which "most clearly link that faith
with the other great faiths of the world."

I concluded my speech by pointing out that "the greatest historical
weapon in the arsenal of Iran has not been its armies and material wealth. It
has been its culture. Armed with a rich language that can be traced by written documents over a period of some two thousand and seven hundred
years, beneficiary of historical synthesis of many brilliant civilizations, the
Iranian culture has survived and thrived. Throughout history, Iran conquered lands and people and in turn was conquered, reconquered by Mace-
donians, Arabs, Seljuks, Turks, Mongols, Tatars, and Uzbeks. Yet each time,
the Iranian culture conquered the conquerors of Iran, made them its con-
verts, and brought the rebirth of the Persian state, demonstrating time and
time again the brilliance of the Iranian culture."

* I met Mr. Alam again socially in 1976, and in 1977, I received a note from him asking for
my help to set up a new university in Iran's Kerman region, at one of his family estates. (He was
a great landowner.) While in Iran, I visited him in his residence, and we discussed his wishes
and plans. I was very excited about the idea of a new university and my potential role. I thought
it provided me an opportunity to pay my dues and gratitude to the country of my birth. The
very fact that I was even asked to help Mr. Alam astonished me. He wanted an independent
voice and forthright answers. I was flattered. Unfortunately, our discussions did not result in
concrete actions. Mr. Alam was afflicted with cancer and ailing. The Iranian Revolution put an
end to the prospect and my possible role as an educational consultant.

In 1976, as we were celebrating the Bicentennial, Iran, having celebrated the 2,500th anniversary of the Achaemenid Empire, was also celebrating the fiftieth anniversary of the Pahlavi dynasty. IranAir inaugurated its first non-stop New York–Tehran flight. The event was celebrated with great pomp and circumstance. To mark the occasion, the Iranian embassy in Washington, D.C., had invited a number of Americans and a handful of Iranians to be the guests of IranAir and the Iranian government in Iran. It was an extraordinary event. The Boeing 757 resembled Noah's Ark. There was a pair of doctors onboard, one of them the gynecologist of Jacqueline Kennedy, and a pair of newsmen and their spouses, and there were at least three actresses. One was Elizabeth Taylor, who came along with her hairdresser and a dietician. There was a pair of bankers and a pair of oil magnates, including the head of the Standard Oil Company and, finally, a pair of professors. I was one of them. It was most reassuring that the chairman and CEO of Boeing was onboard, too.

I assume the reason I was invited was that the daughter of Mohsen Goodarzi, consul general of Iran in New York, was a student at the University of Pennsylvania. My wife was invited to accompany me on this all-expenses-paid first-class trip to Iran. We faced a major hurdle, however. I was an Iranian citizen and needed entry and exit visas from Iran. My wife, however, was an American citizen. The Iranians considered her to be an Iranian citizen since she had married me. They insisted she could accompany me only if she obtained Iranian citizenship. It was a routine, pro forma act, they explained. She did not have to relinquish her U.S. citizenship. Many an Iranian spouse had obtained Iranian citizenship while retaining passports of their native lands. My wife was adamant that she would only travel with an American passport. Under the circumstances, I informed Mr. Goodarzi that we were unable to accept their invitation.

The consul general was stunned. He said, "Let us see whether we can find a creative solution for your problem." They did, indeed. My wife's U.S. passport received an Iranian visa and mine an entry visa. They were given to us not as a couple, but as individuals. The catch was that each of our visas indicated that we were traveling "unaccompanied." That did not prevent our hosts from listing us as "Mr. and Mrs. Gregorian" in all their official invitations, nor assigning us hotel rooms as a couple. I realized then and there that such "creative solutions" were fraught with potential dangers and problems.

The trip was memorable. We went to Tehran, Isfahan, and Shiraz. There were fabulous garden parties and concerts and visits to the royal palace in Tehran and, of course, Persepolis. The visit to Persepolis, my third, was again an overwhelming experience.

An extraordinary opportunity preoccupied me during the 1975–1976 academic year. I had made the acquaintance of Professor Adolf Klarmann, who taught Austrian literature at the University of Pennsylvania. When I visited him in his office, I saw a death mask on the wall. It was Franz Werfel's. Professor Klarmann, I discovered, was the general editor of the complete works of Werfel. We talked about Werfel and his various writings, including the *Forty Days of Musa Dagh*. I told him that I had read it in Armenian when I was a young boy in Tabriz and that it had left a great impression on me. By the way, I asked, when did Franz Werfel die? 1945 was the answer. Where is he buried? Rosemont Cemetery in Los Angeles was the response. How come Austrians have not transferred his remains to Vienna? I asked. You know theirs is a slow bureacracy and a slow process! was the answer. My God, twenty years have passed and they still have not done it yet? Then I will transfer the remains to Vienna, I said with great authority and passion. Professor Klarmann got very excited. I wrote to Rosemont Cemetery. We needed money and legal authorization by a blood relative of his. Since his family was wiped out during the Holocaust, Professor Klarmann found one relative in either Hungary or Israel. We got his signature. The daughter of Alma Mahler, Werfel's last wife, sent her permission from London. I provided funds for exhuming his remains and their transportation in a coffin to Vienna.

There was a great deal of social and political commotion in the literary and artistic circles of Vienna. Anna Mahler sculpted a monument. We organized an international symposium on Werfel. My only condition was that his monument should be unveiled either on the Warsaw Uprising or Armenian Genocide commemoration dates or else on Israeli Independence Day, and that I had to remain in the background. All kinds of groups took credit for the pending transfer of Werfel's remains to Vienna. Unfortunately, Professor Klarmann died before the event. His widow, Isolde, revealed that I was behind the initiative. The Austrian government invited Isolde Klarmann, my wife, and me to the unveiling of the Franz Werfel monument in the Pantheon of Austrian writers. The government awarded Klarmann and me the Gold Medal of Honor of the City and Province of Vienna. There was a fancy state luncheon and dinner. What surprised me was the citation of the decoration. There was no mention of Franz Werfel, the Jews, the Holocaust, or the Armenian Genocide. The medal was awarded to me "for organizational and administrative talent." In my remarks, I rectified that by discussing the importance of *Forty Days of Musa Dagh*. It was written about Armenians but was also, I thought, a metaphor for the Jews, for their trials, and the impending dangers facing them. After all, we all knew about the significance of forty days, the fact that the Musa was Moses, and Dagh was a mountain. It was about the historical plight of both the Armenians and the Jews. And, yes, incidentally, it was published in January 1933, and every Jew in Austria and Germany must have read it for what it was: a warning.

I don't think the Austrian Jews liked my remarks about anti-Semitism and the Holocaust. They did not believe it was the appropriate time to raise the question of Austrian anti-Semitism. Franz Werfel was very religious. According to Professor Klarmann, he had flirted with Catholicism but did not convert. He could not chose between Judaism and Catholicism. Under the circumstances, I asked the Armenian Bishop of Vienna to bless his grave and monument in the presence of many officials and dignitaries. But I don't have a deacon, he said. I'll be your deacon, I told him. I know the appropriate prayers. Thus, in 1976, this former altar boy from Tabriz participated in the blessing of the Werfel grave.

In 1978, several events took place at Penn that had a major impact on the university and many lives, including mine. With the support of the majority of the faculty, the administration decided to discontinue the School of Allied Medical Practices as a measure of fiscal responsibility. This created an uproar. Students, faculty, and minority groups attacked the decision as unsound, irresponsible, and opportunistic. They pointed out that the school was one of the best of its kind, and that an aging America needed the services of such a school to provide competent professionals for health care, auxiliary services, physical therapy, etc. The decision to close SAMP created a great deal of ill will toward the provost and the president. There were votes of no confidence, student organizing, and national appeals to reverse the decision.

On March 2, 1978, while I was addressing several hundred prospective students at the university museum, there was a student rally in front of College Hall, the main administrative building. It was sponsored by the Undergraduate Assembly to protest the announced cuts in the university budget that would discontinue the intercollegiate hockey and gymnastics teams and end the professional theater in the Annenberg Center. At the end of the rally, several hundred students occupied College Hall.

By the time I arrived in my office, students had filled the entire hallway, including the entrance of my office. All offices were shut tight, except mine. This bunker-siege mentality backfired. Students got emboldened. They formed a Student Committee on University Priorities (SCOUP) and issued five demands:

To reinstate the hockey and gymnastics teams as well as the
   professional theater.

To form an ad hoc committee to ensure access to any and all pending
   decisions being made by the administration.

To establish and empower a Student Committee of University
   Priorities (SCOUP) with the right to veto or rescind decisions
   which affect all students.

To implement nonvoting representation of students on the Board of
   Trustees. All trustee meetings must be held during the time in
   which classes are in session.

To ensure the right of all upcoming graduates to have the sole say
   over the choice of graduation speakers.

The organizers of the sit-in and the student spokesmen were members of
the Undergraduate Assembly and the student government. They were not
radicals. Hundreds of students who stayed overnight were fed by the university's Dining Service and received free sandwiches from the Student Activities Council. Security officials allowed a rock band, Wonder Drug, to
perform as long as students did not bring any kegs.

The administration did not know how to handle it. Normally, the vice
provost for university life took care of such situations. The incumbent was
not up to the task, so it was kicked upstairs to the provost. The provost had
to consult with the president, who was, unfortunately, in Barbados. There
was tension between the president's staff and the provost's. Students passed
yet another resolution that "Meyerson must be contacted and asked to return at once to meet with students. If he refuses, he will be asked to resign."
There was a bomb threat. Penn security considered evacuating the building
but, fearing that students would probably refuse to evacuate, they simply
searched the stairwell. Students occupied College Hall for four days. They
had begun negotiations directly with the provost and then, upon his return,
with the president himself. Two bad decisions were made. The first was to
cover the negotiations live on campus TV and radio, which turned the College Hall event into a happening. The second, which had disastrous reper-
cussions, was the president's decision to invite several trustees to take part in
the negotiating sessions.

These actions brought more demonstrations both from within and without the campus. The president, provost, two vice presidents, vice provost,
and a dean or two were sitting across the table from undergraduate freshmen and other students, discussing the university's governance, finances,

and priorities. Everybody had passed the buck to the provost and the president. Faculty members who had initially considered the incident as a conflict between students and the administration became incensed. The feeling was that out there at College Hall, people were discussing all kinds of important matters without faculty consultation or its involvement. They asserted that the university governance issues, finances, and priorities were faculty prerogatives. They criticized the administration for a failure of leadership.

In my opinion, both the provost and the president were ill served by competing, unimaginative, indecisive subordinates. Neither should have been involved directly. They should have assigned two or three individuals to deal with the students and brought in faculty as a counterweight. The president should never have asked the trustees to be participants. They were a policy group, not part of the university's management.

The faculty began circulating a petition calling for an emergency faculty meeting, asking for a no-confidence vote in the president and for his resignation. To delay the matter, the university Senate established an ad hoc fact-finding group. The group met with trustees, the president, the provost and the deans. It soon became clear that the president could not resign in the midst of the campaign. Eliot Stellar, the provost, a great scientist, a wonderful, generous, and kind man, had to take the fall.

Dean Louis Pollak and I drafted a resolution in support of Eliot. All the deans signed except the dean of SAMP. I attempted to add President Meyerson's name to the resolution, but several deans demurred. They believed that the president or his administration had mishandled the situation. The university Senate's ad hoc committee report criticized the provost and the president though it did not ask for their resignations. The trustees were part of the behind-the-scene settlement to prevent a vote of no confidence in the provost and the president. In April, the provost resigned, effective December 31. At the beginning of the 1978 academic year, the president announced his decision to retire in 1981, upon the completion of the Campaign for the Eighties.

President Meyerson had publicly criticized Judy Gleason, one of my secretaries, who, in my absence, had not locked the doors of the dean's office during the sit-in. I took it as a criticism aimed at me. I said, "I do not want my secretary to be a scapegoat. If you want one, I'll be happy to assume that role. I, therefore, submit my resignation." There were no takers however.

The changes in the university leadership coincided with changes in trustee leadership. During 1976–78, there were persistent rumors that five or six Philadelphia trustees spearheaded by John Eckman, CEO of Rohrer

Group (Maalox), were unhappy about the fact that the University of Pennsylvania Board of Trustees was headed by Donald T. Regan, chairman of Merrill Lynch and a Harvard graduate. They were supposedly unhappy about President Meyerson's "imperial presidency." They wanted Philadelphia-based trustees to have a leadership role. The rumor was that they threatened to force a vote of no confidence in Chairman Regan. Don Regan, who ran the board along with Bob Dunlop and Thomas Gates Jr., was in the midst of restructuring Merrill Lynch. He resigned as chairman. Dunlop, Gates, and other trustees did not want to reward John Eckman, so they proposed Gates, as a Philadelphian and Penn graduate, to be Penn chairman. He responded that unless there was a unanimous vote he would not accept. Since there was not, he declined.

The opponents of John Eckman and his four or five colleagues then chose a compromise candidate, Paul Miller Jr. Eckman and company thought this was a Martin Meyerson–engineered solution and never forgave him. The College Hall events and faculty ad hoc report came as handy ammunition for those who tried to sideline President Meyerson.

Within days of the provost's announced resignation and the president's retirement, a consultative committee on the selection of a new provost was set up. It was headed by none other than Professor David DeLaura, formerly of the University of Texas. Within ten days, the committee, according to the press, had narrowed the list of its candidates to four: Ralph Amado, professor of physics and a former Faculty Senate chairman; Dan McGill, professor of insurance at the Wharton School, who was heading the faculty committee examining the performance of the Meyerson administration; Associate Provost James Freedman, professor of law; and me. Professor Freedman informed me that he was withdrawing his name in support of my candidacy, and that he would be happy to work for me or with me.

On Monday, September 18, eleven deans of the University of Pennsylvania (minus two of us) met with President Meyerson at his residence to give their opinions about candidates. According to the *Philadelphia Evening Bulletin,* all eleven supported my candidacy. On Wednesday, the president offered me the position. I spent Wednesday evening at his home. Paul Miller Jr., the new chairman of the Board of Trustees, was there. The joyous occasion was marred by a phone call. It was a trustee from Massachusetts. He told me, "Don't think this will be a stepping-stone. You'll be president of the University of Pennsylvania over my dead body." I was shaken. Both Meyerson and Miller calmed me down: "Don't worry. That is the opinion of only one trustee."

I consulted with my wife and sons, several friends, including Judge Louis

Pollak, former dean of the law school at Penn, and Irving Kravis, chair of the Faculty Senate (with whom I had become friendly). Judge Pollak told me it was my moral obligation to accept the offer. Professor Kravis said, "You have no choice but to take the job. It is a dumb personal decision but a good one for the university."

The news of my appointment was received with much enthusiasm. The *Daily Pennsylvanian* editorial cast me in the role of the "Messiah of the University," saying that "the trustees, faculty, and students have turned to Gregorian to restore stability and self-confidence." (" . . . he has an impressive ability to bring people together.") The Undergraduate Assembly chairman Mark Lerner, who had been active in the College Hall sit-in, commented that the greatest asset I brought to the position was that "while he listens to everyone, he will be his own man."

In presenting my candidacy to the board, President Meyerson said: "My conclusion was that the times and circumstances demanded one talent in preference to all the others—part flamboyance, part diligence, and a determined and very special devotion to our university." The Executive Board of the Trustees approved my appointment by acclamation.

Two or three weeks after my appointment as provost, the Faculty Panel on Administrative Functioning of the University, established in May 1978 by the Faculty Senate, issued its report. It "strongly recommended that the traditional division of responsibilities between the president and the provost be preserved" and that the provost "be given primary responsibility for directing those functions that are central to the educational mission of the university." In a sense, the report was recommending that the provost be chief academic officer, and the president chief executive officer of the university. The panel met separately with Meyerson, Paul Miller, and me. I promised to implement its recommendations: strong provostship with emphasis on the academic mission of the university, transparency, consultation with faculty, and good communication with the campus.

I assumed the position with a great mandate from the faculty, the president, the board, the students, and, what was most unusual, my fellow deans. My immediate task was to restore the faculty's morale, regain their and the students' trust in the university administration, and mobilize the university community's efforts to assist the deans and the president to realize the $255 million Campaign for the Eighties. An additional objective of my own was to strengthen Martin Meyerson's moral and executive authority on campus by treating him with respect, even affection, in an attempt to dispel the prevalent notion that he was as powerless as a lame duck.

In the meantime, however, President Meyerson was facing another reality. Whereas the former trustee chairman was criticized by some for his absentee "imperial chairmanship" and for giving the president great freedom of action, Paul F. Miller Jr., the new chairman, was determined to be "a hands-on" chairman. In an interview with the *San Francisco Chronicle* (April 21, 1979), Miller stated his position: "I look on trusteeship in a different light. . . . Trustees traditionally look after investments, glance at the budget, and hire and fire the president. That's about it." But with Miller as chairman of the University of Pennsylvania, he added, things would be different. "We will push hard for evidence of good management on campus," he said. "Trustees are the only people in an educational institution that are devoid of self-interest. I firmly believe that management monitoring, as practiced by corporate directors, is perfectly compatible with the educational world." The *Chronicle* added: "Miller's role as an activist trustee became abundantly clear when, a few days after he took over as chairman, he carved out a modest office space in one of the university's administrative buildings. No other chairman had ever done that, the others preferring to make what amounted to ceremonial visits to campus."

In fact, the office was not modest. It was the former office of Paul Gaddis, the vice president for management and finance and it was in College Hall. The Secretary of the Corporation and her staff became the chairman's de facto staff. Miller held regular meetings with the vice president for budget and finance, as well as with other subordinates of President Meyerson. He left the impression that the presidency was in receivership.

My first task as provost was to put together a new administration. Robert Dyson, noted archeologist and former associate dean, was named dean of the Faculty of Arts and Sciences. Benjamin Shen, chairman of the departments of astronomy and astrophysics, was named associate provost; Louis Girifalco of engineering became vice provost for research; Janis Somerville was named vice provost for university life; and Dean Jean Brownlee, former dean of the College for Women, was nominated to be special assistant to the provost for alumni and Philadelphia affairs. Management professor Ross Webber was appointed faculty assistant to the president and the provost to study the university's administrative structure, its strengths, weaknesses, and possible remedies.

At the end of my first anniversary, we held an academic planning retreat that brought together the president, the provost's staff, the Council of Academic Deans, and the vice president for budget and finance to discuss the future "scale and scope" of the university and to evaluate the impact of responsibility center budgeting. One hundred of the university's top academic decision makers were in attendance. The outcome was positive. We began to draw up a blueprint for post-campaign Penn.

It was inevitable that in the midst of all these activities there would be speculation as to whether or not a "powerful" activist provost, by asserting his authority, would impinge on President Meyerson's authority. The fact was that we worked well together. I had to stress publicly that there was only *one* administration, Martin Meyerson's, of which I was the chief academic officer. The president and I appointed a long-range planning committee to combine both academic and nonacademic planning in a more cohesive process.

My life was not completely anchored around the university, however, for shortly after our return from Iran, I applied for U.S. citizenship. I was only the second immigrant to assume the post of provost of the University of Pennsylvania. The first was William Smith, the first provost of the University of Pennsylvania, imported to Philadelphia by Benjamin Franklin. I did not want one of William Smith's successors not to be a U.S. citizen.

To be a citizen, I had to take an examination. My examiner, who was an alumnus of the University of Pennsylvania, was excited to have the opportunity to examine the provost of his alma mater. He wore a Penn necktie. We were both worried that I might stumble on a question or two and I missed one: How many amendments does the U.S. Constitution have? "Twenty-nine." "Provost Gregorian, the Constitution has only twenty-eight amendments," he said. I was fast with a retort: I was counting the Equal Rights Amendment as a done deal. "Not so," he said, relieved. "It has not been approved yet."

The citizenship ceremony was a very special occasion. My family and many friends were present. The federal judge who presided over the ceremony was my friend Louis H. Pollak, former dean of Yale law school, and, later, of the University of Pennsylvania. I was asked to speak on behalf of the new U.S. citizens who were naturalized along with me. As the ceremony was about to begin, I became nervous and tense. Suddenly, the loudspeaker called my name, instructing me to proceed immediately to the judge's chamber. I did so with trepidation. I wondered whether there was a last-minute legal glitch. I was relieved to find out that federal judge Norma Shapiro wanted to give me a "big hug."

As the official ceremony began, and as I prepared to take the oath of citizenship, I became emotional and even teary. I felt as if I were getting married.

After the citizenship oath was administered, Judge Louis H. Pollak intro-

duced me and made some remarks, and then I rose to speak on behalf of all
the new citizens.

Your Honor, fellow former immigrants and now citizens, distinguished
guests: We, the new citizens of this United States of America, come
from some twenty-seven countries, from many cultures, from many
continents, many faiths, races with many colors, many languages,
many accents, of different socioeconomic backgrounds and of different political persuasions, but whether we came to the United States for
economic opportunity, political or religious asylum, education, security, reunification with our families and relatives, we all share a common faith in America. America is a democracy. It has profound faith in
human dignity and freedom and men's and women's potentialities.
That faith and principle are manifested in America's historical commitments. However one defines democracy as a political system,
whether it's government of the people, by the people, for the people or
a system that embodies sovereignty of the people where, according to
Alexander Hamilton, the people may be said to be entirely masters of
their own destiny and fate, the essence of the American proposition
has always been that free people can be trusted to know what's good
for them. In this connection, we share the vision of Walt Whitman that
democracy is the essence of the American spirit and the purpose of
America's existence, and that democracy's aim was and must be the
perfection of human beings, a kind of training school for making first-
class men living lives of love and noble aspiration. We share Woodrow
Wilson's notion of democracy that it exists for the purpose of reducing
inhumanity and maximizing hope. That's a quality that makes the
principle of the dignity of the human being and guarantees legally political equality of the individual, that gives recognition to individuals
and helps to create a society that provides political and potentially or
actually social and economic opportunity for the mass of men.

We agree with Wilson that by "morality" we mean the enhance-
ment of the human being and that in the political sphere democracy is
morality of a higher order, for it involves respect, justice, and hope, for
it releases the energies of every human being.

We share the legacy of Franklin Roosevelt and his view that American democracy's freedom must include freedom from want, freedom
from insecurity, and freedom from fear.

In addition to democracy as the embodiment of human dignity,
freedom, and self-determination, we share the common vision of a

pluralistic, nonparochial, cosmopolitan, and international America, America where faiths, cultures, races have coexisted in a microcosm of humanity. In the words of Herman Melville, we are not a narrow tribe of men. No, our blood is that of the blood of the Amazon, made up of a thousand noble currents all pouring into one. We are not a nation so much as a world.

While not abandoning our identity and our past, as new American citizens we share Thomas Wolfe's confident assertion of America's dream when he says, and I quote: "I think the true discovery of America is before us. I think the true fulfillment of our spirit, of our mighty and immortal land is yet to come. I think the true discovery of our democracy is still before us. And I think that all these things are certain, as certain as morning, as inevitable as noon."

The preamble of the United States Constitution states, and I quote: "We, the people of the United States, in order to form a more perfect union, establish justice, insure domestic tranquillity, provide for the common defense, promote the general welfare, and secure the blessings of liberty to ourselves and our posterity, do ordain and establish this Constitution for the United States of America."

We, the new citizens of the United States, like many other immigrant forefathers of ours, have come not only to enjoy the benefits of America but to contribute to its development, to its growth as well as to its welfare. We have come to contribute to the achievement of what is left undone or unfinished in the agenda of American democracy. We have come to contribute to that perfect union. For us, America is not just its past but also its future. It's not an actuality but it's also a potentiality. We have come to share its past heritage and the responsibility of its future mission.

Your Honor, we are delighted and proud that on the eve of the Bicentennial of the United States Constitution, Tricentenary of the City of Philadelphia, cradle of American independence, under jurisdiction of one of America's prominent judges like you, we are joining the American nation in order to become part of its historical struggle and quest for human dignity, freedom, self-determination and social justice.

*   *   *

In early December 1979, President David Saxon of the University of California called me to say that the University at Berkeley was seeking candidates for the position of chancellor. For a moment, I thought it was a joke.

After I obtained my Ph.D. from Stanford in 1964, whenever I was asked what I planned to do with a Ph.D. in history, I would say that I was going to be chancellor of UC Berkeley. Friends and strangers alike would roar with laughter and I was the butt of a practical joke or two. "Roger Heynes, the president of the University of California, is on the line. He would like to know whether you would be interested in accepting an offer to be chancellor of Berkeley."

This was not a joke. Saxon informed me that they had a short list of candidates and I was one of them. "Would you be willing to fly to California and meet with the members of the search committee? I chair that committee." I was thunderstruck! The only career fantasy of my life was no longer a fancy dream. But the invitation put me in an awkward situation. I informed President Meyerson and Chairman Miller that during the past seven years I had received numerous inquiries from "headhunters" and all sorts of presidential search committees. I had turned them all down. Indeed, in 1978, I had declined the chance to lead the University of Massachusetts system. My Stanford classmate Judge Stephen Breyer (now Supreme Court Justice Breyer), who was the chairman of the search committee, had made a compelling case for the institution. He had even enlisted David Riesman, who had said they would be willing to wait a year. But Berkeley was different. I asked for their permission to meet with David Saxon and the search committee. I had a great meeting with the committee, tough and honest. When one member asked whether I was taking certain positions to please the members, I shot back, "No. I am here to be persuaded by you to be chancellor of Berkeley, not the other way around. I give straight answers to straight questions." I was amazed at myself. It sounded so arrogant, but the committee members asked me to come back. I met the chairman of the Board of Regents and Ed Carter, one of the most influential UC regents, in Los Angeles, at Carter's extraordinary house in Bel Air. In my presence, he called David Saxon and said, "On a scale of one to ten Gregorian is a thirteen—grab him," or words to that effect. I was practically in a trance.

Before I bid good-bye, Ed Carter gave me some advice. "When you receive UC's formal offer, two individuals who are friends of yours, Martin Meyerson and Franklin Murphy (former chancellor of UCLA and CEO of Times Mirror Co.) will advise you to decline our offer. Ignore their advice. Martin Meyerson wanted to be chancellor of Berkeley. It will be very hard for him to see his provost get the job he did not. Franklin Murphy wanted to be president of the UC system. He did not get it. He would advise you to ignore our offer, too."

In subsequent days, I consulted my mentors at Stanford, David Riesman and Reginald Zelnik. They all said that I should seize the opportunity. Martin Meyerson and Franklin Murphy both advised me to decline it. After all, I had a great future at Penn. Franklin Murphy said both in private and public that Miller and I were destined to be a great duo for Penn.

Before I could sort things out, on January 17, the *Daily Californian* and Berkeley's *Independent Gazette* reported that UC Berkeley had narrowed the list of the candidates for chancellor to four: Earl Cheit, dean of Berkeley's Business School, Vice Chancellor Ira Michael Heyman, President Steven Muller of Johns Hopkins University, and me. The same day, the Penn trustees announced the membership of the presidential search committee. I received urgent calls from Walter Annenberg, Donald T. Regan, and scores of other trustees, including Sarkes Tarzian, urging me to stay at Penn. Paul Miller urged me to decline the Berkeley offer because my future belonged to Penn. I was a logical candidate for the presidency of Penn. Many faculty members called with the same message. So did many deans. If I decided to leave for Berkeley the university would have a lame-duck president, a lame-duck provost, and a lame-duck Campaign for the Eighties. Many pointed out that it was clear to everyone that being provost was the first of a two-step process designed to land me the presidency of Penn. My departure, I was told, would constitute a great setback for the university. A few individuals reminded me that it was not *right* to accept the provostship and leave my post after only two years.

I paid another visit to Berkeley. Upon my initiative, I met with Chancellor Bowker, who was retiring. I was told his candidate was Vice Chancellor Heyman. I discussed with him major problems confronting Berkeley. I also met with a handful of Berkeley's prominent scholars. I raised the issue of the calendar and the merits of a semester versus a quarter system. Finally, I met with the chairman of the history department. We discussed my appointment as professor of history. I joked that their department was so good that I had taken the circuitous route of joining their department by becoming the chancellor of Berkeley! I met again with David Saxon, some trustees, and other officials. The ball was in my court.

I was torn between duty and opportunity. My friend Reggie admonished me: this is the first time a war has been won, but you, the general, refuse to accept the victory. I vacillated. In the mornings, I would decide to stay at Penn; in the evenings, prompted by telephone calls from the West Coast, I would decide to go to Berkeley. I think I aged five years during that week. My family agonized with me. They had lived in Beirut, California, Texas, and Pennsylvania. Should we uproot ourselves once again to go to California? That was the question. One evening several close friends and our family discussed the matter one more time. We resorted to secret ballots to express our true choices. We were divided. The decision was left to me. On February 4, I notified David Saxon that, with great sadness, I could not accept the chancellorship. I had agonized far too long. He expressed his profound regret.

I knew that cemeteries are full of irreplaceable people. I knew that nobody is indispensable, but I felt that I had a moral obligation to stay at Penn. I could not leave in good conscience. I had to provide continuity and stability. My departure would have caused severe problems for the university in such areas as budgeting, academic planning, fund-raising, and the tenure appeal process. The admonition that it was not *right* to take a major responsibility and then leave after two years tipped the scales.

In turning down Berkeley, I had made no deals with anyone about the presidency of Penn. For me, there was no connection. But in many people's minds, there was. The dean of the Wharton School, Donald Carrol, made a comment that was typical: "I would think that Dr. Gregorian is the odds-on favorite to become the university's sixth president. But I think he was the odds-on favorite before Berkeley arose."

Even though I had made the right decision, I nevertheless had great regrets about it. All I could think of was what might have been. Berkeley had my undying gratitude and affection for making my dream a reality. That great university had offered its leadership to a Stanford graduate, an Ivy League provost, Iranian-born, and it had done so in the midst of the U.S. hostage crisis in Iran. I could visualize the headlines: BERKELEY DOES IT AGAIN. AN IRANIAN NAMED AS ITS CHANCELLOR.

During my almost two-year tenure as provost, I continued to enjoy the support of the faculty, the staff, the students, and my fellow deans. Trust, collegiality, and transparency were restored, along with accountability. The Campaign for the Eighties achieved its $255 million goal. A preliminary academic and budgetary blueprint was developed for the 1980s. The university's academic standing rose nationally, and its budgets were balanced. As promised, I ran an open administration. I visited all the schools and dormitories and, along with the president, paid visits to Penn alumni both in Pennsylvania and elsewhere. In addition, we established various international linkages with some European, Israeli, Arab, African, and Latin American institutions of higher learning.

My relationship with President Meyerson remained cordial. I did everything possible to restore his standing with the faculty, defending him, praising him, giving him due credit, attributing all my initiatives to his leadership and vision. There were some tense moments, however. When in August

1980 he left for China, the issue arose as to who should serve as acting president. According to rules and tradition, in the president's absence, the provost acted on his behalf. There was a "strong suggestion" that maybe Dr. Thomas Langfitt, the vice president for health and human affairs, should be named acting president. That suggestion, which came from a trustee, was shot down by the chair of the Faculty Senate and the Council of Deans. During the month of August, I served as acting president. In President Meyerson's absence we settled a protracted and highly disruptive Teamsters strike.

President Meyerson was under tremendous psychological pressure. The announcement of the presidential search process had highlighted his lame-duck status. That many faculty members, deans, and students were treating me as if I were the designated future leader of the university was of course irksome. The vice president for budget and finance and the vice president for facilities had boxed Meyerson into an untenable position. The two vice presidents had direct access to Chairman Paul Miller, consulted with him regularly, and then informed President Meyerson that such and such action was "favored" by the chairman or he found it "helpful." In other budgetary matters, the president was caught between the vice president of budget and finance (who enjoyed the chairman's support) and me (who enjoyed faculty, dean, and student support).

Prompted by the vice president for budget and finance, the president wrote an official memorandum to me stating that, while he was in China, there could be no staff hiring. He even specified that the vice provost could not hire a replacement for her secretary's job. I received a letter inquiring formally whether I had used Tarzian Chair funds to buy a car for personal use. Thank God, I had kept all the correspondence with Mr. Tarzian, our trustee-benefactor. He had pleaded with me to use one of his company's leased cars. He also paid for the insurance. The university had incurred no cost, even for mileage or gas. The episode made me angry. For a brief moment, I felt as if I was back in Texas, that, once again, "dark forces" were trying to find some kind of financial "irregularity" or other "problems," to cast doubts either about my character or my "management style," so as to influence the opinion of trustees that I was a "controversial" character or, at the least, an absentminded one.

Since I was beholden to the deans for their support, questions were raised as to whether I would be able to resist their pressures for budgetary concessions or administrative favors. The deans were sensitive to the same charges and they took it very well, even when I rejected their requests. I found, on occasion, humor to be a welcome medicine. When my dear friend Robert Marshak, the dean of the veterinary school, came to see me with an urgent request for a $1 million budget for the Big Animal Hospital, I read his proposal. I found it first rate, and I told him so, but I also told him with a straight face that I was disappointed in him. If it was such a great project, how come he was asking for only a million? That certainly was not enough. How much should he be asking for? he inquired. Two million. Okay, I am asking you for two million, said Marshak with great enthusiasm. Now, Bob, guess what? I am turning down a two-million-dollar project, not a one-million-dollar project. He was stunned. Then we both laughed. The fact was that I did not have the money. We would have had to raise it.

Don Carrol, the dean of the Wharton School, a Quaker, had a brilliant mind and was a hands-on dean, who enjoyed the support of his faculty, the alumni of Wharton, and many trustees. He was a force to be reckoned with. He and I had fought many battles over the university's budget, but in spite of it, we were good friends. We trusted each other. Unfortunately, he disliked President Meyerson and, on several occasions, he threatened to resign. Once President Meyerson came to my office to fetch me. He said, "Dean Carrol is in my office threatening to resign over the issue of the reconstruction of Dietrich Hall." I went to see him. I asked him what the problem was. He said, in effect, Meyerson wants me to come up with $10 million in cash before I can embark upon the project. My answer stunned them both. Ten million is not enough. You have to put up twelve million! Okay, he said. I'll do it for you, but not for Meyerson. No, I said. You are doing it for the university. You are complying with the existing university rules and regulations.

The campus was curious about my relations with the students. After the 1979 tumultuous sit-in, students had become visible and active on many issues. I had spent considerable effort on the undergraduate curriculum, the quality of undergraduate teaching, and student housing, as well as other services that catered to the students. One of my first acts as provost was to announce that I did not accept demands; requests, yes, petitions, yes, but demands, no. I was tested. Students collected thousands of signatures demanding that I make eight major Christian and Jewish holidays official university holidays. This was a request. I was told that the president had agreed to it during the 1979 sit-in negotiations.

I discussed the issue with the university's chaplain and various university-based priests, ministers, and rabbis. I contacted the cardinal's office. Then I issued a report reminding everyone that ours was a *secular* institution; therefore we would not observe religious holidays as official holidays. We will, however, not give exams before and during those holidays. This decision resolved a difficult situation to the satisfaction of most of the students and their parents.

There was another petition containing a couple of thousand signatures, demanding that we authorize the operations of a for-profit, nonuniversity "head shop" in Houston Hall (the student union). Not only did I reject it but we evicted the shop. I turned them down on the basis of its being a non-university activity. It was not until later that I learned that a "head shop" sold drug paraphernalia. I paid a penalty for that decision however. At the commencement that year, three of the proponents of the head shop streaked on the stage, shocking everybody, especially the fiftieth reunion class. I remember my words: "Ladies and gentlemen, don't worry. They are not Diogenes searching for real men." The crowd burst out laughing.

There was also a great deal of speculation about my relationship with the members of Penn's African-American community with whom I had a great rapport. They had given me great support during my tenure as dean of the Faculty of Arts and Sciences. Shortly after I became provost, several representatives paid a visit to me. The delegation was headed by Professors Ralph Smith of the law school and Houston Baker of the English department. They asked me what promises and commitments I was specifically willing to make to their community. None, I said. You have to wait and judge me by my actions, not by my words. My record as dean of Arts and Sciences should be a guide to you. That was it. They thanked me for my candor. When they celebrated the One Hundred Year Anniversary of Black Presence at Penn, the entire community honored me for my commitment.

Then there was the issue of "sexual orientation," the demand on the part of several groups, inside the university and outside as well, to change the university's policies to include a nondiscriminatory clause about gays. This was a difficult issue at the time. The Penn community had not debated it and was not ready for it. Certainly many of our trustees were not enthusiastic about it. They were unsure about its "legal and moral consequences." Meyerson delegated the problem to me. There were tons of letters and phone calls urging the university to take action. There was a scheduled University Council meeting. The issue was on the agenda. Many outsiders joined to demonstrate on behalf of a policy change. The University of Pennsylvania was, I told the Council, a state-aided university. The State of Pennsylvania was assisting our veterinary school and some other programs. Governor Shapp had issued an executive order changing the state regulation. We had to comply. If I remember correctly, the entire issue took less than a couple of minutes. The administration's resolution passed without dissent and Penn became the first Ivy League institution, or maybe even the first major higher education institution, to adopt an ordinance against discrimination based on sexual orientation. Some advocates were disappointed. They had wanted to "wrest" the policy from the university rather than simply receive it. To my great surprise, I became a "hero" in some gay circles. They thanked me for my "courage."

During my eight years at Penn, I had established cordial relations with a handful of trustees. I socialized with them only during board meetings and alumni or campaign events. The Executive Board was headed by three trustees: Thomas S. Gates Jr., Donald Regan, and Bob Dunlop. I came to know all three of them, as well as Ambassador Walter H. Annenberg and Bernard Segal, very well.

When I first appeared before the Executive Board I was given five to eight minutes to present the Arts and Sciences Report. During that time, Tom Gates interrupted me at least four times. Exasperated, I said, Mr. Gates, you have all the time in the world, whereas I have only eight minutes to present to you the Arts and Sciences Report. Please let me finish, then you can ask all the questions on your time, not mine. He laughed. He told me later, You are a son of a bitch—my kind of son of a bitch.

Don Regan, the head of Merrill Lynch, was miscast in Philadelphia. He always thought big in a city that, for a long time, was not used to thinking big. He was a decisive and supportive trustee and chairman. He once asked me, Who is Penn's competition in the realm of Arts and Sciences within Greater Philadelphia? I answered, Bryn Mawr, Swarthmore, and Haverford. He said, Why don't we acquire them? He said it half jokingly, half seriously.

Bob Dunlop was a devotee of Penn. He was chairman of Sun Oil Company and it was thanks to his leadership that Glenmede Trust (Pew Charitable Trusts) became a major patron of the university. He was politically conservative, with deep religious beliefs and values. He invited me on several occasions to prayer breakfasts. While I was provost, in 1979, with his family's connivance, we organized a surprise birthday luncheon for him in my office. I asked my son, who was a drummer in the Philadelphia Scottish Highland Band, to come with the band and play for Mr. Dunlop. He was moved to tears.

Walter Annenberg and Tom Gates enjoyed each other's company, especially while armed with a pitcher of martinis. I was on the Annenberg School and the Annenberg Center boards. I came to know Walter well. I never solicited him, either for Penn or for any other cause. He had a wonderful sense of humor, hated off-color jokes, hated racism, and disliked any religious leader who took God's name in vain or fomented division. He especially disliked those who thought God would be on their side if only God knew all the facts. He invited me once to visit him in Palm Springs. When I asked for the address, he said it was between Frank Sinatra and Bob Hope Lanes, but he did not give me a number, and he did not tell me that those lanes were many miles long.

In general, I did not spend much time getting to know many trustees of Penn, curry favor, or socialize much with them. I thought the relations with the trustees belonged most appropriately to the president.

The deliberations of the presidential search committee lasted seven months. During those months, the campus press and the rumor mill were fully engaged in speculating. There began select leaks to the press by some members of the search committee, some administrators (mostly from the nonacademic side), alumni leaders, and some major donors. There were regular public assessments in the press of my strengths and weaknesses. On the positive side, it was pointed out that I was a good teacher and that I had done an "excellent job" in putting together a new faculty by uniting five disparate academic and administrative entities during difficult financial times. It was pointed out that I enjoyed the support and trust of the faculty and the students, including women and minorities, and that I had demonstrated my devotion and loyalty to Penn by declining Berkeley.

It was argued that I had established an open administration. The student newspaper noted, "Things are so quiet on campus that last year, students accepted a 13.85 percent tuition hike without a whimper and the faculty hardly complained when they received a salary increase amounting to just one half of the inflation rate." I was described as energetic and dynamic, with good judgment in selecting an outstanding team of administrators and experts. I was praised for my integrity and for not abandoning my core principles, as well as for my "disarming" sense of humor. One of my quotes from Provost Shannon McCure of the University of Massachusetts made the rounds on campus: "The president makes speeches. The student's job is to think. The provost's job is to see that the students don't make speeches and the president doesn't think."

On the negative side, there were anonymous accusations that I was too political: "The university cannot be treated as a political ward." I was flamboyant, too concerned about my reputation and image. It was hinted that I had shied away from making difficult and unpopular decisions. It was even suggested that maybe I had "manufactured" a Berkeley offer to place "undue" pressure on the Penn trustees to bypass their process and "award" me the presidency of the University of Pennsylvania. In her article "A Battle of Great Men" (*Today, The Philadelphia Inquirer* magazine, February 1, 1981), Julia Klein wrote, "Gregorian's public indecision, his very agonizing over the Berkeley job annoyed some trustees, striking them as a Machiavellian way of raising his stock at Penn." It was also reported that many trustees disliked my management style, "which is often seen as disorganized."

I asked Chairman Miller on several occasions about the status of the search and my status. He assured me that everything was progressing smoothly, that I was still one of the top candidates. Two or three times, I volunteered to withdraw formally my name from the selection process. Miller and Meyerson separately dissuaded me. The first time occurred when a prominent trustee, who had told me that I would be president of Penn only over his dead body, was named to the search committee. Don't worry, that's just one vote, I was told. My only request was that if, for whatever reason, I was not their choice, and if they wanted me to remain as provost and be effective, they should give me a month's notice to withdraw my name or at least forty-eight hours. Otherwise, I would be a liability to the new president.

During those seven months, three internal candidates emerged. One was Dr. Thomas Langfitt, vice president for health and human affairs, a distinguished neurosurgeon. His candidacy was favored by Bob Dunlop, a patient of his, several other trustees, and some biomedical and medical faculty members, as well as some members of the university's Budget Office. Dr. Langfitt, it was speculated, would bring "management" and expertise in health affairs, one of the major sectors of the university. John Eckman, who was Dunlop's, Regan's, and Meyerson's Philadelphia resident detractor, pushed forward the candidacy of Ed Stemmler, the dean of medicine, who also enjoyed the support of some medical faculty, the chairman, and several trustees. I gather Stemmler was a board member of Eckman's firm, the Rohrer Group. Then there was my candidacy. I was the faculty's and students' first choice, as well as that of several influential trustees (Gates, Segal, Annenberg, Tarzian, Amsterdam, Trescher). Unfortunately, most of them were retired. They hated to take up any battles that they might not be able to win. It was clear that the trustees had rival candidates. One choice would have been to select federal judge A. Leon Higginbotham Jr. I nominated him. He would have been the first African-American Ivy League president. I would have been happy to remain as provost. The judge, a trustee of Penn and a faculty member, however, was deemed too liberal. He had declined to be interviewed by the search committee.

The situation was becoming awkward for me. There were many pending tenure cases, one of which involved Professor Fred L. Block, a Marxist sociologist. There had been divided opinion whether or not he should get tenure. The case was before the Provost Staff Conference, which considered and recommended all faculty appointments and promotions. I received hundreds of letters from all corners of the country and abroad accusing me of trying to deny him tenure in order to please the university's conservative trustees so that they would anoint me president. One letter stated that I was sacrificing Fred Block on the block of capitalism in order to advance my miserable career. Actually, I was attempting to get a fair hearing for him from a national panel of experts for tenure consideration.

In the midst of these speculations, there was pressure on me to appear before the Search Committee and be interviewed. I did not see any rational justification for it. I had been at Penn for eight years. I was named dean of the Faculty of Arts and Sciences by the trustees by acclamation. I was appointed provost by acclamation. My record was an open book. So were my views given in innumerable speeches and position papers. Chairman Miller and Jacqueline Wexler, along with Martin Meyerson, insisted. There was speculation among some African-Americans that this was an attempt to block Higginbotham's candidacy. They could tell the judge, "He should appear for an interview with the search committee. All the candidates are appearing for interviews with the committee, including the provost."

Two weeks before my interview, an encounter with a very prominent trustee made me angry. He told me, "Several of us don't think you have the social graces to be president of the University of Pennsylvania." At first I thought he was joking. He was not. That statement crushed me. During this period, I spent several days in the University of Pennsylvania's hospital with an extremely high fever. I was shivering helplessly in the midst of the August heat. I had kidney stones. As soon as I got out of the hospital I had to go for my interview.

As I prepared for the meeting, I recalled that I had alienated several trustees. One had been dating a staff member who now claimed that she was being harassed by him. When I was dean of Arts and Sciences, I had taken her case to the provost and the president. Since I knew the trustee in question well (he did not have good relations with the president), I spoke to him about the awkwardness of the situation and our colleague's right not to be harassed. He invited me to his office and played tapes on which he had recorded the accuser's phone calls and insisted that he was the real victim. I told him that he was not a gentleman. "Gentlemen don't tape their unsuspecting 'lover's' conversations." He was outraged. I knew he was certainly not going to vote for me.

In another instance, we needed a new athletic director. I appointed a campus-wide search committee, which included faculty, trustees, athletes, and coaches. I had strict instructions about confidentiality. It was broken. Among the candidates was Gayle Sayers, whom I thought outstanding. The committee members, by leaking his name, did not mention that they did not want Penn to appoint a black athletic director, the first in the Ivy League. In their leak, they mentioned only that he wore too much gold. While we were assessing the qualities of the candidate, one jock trustee said, "We better organize a dinner party and see whether he has table manners and social graces." I was shocked. I said that was a racist remark. I certainly did not have his support, nor that of the trustee who thought it was all right to give checks or expense accounts to prospective Penn athletic recruits. I told him it was against NCAA and Ivy League rules and regulations. I told him, "I will report all infractions." It made him angry.

I disbanded the search committee and appointed another. It gave me the candidacy of Charles Harris, a twenty-nine-year-old African-American. Nobody mentioned race this time, but they all objected to his age. I decided to appoint him. He became the youngest athletic director, not only at Penn but in the Ivy League, as well as the first African-American. That did not win me friends within the ranks of trustees.

When I left the hospital, I felt tired and discouraged. I had been at Penn for eight years, with no leaves. I had worked every summer, and fourteen-hour days. At first, I decided I would not go for the interview and would withdraw my name. I visited Tom Gates. He surprised me. "You don't deserve to be even a dog catcher. You are too naive. You can't trust Paul Miller. They don't want you." I was stunned. I thought I had a good relationship with Paul Miller. He was a successful businessman, an ambitious, savvy investor. He was serious and engaged. His laughter was great, and he loved good company and liked to tell jokes, including some of the off-color, locker room kind. He was tough and direct. For six years, I had a comfortable relationship with him. When he became chairman in 1978, however, our relationship gradually changed.

When he told me I was one of the leading candidates for the presidency, I trusted him. When he advised me not to withdraw my name, I did not. If he did not want me, he should have not have argued against my going to Berkeley. Besides, I had told him time and time again that neither he nor the board owed me the presidency. I expected them to give me a warning, an honorable exit, not only for my sake but for the university's. Otherwise, I told him, I had no choice but to resign. If I was good enough for Berkeley but not good enough for Penn for unspecified reasons, I would be a lame duck.

I had heard about Miller's alleged "unhappiness" with my "management ability" and "flamboyance." If he was unhappy, he never said so to me. I had also heard that some trustees were worried that I was "too ethnic," that I had a "thick accent" and "unruly hair," and that there were serious questions about whether I would be able to raise substantial funds for Penn. One thing was clear: for many trustees, including Miller, I had reached my plateau as provost. I assumed that after Martin Meyerson, they did not want another "ethnic" president for Penn. They wanted somebody from central casting. Paul Bender, professor of law and a member of the search committee, noted that some of the trustees' real concern was the possibility that "Gregorian would be too powerful a president. They probably were afraid of a hands-on, close touch approach. . . . That would have made him an enormously powerful figure. He would have been the University." (Jennifer Allen, "The Library's Social Lion," *New York* magazine, January 16, 1984.)

As I walked in for my interview, my fever was matched by my anger. The smirk on the face of the trustee who had told me that I would be president of the University of Pennsylvania "only over his dead body" was too much. I realized that my anger was directed primarily against Miller. I had trusted him. I felt betrayed; actually, misled is a better word. Since the beginning of the search, I had offered him a great exit strategy. If, for whatever reason, I had told him, I was found unsuitable or unacceptable for the presidency, give me the signal and I'll exit graciously. I confirmed that in April. Miller told me, I'll let you know in June. There was no word from him in June. In July, he told me that there were certain pockets of influential resistance and that it was "not a cinch." I said, "If that is the case, all right. Then you owe me a graceful exit." That had been my only request.

Having been told that I did not have the "social graces" to be the president of Penn, sitting near a trustee who had told me that I would only be president "over his dead body," facing Miller who had not leveled with me about my alleged shortcomings as a leader and never understood that, for me, my dignity and the dignity of my office were more important than my ambition or my security made my blood boil. I felt that I had been, at worst, deliberately deceived, or at least finessed. I told the members that I had heard rumors about their worries about my accent and hair and ethnicity and that I was ready to discuss these "handicaps." Finally, I told them again that they did not owe me the presidency, but that they did owe me a gracious exit. If they did not provide that, my effectiveness as provost would suffer and I would have no choice but to resign. My outburst pleased my detractors and stunned my supporters. When Chairman Miller asked what my first act as president would be, I told him, "to remove your office from College Hall."

I ended my interview by telling the committee, "I hope my remarks have not been trivial." A female trustee told me, "You don't have to be defensive.

You are a great man." The committee members rose and applauded me. That was the greatest send-off.

After I left the meeting, it was reported that Paul Miller referred to me as "an unguided missile." My "favorite" trustee chimed in that I "was too volatile emotionally to be president of a major university."

On September 5, Trustee John Eckman asked to meet me at the Union League, where we had a few drinks. I think he wanted me to solicit his support. I would not. We talked about everything except the Presidential Search Committee. Then I said, "John, I need your help." His eyes lit up. I told him, "You know, we have been successful in procuring Marian Anderson's papers for Penn. I need you to cover the cost of obtaining a bust of her. . . ." I am sure he was disappointed.

On Monday morning, September 15, at nine-thirty, Paul Miller summoned me to his office. He began by saying that he thought I was one of the greatest men he had ever known, and that choosing a new president for the University of Pennsylvania had been one of the hardest, most difficult tasks he had ever had. Then he informed me that the Executive Board had decided to go outside of Penn to recruit a new leader. He then asked me, actually urged me, to make one more magnanimous gesture, to use my powers of "statesmanship" to support the new president and make the transition process a smooth one. I asked him who the chosen candidate was. "I cannot tell you the name. We will be having a press conference." It sounded bizarre that I was being asked to support someone but was not being trusted with the identity of the person I was supposed to support. I remained calm. I went back to my office and acted as if nothing had happened. After a provost staff meeting, I called my wife. "They have kicked you in the gut. Is this the way they reward your eight years of dedication to Penn?" she shouted. I felt like a hurricane victim.

All of a sudden I felt humiliated, betrayed, depressed. I don't know whether it was Richard Yates or someone else who compared being depressed to blindness and deafness. In going blind, the darkness at first is gradual, then all encompassing; in going deaf, one hears less and less until a terrible silence falls all around one.

I felt sad, stupid, and dejected. All of a sudden, I had lost the presidencies of both Berkeley and Penn. That I could understand, and even accept. After all, practically all of Armenian history is full of moral victories only. What I could not understand was the calculated humiliation. My main question was why I was not allowed the opportunity to withdraw gracefully.

When there is an emotional crisis one discovers the essentials: one's family and one's friends. Clare did not want me to come home defeated and be alone and sad. So she spent all day on the phone lining up all of our friends. When I arrived, they were all there, the deans, faculty friends, personal friends, the Vucinichs, Judge Pollak and his wife, and my Armenian friends from Philadelphia. I was not alone. I had the solidarity and love of many but, most important, of my wife and sons.

On my way to Swarthmore, I heard the news on the radio. The president-elect of the University of Pennsylvania was Sheldon Hackney, a former provost of Princeton and president of Tulane University, a very decent man and a good historian. I called the two internal candidates, Edward Stemmler and Tom Langfitt, to alert them of the appointment of the new president. Later in the evening, Paul Miller called to tell me the name of the president-elect. I told him to speak louder. I could not hear him because we were having a big party. I felt good. I did not give him the satisfaction of seeing or hearing me in a state of self-pity or mourning.

*   *   *

On September 16, I submitted my resignation as provost effective October 24, the day of the annual meeting of the Board of Trustees. There were many important issues, projects, and recommendations that had to be submitted to the trustees for their consideration and action. I thought it was the most honorable way to end my two-year tenure as chief academic officer. President Meyerson attempted to dissuade me. I told him that I could cope with rejection but not insult and humiliation. I was not a Mr. Magoo. If somebody spits at me, I cannot pretend it is a raindrop. Meyerson issued a statement: "It had been a very extraordinary privilege to work with him." I issued a conventional statement, asserting that the decision of the trustees had "surprised" me and that I was "disappointed but not bitter." I thanked Meyerson.

I thought that marked the end of a painful episode but I was wrong. The day I resigned, Janis Somerville, the vice provost for university life, came to see me, accompanied by Allison Accurso, chairman of the Undergraduate Assembly (the student government). Accurso informed me that the students intended to protest. I begged her not to do that. Her answer was "We are not going to do it for you; we are doing it for us." She asked me if I would be willing to speak to the students. My answer was no. She was angry. She said the students had to do something to express their frustration. For them, the student protest was a "necessary catharsis." Besides I "should not leave the campus without a tremendous show of support."

The hastily organized noontime rally drew five hundred people. There were many speakers. The *Daily Pennsylvanian* denounced the Penn trustees and the search process. Thus began a tumultuous period at Penn. Each letter, editorial, speech poured salt on my wounded pride. It was a very hard time for my family. Clare was very angry. So were our boys. Vahé, our eldest son, who played football for Penn, was a freshman and lived on campus. It was especially hard for him. He had become an instant subject of sympathy. The day of the student rally, Clare, not wanting Vahé to be alone, attended the rally with him, hoping they would not be noticed. They were. Clare's comment to the student newspaper reflected our family's collective psyche, "I think it's lovely, and it's touching, but there is no looking back."

On September 17, I attended what was to be my last university Council meeting. The Council is the legislative body of the university. It included the president, the provost, various vice presidents, the deans, chairman of the Undergraduate Assembly and the Graduate Student Association, and representatives of the staff. As I entered the room, I received a standing ovation. President Meyerson and Paul Bender, the chairman of the Faculty Senate, were effusive in their praises of me.

I gave my first formal statement to the Penn community. I called for an end to the tense emotional atmosphere on campus and asked the faculty and students to welcome the new president and extend him their support and cooperation.

The entire session lasted twelve minutes. The mood was somber. The University Council, "out of deference to me," adjourned. It was the only time in its history that it had adjourned without completing its agenda.

I thought my formal and conciliatory statement would bring the matters to a close. I was wrong. The student "catharsis" was followed by two other public acts of catharsis. One was on the part of the campus ministry. Seven priests, ministers, and rabbis issued a joint ecumenical letter to their constituencies and the entire campus, telling them that they felt there was a death in the Penn community. The faculty challenged the leadership and the entire selection process and demanded a special meeting of the faculty. Six out of seven Benjamin Franklin professors (the highest-ranking academics at Penn) had submitted a resolution to place my name before the trustees of Penn to be voted for president of the university. On October 14, after a two-hour tumultuous meeting, the faculty voted for the resolution. The university was facing a major constitutional crisis. The faculty was challenging its leadership and the authority of the Executive Board of the trustees. It was also making a statement that I was their choice to be president.

I thought the matter had gone too far. Sure, I was proud that the students, faculty, and even many alumni had demonstrated their support. David

Riesman, who had followed my Penn saga, wrote: "I cannot think of a case in recent academic history of any major university or even a liberal arts college, other than an evangelical one, where there has been such unanimity among the faculty, administration, and both graduate and undergraduate students."

The depth of campus support for me was irrelevant. The fact was that even in the unlikely event that the Executive Board decided to reverse itself, I would have no interest in it.

Under the circumstances, on October 16, I met briefly with the Executive Board of Trustees and informed them that I would be making a public statement to the faculty on October 20. On that day, at a gathering of some fifty to sixty faculty leaders, deans, and the Benjamin Franklin professors, I thanked them for their action and trust and informed them that that very day I had sent a brief note to the Executive Board stating that "I do not wish my name to be placed in nomination for the presidency of the University of Pennsylvania at the October 24 meeting of the Board of Trustees." As I read the statement I was relieved. So was everyone. Paul Miller Jr. welcomed my statement and characterized it as "full of dignity and grace," adding that I was "a man of great stature" and that that stature showed in my statement.

There remained one painful event. I had to attend my last meeting of the Board of Trustees. I hoped to give my report, which always followed the president's, and leave. Unfortunately, the rules were changed. The nomination and selection of president was the number-one item on the agenda, and my report was the last item. To avert any possible criticism of its actions and to comply with the provisions of the "sunshine laws" of the State of Pennsylvania, the board staged an "open meeting" during which a number of the trustees read written questions prepared by the University Council, along with their written responses, about the president designate's educational leadership, administrative and fund-raising abilities, his record on affirmative action, etc.

This charade lasted for half an hour. Then there was the vote. Sheldon Hackney was elected unanimously. The only nonscripted speech was delivered by Sarkes Tarzian, trustee emeritus. With great calm, he said, "I think that it takes courage and it takes stature for a group to admit when they have mishandled something so there will be credibility of that group with the student body and the faculty. . . . Everyone has acknowledged that he [Gregorian] did an outstanding job as dean and an outstanding job as provost. But, in some respects, I think that he hasn't been treated civilly. There has been a shadow cast over his career. If there was a good reason why [his] name could not be submitted to the Executive Board to be considered as a candidate, I think that could have been done diplomatically through his friends or to him personally, or in confidence."

There were some embarrassing moments of silence. Then Bernard Segal, Esq. (formerly a life trustee and a member of the executive committee of the Board of Trustees of Penn), read a prepared statement extolling my virtues and contributions as dean and provost. (In 1997, when Bernard Segal died, my wife revealed to me that Segal had called on her, during my darkest days, to assure her not to worry about financial hardships because he had made provisions to support us in case I did not get a job. He made my wife promise not to reveal this until the day of his death. She agreed.)

To keep my calm, I wrote my grandmother's name, in Armenian, numerous times in order to give myself the fortitude not to show any emotion. I managed it.

My final provost's report would have been anticlimactic. I told the board that my entire report would be mailed to them and that I had only a brief remark. I congratulated Sheldon Hackney. I thanked President Meyerson for his major contributions to the University of Pennsylvania. I said, "For whatever I have done right, please remember me, and for whatever I have done wrong, please forgive me." Almost everyone, with the exception of two or three of my ardent detractors, were moved, some even to tears. Trustee Leonard Lauder hastily wrote a resolution and submitted it to the board for its approval: "The Trustees of Pennsylvania unanimously declare their thanks and appreciation for Vartan Gregorian, for his deep dedication to the University of Pennsylvania, and for his superb leadership and service to both the faculty and students of the University as dean of the Faculty of Arts and Sciences and provost."

The motion passed unanimously. The trustees gave me a standing ovation. A visibly shaken and tearful Martin Meyerson spoke of my "sensitivity and humaneness that is rare among us all" and stated once again that "Vartan has been a teacher to us all."

Before the board adjourned, I brought up one item of unfinished business—my recommendation that Professor Fred Block should be granted tenure. The motion passed.

I left the board meeting emotionally drained and exhausted. Thus ended my administrative career at Penn.

*   *   *

In 1980, after declining the chancellorship of Berkeley and resigning as the provost of Penn, I received an urgent call from a Mr. Bill Bowen of Heidrick & Struggles, a national recruiting firm. He informed me that the University of Miami was ready to offer me its presidency and asked if I would visit Miami and meet with Professor Mentschikoff, the dean of the law school and the chair of the search committee, and Chairman of the Board James McLamore, CEO of Burger King. I went to Miami. I had a wonderful visit. My hosts were kind, considerate, and generous. Dean Mentschikoff was a fascinating person. She was a graduate of Hunter College and had received her law degree from Columbia Law School in 1937. (In 1947, she became the first woman to teach law at Harvard Law School, and in 1951 the first woman to teach law at the University of Chicago. In 1972, she was one of two women to be appointed a trustee of the Rand Corporation. In 1973, she became the first woman to serve as the president of the Association of American Law Schools. Dean Mentschikoff was an international authority on commercial law. With her husband, Professor Karl N. Llewellyn, she planned and drafted the Uniform Commercial Code.) She had assumed the deanship of the University of Miami's Law School in 1974 and served in that capacity until 1982. We had a wonderful dinner, drank lots of wine, and talked for hours about higher education, political theory, and literature. During my three-day visit, I toured the campus, met several faculty leaders, deans, and trustees. By the end of my visit, I was offered the presidency of the university.

"Why me?" I asked. They responded, "We are not the University of Pennsylvania, but we have aspirations and the determination to become a great university and we believe you can mobilize our faculty, students, alumni, and lead us to our goal." I listened carefully and sympathetically. I did not ask about salary or benefits. They volunteered it and used it as an enticement. It was an enormous package and a most generous one. If I was not satisfied with it, they told me, it was negotiable. They spoke of the president's house, its amenities, the president's status in the community, a start-up fund to launch the new presidency, and other perquisites. If I decided to come, I told them, compensation would not be the key factor but rather their determination to make Miami a first-rate institution. I asked them for time to think about their offer. As I left Miami I asked Mr. McLamore for a Burger King certificate. I told him that my sons would be most impressed that I knew the CEO of Burger King.

*   *   *

Thanks to Bernard Segal, I was invited to meet Larry Tisch, the chairman of the Board of Trustees of New York University, which had launched a search for a new president. The search committee, which consisted of trustees and faculty and included, if I remember correctly, some students, gave me a cordial reception.

The Miami offer and my meetings with the NYU presidential search committee boosted my morale. I was pleasantly surprised to find out that several Penn trustees (Bernard Segal, Ralph Saul, Irving Shapiro, David Mahoney, and Thomas S. Gates Jr.) had recommended me for the presidency of NYU. I was gratified that David Saxon, president of the University of California, and Edward Carter, former chairman of the UC Regents, had also joined in the effort, along with Franklin Murphy, former chancellor of UCLA and CEO of the Times Mirror Company.

What astonished me was the support of the presidents of the Rockefeller, Mellon, John Simon Guggenheim foundations, the American Council of Learned Societies, and the Modern Languages Association. I realized I was not alone. Such broad support was soothing and uplifting. Even if I did not get the presidency of NYU, my faith and my self-confidence were restored.

During my interviews with NYU's presidential search committee, I stated that my position vis-à-vis any New York institution was, and always has been, a basic one. No New York institution has any excuse to be mediocre. After all, a great number of our nation's major law firms are in New York, as is Wall Street, the headquarters of most of the Fortune 500 companies, and a majority of our nation's communications networks. Therefore, no law school, business school, or communications school can afford not to be excellent. Some of the greatest medical talent of our nation and its finest hospitals are in New York. The city is the intellectual and cultural center of our nation, with its myriad museums, libraries, theaters, and hundreds of magazines and newspapers in numerous languages. How can any university avoid having the best faculty in the humanities, the social sciences, and the sciences? And, finally, New York is the headquarters of the United Nations.

My advice to NYU was to do what Stanford did in California. Don't be mesmerized by your version of UC Berkeley, namely Columbia University. Chart your own course. Become a central institution in the social, economic, political, cultural, and artistic life of New York. Take advantage of existing institutions. Don't use lack of money as an excuse for not thinking big. What institutions need are great ideas; money will follow. In addition, I urged them to take advantage of many obvious opportunities. I told them they could establish a Dag Hammarskjöld lecture series. Grant a ten-thousand-dollar lecture fee (a big amount in 1980) to each lecturer. Invite members of the International Court of Justice to give the lectures at NYU's Law School. To me, the International Jurists at The Hague resembled the

Maytag repairman: no one called them for assistance. It was a waste of their talents. In three years, NYU, having hosted all the justices, would be able to inaugurate an international law program and/or establish a center at The Hague.

In addition, the UN could add anywhere between five hundred to one thousand adjunct or visiting professors every year or every other year, from the ranks of UN delegates. They would have welcomed an association with a private university, for a dollar-a-year symbolic compensation, in order to be part of a learning or cultural community. On the home front, I recommended that NYU purchase vacant neighborhood properties and transform the neighborhood into a virtual campus. I also suggested NYU make residency in the Village mandatory, beginning with the newly recruited faculty members. As the interview went on, I cited one "crazy" idea after another. Among many other topics, we discussed the curriculum, the necessity of strengthening the liberal arts at NYU, and how to attract outstanding faculty to NYU. At the end I was told it was too bad that my candidacy was an eleventh-hour one because the job had already been promised to John Brademas, the Indiana ex-Congressman.

It was hoped that John Brademas, because of his stature in Congress and his great legislative record, his expertise in matters of education and his contacts in Congress and Washington, would be able to secure federal and private funds for NYU and give it great visibility. If, for whatever reason, John Brademas declined the NYU presidency, I was told I was next in line.

CHAPTER TWELVE

A Rendezvous with the New York
Public Library

In 1981, at a time when I was facing uncertainty about my future and weighing possible and impossible scenarios for my career, I received another telephone call from Mr. Bill Bowen of Heidrick & Struggles. He asked if I would meet with Mr. William Dietel, president of Rockefeller Brothers Fund, a trustee of the New York Public Library, and chairman of its presidential search committee. He told me about the plight of the New York Public Library and the board's determination to find a leader who would help rescue it. His presentation alternated between optimism and pessimism, possibilities and limitations, daring and caution. I told him I used libraries and, even though as provost I had supported the University of Pennsylvania's library, I didn't know anything about their administrative structures or the issues facing librarians and their profession. In Philip Hamburger's two-part *New Yorker* profile, "Searching for Gregorian," Mr. Dietel recalled: "When I did meet him, it was love at first sight. I must confess that we ardently courted him. We were asking him into a tough situation. We needed a charismatic character. . . . [We] realized that any dream we might have of the library's future could be handled by Gregorian."

At the time I told Mr. Dietel I had no interest in the presidency of the Library. He said, "Before you give a final no as your answer, please meet with two of my colleagues." My "interview" with the late Richard Salomon

(1912–1994) and Andrew Heiskell was an amazing event. Richard Salomon was the CEO of Charles of the Ritz. He had revolutionized Madison Avenue with his imaginative marketing of the perfume and cosmetic industries. He had bankrolled the successful careers of Yves St. Laurent, Vidal Sassoon, and a few others. He was the outgoing chairman of the board of the New York Public Library and chancellor of Brown University.

Andrew Heiskell, a legendary figure in the publishing industry, was the outgoing CEO of Time, Inc., a member of Harvard Corporation, and the incoming chairman of the New York Public Library's Board of Trustees. These two men tried to interest me in the presidency of the New York Public Library. Twenty minutes into our interview both declared, "You are our man! We want you to be the president of the New York Public Library. You must be our next leader!" Their decisiveness, their directness, their passion, their vision, and their determination overwhelmed me. Within a very short time we had established an amazing rapport. Here is how *Outsider, Insider: An Unlikely Success Story: The Memoirs of Andrew Heiskell* describes our encounter: "We set up a search committee and hired a search firm. We saw a number of characters, adequate but not sparkling, not the kind of people who would turn a nearly defunct organization into a lively and vibrant one. Then, out of nowhere, a new candidate appeared. Vartan Gregorian. . . . Instinctively I knew he was it. Here was the man who could do the job, and the search committee agreed. We told the search firm, 'Okay, no more. Just make sure we get him.' "

In the book, this is the way Andrew Heiskell describes the situation: "The library was broke. The chandeliers and lighting fixtures all through the main building were dirty and had only two or three bulbs in each. The beautiful Celeste Bartos Forum, now the Library's most important meeting place, had been turned into a warehouse. The gorgeous Gottesman Exhibition Hall had been divided by Masonite partitions into tiny offices for personnel and accounting. The only decent room in the entire building was the board room, but even there the tall curtains fell apart if you touched them."

The New York Public Library, along with other cultural and educational institutions, was hard hit in the late 1960s and especially in the 1970s, when New York City was on the verge of bankruptcy. It had no political clout. According to Andrew Heiskell, "It had no constituency except scholars, children, and ordinary citizens who like to read." He described a down-and-out institution: "The city had cut back so hard on the Library that some branches were open only eight hours a week. . . . Some librarians had to scurry from building to building trying to service the three branches in one week. The marble inside the main Fifth Avenue building, the one with the great sculpted lions guarding the broad front steps was so filthy brown that you would never guess it was marble.

"Inside this building were more than three million books, many of them extremely valuable, gathering dust and crumbling away in stacks that were not air-conditioned. The Library had begged the city for air conditioning for 20 years but nothing happened. [In the past] the Library had a weak board of trustees, and no management worth mentioning." There were projections that the Library would soon lose its entire endowment and accumulate a $50 million deficit. In short, the situation was frightening.

Nevertheless, I declined the Miami offer and, with trepidation, accepted the presidency of the Library. However, I did so with a clear view. I thought that if I succeeded in rescuing and rejuvenating the Library and restoring its central role in the cultural and educational life of New York, it would be considered a "miracle." If I failed, it would be a worthy yet public "martyrdom." Many of my friends had misgivings about my decision. It would be safer to accept a college or university presidency, they advised. Indeed one "sympathetic" New York–based trustee of the University of Pennsylvania told me to see a psychiatrist.

There was another crucial factor that attracted me to the New York Public Library and that was the city itself. Céline, the writer, once described New York as a standing city. To me it was a soaring, aspiring, proud, and impatient city, a city always on the move. Whereas passion and emotion were suspect in Philadelphia, they were part of the social fabric of New York. New Yorkers were not afraid of energy, flamboyance, and panache. I was struck by the deep feeling and intense commitment the trustees and the librarians had for the Library. The excitement of the trustees, especially that of Andrew Heiskell, Richard Salomon, and Bill Dietel, infected me. I knew I had reliable partners for a long, arduous struggle. As I accepted the job I quipped: "I know you! When the lions [the Library's two lions, Patience and Fortitude] are hungry you feed them the starving Armenians. . . ." I told them that even though we faced monumental problems, even though the odds were against us, I was sure that together, with hard work, imagination, and stubborn determination we would rebuild the Library and make it stronger. I told them New York was full of chutzpah and I was full of chutzpah. We would do our best.

In his announcement of Andrew Heiskell's and my appointments as chairman and president, respectively, Richard Salomon praised us for our past "accomplishments" and "contributions" and expressed his conviction that we would make a great team and that I would make a "superb president." But what astonished me was his assertion that "Neither he [Gregorian] nor Andrew Heiskell has ever failed in any endeavor, and with their leadership the New York Public Library is destined to achieve new eminence as a world cultural and education institution." Those were scary words, food for hubris.

My first Library board meeting was held in the Wall Street offices of one of our trustees. Not only was the Philadelphia–New York train late that day, but I had the additional misfortune of having a newly arrived Soviet émigré as a cabdriver. He did not know how to get to Wall Street. I was very angry, so I cussed him in Russian. I told him angrily: "I am late to my first board meeting!" "Do you think you have problems?" he answered. "I have to go to the bathroom." I could not help laughing.

Once I got there, half an hour late, the tone of the meeting and its agenda frightened me. The board had under consideration several "realistic" measures: how to "deaccession," a euphemism for how to "sell" some of the Library's prized collections, cut additional service hours of the branch libraries, close some of the branches, follow the example of the Metropolitan Museum of Art and other cultural institutions and charge an admission fee, or at least levy "voluntary" contributions from the Library's patrons. . . .

I asked for time to review the strengths and weaknesses of the New York Public Library, its four research and eighty-three branch libraries. I found out that even in the midst of all its fiscal problems and physical handicaps the core of the Library was still functioning normally. Throughout the Central Research Library, librarians were working indomitably, scholars were poring over materials in the reading rooms, and prints lined the halls in low-key displays. But against what odds! Hours of service had been curtailed years before, and indeed, the building was closed all day on Thursdays. Thousands of books had to be kept out of circulation, languishing in storage areas until they could be catalogued and put on the shelves. Older volumes, subjected to the hazards of heat, sunlight, dust, and grime, were silently crumbling to dust. The marble and beautiful woodwork were scarred, ornate ceilings and walls were obscured by temporary partitions.

Outside and in, the building looked shabby, suffering from neglect. Bryant Park and the immediate surroundings of the Library were infested with drug dealers, pimps, and "the criminal element." The back of the Library, facing Bryant Park, had become New York's longest urinal. After hours, neither the park nor the Library was considered safe. The rich holdings of the Library, the dedication of the librarians, their professionalism, and their expertise were the main forces keeping the Library an ongoing, viable, central institution.

The conditions at the main research library appeared idyllic in comparison to the plight of the eighty-three branch libraries throughout Manhattan, the Bronx, and Staten Island. Buildings, some of them donated by Andrew Carnegie as a gift to the City of New York, were crumbling, their collections dwindling. You needed an elaborate timetable to know which branches were open in the mornings, for how many hours, whether or not there were any libraries open in the evenings or even on weekends. Libraries could no longer accommodate schoolchildren: they had neither the manpower, nor the materials, nor the hours, nor children's librarians. Branches were dark, dirty, and unsafe. They were gradually becoming a haven for the homeless. The morale within the branches was, needless to say, very low. Job security was the primary and immediate preoccupation of the librarians and their union: the hours, the collections, development, and educational outreach were sidelined.

In addition, there was tension between the research librarians, equipped with advanced degrees, who served "the scholarly community," and the branch librarians who served "the general public." The research librarians were the beneficiaries of public (city) funds earmarked for building maintenance and private funds for acquisition, cataloguing, and publications. In addition, they received state and federal funds for preservation and education outreach. The branch libraries were maintained primarily by public funds (mainly city and some state). While they received some federal funds for programs, they received meager private funds from neighborhood support groups (who sold baked goods at annual benefits), book sales, and book fines. Private philanthropies and charities, by and large, stayed away from the branch or circulating libraries, as they were considered to be the city's responsibilities.

My first act as president was to acquaint myself with the institution, its four research libraries, and eighty-three branch libraries, the librarians and the staff, their needs, aspirations, and frustrations. Some librarians resented me because I was not a librarian. They were angry that the three most important libraries in the nation—the Library of Congress, the New York Public Library, and the library at Harvard—were all headed by historians. They saw this as an affront to their profession.

I decided to have a general meeting of the librarians, and I was candid with them: I had come as an educator who loved books and learning and respected librarians as educators. I addressed them as "my fellow educators." I visited other major libraries of our nation, including the Library of Congress and Harvard's libraries, to learn about their problems, the challenges they faced, and their planned responses. Next came our donors. I visited many benefactors or wrote to them, thanking them for their past support of the library, explaining that we had never taken their support for granted and never would, and that we simply appreciated their civic spirit and generosity.

Last but not least, I began to visit City Hall, to pay my respects to the mayor, the controller, commissioners, members of the City Council, the speaker of the City Council, the borough presidents, members of the Board of Estimate, and the leaders of the State Legislature in Albany. (In 1981, the Library gave a reception in honor of its new chairman and president. The reception was for public officials to meet the new team of the Library. There was a large bottle of Soave Bolla white wine, twenty-five plastic cups, and some potato chips. Only two city councilmen showed up. They stayed five minutes and left. Andrew Heiskell and I drank a toast to each other.) And, of course, I paid a visit to the Roman Catholic cardinal, who was a member of the Board of Trustees of the Library. About seventy-five years earlier, the Library had acquired the libraries of the Catholic Archdiocese of New York. Hence it was customary to have the cardinal of the New York Archdiocese as a board member. Cardinal Terence Cooke won my heart instantly. He promised his help.

I had one simple message for everyone: the New York Public Library is a New York and a national treasure; the collections of the Research Libraries are an incomparable treasure, and they deserve to be better known, better respected, better "treasured," and better housed. The branch libraries constitute a precious and viable network of educational institutions in eighty-three neighborhoods. They provide educational support services to families, children, individuals, businesses and immigrants. The branch libraries have *made* lives and *saved* lives. The New York Public Library is not a luxury. It is an integral part of New York's social fabric, its culture, its institutions, its media, and its scholarly, artistic, and ethnic communities.

The Library was built as a civic monument, as a symbol of New York's openness and importance. It was a monument dedicated to knowledge, and hence progress. It deserves the city's respect, appreciation, and support. No, the Library is not a cost center, I told a representative of the city's Office of Management and Budget; it is an investment in the city's past and future. My final message was that democracy and excellence are not mutually exclusive; they are compatible. Finally, I stated that the New York Public Library is not in need of charity, it is in need of philanthropy. I told the trustees that it must become clear to the whole world that the Library is a high penalty organization—donors and government officials must feel that the price of their *not* supporting it is too high for this community to pay.

*   *   *

Andrew Heiskell was the perfect chairman of the board. Having served as chairman and CEO of Time, Inc., he understood the difference between leading and managing. He helped set guidelines and policies and extended his time and energy, but he never micromanaged. During his chairmanship and my presidency, we never disagreed. (Well, that is not entirely true. We disagreed on several occasions when he wanted to raise my salary and I declined.) From the very beginning, our relationship was one of friendship, even kinship. The irony that both of us were born abroad—Andrew in Naples, Italy, and I in Tabriz, Iran—and that we were entrusted with the fate of the New York Public Library did not escape us. I would describe Andrew as an Italian WASP: he believed in tradition, honor, dignity, integrity, fairness, and fair play. His word was his bond. Owen Wister, the nineteenth-century Philadelphia WASP, joshed that in Philadelphia even moderation should not be excessive. Andrew had an excess of passion, exuberance, and zest for life. He was an immoderate WASP.

I identified with Andrew Heiskell for another reason: he was sui generis. He was born of expatriate parents and spent a nomadic childhood in a series of European hotels. He did not go to school until he was ten. He never graduated from college. He knew nothing about America when he arrived here at age twenty, at the height of the Depression. Ten years later, at thirty, he had become the publisher of *Life,* the most successful new magazine in the United States. Later, for twenty years, he served as chairman of Time, Inc.

*   *   *

On December 8, 1981, Mrs. Vincent Astor gave a black tie party in honor of Clare and me to introduce us to New York society. Three or four weeks before, she had given a party in honor of President and Mrs. Ronald Reagan. What amazed me was that the list of invitees to our dinner was substantially the same as that for the president of the United States.* When I expressed my surprise and awe, Mrs. Astor told me, "The president of the New York Public Library is an important citizen of New York and the nation. He represents one of New York's and the nation's major institutions. . . ."

---

* The list of invitees included The Honorable Douglas Dillon, chairman of the Metropolitan Museum of Art; William S. Paley, chairman of CBS, Inc.; Barbara Walters, anchorwoman; Franco Zeffirelli, the director (Mrs. Astor informed me that he was working on *La Bohème*); Mr. and Mrs. Douglas Fairbanks; Mr. and Mrs. H. J. Heinz (he was the chairman of Heinz "57 Varieties"; his wife, Drue, was the publisher of *Antaeus*); Mr. and Mrs. John Chancellor, anchorman at NBC; Mr. and Mrs. Lewis Preston, chairman, Morgan Guarantee Trust Co. (later president of the World Bank); Mr. and Mrs. Felix Rohatyn, senior partner, Lazard Frères; Mr. and Mrs. Victor Gotbaum, president of the Municipal Workers Union; The Honorable and Mrs.

I felt as if Clare and I were at a debutante party in Mrs. Astor's magnificent Park Avenue apartment. It was decorated with great care and taste; the library was lined on three walls with handsomely bound editions of classic English, French, and Russian literature, including Shakespeare, Pushkin, Voltaire, Dostoevsky, Tolstoy, Dickens, George Eliot, et al. The library and living room were decorated with rare drawings and nineteenth- and twentieth-century European paintings, and mementos and gifts from all over the world. The library was painted deep red; the dining room was green with pink curtains. It seemed as if the entire apartment was filled with books, chintz, clocks, and flowers. The cocktail napkins and shiny silver matchboxes bore the initials of Vincent Astor.

Waiters served on nineteenth-century fine china with crystal glasses. Mrs. Astor looked splendid in her black velvet dress and her emerald necklace and earrings. She gave a fabulous toast to the New York Public Library and its new "educator guardian." The entire evening, Mrs. Astor, her guests, and her apartment seemed unreal. I had read about or seen most of the guests on TV but never thought I would be in one room with all of them, and that the occasion would be a dinner in our honor. Even in my wildest dreams, I would never have imagined that one day I would be honored by Mrs. Astor and, thanks to her, become part of New York society. But there it was! I sat at Mrs. Astor's right, I looked at all the dignitaries and glamorous people, the elegant apartment, and reflected on the distance between 1699 Church Street, Tabriz, Iran, and 778 Park Avenue, New York.

Mrs. Astor was both smart and shrewd. She sensed instantly that Clare

---

Abraham Ribicoff, the former senator and governor of the State of Connecticut; Sir Fitzroy McLean, wartime hero, writer, and authority on Tito and the Balkans; Sir John Pope-Hennessy, curator of the Department of European Paintings at the Metropolitan Museum of Art; Peter Glenville, producer; David Bathurst, chairman of Christie's; Enid Haupt, philanthropist (sister of Walter Annenberg); Mrs. Moss Hart (Kitty Carlisle Hart), chairman of the New York State Council on the Arts; Mrs. Henry Kissinger; Mr. Henry Ess of the Sullivan and Cromwell law firm (Mrs. Astor's lawyer); Mr. and Mrs. Arthur Schlesinger Jr., historian and professor at CUNY Graduate School; Dr. and Mrs. Gerald Edelman, Nobel Laureate and holder of the Astor Chair in Immunology and Virology at Rockefeller University; Mr. and Mrs. Oscar de la Renta, fashion designer; Mr. and Mrs. Archibald Gillies (she was director of the Vincent Astor Foundation and he was with the Walter Thayer Foundation); Mr. and Mrs. Samuel F. Reed, president of American Heritage Publishing; Mr. and Mrs. Barney McHenry, president of the Wallace Foundation and a member of the board of the Reader's Digest Foundation; Mr. and Mrs. Augustine Edwards (Mrs. Astor described them as two prominent Chileans. He was a banker and a businessman.); and last but not least, Mr. and Mrs. Ezra Zilkha, the banker (Mrs. Astor's note indicated for our benefit that Mr. Zilkha was originally from Iraq and Mrs. Zilkha from Iran.) Naturally all those invited showed up. No one turned down an invitation from Mrs. Astor.

and I, coming from another world, the world of academe, would take time to get accustomed to, not to mention accept, the high society of New York, its glitzy parties, its opulence. In her interview with Philip Hamburger of the *New Yorker,* she said: "One thing did worry me about Vartan and Clare Gregorian when they came here from Philadelphia. After all, they were part of the grove of academe down there. A quiet life. And suddenly they are thrown in with a ritzy crowd and money. I worried about Clare. It wasn't her style. The pace worried me. The different dinners every night. The fundraising. But it has quieted down now, and they have settled in."

Mrs. Astor was right of course. Clare, whose lineage on both sides is the Mayflower, had always shied away from glitzy, ostentatious, nonintimate parties. In my case, throughout my academic careers at San Francisco State College, the University of Texas at Austin, and even the University of Pennsylvania, my range of activities was confined to the academic, cultural, and educational realms. While I was outgoing, my sociability was confined to university campuses, their constituents, and their formal affairs.

I first met Mrs. Vincent Astor in one of the conference rooms of Time, Inc. She asked me about my family and made me feel at ease by simply telling me that "my friends in Philadelphia like you, respect you, and think highly of you." That was it. As she was getting ready to leave, she said: "I like you and I'll help you any way I can." As the saying goes, it was love at first sight. Thus began a more than two-decade, very close, wonderful friendship. She became a vigorous supporter, a mentor, and a major benefactor of the Library. We danced, dined, drank, had tea, and had wonderful conversations about the Library, New York, history, and literature. My wife once told me that if Mrs. Astor were just five years younger, she would not have left me alone with her, for Brooke was a big flirt.

Since Brooke Astor was the honorary chairman of the Library's Board of Trustees, I read everything I could in order to get to know her, including her two-volume autobiography, *Patchwork Child* and *Footprints,* her poems, her novel, *The Bluebird Is at Home,* her many articles, and scores of articles about her. In 1959, when her third (and last) husband, Vincent Astor, died, Mrs. Astor inherited his fortune: $2 million in cash, some $65 million in investments, and, of course, the Vincent Astor Foundation with $67 million in assets. The mission of the foundation was a broad one: "the alleviation of human misery." By the end of 1997, when the foundation closed its doors and went out of business, having spent its entire capital, it had donated $193,317,406 to New York's cultural, educational, scientific, and social organizations and major institutions, primarily to the city's "crown jewels": the New York Public Library, the Metropolitan Museum of Art, the Morgan

Library, the Metropolitan Opera, the Brooklyn Museum, the Rockefeller University, the Museum of Modern Art, the New York Botanical Garden, the Bronx Zoo, the Museum of Natural History, and Carnegie Hall.

In charting the course of her philanthropy, Mrs. Astor had two fundamental guidelines: first, since Vincent Astor's fortune was made in New York, her efforts would be concentrated in New York. "The money came from New York and therefore it should be invested in New York." And she was determined to give away the entire assets of the foundation and her entire fortune while she was alive. She was adamant that no grants would be made unless she had first-hand knowledge of the needs, aspirations, record, reputation, and integrity of a given organization, association, or institution.

By 1997, her foundation's 2,698 grants had rescued museums, libraries, churches, and settlements. In the process, she had come to know the City of New York, all its boroughs and segments of its society very well, crisscrossing from Harlem to SoHo, assisting underprivileged young people and struggling institutions, as well as serving as a trustee of many of the city's major educational and cultural institutions, including the New York Public Library, the Metropolitan Museum of Art, and Rockefeller University. There is not a single sector of New York that has not been touched by her generosity. In dispensing the assets of the foundation and her fortune, Mrs. Astor told everyone that she had "a lot of fun." The three institutions that received the largest grants from Mrs. Astor were the New York Public Library ($24,600,000), the Metropolitan Museum of Art ($21,000,000), and the Bronx Zoo ($11,800,000).

Mrs. Astor was already a legendary figure when I came to New York in 1981. She was hailed as an "anchor of New York Society and Philanthropy," as "the Social Arbiter of New York Society," as "New York's Unofficial First Lady." It was not the size of the Astor Foundation, nor her largesse that had won her that status. It was her irrepressible personality, her style, her spirit, her manners, her sense of humor, and the fact that she embodied grace of mind, body, and movement, and that she was highly disciplined and always in charge that set her apart. Along with her philanthropy came her interest, compassion, and promises of hope and continuity coupled with class without condescension or noblesse oblige. She was comfortable with everyone. She had genuine interest in people and their plight. She was an avid reader and writer. She was a good listener. She did not engage in gossip, she was not afflicted with envy. She loved life and people and had mastered the art of conversation. She sent thank-you letters, letters of condolence and congratulations to the famous and the ordinary alike. She believed that she had to dress well, not for some occasions but for all occasions, as a sign of respect for New Yorkers.

Once, when a thief attempted to rob her on Fifth Avenue, she turned to him, extended her hand, and said, "I'm sorry, but I don't believe we've been introduced. I am Mrs. Astor." He must have been dumbstruck for he left her alone. . . . She loved to dance until she got tired and she loved to flirt even at the age of eighty (and even now at the age of 101!). She had a wicked sense of humor. She told me a journalist once asked her whether she was a lesbian. No, my dear, I am an Episcopalian, she replied. She once addressed a gathering of proud philanthropists, quoting Thomas Wilder: "Money is like manure. So what we have done is spread around manure. And I have been raking it."

One day in the mid-80s I received a phone call. Mrs. Astor asked me if I was standing or sitting. I told her I was standing. "Sit down," she said. I sat. "I have decided to resign from all other boards and dedicate myself to the Library and you." I was speechless. Her decision sent shock waves in the nonprofit sector. Newspapers gave it wide coverage. It was a heaven-sent gift to the Library.

Mrs. Astor is one of the few people I know who still pens her own letters. In 1986, on her birthday, I gave her a copy of *The Education of Henry Adams*. Her thank-you note read:

> As you well know, it brings back the one visit I had with him in Washington Square when I was eleven years old.
>
> Mother said I would never forget that visit, and I never have.
>
> Also, another link is with Henry Cabot Lodge. If it was the old senator, I did not know him. But if it was his grandson, Henry Cabot Lodge at the United Nations, I knew him very well. When I was thirteen years old, dancing around a Christmas tree with a lighted candle at the house on DuPont Circle in Washington, Henry Cabot Lodge, then about nineteen and very good-looking, was standing at one side, and I fell instantly in love—to no avail.
>
> Thank you for sending such a glorious gift—it will have a treasured place in my library.

I asked her one evening about the secret of her longevity. She responded: Be an optimist, be curious, read every night, don't meet the same people all the time (sooner or later they become lazy, boring, and repeat themselves), don't be a cynic, don't envy or be jealous (these sentiments are corrosive and they diminish you), spend some time in solitude in order to reflect, meet different people, young people, travel, and, if you are rich, adhere to the Gospel of "the Joy of Giving."

When I was a sophomore at Stanford, I heard an interview with Marlene Dietrich on the radio. If I am not mistaken the interviewer was Mike Wallace and he asked her: What is the most important thing in life? Her answer had astonished me: "How to overcome the routine in order to do the essential." Brooke Astor managed to conquer the routine; she was engaged in the essential business of New York and all of its citizens. I had never met anybody like her before and I am sure I never will again.

Richard B. Salomon was an extraordinary man, a born leader, a great entrepreneur, and a philanthropist par excellence. He was a highly cultured person, well read and curious, with refined taste. He was a passionate man. He was recruited by Mrs. Astor and served as chairman of the Library's Board of Trustees for four years (1977–1981), during very trying times. It was his appointment that kept Mrs. Astor's interest in the Library. Otherwise discouraged, she was ready to walk away. Dick Salomon held the Library together, thanks to a $5 million gift from Mrs. Astor. He began the recruitment of new trustees. One of his recruits was Andrew Heiskell.

Richard Salomon, Andrew Heiskell, and Brooke Astor worked as a wonderful team. Richard Salomon paved the way for individual giving and business and Jewish philanthropy; Andrew Heiskell went after individuals and major corporations, his former pals; Mrs. Astor opened the doors of New York society and its philanthropy. They helped me make the case for the New York Public Library, making it a civic project that was both honorable and glamorous.

But first we needed a plan, a strategy, and a timetable.

My basic plans for the Library, approved by the chairman and the Board of Trustees, consisted of seven steps:

1. Get a firsthand knowledge of the institution, its history, and its constituencies
2. Assess the strengths and weaknesses of the Library's central administration
3. Recruit a strong management team
4. Make an institution-wide needs assessment
5. Strengthen the Library's Board of Trustees
6. Publicize the centrality of the Library in the life of New York and the nation
7. Launch a major capital campaign

My first act at the Library was to assess the strengths and weaknesses of the central administration. McKinsey and Co. assisted us in the analysis. We recruited two outstanding executives: John Masten from New York City's Office of Management and Budget and Gregory Long. The former reorganized the financial and administrative structure of the Library, and the latter headed the Library's Development Program with inspiration, imagination, and energy. In addition, I recruited Joan Dunlop, a first-rate executive assistant who had worked for the Ford and Rockefeller foundations and had served as assistant to John D. Rockefeller. Richard (Dick) De Gennaro, former librarian of the University of Pennsylvania, David Stam, a very able director of the Research Libraries, and Edwin Holmgren, the director of the Branch Libraries, constituted the academic leadership of the New York Public Library.

The Library's enormous collections and vast services, its complex relations with the city and the state, ever-increasing federal rules and regulations, management of eighty-seven separate sites, intellectual property issues, many intricate legal contracts, and work-related personnel issues required a legal officer. The Library did not have an in-house lawyer but had relied on outside law firms. We established such an office, not only to save money but also to protect the Library, its rights, and its personnel vis-à-vis myriad constituencies.

The Library, for generations, had served the needs of the scholarly and professional communities of New York and those of its individual citizens. I believed that it had a central, educational, and cultural role as well; along with the acquisition of collections, information, and data it had to have a credible, determined, forceful program to disseminate knowledge, culture, and scholarship. We inaugurated a vigorous public education program and an ambitious exhibitions program under the aegis of highly motivated, extremely able, and effective professionals.

We reorganized the Library's public relations office. Its role was to tell the public what was right about the Library, how vital and central it was in the life of the city. It was not to take credit for the doomsday stories just because these stories were published in the *New York Times* and the *Wall Street Journal*.

My first year at the Library was consumed by efforts to get to know the cast of characters that had kept it functioning under great constraints and difficulties—a dedicated group of librarians who had great pride in their profession and were dedicated to the mission and the legacy of the Library. Next came the city officials, the mayor (Ed Koch), the comptroller (Harrison "Jay" Goldin), the presidents of the boroughs of Manhattan, the Bronx,

Brooklyn, Queens, and Staten Island, followed by the small and important benefactors of the Library as well as civic, educational, and cultural leaders of New York. The governor of New York and the state legislatures presented yet another challenge, not to mention the National Endowment for the Humanities and the National Endowment for the Arts. In making our case to public officials, we relied on the prestige of our board and on citizens' groups in the five boroughs who made the case to millions of library patrons, and also on all the major campaign contributors to elected public officials.

Andrew Heiskell's memoirs recount our difficult first year: "Staff morale was terrible. They had been hit so often, there had been so many firings, that they practically had their arms up over their heads, waiting for the next blow. Greg (that is what Andrew called me) and I made a major decision. We told the staff: *No more talk about what's wrong with the Library.* From now on we will say only what's good about the Library, even if you can find only one small thing.

"This sounds funny, but without having achieved anything substantive during the first year, just stopping the bad talk and spreading the good talk made a difference. It also made a difference that this character Gregorian immediately got embraced by the entire city. Or perhaps he embraced the entire city. I am not sure which. Within six months he knew Mayor Koch and philanthropist Brooke Astor better than I who had lived in this world for years. He sold the importance of the Library: why we needed the money, what would happen if we didn't get it. He sold this to the city, to the state, to the feds and to private citizens."

What made me an instant "celebrity" in New York was not the mission of the Library but its quest to find a residence for the Gregorian family. The Library's presidents and directors had all been New Yorkers. Unlike many universities and cultural institutions, it did not have a residence for its chief executive officer. Richard Salomon made me an extraordinary offer: "Why don't I give you a loan of up to $600,000 to help you buy a co-op apartment? When you finish your mission at the Library and decide to leave, you can sell the apartment. If there is a financial loss, I'll assume the responsibility. If you make a profit, we'll split the proceeds."

I suggested that he give the money to the Library and restrict it to the purchase of an apartment for presidents of the Library. He agreed. The Library thus received a major gift and began a search for a suitable real estate investment in the city. The search lasted for seven or eight months. At first Clare and I commuted to New York from Philadelphia. I went to work and she went in search of an adequate apartment. In the middle of all of this, all hell broke loose.

At a cocktail party at a Park Avenue apartment, a *New York Times* reporter overheard a conversation. On November 23, 1981, the *Times* ran an article with the headline: PUBLIC LIBRARY SEEKS TO BUY APARTMENT FOR ITS PRESIDENT. It mentioned 1120 Park Avenue as a possible choice. "The move by the Library has met with opposition from the Board of Directors of the luxury building. One of the directors, Robert W. Pleasant, said he was strongly against the Library's buying an apartment in the building. "The way things are going these days, it's very likely that the president of the Library could be a member of a minority group. . . . And no matter how we feel about it, we've got to protect our investments. With a member of a minority group living in the building, the value would go right down like that. 'What right has the Library to go off and spend $400,000 for a co-op for its president when it is pleading poverty and begging for nickels and dimes from children. . . .' "

That was a valid criticism and could have been easily dealt with by explaining that a donor had given a restricted gift for the specific purpose of purchasing a residence for the incumbent and future presidents of the Library.

Heiskell and Salomon wrote letters to the *New York Times* noting the disadvantages of the New York Public Library's attracting a leader without being able to provide housing like other major cultural and educational institutions. They referred to the segregated funds earmarked for this purpose. Clare and I were appalled. I was apprehensive about the impact of this publicity on the Library's fund-raising efforts and our plans for its future. I wrote Heiskell and Salomon that, in view of market conditions, high interest rates, and protracted negotiations "as well as certain practices and attitudes of co-ops vis-à-vis nonprofit organizations," a co-op purchase at this time was inimical to the interest of the Library.

I thought a brief interlude would give us a chance to reassess. But unfortunately the criticism was not confined to money. There was a concern expressed that once I got in, "all kinds of people" would clamor to get in. The attention switched to the issue of discrimination and racism when Sydney H. Schanberg, the Pulitzer Prize–winning columnist of the *New York Times*, wrote a column, "Mr. Pleasant Regrets . . ."

"In short," he wrote, "Mr. Pleasant was telling us, you let an Armenian Trojan Horse in today and the next thing you know there'll be a black or a Puerto Rican—and there goes the neighborhood." Mayor Koch offered me

Gracie Mansion as a residence. African-American landlords in Harlem invited us to move to Harlem. Many landlords invited me to look at their buildings, and many organizations sent letters of solidarity and protest.

The *New York Times* article and Schanberg's column made my name a household word. I was "famous," a "celebrity." Eventually the Library did buy a condominium in Carnegie Hill Tower (Ninety-fourth Street and Madison Avenue). Thus ended the controversy. In 1988, when I left the Library to become the president of Brown University, the Library offered to sell me the apartment at purchase price. By then it was valued at over $3 million. I declined. I did not want to become a millionaire at the expense of the Library!

One irony is that during my tenure as president, many millionaires, even billionaires, and many famous people who wanted to buy a co-op or condominium on Fifth, Park, or Madison Avenues requested letters of recommendation, asking me to vouch for their good social standing. . . .

I decided to use the apartment controversy as an opportunity. It gave me the stage, the visibility, and the opportunity to focus the public's attention on the Library's mission. I stressed the fact that New York could not claim to be the cultural capital of the world or even our nation without its monumental New York Public Library. After all, it embodied not only the memory but also the spirit of New York.

During the eight years that I was president of the Library—and ever since—I have been on a troubadour's journey, singing the praises of libraries to anyone who will listen. I have traveled the country on this mission, north, south, east, and west, and my song always includes Andrew Carnegie's lyric that "The free library is the cradle of democracy." In June 2002, I had an opportunity to speak at the White House on the occasion of a conference on school libraries hosted by First Lady Laura Bush. Into this speech I poured all my thoughts, speaking from my heart about my passion for libraries and for books.

When Charles Dickens moved into Tavistock House, the home of his dreams, he took care with the arrangement of his study. To ensure his privacy he installed a special hidden door, made to look exactly like part of an unbroken wall of bookshelves, complete with dummy books. Dickens had no difficulty in coming up with ingenious titles for his artificial books. One was called *Cat's Lives* (nine volumes), *The History of a Short Chancery Suit* (twenty-one volumes), a seven-volume magnum opus, *The Wisdom of Our Ancestors,* which included the individual titles *Ignorance, Superstition, Dirt, Disease, The Block,* and *The Stake. The*

Virtues of our Ancestors, on the other hand, was so slender that the title had to be printed on the spine sideways. Then there was a three-volume work entitled *Five Minutes in China.*

Let us now turn to real libraries, which are as old as civilization—the objects of pride, envy, and sometimes senseless destruction. From the clay tablets of Babylon to the computers of a modern library stretch more than five thousand years of man's and woman's insatiable desire to establish written immortality and to ensure the continuity of culture and civilization, to share their memories, their wisdom, their strivings, their fantasies, their longings, and their experiences with mankind and with future generations.

Let us now turn to real libraries, which have always occupied a central role in our culture. They contain our nation's heritage, the heritage of humanity, the record of its triumphs and failures, the record of mankind's intellectual, scientific, and artistic achievements. They are the diaries of the human race. They contain humanity's collective memory. They are not repositories of human endeavor alone. They are instruments of civilization. They provide tools for learning, understanding, and progress. They are a source of information, a source of knowledge, a source of wisdom; hence they are a source of action. They are a laboratory of human endeavor. They are a window to the future. They are a source of hope. They are a course of self-renewal. They represent the link between the solitary individual and mankind, which is our community. The library is the university of universities, for it contains the source and the unity of knowledge. The library is the only true and free university. There are no entrance examinations, no subsequent examinations, no diplomas, no graduations, for no one can graduate—or ever needs to!—from a library.

Above all else, libraries represent and embody the spirit of humanity, a spirit that has been extolled throughout history by countless writers, artists, scholars, philosophers, theologians, scientists, teachers, and ordinary men and women in a myriad of tongues and dialects.

The library, in my opinion, is the only tolerant historical institution, for it is the mirror of our society, the record of mankind. It is an institution in which the left and the right, the Devil and God, human achievements, human endeavors, and human failures all are retained and classified in order to teach mankind what not to repeat and what to emulate.

The library also marks an act of faith in the continuity of humanity. The library contains a society's collective but discriminating memory.

It is an act of honor to the past, a witness to the future, hence a visible judgment on both.

The existence and the welfare of the library are of paramount importance in the life of a society, in the life of a community, the life of a university, the life of a school and a college, the life of a city, and the life of a nation.

Indeed, the library is a central part of our society. It is a critical component in the free exchange of information, which is at the heart of our democracy. In both an actual and symbolic sense, the library is the guardian of freedom of thought and freedom of choice; hence it constitutes the best symbol of the First Amendment to our Constitution. For what will be the result of a political system when a majority of the people are ignorant of their past, their legacy, and the ideals, traditions, and purposes of our democracy? "A nation that expects to be ignorant and free," wrote Thomas Jefferson, "expects what never was and never will be."

Through the development and spread of the academic and private libraries, and the central role that our public libraries and school libraries have assumed, we have come to view the library not only as a source of scholarship, knowledge, and learning, but also as a medium for self-education, progress, self-help, autonomy, liberation, empowerment, self-determination, and "moral salvation," as a source of power. That is why the library was dubbed the "People's University" by Emerson and the "True University" or the "House of Intellect" by Carlyle.

Libraries are not ossified institutions or historical relics. Libraries and museums are the DNA of our culture. Cemeteries do not provide earthly immortality to men and women; libraries, museums, universities, and schools do.

To prepare a master plan for the Library and to get ready for a campaign, we undertook a self-assessment. Every sector examined its immediate needs and long-term aspirations. We integrated all the submissions into a single planning document and subjected it to a cost analysis. The total cost amounted to a billion dollars. We knew we could not possibly raise that much money. We scrutinized all the plans again to determine the basic needs, then prioritized them and costed them out again.

On this second round, the projected cost of meeting the Library's needs was $479 million. We hired a national fund-raising consulting firm to assess our chances of launching a capital campaign. Their evaluation was that at the maximum we would be able, if lucky, to raise $300 million, half in public funds and half in private. But they cautioned us that even that amount was unrealistic unless the board itself put up a "sizable amount." We trimmed our plans to fit the $300 million goal. Then Andrew and I went to the board and said: "This is what we recommend. But it will only happen if the board shoulders its share of the responsibility."

The board members were stunned. New York was still recovering from its financial woes and no cultural institutions in New York had aimed so high. We were on untested ground. When he was asked what we meant by "sizable amount," Andrew Heiskell said: $45 million. It was a huge amount for a board that included many academics, civil servants, and few rich individuals. After a couple of minutes of endless silence, the board voted that it would put up the $45 million before we went public with the Library's campaign. The board's endorsement marked the beginning of an arduous campaign, marked by joy, disappointments, surprises, action, accomplishment, and gratification. Andrew called the board's action a "gallant act." I called it a "noble one."

How to raise the first $45 million was a great challenge. As Andrew notes in his memoirs: "The whole trick on this kind of drive is to set the right level of giving. The first big contribution is called 'the lead gift.' It pretty much determines what everybody else is going to give. It is extraordinary to what degree it does. The level of the lead gift means more than the name of the donor. But if the first donor also happens to be prominent, really connected and therefore setting a clear example, that is all to the good.

"In our case, Brooke Astor, Mrs. Astor, was obviously the lead gift. She would set the level for good or bad. If she ended up giving $2 million then everybody else would give proportionately and we might as well forget the whole thing.

" . . . Naturally we—Greg, Dick Salomon, and I—talked to her as sweetly as we knew how. . . . It took six months. Time went on and on, and we could not ask any other trustee to give until Brooke set the level. One day she said, without preamble, 'I am going to give ten million.' Period. No conditions, no nothing. 'That's it as far as my foundation is concerned. This is my last big gift.' "

As we waited for Mrs. Astor's decision, we tried to strengthen our links to the community with the addition of many civic, cultural, and business leaders to our board.† The ranks of new trustees included several prominent

† Kenneth S. Axelson, Bill Blass, Carter Burden, Bob O. Evans, Ann G. Getty, Seymour M. Klein, Carolyn Roehm Kravis, Charles Marshall, John P. Mascotte, Hamish Maxwell, Susan M. Newhouse, His Eminence John Cardinal O'Connor, Anne E. Reed, The Honorable Abraham A. Ribicoff, Elizabeth F. Rohatyn, Marshall Rose, Sonny Sloan, Saul P. Steinberg, Alfred R. Stern, John C. Whitehead.

novelists, such as Carlos Fuentes, Toni Morrison, Tom Wolfe, and the biographer Barbara Goldsmith. The list also included Harold Prince, the Broadway producer, philanthropists such as Sandra Priest Rose, Dorothy Cullman, Annette de la Renta, Ace Greenberg, Robert Menschel, and Larry Tisch, among others. We had a fashion designer or two. To those who objected about the latter appointments, my answer was simple: our strong one-million-plus picture collection, not to mention the Performing Arts Research Center, was being heavily used by the theatrical, advertising, and fashion industries. We needed their support.

The ranks of the new trustees also included Marshall Rose, chairman of the board of the Georgetown Group, Inc., a privately held real estate development and financial services company. Marshall Rose proved to be a great catch for the Library. He was an ideal candidate, a man of high energy and integrity, with very few board affiliations, who was ready to share with us his time, his wisdom, and his wealth. It became apparent that we had managed to find another born leader to join Andrew, Dick, and Brooke.

The wisdom of our choice was evident in Marshall's first recommended real estate transaction. The Library, which had in the past sold its air rights on Donnell Library (across from MoMA on Fifty-third Street) for a pittance, had rented a huge garage deeded to us for some fifty thousand dollars a year. It was on a long-term lease. We wanted to sell the garage. In what we saw a liability, Marshall saw an opportunity. He told us the garage was a valuable property separating two buildings. He managed to sell it for some $3 million.

Andrew and I turned over the supervision of the entire real estate holdings of the Library to Marshall. He oversaw our renovation plans for the Central Research Library at Forty-second Street, the Schomburg Center for Research in Black Culture, the Library for the Performing Arts, and many of our branch libraries. He joined Andrew Heiskell, Richard Salomon, Dan Bideman (of Business Improvement District), and me in spearheading the restoration of Bryant Park. The Library had a great depository on Tenth Avenue that housed our patent collection and periodicals. We did not know what to do with it. Eventually, Marshall managed, through creative fiscal and real estate deals, to transform and transfer it to the former B. Altman's department store on Fifth Avenue, creating a 100-million-dollar Science, Industry, and Business Library (SIBL).

During my first one hundred days, I agreed to be the main spokesman for the Library. We made a tactical decision not to announce all our incoming gifts and grants at separate intervals but rather to accumulate and announce them all together. On September 9, 1981, we announced that the Library had received several grants totaling some $10 million. The grants were from the National Endowment for the Humanities, the U.S. Office of Education, the City of New York, and the State of New York.

Announcements in New York are routine, but newspaper and television coverage of them are almost always uncertain. On September 7 or 8, the late Laurie Johnston of the *New York Times* called to inquire whether it was true that the Library was getting ready to announce the sale of its Audubon prints and other rare items to cover its operating costs and save its dwindling endowment. I told her that was not true. What was true, however, was that we were ready to announce several major gifts to the Library, worth some $10 million. I implied that perhaps she was angling for an exclusive report. She came right away. The coverage and the headline were music to my ears, soothing for my eyes: MAJOR NEW FUNDING BRIGHTENS PUBLIC LIBRARY FUTURE: OFFICIALS ANNOUNCE $10 MILLION IN INCREASED ALLOCATION. In a subsequent article, she reported that the Library had balanced its budgets for two years in a row; that the last years' projection of a $52 million cumulative deficit by 1985 "no longer holds"; and that the Library's message is: "We are not in a holding pattern anymore; we are in a position to move forward."

Arthur "Punch" Sulzberger, the publisher of the New York Times, Inc, gave a lunch in honor of Andrew Heiskell (his brother-in-law) and me at the New York Times headquarters. The editor, the managing editor, and various important reporters of the paper were present.

Andrew and I gave a report. The issue, we said, was not whether the New York Public Library would survive or not but rather the quality of its survival. Sulzberger asked a crucial question: What do corporations do for the Library? My answer was "Let us take the case of the New York Times, Inc. We will gladly give back your ten- to twenty-thousand-dollar annual contributions if you house dozens of the Library's microfilm readers, preserved specifically for the readers of the *New York Times,* since the paper no longer has its own morgue."

There was an awkward moment. I had made my point. The New York Public Library's welfare was everybody's business: newspapers, magazines, publishing houses, institutions of higher education, as well as the entire school system, law firms, business firms, artists, architects, scientists, fashion designers, members of the performing arts professions, a myriad of immigrants, genealogists, cartographers, city, state, and federal agencies, etc., etc.

I told them that the libraries and museums were in the immortality business. They were the only institutions that granted and preserved immortality on earth. Most buildings, even the tall ones, could not guarantee it, neither could cemeteries. It is the libraries and librarians that buy, catalog, circulate, preserve, and disseminate the works of our writers, composers, scientists, and scholars. They are your best allies, I told the editorial board, don't neglect them. You help yourself as well as preserve one of the "crown jewels" of New York.

My heartfelt plea left a visible impact on the publisher, editors, reporters, and especially Arthur Gelb, the managing editor. He became the Library's biggest protector. He assigned reporters to cover every aspect of the Library, every major activity. He did not have to prod his reporters; they got caught up in the Library's struggle to educate the public and emphasize its central role in the city and the nation. They conveyed their passion and their love of the library, and their enthusiasm became infectious. Abe Rosenthal, the editor of the *New York Times,* once complained to Arthur Gelb, half jokingly, that there must be something wrong with the *Times,* as a day had passed without a New York Public Library story.

As part of our campaign to extend the right of ownership of the Library to America's writers, we held a Literary Evening at the Library. It was Salomon's idea to have twenty-one distinguished writers act as hosts to twenty-one tables for dinner. The cost of the meals, the décor, and the administration overhead was to be underwritten by twenty-one benefactors. Each benefactor and their eight guests would join the hosts. The proceeds would go to purchase books for the Library.

Would writers come? Would twenty-one benefactors agree to pay ten-thousand dollars for the privilege of dining with an author? Should there be speeches? How would research librarians react to a dinner in their beloved quiet reading rooms? Would foodstuffs attract vermin, etc., etc.?

Writers accepted with enthusiasm. Benefactors gave readily. Librarians agreed. Everyone invited came. Publishers provided the books of those being honored. We decided to call the honorees Literary Lions, after Patience and Fortitude, who guard the front stairs on Fifth Avenue. We purchased small and elegant gold medallions, with a lion's head, patterned after the lions of the Achaemenid Persian Empire.

The dinner yielded $1,200,000, $1 million of which was a surprise gift from Enid Haupt, philanthropist, editor, publisher, and the sister of Ambassador Walter Annenberg. She said, "Books are the most important thing in life besides nature." Her gift was the first million-dollar gift that I received my first year. Then, in December 1981, with great fanfare, we dedicated the new Castle Hill branch library in the Bronx. It was an important symbol, stressing that the branch libraries were not going to be left out. "The Literary Lions" dinner became such a success that we raised the price to twenty-five thousand dollars. I called it "the privilege" of hosting a dinner table in honor of an author. The success was guaranteed by exclusivity: only twenty-one tables and 210 guests. The media coverage brought forth many requests to underwrite the costs of the liquor, decorations, and food. The success resulted in intense pressures on me from many powerful, or prominent, rich individuals to "own" a table. I was told the price was not a problem.

Our efforts to publicly recognize our writers and scholars as worthy representatives and symbols of America's creativity, and the Library as the repository of our heritage, traditions, and memory, met with success of another order than money. One outcome was the recruitment of poets, writers, scholars, artists, and scientists as surrogate spokesmen of the Library. They became its intellectual shareholders. In eight years, 175 poets, writers, and scholars had been honored as Literary Lions.

There was pressure to recognize others of creative achievement, especially the performing arts. After all, New York is the cultural capital, and the Library has one of the great performing arts research centers at Lincoln Center. We began an annual Performing Arts Lions dinner. It was a success, though it could not match the cachet of the Literary Lions. After all, there were the Kennedy Center awards, the Oscars, Emmy, and Grammy awards, and many others for performing artists.

Educating New York's establishment about the Library was not sufficient to preserve, rebuild, and expand it. We needed the voice and the will of the people of the city. We needed to recharge those who had taken it and its many roles and services for granted. We had to change attitudes, but to change attitudes we had to challenge them. Words were not enough. Practically everyone in New York waxed eloquent about every worthwhile cause and institution. We had to demonstrate our vision through major, durable, credible, and dramatic deeds. We needed a campaign to build, restore, and expand the Library and its services. To prepare a major campaign, we needed experts, a plan, and money.

We borrowed from the Metropolitan Museum of Art the services of Arthur Rosenblatt, its resident architectural consultant, on a part-time basis. We asked him to survey the Central Research Library building at Forty-second Street and Fifth Avenue. Overwhelmed by the neglect of the physical plant and the infrastructure, he asked "How much money have you requested from the city?" "Only $600,000," I answered. "My God!" was his reaction. "The Met gets ten million, the Brooklyn Museum from six to seven million. You should ask for at least five million." The deadline for the submission of a request to the city's capital budget was around the corner. We worked for several days to prepare a proposal for the city. Whatever you ask for, Rosenblatt advised, the city will cut that amount drastically. I guess we asked for ten million. We were in a state of shock. No one had ever asked for that much money from the city. Our request elicited an initial negative reaction from the city's OMB.

In the meantime, for $86,000 we erected a beautiful blue fence at the corner of Forty-second and Fifth Avenue. In big white letters, we listed the names of the top political leaders of the city: the mayor, the comptroller, the borough presidents, the chair of the Board of Estimate, etc. It said simply: The Future Construction Site of the New York Public Library. The fence accomplished three goals: it advertised rebuilding, it cut the flow of drug dealers between Forty-second and Bryant Park, and it put pressure on the city. The OMB and the Library played a cat and mouse game. Every time the mayor visited the Library or its vicinity, I was there but so was a representative of the OMB to make sure we did not wrest a major commitment from the mayor. We took photographs of every horrible scene, every grubby detail we could find in the Library and put them in a slide show. They were not pretty pictures. We had a big dilemma now: how to impress the city, our trustees, and potential benefactors without depressing them and discouraging potential supporters by overwhelming them. We did not want to convey the impression that we were hopeless. At the end, we received $4.7 million from the city.

We installed a temperature/humidity control system in the book stacks, air-conditioned the public rooms, reading rooms, and offices of the Central Research Library, relandscaped the Plaza (the entrance to the Library), restored the façade, cleaned the entire building, constructed a ramp to provide handicap access to the Central Research Library, and built a Library shop and a café on the Plaza. We repaired and replaced the roof of the library and its lead pipes.[‡] Most important, we provided some one hundred miles of additional book stacks under Bryant Park. The city provided $16.6 million for the project, and trustee Ann Getty donated $1 million for the topsoil in my

---

[‡] The list of restoration, renovation, and repairs of the main building included the Brooke Astor Reading Room for Rare Books and Manuscripts; the Public Catalog Room (now the Bill Blass Catalog Room); the McGraw Rotunda; Room 316, now the Edna Barnes Salomon Room for exhibitions of the Library's Special Collections; the Celeste Bartos Forum (it had been used as a warehouse); the DeWitt Wallace Periodicals Room; D. Samuel and Jeane H. Gottesman Exhibition Hall (previously it had been divided by Masonite partitions into tiny offices for personnel and accounting); the Jewish Division (now the Dorot Jewish Division, thanks to the munificence of Joy Ungerleider-Mayerson), along with the Oriental, Slavonic, and Economic and Public Affairs Divisions; and the Astor Hall.

honor. I joked at the time that maybe I should be buried in those stacks, since the "Gregorian topsoil" was paid for.

The sight of the cleaned and restored Library was spectacular. The lions were smiling. I believe the Library, the first cultural or municipal institution that decided to be washed, cleaned, and reconstructed, heralded the reemergence of a new energized, determined New York.

A restored clean, sparkling, modernized Central Library building would not satisfy the Library's mission, however. That mission mandated the constant acquisition of new materials for its growing and changing collections and their maintenance in usable condition. In addition, it required the presence of a competent, dedicated professional staff to provide the highest quality public service. And, yes, the Library had to be open and accessible. It pained me to see the Library closed or to have drastically reduced hours of service. I had to remind the public and its officials that even during the Great Depression of 1929 the libraries had remained open all day, evenings, and on weekends. I thought a closed library was the most uncivic institution, its locked doors a wasteful, even sinful act. It was with great pride, therefore, that we managed to open the Library six days a week and increase its hours of access from a low forty to some sixty hours a week. Service was extended to Monday, Tuesday, and Wednesday evenings and all day on Thursday.

When we opened the Library's doors, I was alerted and waiting for the first patron. It was none other than Jacqueline Kennedy Onassis. She wore blue jeans, a nice jacket, and dark glasses. We celebrated the occasion with a cup of coffee in my office. Mrs. Onassis, an avid reader and a patron of the Library, was there in her capacity as an editor at Doubleday publishing house. (Mrs. Onassis and I became good friends. We discussed several book projects. She picked one idea: the diary of a German soldier in Napoleon's army. I was touched by her generosity when she dedicated that book, her last, to me.)

In the 1980s, one of the major achievements of the Library was the completion of two major projects initiated by Richard Couper, my predecessor, Richard Salomon, and James Henderson, the director of the Research Libraries. One was the publication of the eight-hundred-volume *Dictionary Catalog of the Research Libraries of the New York Public Library*. It contained, in book form, some nine million entries of the Research Libraries' main card catalog prior to 1972. The project was begun in 1978. The other major project was the installation of CATNYP (1988), an online card catalog designed for the post-1971 acquisition of the Research Libraries.

The Library's three main functions to acquire, to catalog, and to circulate required a fourth: to preserve. We had to protect our collections, indeed, save them from the deteriorating effects of air pollution, humidity, heavy use, and the decay of acid paper. In addition to the installation of temperature and humidity control systems and air-conditioning, we constructed and equipped the Goldsmith-Perry Preservation Laboratory, a state-of-the-art facility. Together with Barbara Goldsmith (later a trustee of the Library), we brought together prominent authors and major publishers to issue a joint manifesto pledging not to publish their works on acid paper.

But what really captured the public's imagination was the Central Library's big project—to dust its eighty-eight miles of bookshelves. They had not been dusted in seventy-five years. As Andrew Heiskell put it: "All the dust and dirt of the City was inside the Library." The cost of cleaning was $1 million. Hamish Maxwell, the chairman of Philip Morris Company, underwrote the cost. A slew of Russian émigrés, whose specialty was to clean books, were given a contract. The *New York Times* gave it great coverage. In addition to cleaning the books and the shelves, we discovered in the process of an inventory that we had some 100,000 more volumes than we thought we had. Evidently some of the users of our card catalog, instead of copying the information on the cards, had simply taken the cards, thus condemning many books to the realm of the unknown.

Our acquisition, preservation, renovation, and modernization plans were not confined to the Central Research Library. We extended them to two other research libraries: the Schomburg Center for Research in Black Culture, one of the greatest national repositories of the history of African-Americans, and the Performing Arts Research Center. We built a new theater and an exhibitions gallery and refurbished the Old American Negro Theater Auditorium at the cost of some $23 million.

Within Lincoln Center, we renovated the Performing Arts Research Center, opened it six mornings a week, expanded and modernized the Rodgers and Hammerstein Archives, as well as the conservation lab of the Dance collection (it had been closed for ten years), and cataloged years of backlogged materials.

One of our great accomplishments in the 80s was the revitalization of the eighty-three branch (circulating) libraries. The renovation and restoration of the Countee Cullen branch in Harlem led the way, as did the restoration and modernization of the Yorkville and Aguilar branches, thanks to the generosity of Sandra Priest Rose. These set high standards for other branch libraries.

Between 1981 and 1989, thanks to the concerted efforts of our trustees, members of the Branch Library Council, the administration of the Library, and, most important, the citizens of New York, who were its patrons, the branch libraries' operating budget increased from some $29 million to about $60 million. This 100 percent increase not only covered most inflationary cost increases but also made it possible to make many improvements. We hired some four hundred new staff members, doubled the Library's book and materials budget by 100 percent (to $7.5 million), and began to acquire some 800,000 to a million items a year. We expanded the children's reading room collections with new books, videocassettes, and microcomputer software designed specifically for children and extended the Early Childhood Program into neighborhood branches and disseminated it nationally. In addition, the Library was able to replenish and revitalize its foreign language collections (Hispanic, Chinese, etc.) and circulate some 10 million items to its one million library card holders, a 20 percent increase in circulation. We opened seventy-five branches five days a week, and forty-nine branches were provided with weekend service.

Between 1981 and 1989, we also completed twelve major capital projects. We dedicated the mid-Manhattan Library, the headquarters of the branch libraries that housed, among other things, its unique one-million-strong picture collection. We opened four new branches (Eastchester, Parkchester, Belmont, and New Amsterdam), relocated four branches to new, more spacious and modern rental quarters (Sedgwick, Cathedral, Castle Hill, and Todt Hill), and completely renovated three branches (Yorkville, Epiphany, and St. George). Finally, we introduced the first microcomputers for public use in the branch system and installed the Automated Circulation System, an online computerized system for the book circulation. Library-wide initiatives launched in the 80s included eight Centers of Reading and Writing in the Bronx, Manhattan, and Staten Island to teach functionally illiterate adult New Yorkers to read.

The renaissance of the New York Public Library was made possible by the success of a private-public partnership that raised $327 million. A major outcome of that successful campaign was the Library's ability to expand the base of private and governmental support for ongoing operating costs. By 1988 we were able to secure $10 million a year. In addition, we obtained some $70 million of gifts-in-kind from individual collectors and benefactors.[§]

During and in the aftermath of its successful campaign, the Library man-

---

[§] The Carl H. Pforzheimer Shelley and His Circle Collection; the Leonard Schlosser History of Papermaking Collection; Max Ernst's work as a printmaker; the papers of Truman Capote; the CARE archives; the Toscanini Legacy; the papers of William Schuman; the Lucia Chase Collection; the Frank Loesser Collection; an important assemblage of Louis Gottschalk material; the Boris Aronson Collection of Designs for the Theater; the Melville J. and Frances S. Herskovits Collection.

aged to inaugurate a successful exhibition and education program. Between 1984–1989, some forty exhibitions were mounted. We launched a new publication program. The Library's educational outreach programs attracted thousands. The branch libraries sponsored some sixteen thousand different events and activities. In 1988 alone, the Central Research Library organized more than 350 special events. The educational activities were a great source of recruiting support for the Library and its mission.

In his memoirs, Andrew Heiskell writes that when I was appointed as president of the Library, "Greg realized it was a perilous job. A huge amount of work had to be done at great cost over a long period of time before we could turn the monster around." I was happy to report to him that after eight years of incessant work, teamwork, by 1988–89 we had succeeded in rescuing the New York Public Library and reestablishing its central educational, civic, and cultural preeminence in New York. For me it was a wonderful, exciting, enormously satisfying journey. I came to believe in miracles.

The Library's renaissance would have been impossible without the leadership of Andrew Heiskell, Brooke Astor, Richard Salomon, Marshall Rose, and the generous, caring, and committed Board of Trustees. But most of all, the Library's rebirth could not have been accomplished without the devotion and the enduring hard work of a wonderful group of librarians.

Naturally, none of this success would have occurred without the citizens of New York, their pride in the Library, their faith in our democracy, and their ardent belief in equal opportunity. After all, almost all New Yorkers, in one way or another, throughout their lives, had reaped the benefits of the Library: scientists who made discoveries from their research at the Library (for example, Edwin Land, who developed the first efficient light polarizer widely known as Polaroid); aviation executives who located maps for PanAm transoceanic flights over the Pacific; DeWitt and Lila Wallace who used the Library to launch *Reader's Digest;* many writers who wrote seminal works in the Frederick Lewis Allen Room; rabbis and secular Jewish intellectuals who used the Jewish collection (perhaps the only ecumenical Jewish collection in New York); African-Americans and Hispanics who used the vast riches of the Schomburg Center for Research in Black Culture; scores of children who were read their first kindergarten stories by the children's librarians; actors, actresses, fashion designers, ballet dancers, and newspaper reporters who used the Performing Arts Center collections and mid-Manhattan's picture collection; lawyers who benefited from the patent collection; families who found their roots through the Genealogy Division; and all the immigrants who found the Library a linchpin between their new country and their native lands, between a new culture and their ancestral ones. And all of them received these benefits for free, without questions. They were determined that the next generation would benefit from this source of knowledge and power. The New York Public Library was the library of libraries.

As I wrote this chapter, I thought about how much time, effort, energy, and anxiety I had devoted to the Library. It consumed eight and a half years of my life. I was committed to its mission and obsessed by its success. I attended thousands of events, breakfast meetings, sometimes even two luncheons a day, sometimes two cocktail parties or dinners; perhaps even two of those a day. In the process, I gained stability by gaining almost forty pounds. At first I thought my clothes were shrinking until one day I discovered that it was I who was expanding. I felt as if I had to be everywhere, to witness for the Library's cause, to advertise its ambitions, to brag about its accomplishments.

I remember my first luncheon with a Library trustee. I asked my secretary where my predecessor had taken his guests for luncheons. She listed The White Horse, Les Pléiades, La Grenouille, Caravelle, "21," the Century Association, and the Four Seasons. I had never heard of them. The only ones I had heard of were Ararat (Armenian), Dardanelles, Cedars of Lebanon, and some restaurants in the Hilton Hotel and Statler Hilton. I had also heard of Tavern on the Green. I picked Caravelle for alphabetical reasons. I went to the restaurant to wait for Tony Mortimer III. I discovered I couldn't afford it and the restaurant did not accept credit cards or checks. I spotted Richard Salomon. He asked whether he could be of any help. I said, "I'd like you to lend me some money." He gave me a hundred dollars. When Tony ordered a drink, I told him I had stomach problems and only ate some soup and maybe some salad, always counting.

I remember when Cardinal Cooke gave me permission to list his name as a petitioner on the part of the Library in his capacity as vice chairman of the Library's board. I needed his permission to ensure that we and our committed trustees did not have to wait for hours for the hearings before the Board of Estimate to make our case. The moment the mayor, comptroller, and borough presidents noticed that the cardinal was coming, not only did they give us the first appointment but they themselves came (this event was usually relegated to subordinates) to hear our testimony. When it was my turn to testify, I rose to announce that due to an urgent pastoral commitment, His Eminence could not be there and that he sent his regrets. Immediately upon hearing this, all the city higher-ups left, as did the television cameramen and newsmen.

Unaccustomed as I was to testifying before City Council committees, I soon became a regular in the hallways and halls of City Hall. I remember that, while institution after institution was brought before the City Council, several of the City Council members would be reading their mail, eating their lunch, or talking on the phone. So one day I shocked them. I apologized for disrupting their luncheons, their calls, and boring them. I suggested that perhaps I would mail them my statement so that they could read it in their leisure time.

Relations between Cardinal O'Connor, who was Cardinal Cooke's successor, and Governor Mario Cuomo were not cordial. We needed the cardinal's support to secure from the State of New York a $16 million Library for the Blind and Physically Handicapped. I went to see him. We had a good relationship. The cardinal wrote a letter to the governor. It was my hope that this request would provide an opportunity for building a new relationship between them. Months passed and the cardinal's letter remained unanswered. One day I interceded with Mrs. Cuomo, gently, that the cardinal was not an ordinary person: in addition to God, he had a large archdiocese in New York on his side. The governor approved our request. We got our library.

On the day when Mrs. Astor, Richard Salomon, and I were to request a major gift from David Rockefeller, the two of them, who were to make the solicitation, at the last minute, demurred. I was very nervous. I told Mr. Rockefeller, "Don't worry, we're only asking for three million dollars rather than ten million." I was elated when he gave us the three million. Weeks later, at a Rockefeller University event, David, in a very good mood, put his arm on my shoulder and said, "Thank you, Greg, for saving me seven million. . . ."

Mrs. Astor and I failed miserably with Donald Trump. We visited him in his office in Trump Towers. He was gracious but took two or three telephone calls as we were making our case. Mrs. Astor winked at me; we were not going to get anything. She was wrong, however: we got twenty-five thousand dollars. Then there were the three Gottesman sisters—Joy, Miriam, and Celeste—whose generosity overwhelmed me. They endowed the Gottesman Exhibition Hall, the Celeste Bartos Forum, the Miriam and Ira D. Wallach Librarian for Art, Prints, and Photographs, and the Jewish Division, thanks to Joy Ungerleider-Mayerson. One day I joked with them that if their generosity continued unabated, pretty soon the whole library would be named after the Gottesman sisters.

There were some maverick benefactors. One name in particular comes to my mind: Alan (Ace) Greenberg, chairman of Bear Stearns. He once told me, "I'll join your board, but I won't come to the meetings. If you need anything, just let me know." One day, at a reception at Gracie Mansion, he saw a limping Mrs. Astor, who had sprained her ankle, and a tired Gregorian. The very next day a messenger brought to my home a twenty-five-thousand-dollar check, with a note from Ace, saying that he'd seen many performances that advertised the Library's needs but that by putting on such a sad show we had crossed the line. Another day he sent a $385,000 check, saying he didn't know what to do with it and asking me if I would mind taking it and putting it to good use for the Library. On yet another Saturday, a messenger came to our apartment with a note from him, saying, "My children are very open and tolerant, I hope yours are too. Why don't *we* get married?" Later, after I announced my resignation from the Library, he announced that he would pay for the restoration of the Trustees Room, as a parting gift in my honor. . . .

Throughout my term at the Library, I developed a good relationship with Victor Gotbaum, president of the Municipal Workers Union District 37. I went to see him once because I wanted the union's permission to accommodate and recruit several retirees as volunteers. Mr. Gotbaum told me that I was "lucky" because the library union was the most radical union, even Trotskyite in nature, and that they would never be willing to allow recruitment of volunteers because they would cost jobs. "But there were no jobs," I said. "And volunteers would be giving directions and maybe tours so that professional librarians could do their own work." He was not convinced. So I said, Okay, what does it require to be a union member? He said, Union dues. I told him I was willing to pay union dues on behalf of all the volunteers. This would be the first unionized volunteer group. He was astonished. "You're crazy! You'll ruin the labor movement."

At the end, I was able to get at first twenty and eventually two hundred volunteers to give their time, devotion, and even money to the Library. But Mr. Gotbaum was correct in one respect: during my first year, I received petitions from librarians concerning the humidity, the heat, and the unbearable working conditions in the labor-intensive Cataloging Room. I used the first $300,000 private gift that I raised to air-condition the Cataloging Room. I received a letter from a union member accusing me of being a Stalinist: he charged I was air-conditioning the room to make workers work harder. I got an apology from a union district representative.

*   *   *

In the 1980s, there was official apprehension about national security. There were fears of Soviet or other Communist spies visiting our libraries and obtaining scientific and technical information that might be used against our nation. Libraries and librarians were asked to keep a watchful eye and report to the FBI any curious and inquisitive "suspicious types" who might prove to be alien agents. There were several problems with the request. First, it went against all the principles of libraries and librarians and their value systems. The Library had a strict privacy policy. Furthermore, we did not ask for IDs from any of our patrons. Our circulation records were to be sealed for a century and were, therefore, unavailable. What one read was nobody's business. Even if we could overcome those hurdles, it was a fact that there were many in the great metropolis of New York who looked "suspicious." After all, there were so many beards, so many guises, so many foreigners, and so many immigrants, not to mention UN diplomats. Besides, we were not trained as detectives or security agents.

I pointed out these facts to the late Jim Fox, the head of New York's FBI field office. In addition, I drew his attention to the obvious fact that any government, agency, or individual who wanted to read our scientific journals could certainly afford to subscribe to them rather than send a spy to read and copy them. In the end, what impressed Mr. Fox was when I said, Suppose we agreed to be "monitors" or "lookouts" for our government—I am afraid if I walked into the Library, if I were not its president, the librarians would have to report me. Mr. Fox laughed. My point, he said, was well taken.

In the middle of the eighties, we decided to do something on behalf of the New York City public schools. There were many outstanding public schools that were respected nationally and internationally (Bronx Science, Stuyvesant, Hunter College High School, etc.), but the overall quality of the school system was uneven and weak. A national commission report issued in 1983, *A Nation at Risk,* described the terrible state of our public school system and how it affected our nation's future, even our national security and international standing. We decided to focus on the valedictorians of New York's schools and, through them, the school system. With a gift of a thousand dollars a year from the Merchant's Bank of New York, we decided to hold an annual Minerva (Goddess of Wisdom, the Library's emblem) Awards Ceremony in honor of the city's valedictorians.

The annual event was held at the Central Research Library. We invited prominent public figures (Mayor Ed Koch; Barbara Walters; I. M. Pei; the actor Ben Vereen; Harrison "Jay" Goldin, the comptroller; and many others), preferably former valedictorians themselves, to address the honorees. We asked publishing houses in New York to provide the valedictorians with "meaningful gifts": dictionaries, anthologies, encyclopedias, and other reference books. We invited teachers, the chancellor of the school system, principals, superintendents, and most important, all of the parents. They all came.

The Merchant's Bank gift bought punch and cookies. Ever since, the annual Minerva Awards Ceremony has become a major event, a must for politicians to attend. Encouraged by its success, we persuaded the mayor and the late Richard R. Green, the chancellor of the school system, to join us in issuing one million library cards to all the students of the New York City public schools. In addition, we participated in the "corridor plan" to develop a partnership between the city's libraries, museums, major performing arts centers, and the school system to benefit the curricular needs of the public schools.

My first Christmas and holiday season at the Library was not a pleasant one. The façade of the Library was dark and dirty. The two giant wreaths that graced the necks of our two venerable lions were stolen. New Yorkers helped pay for their replacement. I did not want the Grinch to steal the holiday season, so I contacted Gordon Davis, then the parks commissioner, and he agreed to have guards posted to protect the wreaths.

We decided that the best way to celebrate the holiday season was to decorate the Library's Astor Hall, to open the entire Central Research Library and its divisions, to provide music, choral and brass, to provide mime, magic, storytelling, and to encourage grandparents, parents, and their children and grandchildren to attend an annual family gathering at the Library. We invited all of our patrons, friends, and sponsors to come and celebrate the holiday season with us. Mrs. Astor, the president of the Library, many trustees, and librarians all lined up to greet some eight to twelve thousand individuals.

I told the trustees that the citizens of New York are our true stockholders. The holiday parties not only conveyed goodwill and joy and hope but also bonded thousands of individuals and their families to the Library. I remember all those I welcomed at the door, who handed me envelopes full of dollar bills and big checks. It was as if they were coming to a wedding, christening, or bar mitzvah. The one that touched me most was a social security check from a nursing home resident.

There were also moments of anxiety and pride. One day the president of Brazil got stuck in the elevator. The visit of the defense minister of France, François Leotard, was nerve-wracking because I bragged to him that we had something on practically any subject. Let us see, he said, whether you have my wife's dissertation on a certain region of France in your Genealogy Division. With trepidation I asked our librarian. We had it. It was a Gallic victory for me.

*   *   *

Saint Patrick's Day, a great day for New York, used to be one of the worst days for the Library. Hundreds of boisterous young men, most of them underage high school students, would stream to the Central Research Library to use its public bathrooms. They bothered the patrons and jostled with our unarmed security guards. We came up with a solution. I invited the New York Police to make the Library its central command headquarters for Saint Patrick's Day. We offered them free doughnuts and coffee. The sight of hundreds of blue-uniformed officers provided the best deterrent.

Occasionally, the Library's Astor Hall would be used for major social events. One of these was the fashion industry's Lifetime Achievement Award, one of the most important events in the world of fashion designers. Ordinarily one would not associate the Library with the fashion industry, nor fashion with Katharine Hepburn. Imagine my surprise when the great actress Katharine Hepburn was invited to receive this award! Ms. Hepburn had accepted the award, but she had declined to attend the luncheon itself. Instead, she asked to dine with me alone in my office. Naturally, I was thrilled. I was sitting with several great fashion designers in Astor Hall. I apologized to them—I am sure I will see you all again, but Katharine Hepburn? Only once in a lifetime does one get an invitation to dine with her. So I left the company of designers for her.

As I entered my office I saw an unbelievable sight. The legendary actress was standing on my table surveying the wood-covered panels in my office, including the eighteenth- and nineteenth-century portraits of John Jacob Astor, Benjamin Franklin, and Shelley's parents by George Romney. We had a wonderful lunch. Her self-confidence and independence, that she had arrived in plain black slacks and shirt to receive the fashion industry's high award, seemed to me a signature mark of her stubbornness and independence. When the time came to receive her award, we walked down to the hall. She said a few nice words and left.

Another memorable woman I met was Her Majesty Farah Diba, the ex-empress of Iran. The occasion was a great birthday bash given by John Kluge for his then-wife, Patricia Kluge. I had never met Mr. Kluge, and my colleagues at the Library were eager for me to make his acquaintance. My wife and I went to the event at the Waldorf-Astoria. To my great surprise, I was seated at Table 1. I told the manager of the event that there must be some mistake. Not at all, she answered. Her Majesty Farah Diba has specifically asked that you sit next to her. It was an unbelievable evening. We had a wonderful talk. Then she said, "Let us dance." I was petrified. Me dancing with the former queen of Iran? I was nervous. She made me feel at ease.

Then I said, "Your Majesty, if my grandmother were alive, she would be shocked beyond belief. I am sure she would tell me, 'Hey, you, little Vartan. Who do you think you are, dancing with the queen?' " She responded, "If my grandmother was alive, she would have said the same thing!" (Years later, in 1988, when I assumed the presidency of Brown University, the ranks of its student body included the sons and daughters of many prominent American and international parents. I was amazed to find out that the late Leila Pahlavi, the daughter of the late Shah and Farah Diba, and Bahram Pahlavi, the son of Prince Gholam Reza Pahlavi, the Shah's brother, were students at Brown. What a historical coincidence, an Iranian-born president of an Ivy League university was in charge of the education of the Shah's daughter and nephew. That would have really impressed not only my grandmother, father, and stepmother but also my elementary and middle school teachers and friends in Tabriz!)

*   *   *

My life at the Library wasn't all movie stars and royalty! There was, for example, the nagging problem of Bryant Park. For eight years, Heiskell, Marshall Rose, Dan Bideman, and I sought to take over the management of Bryant Park, restore it, secure the perimeter of the Library, and make the park safe. These eight years included hundreds of visits to different constituencies, to interested parties, to donors, to restaurants, to municipal authorities, to City Council members, to the Board of Estimate, to mayoral agencies, to the Municipal Arts Society, Parks Council, Arts Commission, and on and on. I remember one time when Heiskell and I waited in a church basement until eleven P.M., trying to convince a community board to rescind their opposition and approve our plans. We tried to persuade them that as a nonprofit organization, we were not privatizing the park for profit but rather for the use of the public. It was a rough meeting. I was, however, armed with two editorials. One was Lenin's 1913 *Pravda* editorial about the Library (he had just read the first annual report of the Library), wherein he praises the Library and suggests, albeit briefly, that what Russia needed was a similar institution where citizens would have free access to information and knowledge.

The second one was an article in *Literaturnaya Gazeta,* a Soviet periodical, which stated that they understood perfectly why the Library was the venue or setting for a conference on Soviet dissidents. After all, they noted, the entire wall of the back of the Library, facing Bryant Park, was a long urinal, where pimps, prostitutes, and drug dealers were purveying their wares and that, therefore, the Library, Bryant Park, and the dissidents were in the right company. That left a great impression on the community board leaders and they came onboard.

As we restored and renovated the Library, the masterpiece of architects Carrère and Hastings, cleaned its brass lamps, chandeliers, marble, and façade, I got only one major criticism. The *Village Voice* stated that the Library was looking too luxurious and that we were wasting money on nonessentials. To my delight, Howard Fast, the former Communist writer, wrote in my defense. He said something like "He's doing everything to rescue and regain the majesty of the Library and its centrality, so they should keep quiet and mind their own business. Otherwise they should provide alternatives." It was during this period that I described the Library as the "People's Palace," a term that Norman Mailer and many other writers subsequently popularized. One evening when Clare and I were having a quiet dinner at Parma, an Italian restaurant, a rich, middle-aged woman approached us and practically shouted at me, "What's wrong with me?" We were perplexed. "How come," she said, "you never ask me for money?"

The trustees of the New York Public Library, particularly its leadership, were very worried about the range of my activities, my pace, my workload, and the interminable hours that I spent at the Library or in activities related to the Library, including on the weekend. They noticed how frantic I was to keep so many public and private commitments without displaying signs of fatigue or exhaustion and to project perennial confidence and optimism. So Bill Dietel, Richard Salomon, Andrew Heiskell, and several other trustees organized a surprise party for me at one of the private rooms at "21." To boost my morale, they gave me pep talks, a needlepoint pillow with a lion on it (courtesy of Edna Salomon), and an amazing drawing: I was sitting on a throne, bearing a crown (adorned with New York landmarks guarded by Patience and Fortitude). Underneath this huge framed drawing was written: "Greg XI." I was crowned King of the Library and New York. They needed a song, however, and they sang in unison, to the tune of "From the Halls of Montezuma," the following lines: "To the stacks of the New York Li-bra-ry, From the halls of the U. of P." That did it. It replenished my batteries.

I have been asked many times what the source of the stamina was that enabled me to endure and overcome a myriad of political, administrative, and bureaucratic hurdles. The answer is simple. I considered the presidency of the Library a mission, not a job. I believed in the Library's role as the cradle of democracy and knowledge. I considered myself the guardian of some 30 million items—millions of memories and stories, the cultural legacy of our nation and humanity. I was always in awe in the presence of such a great and endless source of knowledge. I was proud and gratified that a boy who used to borrow and rent books in Tabriz was given an opportunity to acquire and lend books to hundreds of thousands of citizens and noncitizens. I felt privileged to defend the rules of privacy and the First Amendment of our Constitution. Whenever I felt discouraged or lonely, all I had to do was go to the main reading room of the Central Research Library and take a look at the eight-hundred-seat reading room, with its ornate 1911 tables, Tiffany lamps, and hundreds of individuals, reading, writing, reflecting. Or else I would visit a branch library and witness firsthand how it affects the lives of children as well as grown-ups, native Americans and thousands of immigrants. I always returned to my office full of inspiration, stamina, high morale, and determination. My work and the work of my dedicated colleagues had meaning and immediate impact. Also, I was born energetic.

After eight and a half years at the helm of the Library and a successful capital campaign, I had seen the reemergence of the New York Public Library as the intellectual, scholarly, and cultural repository of New York and the nation, with a robust public education outreach agenda in the form of exhibitions, lectures, and publications. Most important of all, the Library was able to provide millions of New Yorkers and Americans across our land with *free* access to information and knowledge. My mission was accomplished. Once again the citizens of New York had reclaimed the Library as *their* library.

In 1987, the ever-active Bill Bowen of Heidrick & Struggles began once again to hover over the Library, trying to interest me in the presidencies of several universities and foundations. I told him and the trustees that I was not ready to leave. I still had unfinished business. We needed to secure the Library for the Blind and Physically Handicapped and Bryant Park, as well as secure the renewal of our NEH funding. I did not want to give excuses to city, state, or federal officials to delay or defer their commitments using the transition of leadership at the Library as a convenient rationale. On July 20, 1987, Mrs. Astor wrote: "Thank Heavens you turned Bill Bowen down! Every day I pray to God that you will have the strength to stay at the Library. If you left it, it would be as though an earthquake, a tornado, and a thousand bulldozers had touched the Library. I don't think we could ever recover from it."

Mrs. Astor was most generous but wrong. A year later, once we had secured the Library for the Blind, the NEH funding, and the legal and financial instruments for Bryant Park, I decided it was time to relinquish my post to new leadership. The Library did not collapse. The late Tim Healy, the president of Georgetown University, succeeded me. Upon his premature and unfortunate death, Paul LeClerc, the president of Hunter College, assumed the Library's helm. It continues to thrive.

The sign on Henry Rosovsky's desk, when he was the dean of the Faculty of Arts and Sciences at Harvard, read: "Cemeteries are full of irreplaceable people." I knew that the success of a leadership can be measured by what kind of talent and structure one leaves behind. With that in mind, I knew I could leave the New York Public Library in good conscience.

CHAPTER THIRTEEN

Brown University

In 1980, when I resigned as provost of the University of Pennsylvania, I retained my professorship. In 1981, when I joined the New York Public Library, I was granted a leave of absence from Penn. My sabbatical scholarly leave, granted for my eight years of service to Penn, was postponed. In 1984, I received a cordial note from Professor Al Rieber, chairman of Penn's history department, asking me to teach a course. I agreed. The next thing I got was a lengthy letter from Paul Miller Jr., the chairman of the board. The carefully written letter basically gave me two choices: return to Penn or resign from Penn. No other arrangements were acceptable.

As far as the sabbatical was concerned, it was mine only if I resigned from the Library and rejoined Penn as a *full-time* faculty member. However, in case I decided to remain at the New York Public Library, as a gesture of goodwill, Penn was willing to grant the sabbatical whenever I left the Library to assume a position at an academic institution. The sabbatical was to help my "transition." The sabbatical compensation, however, instead of being based on my provost salary, would be equal to the salary of the chairman of the history department of Penn at the time of my move. I was given a couple of weeks to either resign from Penn or rejoin it.

On June 30, 1984, I submitted my resignation to the University of Pennsylvania faculty. The news of my resignation reopened old wounds and brought several hundred communications from students, alumni, and faculty members. It was covered by Philadelphia newspapers, as well as national media. The president and the Board of Trustees of the New School for Social Research named me university professor. New York University named me professor of Near Eastern Studies and professor of history. I was also named chairman of the board of visitors of the Graduate School and University Center of CUNY. I am sure all these acts were prompted by solidarity.

In 1988, Penn invited me, over the strenuous objections of some trustees, to receive an honorary degree. I accepted the invitation. Several trustees boycotted the commencement. Sheldon Hackney introduced me as a "galvanizing humanist" and "born teacher who exemplified the ideals of Benjamin Franklin [Penn's founder]. The trustees welcome your return to this, his [Franklin's] University." As the throngs of faculty, students, and alums cheered wildly, all of a sudden I felt very peaceful. I realized that was the *real* enduring Penn I had loved.

The Penn commencement of 1988 was a kind of catharsis for me. It cleared my soul of anger. My wife and sons did not attend the commencement. Clare did not want me to accept anything from "their hands," as "they were not worth it." The *Philadelphia Inquirer* described my presence "as a triumphant return to the Ivy League campus." The *Daily Pennsylvanian* editorial simply stated, "An honorary degree: too little, too late." Penn trustee Saul Steinberg endowed a professorship in my name at Penn's English department.

Following Philip Hamburger's 1986 two-part profile in the *New Yorker,* "Searching for Gregorian," I received a number of inquiries from assorted universities and colleges asking whether I was interested in being an active candidate for their presidencies. David Kearns, chairman and CEO of Xerox and chairman of the Board of Trustees of the University of Rochester, made a great pitch for it. I declined. There was a wonderful dividend, however. The two of us became great friends. Then there was the astonishing news, reported by the *New Haven Register,* that I was one of the leading candidates for the presidency of Yale University and that not only was I on the committee's short list but that I was on the top of that list. I was very surprised. No one had contacted me.

Later, the *New York Times* reported that the list was reduced to Maxine Singer, Benno Schmidt, and me. Ted Fiske, then the *New York Times* education editor, called me for confirmation that the Yale board representatives were about to offer me the presidency. I told Ted that I had no contacts with

Yale. I don't think he believed it. I told him Benno Schmidt is their choice. And he was.

By 1988, the New York Public Library's renewal was on course, its fund-raising efforts were a success, the Library had a great administrative team, and a great Board of Trustees. Its relations with the city, the state, and the various federal agencies were great. So was its physical infrastructure. Its endowment had grown; its budget was in good shape. I had done what I came to do. Eight years of constant fund-raising, community activism, and a myriad of social events had taken their toll. I was afraid of hubris. Volumes of articles written about the Library's renaissance had portrayed me as a fund-raiser par excellence, a cultural impresario, a high-society icon. Thanks to many society events, Clare's and my names were in the society columns. Pretty soon, I was simply Gregorian.

There was even juicy gossip about me. Eleanor Lambert wrote a column once about the social scene in London, mentioning that Johnny Carson and his fourth wife were there, as were Abe Rosenthal of the *New York Times* and his new wife, and "soon-to-be married" Vartan Gregorian, president of the New York Public Library, and Dyan Cannon, one of Cary Grant's ex-wives. She reported that we were the toast of London. Clare and I were fascinated. The problem was, I did not know Dyan Cannon, I was still married, and I was not in London. I found out that it was Kirk Kerkorian of MGM who was dating Dyan Cannon. I assumed Eleanor Lambert had heard of me but not of him, hence she had "corrected" the record.

I was eager to rejoin the academic world. I missed teaching, the students, the intellectual and artistic ferment of our universities and even, believe it or not, its academic politics. My friend Bill Ziff once remarked to a reporter: "He [Gregorian] would never be fully himself until he was the president of a great university." He also said, "I think he has a feeling of destiny about that." I alerted Andrew Heiskell and Brooke Astor that I longed for the career of scholarship and teaching that I had pursued for twenty-two years before joining the Library.

Out of the many prospects, I chose three: the John D. and Catherine T. MacArthur Foundation, the University of Michigan, and Brown University.

A four-member delegation of the Board of Regents of the University of Michigan headed by Paul Brown, the chair of the presidential search committee, came to interview me in New York. The other regents were Philip Power, Dean Baker, and Nellie Varner. The presidential search committee had done very good due diligence. They had gathered a lot of information and talked to and interviewed many individuals about me. We discussed the challenges facing U.S. higher education and Michigan. We had an honest exchange of ideas about every major issue, from affirmative action to the urban plight of Detroit, the poor quality of the public schools, and the needs of the Flint and Dearborn campuses of the university. The regents expressed a desire to meet my wife, informing me that a state law or regental law required it. You are hiring me, not my wife, I replied. If you want to meet her you can invite her for dinner. She may or may not come. They did invite her to Michigan State. She declined. However, she joined us for dinner.

Regent Baker raised the importance of the spouses and their participation in the life of the university. He cited Sissela Bok, spouse of Derek Bok of Harvard as a nonparticipant in the social life of Harvard. Clare said, "She's my hero." The interview went well. Clare's independence and erudition impressed the regents. Dean Baker asked me, If you are so good, how come Penn did not select you as its president? Ask them, I said. The regents offered me the presidency. The chairman of the committee, Paul Brown, who was also chairman of the board, wanted to meet me privately to discuss the issues of salary and benefits. Regent Baker entered the room. I don't trust him, he said about Brown. I would like to be present at your salary discussion. I was taken aback. For the first time, I realized that there was tension between him and almost the entire board. I told the regents that I would give my answer by the first week of June.

I told them about Brown University. Richard Salomon, the great benefactor of the Library and former chairman of the Library's Board of Trustees, was chancellor of Brown University. We had become great friends. Clare adored him and we both adored his wife, Edna Salomon. I had met with the presidential search committee of Brown several times. Salomon and Professor Martha Nussbaum headed the search process. I was offered the presidency of Brown University, too.

Clare and I debated the merits of these positions. In her heart, she was leaning toward Brown because her family was nearby. Her mother, brother and sister-in-law and their family were on Martha's Vineyard, her two sisters were in Philadelphia, and many of our and our children's friends were in the East. Besides, she told me, you can't break Dick Salomon's heart. Many friends advised me to take Brown. It was small, it was private, it was an Ivy League university, and one didn't have to deal with a state bureaucracy and the headaches of a huge athletic empire. Besides, they said, because Brown is small and weak, you may be able to leave your imprint on it and take the institution to another level of excellence.

The day I was supposed to give my response to Michigan, I got a call from Regent Baker. He told me, "I know you are the unanimous choice of everyone, but you are not my choice. If you accept the position, I am going to fight you. I believe you will be a poor president. You'll be too focused on Detroit and minorities." He reminded me that he had nothing against minorities and that he was a contributor to the NAACP. He raised the same question again, If you are that good, how come Penn did not name you president? (I am sure he must have talked to some of my "favorite" Penn trustees.) He also pointed out that, in the *New Yorker* profile of me, my executive assistant Joan Dunlop was quoted as saying that I was disorganized; that, he said, had sent up red flags for him. I did not argue. I thanked him for his candor.

That same day, an eager Paul Brown called me. He was ready for my positive response. I told him of Regent Baker's call. It is outrageous, he said angrily. He had no right to call you. His is a lone and isolated voice. Authorized or not, Dean Baker had called me. He had reminded me of the fact that he had been elected by the people of Michigan as a regent, and that he was going to be my full-time resident detractor.

Almost all the Michigan regents called to pledge their support and apologize for Baker's behavior. Governor Blanchard of Michigan called me. The head of the Republican Party of Michigan called to assure me that Dean Baker was not representative of the Republican Party. Faculty and alumni leaders of the University of Michigan called. Harold Shapiro, president of Princeton and former president of the University of Michigan, called me, so did Robin Fleming, president emeritus. The venerable Alex Manoogian, the eminent Armenian corporate leader and philanthropist from Detroit, called.

On June 6, 1988, I sent a letter declining the presidency of Michigan. I have wondered all these years what would have been my decision had Regent Baker not called me. Who knows? Maybe even without Dean Baker's call, Brown would have been my choice. But Baker's intervention made the call certain. On August 31, 1988, Brown University announced my appointment as its sixteenth president. The reaction of the university's governing board, the faculty, and students was uniformly positive and enthusiastic. The *Brown Daily Herald*'s editorial gave me a great welcome: "Gregorian is somehow very much the way Brown likes to see itself: serious in purpose but not self-serious, an achiever who is not uptight. . . . He thinks the big thoughts and expresses himself with conviction and distinctive eloquence. We're pretty psyched."

Brown students and faculty, knowing my Stanford background, were worried that I might gut their "new curriculum" devised and launched in 1969 that had been a successful source of recruiting outstanding, self-motivated students to Brown. The curriculum allowed Brown students to choose their courses during the first two years without specific requirements.

During the last two years, they had to enroll in an academic major (concentration). To encourage the students to be academically adventuresome, the pass-fail grade was set up. At my first press conference and afterward, I was always asked two questions. One dealt with the curriculum; the other with fund-raising. Reacting to my appointment, *The New Republic* had reported that my first task was to reform the Brown curriculum. My answer was simple. "When we deal with the curriculum, the accent should not be on flexibility alone but on intellectual content and rigor. Flexibility is a means. The end ought to be an education that is intellectually exciting and stimulating, so that when people leave Brown they not only know *how* Brown made it easier for them but also how Brown made it easy for them to be intellectually challenged."

When I arrived on campus, Brown was celebrating the twentieth anniversary of its "new curriculum." As I indicated, I had many questions about it. What did it have in common with that of other Ivy League schools? Did the wide range of course choices help students make the most of their Brown education or were they getting lost, like kids in a candy store? Did the curriculum have rigor, did it balance between the humanities, social sciences, physical sciences, and natural sciences?

I asked Sheila Blumstein, the dean of the college, to conduct a thorough review. One major concern that arose from the review was that with approximately 1,800 courses to choose from, students might need more guidance in achieving both breadth and depth in their courses of study. As a consequence, with the assistance of the faculty, we published *The Guide to Liberal Learning,* which defined various components of a liberal education, and listed some 250 university courses that were exemplary in their scope and depth.

Another positive result of the review was the development of a Curricular Advisory Program to ensure better faculty advising for freshmen and sophomore students. Faculty of all ranks advised the undergraduates. We also began to publish the best research papers and projects of our graduating seniors. Since 1984–85, Brown's undergraduate curriculum also included an innovative eight-year Program in Liberal Medical Education (PLME).

Our efforts were not confined to undergraduate students. To help graduate education, we established fifty annual dissertation fellowships and ten awards for Excellence in Teaching. In addition, Brown set up a Center for the Advancement of College Teaching to initiate and prepare the graduate students for the teaching craft.

As far as fund-raising was concerned, my stated position was "the responsibility for fund-raising lies with the corporation. The faculty has to help, too.

Fund-raising will be an important component of my job, naturally, but not *the* most important. No amount of money will give a university direction. I'd like to strengthen Brown's mission and provide it with clarity of purpose and to continue the self-confidence the faculty has."

The reaction of New Yorkers to my appointment as president of Brown was positive mixed with sadness. The *New York Times* published an editorial: "New York Loses a Lion." Robert F. Wagner Jr., then president of the New York City Board of Education, noted that I "had made the Library a central part of the life of the city, reminding people that libraries were engines of hope." Arthur Schlesinger Jr. described me as a great "cultural impresario" with the "talents of a missionary and a showman." The most fantastic remark of all was from Barbara W. Tuchman, the historian and a trustee of the Library, who compared me to Franklin D. Roosevelt in my "ability to communicate enthusiasm and lift morale."

As we got ready to leave New York, the Library gave us a great send-off. The black-tie affair, sponsored and paid for by the trustees of the Library, was an extraordinary party. It was put together by the brilliant Gregory Long, the vice president for development. It gathered the trustees, the administration, and the great friends and patrons of the Library. There was fun, nostalgia, gaiety, goodwill, magic (by Trustee Ace Greenberg). There was music, poetry, readings, and recitations. Clare and I were enchanted and deeply touched by the exuberance, the warmth, and the kindness of everyone who attended the party.

The Library, as a parting gift, presented us with three volumes of letters. Everyone present, even those friends who were absent, had written letters and compositions. Several hundred letters contained accolades, gratitude, affection, humor, and even some satire.

One of the more original submissions was from Hal Prince, who sent me a bona fide contract to play the lead role in *The Phantom of the Opera*. The most unusual tribute came from Walter H. Annenberg who described me as one of "Nature's Noblemen." The most surprising accolade came from the quiet and private Harrison E. Salisbury of the *New York Times*. He claimed that I had "brought Florence and Athens and, yes, Carthage to us, and I bow down to the majesty of his gifts." The most ambitious project was proposed by James Billington, the Librarian of Congress, who wrote an outline for a book, entitled *The Lion in the Apple: A Modern Saga of Urban Adventure,* with sixteen chapters. Dan Boorstin, Librarian Emeritus of Congress, wrote, "Your work at the New York Public Library is an inspiration and a catalyst for the world of public libraries. Your talents are so intensely personal and yet so abstractly intellectual that they are hard to imitate." Ossie Davis, the

actor, who was co-chair of the Schomburg Commission for the Preservation
of Black Culture, wrote:

From One Schomburger to Another

The University of Brown
Speaking blackly
May one day call him
Booker T. Gregorian

While we
Had he kept his rank in our battalion
Would gladly have named him
Vartan Luther King, Jr.

The greatest tour de force was a lengthy poem from Calvin (Bud) Trillin,
entitled "Gregorian Saga" (later published in the *New York Times Book Review*,
a historical first).

I

At Penn, in a prestigious chair,
They had a man considered rare.
He had the requisite degrees
But would, at times of stress or *crise,*
Ignore the folks with Ph.D.'s
And quote his granny from Tabriz.
And she knew everything.

He spoke six tongues (or was it eight?).
In all of them he could orate
On Plato or on quantum particles.
In none of them did he use articles.
But Clare, his wife, would patiently
Remind him of the "a" or "the."
And she knew almost everything.

At Penn, he soon became a dean—
The fastest talking dean they'd seen.
As provost he could feel his oats.

His drive, his warmth, his granny's quotes
Seemed sure to make him president.
If not, he'd surely fold his tent
And leave, just after saying, "Bah!
They really should have made me Shah."

   Your nine o'clock appointment's here.
   You have six calls, and then you're clear.
   And, Greg, if I may be so bold,
   I hope you know that Mayor's on hold.

II

In Gotham, at the great repository
Of knowledge that's the center of this story,
Truth seekers went to find what they were seeking.
They found instead the roof above them leaking.
They found collections crumbled, tables pitted.
They found on Thursday they were not admitted.
In reading rooms they found such sad decay
At one point even flashers stayed away.

This marvel was about to crash.
It needed someone with panache.
And most of all it needed cash.

When Heiskell came, he found malaise was chronic.
He called on high for wisdom Salomonic.
With Tilden gone and Lenox just a Hill,
It fell upon the Astors to fulfill
The role of founders—keepers of the flame.
And luckily, the one who bore the name
Turned out to be the once and perfect dame.

The place they loved was at the point
At which they quickly must anoint
A saviour who could save the joint.

They listed all the attributes they sought
In this, the second saviour God had wrought.

It should be one whose high-toned speech was free
Of simple words—such words as "a" and "the."
And one who had no tiresome aversion
To speaking Greek, or maybe even Persian.
And, not to judge one on appearance solely,
It might be nice if he were roly-poly.
And most of all, they prayed, down on their knees,
For someone with a granny from Tabriz.
Such qualities are hard to find. But then
They heard there was this perfect guy at Penn.

    At one you meet a wealthy bunch
    Of bankers at the bank for lunch.
    Till then, your day is full I'm told,
    And, Greg, the Mayor is still on hold.

III

He came, he saw, he ate and drank
With wealthy bankers at the bank.
And wealthy yachtsmen on their yachts,
And wealthy moms with wealthy tots.
And once, just once, a wealthy poodle
Who had been left a lot of boodle.
And newly wealthy arbitragers
Whose flags of choice were Jolly Rogers,
And wealthy folks with cash so old
That some of it was growing mold.
It's said, by someone indiscreet,
He'd grab the wealthy off the street.
And they enjoyed it.

Although it wasn't always pretty,
He nudzhed the state, he nudzhed the city.
Foundations felt their assets fall
The moment that they took his call.
Evangelistic, bold and brash,
He generated more than cash.
He got New Yorkers thinking hard

About what those two lions guard—
The books, the prints, the monographs,
The songs, the facts, the tears, the laughs,
The thoughts of saints, the thoughts of sinners,
The wealthy eating fancy dinners.

The roof was fixed, new rugs unrolled,
The temperature of books controlled,
Old rooms restored, new rooms unveiled,
And writers of distinction hailed.
Exhibits came, endowments grew,
The place stayed open Thursdays, too.

And, finishing a fourteen-hour day,
Gregorian was often heard to say,
"Hey look—I'm having fun. I'm having blast."
He was—presiding over this vast cast
With bear hugs here, and fourteen speeches there,
And somehow looking none the worse for wear,
Despite his well-coifed Brillo pad for hair.
He made the place the center of the town.
And then he said that he would leave for Brown.

   The senator will be here soon.
   You have two luncheons, both at noon.
   The reading room is freezing cold.
   The Mayor's getting old on hold.

IV

And now he is Rhode Island bound
In Providence he thinks he's found
A tranquil place—a place where he
Can write about philosophy,
As he presides as chief Brown bear,
And brings a little culture there,
And talks of Plato, such as that,
And eats the food of Ararat.
It sounds so good.

But what he'll find in several weeks
Is Brown has roofs, and roofs have leaks.
And Brown has books, and books get old.
Their temperature must be controlled.
He may find walls decaying or
Curriculum in need of core.
He'll have the usual on his plate.
So Socrates will have to wait.

'Cause back he'll go into the fray—
Another fourteen-hour day.
To find Brown grads he'll shake the trees,
And say, "You'll pay for those degrees."
He'll patch the holes that paint disguised
And make the place all Vartanized.
He'll speak in every nook and cranny,
He'll quote from Locke, he'll quote from Granny.
And Clare will do her best to see
That he says "a" and even "the."
We hope it's fun. We hope it's blast.
We hope he's happy—Shah at last.

As I read the outlandish tributes I felt proud, happy, and sad, as if I were attending my own funeral and hearing endless eulogies. Was this the end of my public life? What was I to do with the rest of my life? What could I possibly do to top the New York Public Library?

There were many farewell parties, including Mrs. Astor's. Barbara Walters also threw a party for us. When she asked what kind we wanted, we said a small one in an intimate setting. She held it at Mortimer's. As Clare and I arrived, we saw the Brown University flag at the entrance of the restaurant. Once inside we were speechless. At least, I was. Barbara had re-created the ornate office of the president of the New York Public Library with enlarged color photographs that covered the entire dining room of Mortimer's.

*   *   *

April 9, 1989, was my official inauguration. I had just celebrated my birthday. I was anxious. It was as if I were getting married to an institution in a public, solemn gathering in the presence of multitudes of strangers as well as my family, relatives, friends, teachers, and mentors. I had worked on my inaugural speech, writing and rewriting up to the last minute.

Five thousand people attended the inauguration ceremonies. I was happy that my entire family was there. Vahé came in from St. Louis. Our son Raffi, who arrived from London, surprised us with happy news. He was engaged and his fiancée, Bernadette, had accompanied him to Providence. My sister and my brother-in-law had arrived from Iran, along with their three children who lived in Boston. My sisters-in-law were there, along with my best man, Isaac (Clare's brother) and his wife. Childhood friends from Beirut, as well as classmates from the Collège Arménien, and scores of Armenian friends from Philadelphia and California were also there. The Rhode Island Armenian community, one of the oldest in the United States, was there in force. It was as if I were present at a *This Is Your Life* TV show!

As the ceremonies began, Charles Tillinghast, the senior member of the Board of Fellows and chancellor emeritus, read the "Inauguration Engagement." Chancellor Alva O. Way presented me with the University's Charter, the Chain of Office, and the Manning Chair—all were symbols of the Brown presidency.

There were greetings from New York. Brooke Astor captivated the audience by simply telling them that all the time I was in New York, she knew that what I really wanted to do was to look once again into the eyes of students and stir their intelligence and talk to them and have fun with them and cause excitement within them. "You are going to have the best time you've ever had."

Andrew Heiskell quoted Bart Giamatti: " 'Being president of a university is no way for an adult to make a living. It is the mid-nineteenth-century ecclesiastical position on top of a late-twentieth-century corporation.' Strangely enough, I think for [V.G.] these two characteristics are not necessarily a contradiction; they are not mutually exclusive. He can do it."

My friends Eliot Stellar, president of the American Philosophical Society; Stanley Katz, president of the American Council of Learned Societies; and Hortense Calisher, president of the American Academy and the Institute of Arts and Letters, spoke. James O. Freedman of Dartmouth spoke on behalf of the Ivy League. There were warm greetings on behalf of the faculty, undergraduate and graduate students, the Alumni Association and the Parents Council. All of them pledged their assistance in making my presidency a success.

*   *   *

My inauguration ceremony was noteworthy for another reason. For the first time I had my past and current mentors, benefactors, and friends under one roof. At long last, I was able to pay public tribute to my alma mater, Stanford University, and its faculty, who gave me an excellent education. I thanked the faculties of San Francisco State College, the University of Texas at Austin, the University of Pennsylvania, the New School and NYU. I acknowledged my particular debt to John Silber, president of Boston University, who gave me my first academic administrative position at Texas, and to President Martin Meyerson and Provost Eliot Stellar of the University of Pennsylvania, who appointed me founding dean of the Faculty of Arts and Sciences and the twenty-third provost of the University. I expressed my gratitude to my friend Judge Louis Pollak, who presided over the ceremonies that granted me U.S. citizenship. I highlighted my admiration and affection for three extraordinary individuals—Brooke Astor, Andrew Heiskell, and Richard Salomon—and conveyed through them my gratitude to the trustees, staff, friends, and benefactors of the New York Public Library for the privilege of serving the Library. I thanked the Brown Corporation for giving me an opportunity to serve our youth and our nation.

In my inaugural address, I reminded everyone about the humble beginnings of Brown. During its first four years (1765–1769), the college had one professor. In 1770, the tuition was twelve dollars a year and the annual room rent five dollars. As late as 1827, when Francis Wayland, the fourth president of Brown, assumed his post, the college had three professors, two tutors, and ninety students. Its property consisted of two college buildings used as lecture rooms and dormitories. In 1827, the total funds of Brown amounted to thirty-four thousand dollars. That fund remained the same as late as 1850. That year, President Francis Wayland, with his usual candor, acknowledged that "the college has not for more than forty years received a dollar from private or public benefactors." All of these facts were mere reminders to Brown that, in 1989, on the eve of its 225th birthday, it could take great pride that during that time span it had managed to transform itself from a small, fragile, parochial, regional institution into one of our nation's outstanding institutions of liberal learning.

I pointed out that in this Age of Information "the world was wallowing in detail, drowning in information but starved for knowledge" (John Naisbitt, *Megatrends*), that in addition to an explosion of information and knowledge, we also faced dangerous levels of fragmentation of knowledge, dictated by the advances of sciences, learning, and scholarship, that the modern world is inclined to think that there was no knowledge but specialized knowledge. The university, which was to embody the Unity of Knowledge, had become intellectually a multiversity. The Unity of Knowledge had collapsed. The very concept of an educated and cultured person had also been fragmented.

I noted that the question of integrating knowledge once again highlighted the importance of liberal learning. Liberal education does more than acquaint students with the past or prepare them for the future. It gives them a perspective for reflection upon the nature and texture of their own lives. It provides them with standards by which to measure human achievement and to recognize and respect the moral courage required to endure human anxiety and suffering. I advocated the case for a proper balance between narrow professional training and broad humanistic education. If ever the world cried out for breadth of view and length of perspective, surely it is now. If ever there was a danger that a narrow professional view would make people insensitive to the needs of all outside their particular professional enclosures, there is such a danger now. "We ought to realize that a lopsided education is both deficient and dangerous, that we need a proper balance between the preparation of careers and the cultivation of values. Unless such a balance is restored, career training may be ephemeral in applicability and delusive of worth, and value education will be casual, shifting, and relativistic."

I reminded the Brown gathering that it was Alexis de Tocqueville, the author of *Democracy in America,* who coined the term "individualism" to describe the American character. He believed that the delicate balance between freedom, equality, and social order must be weighted by enlightened self-interest, public morality, and patriotism. He had hoped that long-term self-interest and compassion would override short-term gratification and excesses of materialism and that individuals would learn that what is *right* is also *useful.*

I said, "In a healthy individualism and in the individual, there is a balance between the personal component of the self and the community or the social component. Neither component can exist by itself. In separation each is an abstraction with no content."

I concluded by stressing that the American university cannot afford the luxury of transforming its first two years of instruction into remedial work to meet the woeful inadequacies of our public school system. I advocated the strengthening of our public school system and the rescuing of our high school system. "We have to prepare our students for the twenty-first century. We cannot condemn our youth to economic and technological subjugation nor witness passively the *emergence of a permanent underclass.*"

*   *   *

Once in office, the university atmosphere rejuvenated me, and I was delighted, finally, to remember how wonderful and impossible students could be. My experiences at San Francisco State, the University of Texas at Austin, and the University of Pennsylvania came in handy in dealing with the faculty, students, staff, alumni, and parents. I came to appreciate former Brown president Henry Wriston's description of the difficulties of the job: the president is "expected to be an educator, to have been at some time a scholar, to have judgment about finance, to know something about construction, maintenance, and labor policy, to speak virtually continuously in words that charm and never offend, to take bold positions with which no one will disagree, to consult everyone, and follow all proffered advice, and do everything through committees, but with great speed and without error" (Wriston, *The Structure of Brown University,* 1946).

In 1988, the core of Brown University, which had the lowest endowment in the Ivy League, was roughly the size of the Faculty of the Arts and Sciences at the University of Pennsylvania (528 faculty, 7,500 students), not counting the biomedical facility. The university was struggling to maintain a proper balance between its undergraduate and its graduate programs, its academics and its athletics, and the preservation of a historic campus while meeting the needs for renovation and modernization.

My first step as Brown's sixteenth president was to put together an administration. I recruited most of the talent from within the university. I wanted to send a message to the campus, as an incoming leader, that Brown had sufficient talent to govern itself and that institutional loyalty pays off. The second measure was to launch some twenty internal studies to determine the state of the university's resources. We conducted the first complete inventory of the university's physical assets—artwork, buildings, equipment, everything. We also investigated many other aspects of the university, including its academic centers and institutes, the athletic program, the curriculum, its financial aid policies, and the medical program. These were the necessary ingredients to prepare an overall strategic plan for the university that would link its academic planning with its budget process.

I appreciated the fact that Brown's needs were great because that presented me with exciting challenges to build, to leave a mark not only as a fund-raiser but also as an educator. Brown was poor in terms of financial resources. In order to compete, it did more with less. Its faculty had no choice but to innovate and collaborate. The faculty considered teaching as one of its central missions. It was not risk averse. It considered research and teaching to be the two sides of the same coin. Innovation was always welcomed and celebrated. Indeed, it was that ability to change that had saved Brown from oblivion in the middle of the nineteenth century. It was President Wayland who, in the 1850s, in order to save Brown, reformed it by introducing science and technology, by allowing the students choice in the subjects they studied. He acknowledged the simple fact that students came to college with different interests and attitudes, intent on pursuing very different careers. He believed that it was only reasonable for a college such as Brown to be aware of the vocational interests of the students and indeed to provide for them. Knowledge, in every form, needed to be communicated by men prepared to teach in disciplines previously neglected or prohibited. It was Wayland who first articulated the idea of a student-chosen curriculum.

Wayland taught me about the importance of ideas, the importance of the curriculum, the importance of the faculty as the core of the university. For nine years, I spent much effort building Brown as a community rather than treating it as a corporation. I was convinced, based on my past experience, that a strong community, a hard-working and self-confident community, clear and confident of its mission, would be the best asset for attracting good faculty, students, and staff. And that, in turn, would insure the loyalty of the parents and alumni. That was my plan at Penn, and at long last, I had a chance to demonstrate its soundness at Brown.

We named endowed chairs, professorships, and lectureships not only after benefactors but after distinguished professors and administrators as well. To honor the memory of our professors and students, we planted trees and set up benches on campus. To honor the spouses (of chancellors, vice chancellors, and presidents), we endowed Teaching Excellence Awards in their name to be awarded annually to the best teaching fellows. We did not forget our dedicated staff. The university's most exclusive medal was named in gratitude for and in honor of John McIntyre, who served the university with distinction as assistant secretary of the Corporation for almost four decades. We named a building after Phil Andrews, a staff member who had served Brown with great devotion for some forty-seven years. While some of these actions required money, others did not. We won the hearts of many international students and parents by flying the flags of all countries of graduating seniors. We received tons of accolades after inviting parents and grandparents of graduating seniors who were educators to march with our faculty during the commencement exercises.

To strengthen our ties as a community, we inaugurated the tradition of Staff Appreciation Day. To meet the needs of faculty and staff, we opened, for the first time, a day-care center and instituted maternity leave benefits to staff women. The tuition assistance program was extended to all part-time employees.

In 1988, union leaders told me that families of campus workers were not formally invited on campus as members of the Brown community and, consequently, they rarely visited—except when they came to protest a labor dis-

pute or walk a picket line. The administration, therefore, organized an annual two-day party to celebrate the entire staff and their families during the
winter holidays. Much of the campus was opened to the Brown community
for their enjoyment. It was wonderful to see children skating with parents
and grandparents and to see so many members of the Brown community
enjoying music festivals, mime shows, and storytelling.

*   *   *

Rebuilding Brown's infrastructure was another urgent goal. In 1993, we surveyed all of our 226 core buildings. The needs were staggering. The cost of
deferred maintenance was set at $73 million. We spent $85 million and renovated 60 percent of student dormitories and academic space.

While building Brown's community, we did not forget Brown's obligation to the rest of society. Brown University was the headquarters of the
Campus Compact, the brainchild of three great educators: Brown's Howard
Swearer, Stanford's Donald Kennedy, and Georgetown's Tim Healy. The
objective of the organization was to harness the altruism and volunteerism
of university and college students for public service and public good. That
effort was launched in 1985. Since then it has become a major national
movement. Today more than eight hundred colleges and universities are
part of the Compact. (In 2000–2001, 28 percent of students of Campus
Compact member campuses participated in public service projects.)

In 1994, Brown University, Johnson & Wales University, the Miriam
Hospital, Providence College, Rhode Island Hospital, Rhode Island School
of Design, Roger Williams Medical Center, and Women and Infants Hospital gathered together to form a partnership known as HELP (Health and
Education Leadership for Providence). It was headed by the presidents of
the four private colleges and the four not-for-profit hospitals in Providence.
The organization helped the city of Providence not only through in-kind service but also with cash ($9 million) and helped raise an additional $11 million from foundations and governmental sources. It provided a school-based
dental-health program that has helped some ten thousand children, improved the quality of art education in thirty-seven Providence public
schools, and supported many other notable educational, environmental,
and health initiatives.

When we launched our campaign for Brown, we called it the Campaign
for the Rising Generation. The goal for the five-year effort was $450 million.
It was the most ambitious capital campaign, not only in Brown's history but
of the state of Rhode Island as well. We raised $534 million (from 55,000 in-
dividuals, foundations, and corporations). All in all, in nine years, from all

sources, some one billion dollars were raised for Brown. When I left Brown on September 30, 1997, its endowment had grown by 260 percent to $1.05 billion from just under $400 million.

In the 1996–1997 academic year, we received some 15,000 applications for admission to Brown, including 2,500 early admission applicants. That same year, *U.S. News & World Report* ranked Brown among the top eight universities in the United States. The campaign allowed us to establish seventy-two endowed professorships for senior professors and twenty assistant professors, as well as ten lectureships. I was particularly happy about the endowed assistant professorships. They gave us the best tools to compete and recruit, successfully, the best available national talent. During my tenure at Brown we recruited more than 270 new faculty members. We managed to keep the faculty-to-student ratio around one-to-ten. Thanks to the campaign, we allocated some $40 million to renovate almost 60 percent of Brown's residential halls.

As a result of the Campaign for the Rising Generation, we were able to double the undergraduate scholarship fund, raising some $50 million for the endowment. Brown also decided that student financial aid and scholarship should be indexed to increases in tuition and fees to ensure this assistance was not eroded over time; in addition, all new donations for student aid and scholarship were to be used to increase the endowment for this purpose, rather than being diverted into easing other budgetary pressures. Thus, all new gifts to the fund were made incremental rather than mere "budget relief." In addition, we raised more than $16 million for graduate fellowships. The library's collection increased in eight years from two to three million volumes.

During my tenure, the Brown administration had a strong interest in seeing faculty become as diverse as our student body. We were mostly successful in recruiting more women and minorities for faculty openings. Of approximately 750 medical and nonmedical faculty, about 100 were members of minority groups and 217 were women. With help from the Henry Luce Foundation, we created WISE, a program for Women in Science and Engineering, in order to encourage the enrollment of women in the fields of science or engineering by matching students with mentors and creating an alumni network to help them find work after leaving Brown. We also celebrated one hundred years of women at Brown.

In the mid-seventies, Louise Lamphere, an assistant professor at Brown, who was denied tenure without due process, sued the university. The case was settled in 1977. The so-called Lamphere Consent Decree required the university, under the supervision of an affirmative action monitoring committee, to standardize its employment practices and criteria and ensure that the proportion of women faculty at Brown corresponded to "the proportion of women in the appropriate pool of available Ph.D's." In 1992, a group of women faculty representing the legal class petitioned the Court to vacate the decree. Trust had been restored between the administration and the women faculty, and between them and me. I was both proud and gratified.

When I left office, I noted with great satisfaction that, without fanfare, Brown's administration was one of the most diverse in the country. We were the first in the Ivy League to have a general counsel and a chief financial officer who were African-American. Women held many senior positions, including dean of the faculty, dean of the college, vice president for development, registrar, controller, internal auditor, budget director, chaplain, university librarian, vice president for physical plant operations, and executive vice president for university relations.

In 1979, the university was contributing fifty cents of every financial aid dollar while the federal government provided the rest. By 1991, Brown was contributing ninety cents and the federal government only ten cents. So we made scholarships an important goal of our fund-raising campaign when we launched it in 1992. We were proud that by 1997, 39 percent of Brown students received scholarships and/or financial aid.

The curriculum was strengthened by course offerings in Judaic studies, Islamic civilization, the languages and literature of Greece, Portugal, Brazil, South Asia, the Middle East, Japan, and Africa. We established the interdisciplinary Center for Race and Ethnicity. We established the Watson Institute for International Studies. To broaden our students' perspectives and opportunities, we strengthened our ties with several universities overseas, including Oxford, Bologna, Turin, Yonsei, Kyoto, and Keio. Locally, Brown and the Rhode Island School of Design, under the leadership of Roger Mandel, strengthened their collaboration in allowing our respective students to enroll in the courses of two institutions.

Another Brown-based group, the Leadership Alliance, worked with historically black colleges and universities, members of the Ivy League, and other leading research universities to identify talented minority children and groom them as prospective faculty for our country's colleges. In our hometown, Brown became the city's partner in an ambitious effort to help eliminate poverty from Providence, improve health care, and develop strategies to revitalize the city. Among Brown's contributions was the Providence Plan, which was designed to help the city chart the course of its economic and urban development and, on a statewide basis, the so-called Gregorian Commission was formed at the governor's request to make sense of the 1991 collapse of credit unions and to suggest reforms. Brown's Center for Environmental Studies helped Providence city schools develop educational programs to warn families and children about the dangers of lead poisoning. The School of Medicine helped bring together expertise and funding to provide health care to the young, the old, and the needy. Our theater, speech, and dance department brought sixth graders from two Providence schools onto the University's stage. And Brown varsity athletes served as tutors, "big brothers" and "big sisters," to children at the public Fox Point Elementary School.

The Brown years were some of the happiest years of my life. My wife and sons loved Brown and Providence. We had great ties with the community. I liked the students, respected the faculty, had wonderful relationships with the staff, and very cordial ties with the entire board. I loved my teaching and my students. It was a wonderful place. In 1995, during my sixth year, there was an opportunity to succeed my friend Michael Sovern as president of Columbia University. The idea of moving back to New York was tantalizing, both for Clare and me, not to mention our children. The fever of New York had never left us. I met with the chairman of the search committee and the entire committee. I was offered the presidency of Columbia. But considering the fact that we still had one more year to finish Brown's Campaign for the Rising Generation, I could not in good conscience leave Brown. I would have if Columbia had been able to wait a year but that they could not do. So I did the right and the honorable thing and declined the offer.

*   *   *

During my years at Penn, the New York Public Library, and Brown University, I had become familiar with the world of philanthropy. I had met scores of individual philanthropists and leaders of many foundations. During my last five years at Brown, I became a pro bono advisor to three extraordinary philanthropists, Walter H. Annenberg, Ted Turner, and Bill Gates. Each one of them was a very complex, maverick, fascinating individual. I had known Walter since my Penn days. We were very good friends. When I became president of Brown University, he sent me a $2 million check to celebrate our friendship. Clare teased me that maybe it was a personal gift. I disabused her of that and told her it was for Brown, and it was. In 1993, he entrusted me to oversee the disposition of his $500 million challenge grant to the nation on behalf of reforming the nation's public school system. He became one of Brown University's major benefactors.

Ted Turner, who dropped out of Brown during his senior year, and I became "pals." He became one of the major donors to Brown. Emboldened by

Annenberg's example and encouraged by him, I went to meet Bill Gates of Microsoft to try to convince him to become a major philanthropist now rather than wait until his retirement. I was ecstatic when he decided to do just that. He and his wife, Melinda, asked me to join the five-member Gates Learning Foundation. I did, again on a pro bono basis.

While at the helm of Brown University, I came to know His Highness the Aga Khan, the spiritual leader of the Ismaili community and a great philanthropist. He was a Brown parent. He asked me to join the Governing Board of the Aga Khan University in Karachi. I learned much while serving on that board. Incidentally, the Aga Khan, who accepted Brown's invitation to give the baccalaureate address, was the first Muslim to do so in the history of Brown and perhaps the entire Ivy League.

I also had the privilege of serving on the board of the Aaron Diamond Foundation, headed by the late Irene Diamond, a wonderful woman. Over several years, the foundation gave away several hundred million dollars, its entire asset.

While I knew about wealth, how to receive it, and how to give it, while I knew about philanthropy, I never imagined that one day I would have the opportunity to lead a major, historically important national foundation.

In 1997, Carnegie Corporation of New York offered me its twelfth presidency. I thought it was providential. We came to New York with great love and nostalgia for Brown. Like the New York Public Library, Brown gave me a great send-off. They named a building quadrangle after me, the first dormitory built during my presidency. They endowed a professorship and fellowship in my name. But what was most touching was the fact that the faculty gave me its Susan Colver Rosenberger Medal. (Established in 1919, it is the highest honor the Brown faculty can bestow. I was the twenty-first recipient. Only two Brown presidents had received that honor—Henry Merritt Wriston in 1976 and Howard Swearer in 1983.) The Graduate Student Association also gave me a medal. Most important of all, the city of Providence named an elementary school after me, and Brown granted Clare an honorary degree for years of service. After the Library, thank God, I had another report card.

POSTSCRIPT

From Tabriz, Iran, to New York City, by way of Lebanon, California, Texas, Pennsylvania, Rhode Island, and numerous other places in between. A poor boy, yearning for knowledge, who—I hope!—became an educated man now at the helm of an organization dedicated to disseminating knowledge to all the world. A dreamer who learned to take action. A wandering Armenian who ended up on the society pages of the *New York Times*. A son who became a father, a man who became a husband. This is the life I could never have expected, the life it has been my privilege to lead. In *Leaves of Grass*, Walt Whitman, writing of a young sailor carefully steering his ship, cries, "O ship of the body—ship of the soul—voyaging, voyaging, voyaging." I think of that line often because, my God, what a voyage I have been on! And it continues for me, day by interesting, unexpected, amazing day.

Now, as I sit in my office, under a portrait of Andrew Carnegie, I am given to reflecting on the long voyage that brought me here, to this office at Carnegie Corporation of New York. Many mentors, friends, and strangers have helped and guided me along the way—as well, of course, as my wife and children—but I sometimes have a bit of a suspicion that fate may have had a hand in the proceedings as well. I first read about Andrew Carnegie when I was twelve and was fascinated by the lives of great inventors like Edison and Fulton, and self-made men like Carnegie. At the time, it would have been lunacy for me to even imagine that one day I might be in America, in New York, and might be entrusted with the task of preserving Andrew Carnegie's legacy and the mission of the philanthropic foundation he created. When I had read about him when I was young, I had great empathy for Carnegie and detected some similarities in our backgrounds: we were both boys from poor families; boys who loved books but could not afford to buy, or even rent, them; young men who traveled to another country to find their destinies. We both knew, in our hearts and in our bones, that education

327

would save us and direct us—that in fact, education is the key to a better life for everyone, no matter who they are or where they are born. "Only in popular education can man erect the structure of an enduring civilization," Carnegie said, and he was, and is, absolutely right.

We had something else in common, too: we both loved books and libraries. When I assumed the presidency of the New York Public Library, I came to appreciate the historical impact of Andrew Carnegie who, in launching public libraries, not only in New York but all over the United States and abroad, must have taken great pride in building libraries and providing books—hence, knowledge—to ordinary citizens eager to read and learn. I certainly was proud and felt triumphant that the boy from Tabriz who was too poor to own his own volumes and was even unable to borrow and rent books ended up lending millions of books to the people of New York, including the multitudes of newcomers who continue to flock here, to the city near the Statue of Liberty.

To this day, the walls of my office are lined with books; people send me books and talk to me about books and I still delight in the weight of a book in my hand. A book, to me, is still one of the most extraordinary creations of man, because it is a gift of knowledge: someone wrote it because he had something he felt was worth sharing with others, including you; someone gave it to you or recommended it to you or you found it by yourself on a shelf in your favorite bookstore. However it came into your possession, a book is a treasure trove that you can carry with you and learn from wherever and whenever you choose. A book contains dreams, ideas, and ideals, it contains notions about reality and utopia, about revolutions and clues about life and freedom and happiness. A library, a place where books can be lent freely to those seeking knowledge, is a testament to men and women's concern and caring for each other and for each other's children—for everyone's children: to construct and cherish a library is to invest not only in ourselves but in future generations. A library is a legacy. A library is a mirror to the past and a window to the future.

Because of the role that books and libraries have played in my life, I am gratified that at Carnegie Corporation, I have been able to help direct one aspect of our focus on international development toward African libraries and librarians, in order to help them create the gateways to tomorrow that will best serve the people of Africa. As someone who has had the opportunity to live in different countries and different cultures, I know how extensive the cultural divide between different peoples can seem, how exotic differing beliefs and customs can appear to be, so it seems to me that knowledge about the world, both its tangible qualities and ephemeral mysteries, and about each other—about our glories and our follies—is the only way to narrow the great gulfs that divide us. The place where we can all find that knowledge is in books and in libraries as well as in the new technologies that enhance our ability to share the precious "knowledge and understanding" that Andrew Carnegie believed in so deeply and sincerely. The dissemination of knowledge and understanding is, in fact, the mandate he gave the institution I now serve, and I am pleased to be one of those entrusted with the task of carrying out his vision.

International conflict was a great concern of Andrew Carnegie's. He longed, especially in his later years, for the advent of what he called "the glorious reign of peace." He witnessed the mounting tensions and conflict that unleashed the calamity of World War I. As a young boy in Tabriz, I had read about the terrible devastations wrought by the Great War, including the deportations, atrocities, and genocides perpetrated against civilian populations. During World War II, I read about huge, fierce battles; tremendous destruction; massive forced migrations of refugees; about hunger, starvation, and illness. At the time, I never imagined that one day I would have the honor and the duty to carry on the work of Andrew Carnegie, who had dedicated himself to the cause of peaceful resolutions to conflict and to working for international peace.

The immediacy and importance of Carnegie's mission was brought home to me anew on September 11, 2001. Early that morning I had left New York and flown west to give a lecture at the University of Michigan. I was not in the city when the terrorists brought down the World Trade Center towers on that heartbreakingly clear end-of-summer morning. Watching from afar was like helplessly watching a beloved friend's agony, and as soon as I could, I made the long, slow trip back to the city. During those endless hours, I was gripped with fear and anxiety about the safety of my wife and son Dareh in New York and my son Raffi in Washington, D.C. as well as the staff of the Corporation. For the first time, I realized that New York really was my city. On that terrible day, I also realized the immediacy and the relevance of Carnegie Corporation's mission. The international conflicts, however, were no longer confined to contending states. There were new actors on the scene now, armed with know-how about modern technologies and fueled by hatred and revenge, alternating between nihilistic and utopian ideologies, and who were not averse to committing mass murder and random assassinations, and to using religion and religiosity to advance or justify their political agendas. Unlike the states that have return addresses, these networks of terrorists have no such thing. They believe in a "dictatorship of virtue and justice" defined only by them. Progress and understanding are not in their vocabulary.

One thing is clear, however: peace will be rooted in understanding how the differences between us—between states, peoples, and nations—cause conflict, and in finding ways of managing those differences instead of letting them explode into hostilities. That is why, at Carnegie Corporation, for many years we have had a program that has gone by different names but always pointed toward the same goal: understanding the roots of conflict and finding ways to make the world a less dangerous place to live, a place in which we must believe that peace is always within reach—perhaps just over the horizon. Toward this end, we have moved from Andrew Carnegie's concerns about World War I, through World War II and beyond, making a troubling progression from Cold War worries about preventing nuclear war to finding ways of preventing weapons of mass destruction—which include nuclear, biological, and chemical arsenals—from spreading not only to the storehouses of hostile states but also from falling into the hands of terrorists.

True peace is not merely the absence of war but also the presence of understanding. Who could have imagined, just a few decades ago, that the former Soviet Union and the United States—the bear and the eagle who had been trying to stare each other down from opposite sides of the world—would have found, instead, that they inhabited common ground? Since the fall of the Soviet Union, Carnegie Corporation has been working with Russian academics, educators, leaders, thinkers, and policy makers to develop that nation's future which, like the future of all nations, depends on the development of its human capital.

Because we share this understanding, this similar national interest in cultivating the nurturing symbiosis between a country and its people, we have, in recent years, been involved in partnerships with Russian universities to create centers of advanced study and education, academic hubs for scholars in the social sciences and the humanities that we hope will become vibrant intellectual communities serving all of Russia and its far-flung regions. What more wonderful, moving, amazing way to end decades of suspicion and mistrust than to agree, together, that the future beckons to us through education? And what more important lesson can there be than what has become clear to me, through the Corporation's work in Russia, as well as in Africa, that there *is* a universal language emerging among the peoples of the world: it is the language of knowledge and of understanding.

Education is the means by which all knowledge is produced. It was Carnegie Corporation that first sounded the clarion call for better early childhood education and care; for research about how children learn and about their cognitive development; for improved middle schools; for educational television for children; and for the right of all children not only to an education but to teaching and learning of great quality, to an education that will truly prepare them to participate and succeed in the world. Since so many other foundations and advocates have taken up that mission, we have begun to delve more deeply into just what is the essence of "a good education." One answer lies in the quality of teachers; that is, the quality of knowledge and skill they bring into the classroom. We are spearheading the effort to create better schools of education so our teachers will be *effective* teachers.

Simultaneously, we are investigating the nature of the best environment in which instruction should take place. The culture of American education was shaped in an earlier age, when children needed preparation for a world that relied primarily on physical labor and, by today's standards, on simple machinery. We have now long left behind the age of the industrial worker and passed into that of the "knowledge worker." Almost every job now requires the ability to understand complex information, a mastery of evolving technology and the skills to synthesize the two. Schools must change. At the Corporation, this imperative has taken the form of initiatives aimed at redesigning large urban high schools and of working with school systems across the country to bring about a fundamental reformation of secondary education, reshaping our schools into learning communities with cultures that support high expectations, inquiry, effort, persistence, and achievement by all.

In recent years, there have been troubling indications that Americans, both those born here and those, like myself, who have come as immigrants, often have little acquaintance with the history of this nation, little knowledge of its extraordinary Constitution, of the struggles that generations of leaders and everyday citizens have gone through to obtain basic rights for immigrants and for women and minorities and for countless other disenfranchised groups who now carry with them the same hefty and invaluable portfolio of social and civil rights as every other American citizen. They even have the right to be apathetic about their rights! But if they are, it's a tragedy for them, which I can only hope does not turn into a greater tragedy for the nation. Ours is a *participatory* system that depends on the constant attention, affirmation, and adjustments that only an actively concerned citizenry can provide. The goal of the Corporation's support of programs aimed at reforming our system of campaign financing is to open up the political process to every citizen who wants to serve his or her country, as is our work with those who are finding ways to encourage new Americans, young Americans—all Americans!—to become involved in a genuinely hands-on way with this shared and never-ending work in progress that is our nation.

All that is not to say that I am not aware of this nation's flaws, which arise from the frailties we all share as human beings and from the distance that lies between our aspirations and our achievements. Last year, on July 4, I gave a speech at Monticello, the home of Thomas Jefferson, where I spoke to the newest Americans who had just that day been sworn in as citizens. To them I said, "America is not perfect, but it is perfectable," which I truly believe. At the ceremony in which I was sworn in as a citizen in 1979, I was asked to speak, and I remember that I touched on how people come to this country for different reasons—some in the hope of economic betterment, some for religious freedom, some for political asylum—because the American dream means different things to different people. For me, though, that dream has always been the dream of freedom. My joy in being an American has been the joy of freedom—the freedom to think, to write, to create, to wonder, and to agree or dissent, as I choose. To experience that joy, I am grateful to have been given both the privileges and obligations of citizenship, and to help guide an organization that also holds them dear.

In one of his later poems, Robert Frost tells the tale of a king who has gone to the unimaginable length of selling himself into slavery so that his son can have the money to explore the world and find his destiny. Says the king of his gesture toward his child:

> I looked on it as a Carnegie grant
> For him to make a poet of himself on
> If such a thing is possible with money.

My "Carnegie grant" has been the legacy passed down to me by Andrew Carnegie himself, who said that he wanted the philanthropies he had begun "to do real and permanent good in this world." I had no money, so I have learned, through Carnegie's legacy, what is possible to do with money: give it away! In much the same way, I had learned earlier, how a boy who had no books could grow up to be a man dedicated to using the resources of many to provide books for millions. So perhaps, though I have not made a poet of myself (well, not yet, anyway!), I am, at least, continuing on the path that has led me here from halfway around the world and sometimes back again; led me to learn and teach and strive and struggle. Led me to sit beneath the portrait of Andrew Carnegie, my immigrant predecessor with whom I have so much in common (though there is one important dissimilarity between us—I am slightly taller!), and sip my tea and contemplate. My hope, which, as a teacher myself, I think of in teacherly terms, is that at the conclusion of my presidency of Carnegie Corporation of New York, I will have a report card that will make Andrew Carnegie proud.

ACKNOWLEDGMENTS

In writing a volume that focuses primarily on six decades of my public life, I have been compelled to be selective about events, episodes, and individuals who have greatly influenced the course of my path. Space alone is an obstacle to comprehensiveness; in this volume I have been able to acknowledge only some of those who have been instrumental forces in my life. Of course, there are many others who have also earned my thanks and gratitude for their kindness, friendship, and help.

In Tabriz, there were many childhood and teenage friends who gave me their friendship, solidarity, and family hospitality: Varoujan Arakelian, Boulik Babyan, Parouyr Parouyrian, Kajouk Kraskian, Norik Vartanian.

I am indebted to Sisak Arakelian, Vanik Jhamharian, and Hrayr Khalatian for recruiting me as a page for the Rostom-Kaspar Library of the Armenian Prelacy in Tabriz. That library saved my life.

Ter Karapet, the vicar of St. Sarkis Armenian Apostolic Church in Tabriz, who had performed the marriage ceremony of my parents, baptized me and my sister, and, in 1966, baptized our two older sons, Vahé and Raffi, had recruited me as an altar boy. The Church provided me with stability, solace, ritual, and moments of serenity.

Edgar Maloyan, the French vice-consul in Tabriz, entirely changed the course of my life by helping me go to Beirut. Hrayr Stepanian also helped make that possible. Without that gesture, I could not have obtained a passport. I am grateful to both of these benefactors.

I am indebted to all my Armenian, Persian, Russian, and Turkish teachers, who instilled in me the love of books, reading, literature, and history. Thanks are due to my teachers at the Collège Arménien in Beirut, who inspired me to become a teacher, too. I am particularly grateful to Garo Sassooni and Lola Sassooni (the head of the Armenian Relief Society) without whose intervention and support I could not have stayed alive during my first year in Beirut.

During my high school years in Lebanon, I enjoyed the kindness and generosity of three expatriate Armenian families from Iran: Mkrtich and Hasmik Khanjian and their children, Achik and Melkon; Grikor "Mkho" and Gohar Mkhitarian; Dr. Hambartsoom and Vartoush Markarian and their children, Nigol, Annik, Levik, Armen, and Viguen. They became my surrogate families. Without them, my holidays and so much else would have been bleak indeed.

Dr. Aram Baghdassarian, Dr. Yeghik Konyalian, and Dr. Samuel Semerjian were members of the governing board of the Collège Arménien. They took care of the entire student body's eyes and ears as well as dental problems. We also received physical examinations and vaccinations without charge.

Six classmates of mine, Hrayr Ayvazian, Sahag Baghdassarian, Ara Gharibian, Garo Haikakanian, Vazken Ter Kaloostian, and Hrayr Tookhanian, provided me with bonds of friendship and the hospitality of their families. Sahag has throughout my life extended his friendship and support to me and my family as have Nigol and Maral Markarian.

In 1969, I dedicated my book, *The Emergence of Modern Afghanistan,* to Antoine "Sir" Kehyayan, my wonderful English teacher at the Collège Arménien. He taught me English and has always been my friend and mentor. It was he who filled out my college application forms to Stanford and UC Berkeley.

To the protection, benefaction, affection, and friendship of my mentor, Simon Vratzian, I owe everything.

An Armenian-American couple, Lem and Queenie Amirian, were a source of warm Armenian hospitality to me in Palo Alto. I spent many Armenian holidays with them. At Stanford's International Center, Dr. Werner Warmbrunn, the foreign student advisor, and Inez Richardson, formerly of the Asia Society, both gave me sound advice and protection as well as part-time employment. Among the many gifts that Stanford gave me were scores of friends, led by Reginald and Elaine Zelnik of Berkeley. They have been our faithful friends for more than four decades.

My family and I are grateful to John and Kathryn Silber for three decades of friendship. To Martin Meyerson, I owe much gratitude for recruiting me to Penn, appointing me to the deanship of the Faculty of Arts and Sciences, and naming me as provost. During my tenure as the dean of the Faculty of Arts and Sciences and later as provost, I enjoyed the cooperation, friendship and support of my fellow deans, particularly Donald Carrol (Wharton), Walter Cohen (Dental School), Bob Dyson (Arts and Sciences), James O. Freedman (Law), George Gerbner (Annenberg School), and Bob Marshak (Veterinary School). And, of course, our most valued friends and colleagues were the Honorable Lou Pollak (former dean of the Law School) and his wife, Kathy, and Claire Fagin (dean of the School of Nursing) and her husband, Sam.

One individual who provided extraordinary service was my friend, Manuel Doxer, who managed the finances of the Faculty of Arts and Sciences and later those of the office of the provost. I am most grateful to him. Philadelphia became a city of brotherly love for us because of many caring friends. In particular, John and Roxie Sudjian, and the Hovnanian brothers (Hrayr, Vahak, Jirayr, and Kevork) and their spouses (Anna, Hasmig, Lily, and Sirvart). Margy Meyerson, the First Lady of Penn, welcomed us with open arms and extended her friendship and hospitality, as well as her protection, throughout our stay at Penn.

During my tenure as president of the New York Public Library, I enjoyed the help of an extraordinary group of individuals, who made the renaissance of the Library a reality: Gregory Long (vice president for development), John Masten (vice president for budget and finance), Catherine Dunn (governmental relations), Barbara Friedman (controller), Bob Vanni (legal counsel), Richard De Gennero (director of the Library), David Stam (director of the research libraries), Edwin Holmgren (director of the branch libraries). Joan Dunlop, my executive assistant, and Mary Ann Jordan, who succeeded her, were simply invaluable. I extend my gratitude to all of them as well as to my administrative assistants, Bridie Race, Stephanie Offerman, and Grace Pilgrim, for their dedicated service.

My admiration for the Board of Trustees of the New York Public Library is unlimited. In addition to Brooke Astor, Andrew Heiskell, and Richard Salomon, New Yorkers owe a debt of gratitude to Marshall Rose who succeeded Andrew Heiskell as chairman of the Library's board. The vision, energy, and benevolence of all these people was simply extraordinary.

Public officials were vital to the regeneration of the Library. Mayor Ed Koch, Comptroller Jay Goldin, and Ed Sadowsky, chairman of the finance committee of the city council, were particularly helpful. So were David Dinkins, who succeeded Mayor Koch, and Governor Mario Cuomo.

It is the citizens of New York, however, who deserve the lion's share of gratitude. They were determined that the Library must remain open, up to date, accessible, vibrant, and excellent. The *New York Times,* the *Daily News,* the *New York Post,* the *Village Voice,* the *New Yorker, New York* magazine, *WWD, Time, Newsweek,* and scores of other magazines and periodicals, including the ethnic press of New York, were one in championing the cause of libraries in general and the New York Public Library in particular. Scores of writers, poets, scholars, and public intellectuals contributed their names, their time, and their prestige to the cause of their beloved Library, and continue to do so.

My nine years at Brown were happy ones. I was lucky to have the trust and friendship of Chancellor Alva O. Way; Charlie Tillinghast; Chancellor Emeritus and Senior Fellow of the Corporation, Richard Salomon; Chancellor Emeritus, Vice Chancellor, later Chancellor, Artemis Joukowsky; Vice Chancellors Henry Sharp and Marie Langlois.

I thank the late Howard Swearer, my predecessor as president, for his friendship and assistance that was so critical to a smooth transition of administration. I am indebted to Provost Maurice Glicksman; Fred Bohen, vice president for budget and finance; Robert Reichley, vice president for university relations; and Beverly Ledbetter, vice president and general counsel, for helping the process of the transition. Most of all, I thank Sheila Blumstein, the dean of the college, for her leadership and friendship and for never refusing me her help.

I owe much to my assistants and secretaries at Brown, Stephanie Offerman, Patricia Flaherty, and Karen Culton, for their exemplary and devoted service. They made it possible for me to do my job.

Finally I am grateful to the trustees of Carnegie Corporation of New York, especially to the Honorable Thomas Kean, former chairman of the board, and to his successor, Helene Kaplan. I would also like to thank former chairman of the Corporation's board Newton Minow and the committee he headed that selected me as president of Carnegie Corporation.

I am forever indebted to Heather McKay, assistant to the president for special projects and program associate, for her enormous help with this memoir. Without her, I would have been lost in the wilderness. I owe thanks to Eleanor Lerman, director of public affairs and publications, for her comments and contributions. Thanks are also due to Dorothy Delman, administrative assistant. Jeanne D'Onofrio, my executive assistant, holds my head above water every day. I am grateful to her.

I appreciate the generosity of my friend, Calvin Trillin, for allowing me to include his poem, "Gregorian Saga," in this memoir. Similar thanks are due to Diana Der-Hovanessian for including her translation of Hamo Sahian's poem.

I also would like to express my profound gratitude to Alice Mayhew. Without her, this book would never have been written or published.

I owe to fate the fact that my sister's three children, Ani, Ara, and Armen, came to study in the United States, graduated from Boston University, and settled in Boston. For a quarter of a century, they have been an integral part of my life and family. I am grateful to them for their love. They have always been the treasured link that lures my sister and brother-in-law to America, so that lifetime bonds tying us together never weaken.

There is one person, however, I cannot thank enough. My wife, Clare, has been at the center of my life and career for more than forty years. She is a woman of great talent, erudition, and intellectual vitality, and she is endowed with a wonderful sense of humor. She was once asked how many books she had published. She gave their titles: Vahé, Raffi, and Dareh. She was right. She has raised three wonderful sons. Vahé graduated from Swarthmore High School and the University of Pennsylvania. He obtained a master's degree from the University of Missouri's Graduate School of Journalism and joined the *St. Louis Post-Dispatch* as a sportswriter. Raffi graduated from the Shipley School in Bryn Mawr and the University of Pennsylvania. He obtained a master's degree from King's College London and a doctorate from the Paul H. Nitze School of Advanced International Studies at Johns Hopkins University. He is a military historian and currently works for the U.S. Department of State. Dareh graduated from Trinity School in New York and Boston University. He is also a journalist. He covers the civil courts of New York for the *New York Post*. All three of our sons love what they do and they are very good at what they do.

I consider myself most fortunate for being invited to give the Commencement address to the graduating classes of all three schools from which ours sons graduated. I was proud when they graduated from their respective universities. I was grateful that our sons did not have to face my losses, difficulties, and sufferings as a child and teenager, and thank God that their challenges were different ones and their opportunities many.

Without Clare's love, care, patience, and dedication, our children would not be where they are. Notwithstanding the fact that throughout my career we moved more than thirty times (not thirty jobs), Clare managed to establish a home and a context for the family in each place and helped me to meet the social and institutional obligations of my jobs at Penn, the New York Public Library, and Brown. In addition, she contributed a great deal as a board member to the success of Providence Public Library, Trinity Repertory Theater, and, most notably, Planned Parenthood of Rhode Island, to which she devoted a great deal of time and effort. It was she who started the process which eventually brought Rhode Island its own public radio station. In New York, she served as president of the board of Literacy Partners, Inc., and continues to work with Planned Parenthood on the New York City board. She also serves as a member of the Branch Library Council of the New York Public Library and is on the board of the New 42nd Street Theater.

For all of these reasons and the fact that she has been my main supporter and critic, a major source of moral support, the guardian of my morale, and occasionally the protector of my sanity, I dedicate this book to her and our wonderful sons with gratitude and love.

INDEX

PHOTOGRAPHY CREDITS

About the Author

Vartan Gregorian is the twelfth president of Carnegie Corporation of New York. Previously, he served for nine years as president of Brown University and, prior to that, for eight years as president of the New York Public Library. He lives in New York City.